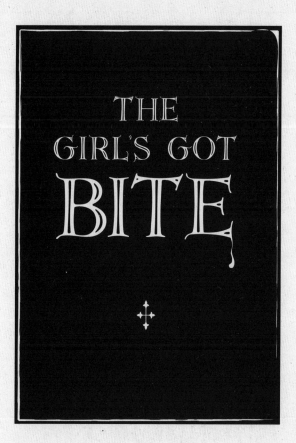

THE GIRL'S GOT BITE

ST. MARTIN'S GRIFFIN

NEW YORK

THE GIRL'S GOT BITE

The Original
Unauthorized Guide
to Buffy's World,
Completely Revised
and Updated

KATHLEEN TRACY

THE GIRL'S GOT BITE. Copyright © 2003 by Kathleen Tracy. All rights reserved. Printed in the United States of America. No part of this book may be used or reproduced in any manner whatsoever without written permission except in the case of brief quotations embodied in critical articles or reviews. For information, address St. Martin's Press, 175 Fifth Avenue, New York, N.Y. 10010.

www.stmartins.com

BOOK DESIGN BY AMANDA DEWEY

Library of Congress Cataloging-in-Publication Data

Tracy, Kathleen
  The girl's got bite : the original unauthorized guide to Buffy's world, completely revised and updated / Kathleen Tracy.—1st ed.
    p. cm.
  ISBN 0-312-31258-X
  1. Buffy, the vampire slayer (Television program)—Miscellanea. 2. Buffy, the vampire slayer (Fictitious character)—Miscellanea. 3. Buffy, the vampire slayer (Motion picture)—Miscellanea. I. Title.

PN1992.77.B84T73 2003
791.45'72—dc21

                            2002045206

10 9 8 7 6 5 4 3 2

CONTENTS

✛

Introduction   vii

1. BUFFY: FROM FEATURE FILM . . . 1
   TO TELEVISION SERIES

2. THE CHARACTERS . . . 26

   The Slayer   26
   The Watcher   27
   Current Main Characters   29
   Recurring Characters   33
   Gone But Not Forgotten   36
   The Dearly Departed   40
   The Big Bads   43

3. A BRIEF HISTORY OF THE VAMPIRE . . . 48

   Vampire Mythology   51
   Vampires in Film and TV   55

4. CAST BIOGRAPHIES . . . 58

Sarah Michelle Gellar   *58*

Anthony Stewart Head   *77*

Nicholas Brendon   *81*

Alyson Hannigan   *85*

James Marsters   *89*

Michelle Trachtenberg   *94*

Emma Caulfield   *96*

5. THE EPISODES . . . 99

Season One   *100*

Season Two   *129*

Season Three   *174*

Season Four   *213*

Season Five   *251*

Season Six   *289*

Season Seven   *326*

INTRODUCTION

✛

As long as there have been demons, here has been the Slayer, one girl in all the world, a Chosen One, born with the strength and skill to hunt vampires and other deadly creatures . . . to stop the spread of their evil. When one Slayer dies, the next is called and trained by the Watcher . . .

lthough loosely based on the 1992 feature film of the same name, the small-screen version of *Buffy the Vampire Slayer* has an identity all its own: Think *Xena* meets *X-Files* in *Beverly Hills 90210*. Ever since its debut on March 17, 1997, as a midseason replacement show for the fledgling WB network, *Buffy* has been singled out for its uniqueness and high quality by enthusiastic critics, with *Entertainment Weekly* calling it that season's "most distinctive and sharply written new show."

The series follows the story of "Buffy Summers," your average, slightly off-center "girl next door"—who just happens to be the latest in a long line of female Slayers fated to protect their generation from the powers of evil. While still a high school student, Buffy was constantly under fire for not living up to her potential and struggled to keep up with her school work. Now, as a young woman raising her younger sister, Buffy struggles to juggle the nuts and bolts of daily living, frequently feeling overwhelmed. But through it all, she remains the Slayer and uses her superhuman strength to battle vampires and other monsters of the night—leaving very little time for a normal social life.

The original cast that brought *Buffy* to life included Emmy-winning former *All My Children* star Sarah Michelle Gellar in the title role; Nicholas Brendon and Alyson Hannigan as Buffy's best friends "Xander" and "Willow"; Charisma Carpenter as the image conscious, boutique-minded "Cordelia," and Anthony Stewart Head as Buffy's "Watcher." David Boreanaz played "Angel," the mysterious stranger who helps Buffy from the shadows. Ironically, the character was meant to appear in just one episode, but the chemistry between Angel and Buffy was so palpable, Boreanaz became a series regular before leaving to star in his own television series, *Angel.*

Whereas the film version ended up more high camp than horror, series creator, Joss Whedon, says the series is his vision of what he originally intended *Buffy* to be. "To me, high school *was* a horror movie," Whedon deadpans. "And that idea can sustain a TV show for years." However, as the series has evolved, Whedon's characters have left high school behind, only to find that life as young adults is equally frightening. "For the series, we've broadened it out. This one community happens to be situated on a Hellmouth, which is a mystical portal, and all kinds of bad things like monsters, demons, and giant insects gravitate toward it. It's not a very good place to go to school"—nor a place conducive to long life spans.

What gives *Buffy* added depth and makes it more than just another spook show is Whedon's allegorical use of monsters and things that go bump in the night to represent the basic fears we all have, about both ourselves and what we really don't know about the people around us.

"When it's somebody's parent or friend who turns into something horrible, it brings up issues that are real and therefore very scary," Whedon explains. "Then there's also your everyday terrors like death, maiming—and life in general."

Welcome to the Hellmouth.

BUFFY: FROM FEATURE FILM TO TELEVISION SERIES

✝

Before there was Sarah Michelle Gellar and Sunnydale, there was Kristy Swanson and Los Angeles. But other than the title, the feature film incarnation of **Buffy the Vampire Slayer** *is as different from the television series as Tod Browning's* **Dracula** *is from George Hamilton's* **Love at First Bite.**

Buffy's evolution from a low-budget feature-film disappointment to one of the most distinctive and stylish television series in recent memory, is reflective of both what's right and what's wrong with working in Hollywood and why it's so important to retain creative control over a project.

It also shows that a good vampire story just won't stay dead and buried.

Buffy Goes to the Movies

When twenty-five-year-old Joss Whedon first got the idea to write his *Buffy the Vampire Slayer* screenplay, his intention was to create a supernatural heroine whose terrifying encounters were reflective of the anxieties all adolescents experience. "The idea behind Buffy was to take someone who is living a normal life, put them in an abnormal situation, and see if they rise to the occasion," Whedon explains. "My idea of the film was that no matter how ill-equipped someone may appear to be to handle their own life, there comes a time when they must take charge of their fate."

That's the artiste's version. On a more superficial level, Joss just wanted this girl to have a little fun: "Yeah, this movie was my response to all the horror movies I had ever seen where some girl walks into a dark room and gets killed. So I decided to make a movie where a blonde girl walks into a dark room and kicks butt instead."

Buffy the Vampire Slayer, Whedon's first screenplay, was optioned in 1988 by Sandollar Productions, the company that was founded by Dolly Parton and her longtime manager, Sandy Gallin. But it wasn't until almost three years later, in 1991, that the script finally passed from the seemingly eternal "development hell" stage to actual pre-production. That's when Sandollar executive, Howard Rosenman, approached the husband-wife team of Kaz and Fran Rubel Kuzui with the script.

Rosenman and his partner, Gail Berman, saw *Buffy* as a small-budget, off-beat independent film. They hoped Japan-born producer Kaz Kuzui, who, along with his wife, Fran Rubel Kuzui, also owned a distribution company that marketed American independent films in Japan, would produce *Buffy* and find Japanese investors to finance it.

The Kuzuis had been a producing/directing team since the couple married. Kaz came to America from Japan in 1977 to work as an assistant director on a Toshiro Mifune film, where he met Fran, who was the script supervisor. They married a year later and when she started spending half her time in Japan, she was hit with culture shock. "I didn't know anything about Japan when I met Kaz," she has said. "I hadn't even read *Shōgun*."

Out of her experiences came the screenplay for the 1988 film *Tokyo Pop*. Although she had no previous directing experience—her background included a master's degree in film from New York University, working as an associate producer at WNET in New York, and as a production manager for PBS—Fran was named the movie's director.

The first meeting between Rosenman and Fran Kuzui didn't go well. "Fran was either an hour early or late and I had a manicure appointment," the producer recalled. "So I asked if she minded if I had my manicure while we talked and she said she didn't. But I later heard through her agent that she thought it was the most loathsome meeting she'd ever had. She hated me. To her, I must have seemed like the clichéd, high-handed movie producer. Which I may have been."

Despite the unfavorable first impression, *Buffy* did end up at Kuzui Enterprises, and then Fran surprised Rosenman by telling him she wanted to direct the film as well. "The instant I saw the title, I knew this was a film I *had* to make," Fran enthused. "Five pages into the script and I was hooked. The more I read, the more I was attracted to the world that Joss Whedon had created. Here's a girl, a high school cheerleader, who's suddenly being told she's part of something else.

"I think all of us, when we're kids, know we're part of *something*, and the process of being an adult is finding the something you're a part of. This is a story about a girl—and it's very important that it's a girl—finding out how powerful she really is."

Once the deal was set, Fran set about changing Joss's script. She says she made Buffy more lovable and asked Whedon to write in a female sidekick for the lead vampire. But the biggest change she made was one of tone, viewing *Buffy* through a pop-culture prism. "I don't understand that approach," Joss admitted at the time, but as the screenwriter he had no say in the matter. It was now the Kuzuis' picture to reshape as they saw fit.

The cast was a curious mixture, with pop culture of the moment integrated with the respected tried and true. Although early in the film's development former *Who's the Boss* star Alyssa Milano was briefly attached to the role, the part of Buffy eventually went to twenty-two-year-old Kristy Swanson, who was just coming off two films, *Hot Shots!* and *Mannequin 2.*

"There are a lot of blondes and they're either funny or they're tough," Kuzui said. "When Kristy walked in wearing a black leather jacket and chewing gum, I knew I'd found my Slayer. You just look at her and know she could kick some tush. The day I met Kristy, I understood that Buffy wasn't just pop and silly."

Despite her youth, Swanson had thirteen years' acting experience behind her. A native Californian, Kristy was born in the well-heeled community of Mission Viejo near San Diego. By the time she was nine, Kristy had decided her future was as an actress, so when a family friend suggested she get an agent, Swanson sent some Kodak snapshots to the Mary Grady Agency, a well-known talent agency for children and young adults. Mary, whose daughter Lani O'Grady was a regular on *Eight Is Enough*, took a look at Kristy's pictures and liked what she saw. Within three days, Swanson had signed with Grady and had been cast in her first commercial, one of the more than thirty in which she would eventually appear.

When she was thirteen, Kristy was cast in her first series, *Dreamfinders*, on the Disney cable channel. With her family still living in Mission Viejo, it meant a three-hour round-trip commute and being tutored while on the set. When the series ended, Swanson returned to school to discover one of the teachers was going to fail her because she hadn't been in class. When her parents couldn't reason with the teacher, they took her out of the school, and, both being teachers themselves, decided to teach her at home, following the local school district curriculum. Kristy "graduated" from high school when she was sixteen.

Although she didn't have to juggle work and school anymore, her age was still a problem and she kept losing roles to older actresses who could work longer hours. So, with her parents' blessings, Swanson filed for emancipation, and, when it was granted, Kristy moved to Hollywood on her own. Within a short time she landed parts in the films *Flowers in the Attic* and *Deadly Friend*.

When asked if she regretted missing the high school experience, Swanson was resolute: "I enjoy characters so I learned to study people—family, friends, everybody. That was more important than going to the prom. My sister-in-law, Jyl, was the model for Buffy. I observed her for weeks before shooting because she had that attitude. No professor can teach you that."

Swanson saw the character as someone going through personal growth. "It's not about 'I'm a woman and I can kick anyone's ass.' It's about change and challenging yourself, getting over your fears and taking one step further. She may walk into the dark room, but she's still afraid. Her biggest fear is, 'What are my friends going to think?' Because in the beginning Buffy knows the price of everything and the value of nothing—she's very shallow."

Interestingly, the movie Buffy was given some of the qualities that would later come to be associated with the Cordelia character on the series: She is consumed with shopping and fashion, bent on running the school social scene and is rather self-involved, with, as Swanson put it, "few concerns beyond what is hip and happening."

Luke Perry was cast as Buffy's boyfriend Pike. Perry was then at the height of his *Beverly Hills 90210* popularity, and was being touted as the next James Dean because of his brooding, bad boy portrayal of Dylan McKay. His fans were exactly the people the producers wanted to attract. Ironically, Perry hoped the comic elements of the movie would give him some distance from his TV alter ego: "I can do more than stand and squint. I'd like to play character parts. Pike is very sweet, he just doesn't expect a lot from anybody or anything. There is a real role reversal in the movie," he noted. "Buffy's the one who's always having to save him, which is a nice change from the way these movies usually work. If Buffy can be seen as a hero, then I suppose Pike is the damsel in distress."

Perry's heartthrob status nonetheless carried over to the film's production. In an attempt to keep his more aggressive fans from tracking his movements, Luke was listed on the call sheet as "Chet," and when filming scenes at the Fashion Square mall in Sherman Oaks, an upscale area in Los Angeles' San Fernando Valley, the producers were forced to hire six extra security guards just to keep the young girls away from Perry.

Swanson revealed that Luke tried to downplay the intensity of his popularity by presenting himself as just an average Joe. "The word 'simple' kind of fell into our vocabulary, because he'd always say, 'I'm just a simple guy.' So I called him Mr. Simple. 'Come here, Mr. Simple.' "

He was chagrined by the teen idolness of it all. "On the first day of shooting, about three hundred people showed up, most of them screaming girls. I was so glad Rutger Hauer and Donald Sutherland weren't working that day because I didn't want these two well-respected, well-established actors to walk on the set and think, 'Oh no—we're making a movie with Frankie Avalon.' "

Donald Sutherland, whose film credits range from *M*A*S*H* to *JFK*, played the mysterious Merrick, whose job it is to instruct Buffy in the ancient art of vampire Slaying. Although he liked the script very much, the title left him him befuddled. "When I first agreed to this," he recalled, "I couldn't even say the title out loud. When somebody asked me what the name of the movie was I was going to be working on, I wrote it down on a piece of paper. They, in turn, fell on the floor laughing."

Rutger Hauer, the Dutch actor who had gained international fame and acclaim in films like *Ladyhawke* and *Blade Runner*, was cast as the vampire Lothos. Among the other credited cast members were a curious collection of actors with pop culture credentials: David Arquette, who at the time was best known for being Rosanna's sister; Natasha Gregson Wagner (Robert Wagner and Natalie Wood's daughter); syndicated columnist Liz Smith; Amanda Anka (Paul Anka's daughter); Sarah Jones (whose father was the Monkees' Davy Jones); and a cameo appearance by *American Graffiti* star Candy Clark, who played Buffy's inattentive mother.

But the most interesting casting was for the part of Amilyn, Lothos' sadistic sidekick. Originally Joan Chen had been set for the role, but left in a dispute over money. The producers had offered her $45,000 and she wanted more. When she didn't get it, she walked just before filming was scheduled to start. That was when Fran suggested the person she'd really wanted all along—Paul "Pee-wee Herman" Reubens. "I had never said anything because it was such a far-out idea," she explained.

At the time, casting Reubens was a risky choice because it would be his first job since being arrested in an "adult movie" theater and charged with indecent exposure, which had effectively ended his career as a children's show host. Reubens agreed to take the role—for $150,000—and, for reasons never clearly explained, the producers attempted to keep his involvement in the film a secret. But on March 3, 1992, the industry trade paper *Variety* reported that "the film's producers and domestic distributor 20th Century Fox and Herman [*sic*] are all under a contractual press gag not to divulge Pee-wee's involvement until production is completed. Sorry, guys."

And except for the press leaks, it would have been fairly easy to keep Reubens' participation under wraps. Like Perry, Reubens had a code name—Beau Hunkus. But unlike the *90210* star, Paul Reubens was virtually unrecognizable in the film, with rat's-nest hair and a goatee disguising his face. And Pee-wee's distinctive nasal preschool voice was replaced by a menacing snarling one. "We decided Paul would play the evil guy and Rutger would play the scary guy," Fran Kuzui said in an interview. "And there's a distinction because usually what you're scared of is not the real evil.

"The thing that's great about directing a vampire movie is that it lets you create your own world. And talk about someone who creates their own world—Paul is somebody who created one of the most unique and, to me, seriously important pop characters ever. Pee-wee Herman is right up there with Mickey Mouse as far as I'm concerned. So I was really interested in what he could do with a character like Amilyn."

Kaz Kuzui later explained the cast mix as a financial necessity: "Luke Perry's name means nothing in Japanese markets or overseas, so we needed to make certain we had international names." But, as it turned out, the need to find Japanese investors fell by the wayside. On the strength of Joss's script and the cast, 20th Century Fox eventually agreed to pick up the $9 million budget in exchange for worldwide rights—on the condition that the movie would be ready for release in the summer. That meant spending only five weeks on pre-production and six weeks filming.

"It was a kid's movie that Fox wanted made quickly so they could release it on the crest of interest in screen vampires," Kuzui explained. "However, it isn't a vampire movie, but a pop culture comedy about what people *think* about vampires." Actually, as conceived by Whedon, it *was* supposed to be a vampire movie as well as a comedy—but by this time, the film had in many ways became completely different from the one Joss had written.

In order to handle the movie's physical demands, prior to filming Swanson had ten days of intensive martial-arts instruction from expert James Lew (*Big Trouble in Little China*) and Pat Johnson, who had worked on *Teenage*

Mutant Ninja Turtles. While filming, Swanson would be coached by the movie's leading stunt coordinator and second unit director, Terry Leonard, whose credits include *Romancing the Stone* and *Apocalypse Now.* "They never asked me if I was a fighter but I did have a dance background," Swanson said. "At the end of the film, I had a lot of bruises and sore bones."

Fran Kuzui takes credit for the martial-arts aspect of the film. "I wanted to find some way for Buffy to slay vampires that had nothing to do with killing, since I was not interested in making a violent film. I am a great fan of Chinese martial-arts films which are, for the most part, pretty bloodless affairs. Since Buffy is a vampire Slayer, not a killer, I had the idea that she would rely on the martial arts as much as possible to get the job done."

Filming began on February 20, 1992—almost four years after Whedon had originally sold the script. The production filmed on location around Los Angeles, including Marshall High School, and on a soundstage built in a converted warehouse located in Santa Monica. What made the nine-week filming schedule particularly difficult was night shooting, which hit twenty-nine consecutive days at one stretch. "The biggest challenge in making this movie was to make it through the night shooting," Swanson said.

"You *become* a vampire when you shoot a vampire movie," Perry joked.

Perry and Swanson got along so well together that they were rumored to be romantically involved. In turn, Kuzui openly enjoyed her younger stars Perry and Swanson, even giving Swanson a silver Celtic cross on a chain with the inscription *To My Favorite Slayer,* but Kuzui's relationship wasn't as warm with some of the other performers. According to Kaz Kuzui, Donald Sutherland and Rutger Hauer were not amused at the tone the film was taking. "They were very difficult," he says directly. "They thought the movie was very serious and became insecure. They tried to make their roles more complex, more emotional"—in other words, the way Joss had originally written the characters. "Rutger tried to be the vampire Lestat from *Interview with the Vampire,*" Kaz continued. "He's very good but he depends on a lot of acting gimmicks."

Hauer acknowledged that it wasn't the easiest of work situations. "It *is* very difficult for me to come into something like this, because it's a supporting role—supporting a lot of young actors." Swanson also admitted to having some problems with her film foe. "Our relationship was hot and cold. He was really trying to screw with me, to get some sort of rise out of me, I guess. He likes to mess with everyone. He'd stare at me with his Rutger Hauer look and it frustrated him because I'd just laugh and say, 'You're not scaring me.' He'd ask me a million questions, like, 'Kristy, what does Lothos mean to you?'

Finally I said, 'Look, does it matter? You take care of your character, I'll take care of mine, and we'll just leave it at that.' "

There was also an uncomfortable moment during a dream sequence in which Swanson and Hauer end up in bed together, which Rutger wanted to play nude. After Kristy asked, though, he complied with her request that he wear pants. Sutherland, on the other hand, was a Swanson favorite: "Donald was unbelievable," she said. "I was blown away by how supportive and sweet he is."

After the production wrapped, Rubel immediately set to work on post-production, having only four months to edit the film before its scheduled release date in late summer. That small amount of time was reduced even further because the studio was so confident the film would be a box office winner, they moved up *Buffy*'s release date to July.

"We really have our summer kind of scheduled around *Buffy*," said Fox's domestic marketing president, Andrea Jaffe. "This is a concept movie and we're going to sell the concept. It's what we have to do." Jaffe wanted to follow the lead of what Disney had done with one of their smaller-budgeted films, *Encino Man*, starring Pauly Shore and then-newcomer Brendan Fraser. Disney had given the film extensive sneak previews which had created a strong word-of-mouth that translated into a healthy box-office performance, making it one of the summer's surprise hits. But Jaffe claimed that, by rescheduling the release date, the film wasn't done in time to do as much screening as she would have liked.

For a small-budget film, Fox gave *Buffy* a relatively large promotional blitz, including an extensive billboard marketing campaign. Actually, the film had more than one campaign. Initially, ads and billboards for the movie showed a cheerleader from the waist down, holding a pompom in one hand and a wooden stake in the other, with the tag line "She knows a sucker when she sees one." Later newspaper ads showed Swanson holding a stake with Perry peering over her shoulder, with the banner: "Pert. Wholesome. Way Lethal." Time would tell whether Jaffe's marketing plan would work.

Although the earlier release date meant going up against stronger competition, Kuzui seemed unconcerned about the switch. "There's probably not really a good time to open a movie. But by August, everybody is just interested in having a good time and I think that's what this movie will provide."

In press interviews promoting the film, Swanson was equally optimistic. "The guys are gonna go, 'Damn!' They're going to think it's cool. I think the girls are going to think it's *really* cool—'I can kill vampires *and* get the guy in the end.' " However, in less-spun moments, she was more ambivalent: "For all I know, it could be really hilarious, or it could really suck."

Buffy the Vampire Slayer opened on July 31, 1992, and died. Even the relatively unsuccessful Meryl Streep–Bruce Willis black comedy *Death Becomes Her* took in more money. The executives at Fox had thought teens would be lining up in droves to buy tickets for *Buffy*, if just to see Luke Perry—but they didn't. Trying to explain why, then-chairman of 20th Century Fox Film Corp., Joe Roth, pointed the finger at the marketing. "We thought we had a campaign that really worked—and obviously we didn't . . . I took my son and his ten-year-old friend to see it," Roth recalled. "On our way out of the theater, the ten-year-old said to me, 'This is a movie for adults, but there's no way they would know that.' I offered him a job."

Beyond that, the movie was generally skewered by the more important film critics. *Time* magazine offered this assessment: "By now you are perhaps dreaming that the summer's most pressing need—for a funny sleeper—has been fulfilled. Wrong. Or as Buffy says, 'Does the word "duh" mean anything to you?' It does to director Fran Rubel Kuzui, whose frenzied mistrust of her material is almost total."

Newsweek's Charles Leerhsen noted, "The film's basic problem is that it fails to create what might be called the vanilla fudge effect—the delicious swirling of the scary and the funny that marked, say, *Abbot and Costello Meet Frankenstein*."

Many critics, such as the *Washington Post*'s, sounded disappointed that such a promising premise hadn't lived up to its potential. "Its comic creativity is patchy; that final match with Hauer is a distinct letdown. *Buffy* is amusing for a time but its destiny is to die in a disappointingly long-winded conclusion."

Michael Price of the *Ft. Worth Star-Telegram* was more pointed: "If it were not for the saving grace of Paul Reubens's show-stopping vampire act, a script too witty for director Kuzui's dreary handling and Kristy Swanson's energetic title portrayal, *Buffy the Vampire Slayer* would be unwatchable." That pretty much summed up Joss Whedon's sentiments as well, who now says bluntly of the film, "The director ruined it."

Although *Buffy*'s disappointing reception did not adversely affect Whedon's career, it was a setback for both Swanson and Perry. Kristy, however, continued her film career, appearing in *8 Heads in a Duffel Bag* opposite David Spade and Joe Pesci, and in Adam's Sandler's *Big Daddy*.

Perhaps the person with the most on the line was Luke Perry, at least as far as his film career was concerned. "I learned I'm not bankable at the box office," he admitted. "I'm no one's first choice for a part. I'm behind fifteen other guys—if I'm thought of at all." Luke Perry would eventually leave *Bev-*

erly Hills 90210 to pursue, among other things, a film career that never came to fruition. Although he had enjoyed minor success with the 1994 film *8 seconds*, based on the life of rodeo champion Lane Frost, Perry's other movies, such as *The Heist*, *The Enemy*, and *Luxury of Love*, have failed to leave a lasting impression. He has fared better on the small screen, appearing most recently in the Showtime series *Jeremiah*.

Fran Rubel Kuzui has yet to direct another film, although she and her husband's Kuzui Enterprises have produced two other films—the 1997 release *Telling Lies in America*, a coming-of-age story starring Kevin Bacon and Brad Renfro; and a 1995 gem called *Orgazmo*, in which a young Mormon actor/preacher becomes the star of a porno film. One of the lead actors in the film, Trey Parker, would later go on to find fame and fortune as the co-creator of the Comedy Channel's animated series *South Park*. Although the Kuzuis are listed as executive producers on the *Buffy* series, they have no creative input at all.

When the final figures were tallied, *Buffy the Vampire Slayer* grossed a little over $16 million in domestic box office, but because the budget had been ultramodest to begin with, the studio managed to turn a small profit. However, nothing could compensate Whedon for his profound disappointment over how his vision of the script had been so thoroughly compromised. But three years later Whedon would unexpectedly get a second chance to do *Buffy* the way he'd originally intended, and he was determined to take full advantage of the opportunity.

Turning *Buffy* into a Television Series

Despite its seemingly quiet, small-town appearance, Sunnydale is actually a hotbed of mystical happenings and a magnet for evil creatures of all types, not just vampires. Why? Because it sits on what is vividly called a Hellmouth: think of it as a Club Med for the demon set.

Unlike the movie, in which tongue-in-cheekiness was substituted for any sense of menace, in this incarnation the sense of lurking danger is palpable. "In the movie, the director took an action/horror/comedy script and went only with the comedy," explains Joss Whedon, who is executive producer as well as creator of the series. "In the television show, we're keeping to the original formula. We take our horror genre seriously. We are not doing a spoof. It's larger than life, but we are very much involved with these characters. This is not *Clueless or Party Girl.* The description I like best is '*My So-called Life* meets *The X-Files.*' "

Welcome to the world of *Buffy the Vampire Slayer,* television style.

The idea for resurrecting the film into a series began in 1995 when Gail Berman, an executive at Sandollar, the production company that originally optioned Joss's screenplay back in 1988, approached Whedon with the suggestion of making the 1992 film into a television series.

"What's ironic is that when I first read Joss's screenplay for the movie years ago, I thought then it would make a great television show," says Berman. "But when the movie came out and didn't do that well, the idea of a series sort of went away." But like the vampires she fights, *Buffy* wouldn't die, becoming a surprising video hit, and Berman exhumed her series idea from the development graveyard.

"I thought about it for a while then decided that I *was* interested because it would be very different from the movie," explains Joss, who would have creative control—something he did not have with the film. "I thought there was an idea in the 'high school horror show' that would sustain a television show and keep it going for years.

"If you look at movies like *I Was a Teenage Werewolf,* you'll see this combination of teen angst and horror has been going on for a long time. So it was a very appealing idea to me for a show, but one I honestly hadn't thought of until they brought it to me."

Not everyone was thrilled with Whedon's decision to go forward with the idea for a series, however: "My agent *begged* me not to do it," Whedon laughs. But Joss ignored the advice because he was being given a chance to do something few screenwriters get to do—get it right the second time and be the man in charge.

"I really hated what they had done to my original script," Whedon says bluntly. "To me, making a movie is like buying a lotto ticket—the writer is just not that important. Being a screenwriter in Hollywood is not all it's cracked up to be. People blow their noses on you. When I went on the set of *Alien* [*Resurrection*], people are nice enough but I'm standing in a corner. On *Buffy,* I'm telling these stories. Not only am I telling them, I'm telling them every eight days," he says, referring to how long it takes to film each episode.

"The movies I write, if they even get made, take several thousand years. But television is a writer's medium so there's a better chance things will come out the way you originally envisioned them. With television, it's like getting to make an independent movie every week. Besides," he says smiling, "it was a way to get back at everyone I went to school with."

Whedon says they worked on the show for about a year before they actually started filming. During that time he ironed out the show's concept and solidified the characters. In the film, Buffy's original Watcher—Merrick—dies. But for the series, Whedon wanted a Watcher who was slightly less strange, though no less confounded by his charge. He also wanted this Watcher to be ever so slightly less surefooted and more human.

The Buffy character was also adjusted. In the film Buffy was a senior, but Whedon made the TV Buffy a high school sophomore. Gone is her preoccupation with clothes and her insider status peopled with a vacuous circle of friends—most of those traits were incorporated into Cordelia, who served as an example of the kind of person Buffy might have grown into had she not been the Slayer—and in their place is a deep sense of angst, and friends who are anything but "in." Also, although she might not be a straight-A student, Gellar's Buffy exhibits far more intelligence than Swanson's. In the film Buffy barely dealt with complex emotional conflicts, but in the series, she would deal with them on a daily basis.

Buffy's mother would be much more than the fleeting joke presence she was in the film. Whedon sought to make Joyce Summers a parent much more grounded in the reality of having to deal with a daughter who seems compelled to do unexplainable things, like burn down the gym and constantly get into fights.

It was also vitally important to set the right tone from the very first scene. Despite the horror premise, Whedon believed that playing it straight would lessen the suspension of disbelief. "We set up the premise that the town is located on a Hellmouth, so it would be understood that our characters know what is going on, know that Buffy is a vampire-Slayer, and would understand that mystical and strange things will happen in Sunnydale."

In March 1996, the WB put the series into development for the 1996–97 season and began the drawn-out casting process. Sarah Michelle Gellar recounts how she first learned of the series: "My manager spoke to the WB and they mentioned they had this *Buffy* show and he thought it would be a great opportunity for me to use my Tae Kwon Do, which I had studied for four years."

The producers had already approached Charisma Carpenter, who was just coming off Aaron Spelling's *Malibu Shores*, for the part of Buffy. But Gellar, who had been set to audition for Cordelia instead, was determined to play Buffy and badgered the producers into letting her read for the lead. "I probably had eleven auditions and four screen tests," Gellar says of the nerve-wracking process. "It was the most awful experience of my life but I was so driven to get this part.

"I had read the script and had heard about how wonderful Joss Whedon was, and I went to audition the week he had been nominated for an Oscar for his *Toy Story* screenplay. I thought, 'I'm going to have this role.' Later, Joss told me I nailed it—but I still went through eleven auditions."

"There was no second place," says Whedon. "We read tons of people and several were staggeringly untalented. Buffy is a tough part; it is a character actress in the body of a leading lady. She's an eccentric. This girl has to look the part of a blonde bimbo who dies in reel two but turns out to be anything but that. You don't find those qualities very often in young actresses who also happen to be beautiful, but Sarah gave us a perfect reading. And then she says, 'By the way, I'm also a brown belt in Tae Kwon Do. Is that good?' "

After hiring Sarah, Whedon offered Carpenter the role of Cordelia instead. The cast, which also included Anthony Stewart Head as Giles and Nicholas Brendon as Xander, was coming together.

Then the series hit a snag. Instead of putting the show on in September, the network decided to hold it for the midseason. Although the delay was disappointing at the time, Gellar says it actually worked out for the best. "The show wasn't ready, so it was a blessing to wait. The extra time really gave us a chance to fully develop and flesh out the show and we're stronger because of it." When they were finally ready to film, a last-minute decision was made to recast the roles of Angel and Willow. Alyson Hannigan replaced Riff Regan and David Boreanaz was cast the night before he was scheduled to show up for filming. The more minor role of Principal Flutie was also recast. The original actor, Stephen Tobolowsky—who has appeared in many movies, including *Groundhog Day* and *Memento*—was replaced by Ken Lerner, brother of Oscar nominee Michael Lerner.

Once his cast was set, Whedon was satisfied he had the right group. He liked all his original characters because they were "either parts of me or parts I wish I had. You know, I took a bunch of pieces and put them on a page and when these guys came in, they not only got them exactly, but since we've been doing the show together, have shaped them. So right now, the characters are a real hybrid with everybody bringing something to their character that wasn't there before. Although the characters started off with me, now they belong to the actors and I just write to them.

"What Sarah brings to the part is her intelligence. At the same time, she's got that hormonal goofiness that makes Buffy not just the Terminator. I'm very fond of everyone in this cast and I've worked with *plenty* of people I can't say that about," he laughs. "It's not easy to find the right balance—people who are mature enough to do the hard work, but who still have that youthful energy that's genuine. It's not easy, but we got 'em."

Executives at the WB were more than pleased with the work Whedon and his cast were doing. Susanne Daniels, then–executive vice president of programming for the network, was one of the series' biggest boosters. "Every once in a while you meet a writer whose passion and vision just blows you away and that's what happened when we met with Joss Whedon for the first time," she says. "As soon as we saw his pilot script, we knew we had something unique, but it wasn't until the casting process, when we met Sarah, that we knew we had our first potential breakthrough show. Buffy is really scary, it's really sexy, and it's really funny. We think it's a show that has it all." The WB, which was going after the same audience Fox went for in its early days, felt *Buffy* would appeal to their target demographic, the 18–34 age group.

Buffy the Vampire Slayer debuted to some of the highest critical praise of any show in the 1996–97 season. *People*'s Tom Gliatto graded it a B+ and added these words of praise: "Sarah Michelle Gellar plays the part (originated by Kristy Swanson in the movie version) with the right degree of put-upon resentment, and the cast—including Anthony Stewart Head as school librarian—is as smooth an ensemble as you could wish for in an hourlong series. All in all, this looks like one of the brightest new shows of the season."

The *San Francisco Chronicle*'s TV critic, John Carman, also lauded the show. "*Buffy the Vampire Slayer* is as surprisingly engaging as the film that spawned it. The Buffy role seems to have been altered a bit for Gellar. This Buffy is primed for martial-arts action, but she's also notably nimbler in the cranium. It's a decent role, and Gellar handles it with wit, confidence, impressive athleticism and a fetching off-center smile. *Buffy* takes itself just seriously enough to ladle moderate suspense between chuckles."

Still, not everyone was enchanted with the series. *TV Guide*'s Jeff Jarvis was one of the few who faulted the show's production values. "I can't decide whether to praise *Buffy* for being different or to make fun of it for being so B-movie cheesy."

But overall, the response was more in line with Kristen Baldwin's brief critique in *Entertainment Weekly*: "Infinitely more entertaining than the cute but forgettable 1992 movie it's based on, *Buffy the Vampire Slayer* is this midseason's most distinctive and sharply written new show."

Gellar felt the series was so different in execution and tone from the film that she never worried about people comparing one against the other. "I look at the series as being loosely based on the movie. In my mind, all we did was take the idea of *Buffy*, not the story or the character. Joss's vision for *Buffy* was something a little darker, a little more on edge, a little less camp. It's really a brilliant idea, that the scariest things in life are things that are based in reality. What scares you the most are things that could possibly actually happen."

Gellar says the original high school setting was the perfect jumping-off place for the series because "I think high school scares everyone. When I was in junior high, I didn't know where I fit in. I tried to be a jock, then I tried to be cool, but I couldn't find my place. I think that no matter how popular you are, or how unpopular you are, high school is a scary place and it is one thing that everyone can relate to; it's one of the few things that everybody has experienced.

"While people might not always relate to the horror aspect of *Buffy*, the situations in our story lines are ones people can relate to—loving a friend, being at an age when you're having problems with Mom, wanting to be an adult and a child at the same time."

That said, Whedon has been adamant about not letting the series become an issue-of-the-week soapbox. "We are not going to get terribly or overtly issue-oriented. The horror isn't just, monsters attack and we fight them. The horror and the stories have to come from the characters, from their relationships and fears—otherwise, it won't really be interesting . . . What I want to get at is the incredibly operatic reactions to small emotional things, to get into the characters' interior lives, even though it's a show with big, horned demons. As I've said before, there will never be a Very Special Episode of *Buffy*.

"The thing that ends up scaring me the most is people. I think the best stuff happens not just by having a monster show up, but when we remember the sort of human relationships people have that are really twisted and scary, and then extend them into horror stories. That's when things really disturb me—when it's somebody's parent or somebody's friend who is turning into something horrible—because it brings up issues that are real, and therefore, very scary.

"In the series, we have taken real-life situations that reflect a grotesque parody. When I get together with my writing team, I ask them, 'What is your favorite horror movie? What's the most embarrassing thing that ever happened to you? Now, how can we combine the two?'

"What's fun about the show is that we never know from scene to scene which way it's going to go. A scene that starts out very dramatically could end up quite funny, or something truly horrible could happen in it. We don't do, 'Okay, now here's the funny part and now here's the scary part.' We never really know what's going to be highlighted until it's over."

To Gellar, it doesn't matter what direction the scenes take. "I love all genres—comedy, horror, action, drama—and what I think is so wonderful about our show is that we have all of those different aspects," Gellar observes. "It's interesting when you go from being a child actor to an adult actor. *All My Children* was really that transition for me, and *Buffy* is really a wonderful opportunity for me to play someone a little closer to myself and situations I've been in—minus the vampires."

Nicholas Brendon, who plays Xander, likes a more macabre aspect of the series: "One thing that I like about the show is that in every episode, somebody dies—and you never know who it's going to be. I mean, you could have a bond with, say me—and then I'm dead. Not that Joss would actually let that happen. So if someone is in danger, they might actually die and not come back, which I think is nice."

Whedon says it was always his intention to introduce characters that wouldn't make it through the end of the season. "Not that we feel we have to kill someone every week, but we like to let people wonder. We like to show people that the peril here is real, that the horror is real and there's something at stake."

"But it's not what you might expect," Gellar points out. "It's not the person you think will die who does."

While some have wondered whether some part of *Buffy*'s success might be a case of lucky timing, Whedon says the premise is timeless. "I have no doubt *Buffy* would have gotten on the air whenever it was pitched. I think horror shows have an important place. People *need* horror stories. They need the Big Bad Wolf and they need something to latch on to, something to project their fears onto. Life's horrible. It's scarier than ever. We are never going to live forever, there is no God . . . so we'll always need these stories for an outlet. But horror had disappeared somewhat in movies which is why it is showing up on television. And it hadn't been on television for a long time, either. It was *The X-Files* that sort of brought it back again."

The second season of the series picked up where the first ended, with lots of critical raves and ever-improving ratings. Of course, ratings are a relative thing, and what was positive for the WB would have been considered disastrous for one of the Big Four networks. But *Buffy* had become the WB's highest-rated show and, more importantly, its most recognizable and talked-about series.

There was some tinkering going on with the show itself. The producers had decided to up the romance quotient, in order to broaden the focus from being strictly suspense and action, and to attract even more women to the show. As a result, the star-crossed romance between Angel and Buffy became the emotional cornerstone of the second and third seasons, until David Boreanaz was given the *Angel* spin-off series and his character left Sunnydale in the third-season finale.

A New Home

For five seasons *Buffy* exceeded all expectations the WB had for it. Sarah Michelle Gellar became a movie star and a fixture on magazine covers everywhere and Web sites devoted to the series and its stars became ubiquitous. More importantly, the show helped the WB establish itself as the network for young-adult females, a sought-after demographic by advertisers. Many at the network credited *Buffy* for helping make the network. The show had also earned the network critical praise by earning Emmy and Golden Globe nominations and making the "10 Best" lists of critics from *Time, TV Guide,* and *USA Today* during its fifth season.

But sometimes shows can become victims of their success, and during the 2000–2001 season the WB sought a minimal license-fee increase to be paid to the producing studio, 20th Century Fox, at the end of the original five-year contract. This was unusual because any show that is on the air that long and is up for renewal usually expects and gets a hefty increase in license fees. To completely understand the bad blood brewing, it's important to know that the 20th Century Fox studio is part of News Corporation, which owns not only the Fox Network but several UPN affiliates as well. The studio balked at the request to lower its license fees—which is the money the network pays the production company for the privilege of airing the show—and let it be known they would be amenable to moving *Buffy* to another network if a deal could not be worked out with the WB. Immediately, UPN expressed interest. Because both outlets were vying to become the fifth major network, UPN and the WB were bitter rivals, and the tug of war over *Buffy* soon turned ugly.

At the end of the fifth season, the WB was paying $1 million per episode. 20th Century Fox wanted more than $2 million, citing the program's continued ratings strength and high production costs. In a war of words played out in the press, then CEO WB Network Jamie Kellner accused the studio of asking for too much and made a final offer of $1.8 million an episode.

While the television community watched the situation with interest, emotions ran high among *Buffy*'s cast and crew. The more Whedon listened to Kellner downplay the show's importance to the network—Kellner saying, "It's not our number one show"—the more the usually easygoing writer burned. "It makes me angry to see this show belittled," Whedon said at the time. In retrospect, he admits, "I was just so turned around by the whole thing." The only time he lost his temper was while filming the fifth-season finale and the WB wanted to honor the show by bringing press on-set for a photo opportunity and a celebratory cake. "The whole thing made me so angry, I had to stop shooting," says Whedon. "I was like, 'Shut it down! I just can't be here right now!' "

Gellar was equally passionate, and in an emotional moment lashed out: "I will stay on *Buffy* if, and only if, *Buffy* stays on the WB. And you know what? Print that. My bosses are going to kill me, but print that. I want them to know."

Reporters did print it and her producers quickly pointed out the error of speaking before thinking. Gellar did a quick about-face and retracted her statement, saying she would stay with *Buffy* no matter where it ended up. When the WB refused to budge past their $1.8 million–per–episode offer, the studio made the deal to bring *Buffy* to UPN, which ordered forty-four episodes to be shown over the course of two years, with a license fee of $2.3 million per episode.

The WB released this official statement: "20th Television has made an inauspicious decision for the television industry by taking one of their own programs off of a nonaffiliated network and placing it on a network in which they have a large vested interest, through their acquisition of Chris-Craft and public comments that Fox and UPN are discussing ways to merge. The WB will continue to develop successful, innovative programming that delivers a high concentration of young adults and teens. We wish Sarah, Joss, and David Greenwalt well."

Sandy Grushow, the chairman of the Fox Television Entertainment Group shrugged off the accusation, saying it was simply a business financial decision. "If News Corporation didn't own a single UPN station we would have made the exact same deal," Grushow said. "We believe that there is enormous upside potential at UPN and, given their passion for the show, given their commitment for the show, we believe they have every opportunity to raise the bar for *Buffy*."

UPN's then–chief executive Dean Valentine said the acquisition of *Buffy* would start a new era for the fledgling network: "We are incredibly pleased to have *Buffy the Vampire Slayer* on UPN, not just because it is one of the best shows on the air and represents a new era in UPN's life and direction, but more importantly because Joss Whedon is one of the finest writers and producers in television. Our main motivation for pursuing *Buffy* so aggressively was to be in business with Joss and with 20th . . . and we're very pleased to have that opportunity."

Gellar tried to explain her earlier outburst: "I love this drama! Of course I had loyalties to the WB. Look at what they've done for me and the show. You have to understand that for five years we had a home. We had a place where we were supported, where we were able to make the show creatively the way we wanted to make it, and the thought of making a move was scary. So of course my first reaction was, 'You want to be where home is.' People ask me if I regret the comment. You can't regret the way you feel. Change is scary. But sometimes change can be for the better.

"Unfortunately, the WB didn't want to make the show the way we wanted to do it. They didn't want to give Joss what he needed to make the show the way it has to be made. And UPN has been incredibly supportive, I think, to make everybody feel incredibly welcome as a whole. And I think they've given us a new excitement about the show. It's like getting to start fresh, so I'm nervous and I'm excited."

The one-hundredth and final WB episode of *Buffy* aired May 22, 2001. It was promoted by the WB as the *series* finale instead of the season finale—a move that fans couldn't help but interpret as an attempt to make viewers think the show had been canceled instead of just moved. But they did put a message at the end of the episode thanking the cast and crew for the five years at the WB. In the end, once the recriminations stopped, the move proved beneficial for all concerned. The WB had the money and time-slots to pursue new, less expensive dramas and comedies, while UPN was suddenly attracting a whole new audience. Most importantly, *Buffy* was guaranteed the opportunity to keep delivering its unique blend of chills and laughs for at least two more seasons.

However, even though Sarah Michelle Gellar is contracted only through the 2002–03 season, there has already been talk that it's possible the series could go on without her past a seventh season. The most persistent rumor is that Buffy's sister, Dawn, could be the next Slayer, although that could only happen if Faith, the once–rogue Slayer who is now in jail, dies, since the Slayer line now goes through her character.

"The show will run as long as it is good," says Whedon. "It is possible that maybe the show stops after seven years. What I do know is that these guys are capable of so much, and the writers have so many ideas, that the show potentially could run for a way, way long time. Eventually there will come a burnout where creatively we'll just be too tired. But right now we're feeling more creative than we have been, so contracts really aren't the point. Contracts get resolved or they don't. People move on or they don't. What matters is that I have another hundred stories to tell, and the people I want to tell them with."

Joss Whedon

There's no question that Joss Whedon has a fertile imagination. He has conjured up some of the most inventive screenplays in recent movie history, from the genre-bending *Buffy the Vampire Slayer* to his Oscar-nominated work in *Toy Story*. His talent is unquestioned. The question is, just what happened to this guy in childhood that so skewed his way of looking at the world?

"Yes, I was a strange, unlovable child," laughs Joss. "I was afraid of the dark and had a very vivid imagination. A lot of things scare me. Actually, everything scares me. I think the thing I was most afraid of was my big brother. So

if you see big brothers being eviscerated in some show of mine, you'll know where that came from.

"The truth is, I like monsters. The thing I like best is when the monsters jump out of the closet or when there are demons with horns. If it's a cheesy horror film, I've probably seen it."

Admittedly a painfully shy adolescent, Joss spent much of his youth escaping into reading—comic books like *Spider-Man*, *Dracula*, and *The Fantastic Four*, and authors Frank Herbert and Larry Niven. "A lot of kids get into comic books, but with me it was deeper, more consuming than with other children. While they were outside playing, I'd be tucked away inside the house with a stack of comic books to read."

Born Joe Whedon on June 23, 1964, he was raised in Manhattan and attended high school at the exclusive Riverdale School in New York, which Joss hated. "Girls wouldn't so much as poke me with a stick," he remembers. During his senior year, Joss transferred to Winchester College, an all-boys school in England that was built over six hundred years ago and is renowned for its academic qualifications. It was during college that he took the name Joss, which means "luck" in Chinese. It was also when he discovered the power of humor. "I started quoting *Monty Python* routines and they accepted me," he jokes. "Actually, I studied the classics and saw a lot of movies," says Joss of his time there.

Whedon returned to America to attend Wesleyan in Connecticut. Originally a Methodist college, Wesleyan is now a small, exclusive university on the Connecticut River with a student body of less than three thousand students.

"College rocked," Joss says. "I mean, I was still miserable most of the time, but in a party way"—and Joss would draw on the experience for the later, post–high school seasons of *Buffy*. Whedon majored in film and when he graduated, he had a degree and a diploma but not much else. "I was broke and without a single job prospect," he recalls.

Not that he was without options. Although it's true he was unemployed, Joss knew what he wanted to do. "Writing is the thing I understand best," he says unequivocally. As it turns out, he was simply joining the family business. His grandfather John wrote for *Leave It to Beaver, The Donna Reed Show,* and *The Dick Van Dyke Show*. And his dad Tom wrote for series such as *Alice, Benson,* and *The Dick Cavett Show,* and produced *The Golden Girls*. "Actually, my father didn't want me to be a writer but after college he suggested I write a TV script so I could earn enough money to move out of the house," Joss jokes.

So Joss got busy and started churning out spec scripts on his typewriter. "I wrote a sickening number of scripts, most of which were returned to me. The rejection notes usually said something like, 'Very charming. I do not wish to have it.' But the thing is, the only way to get a career is to do a lot of it. You have to do the hard work and create the spec scripts. You have to write as many as you can and send them around, even if it takes a large number."

Joss's dream was to get a job writing for *The Simpsons* or *Twin Peaks*. Instead he had to settle for one of the highest-rated sitcoms on television. When he was twenty-five, he was hired as a story editor on ABC's *Roseanne*. "I literally went from working at a video store on a Friday to working on

Roseanne on Monday," says Joss, who vividly describes his experience with the mercurial performer:

"It was baptism by radioactive waste. She was like two different people. One was perfectly intelligent and good to be around. The other was very cranky and not so good to be around. You never knew which would show up. I was on staff for a year and then I quit."

Instead of looking for another television series to work for, Joss turned his attention to feature films and hit a home run on his first at-bat when his *Buffy the Vampire Slayer* screenplay—which he had written while working on *Roseanne*—sold in 1988. "The first screenplay I ever wrote was in high school but I never finished that one, so my first real one was *Buffy*," he says.

One of the biggest drawback to working in features, though, is the time it takes to go from "We love your script; we gotta have it," to actually seeing the movie on film. So while waiting—and waiting—for the *Buffy* movie to be made, Joss worked for a brief stint in 1990 as a co-producer and writer on NBC's *Parenthood*.

When *Buffy the Vampire Slayer* was finally released in 1992, Joss hated what he saw. But despite his disappointment and the mixed reaction to the *Buffy* film, Joss's screenwriting career suffered no setbacks. Over the next two years, he sold two more on spec scripts—meaning he wrote the screenplay first, then sent it around hoping someone would by it, as opposed to being commissioned to write it for a specific producer or production company.

In June 1993, Largo Entertainment bought Whedon's script *Suspension* for $750,000—against a $1 million total price. It was an action/suspense film that took place on the George Washington Bridge, which connects northern New Jersey with Manhattan. Industry insiders described it as "*Die Hard* on a bridge." Largo announced it wanted to begin filming before the end of the year—but it didn't. Perhaps the failure of Largo's *Judgment Night*, which starred Emilio Estevez and Denis Leary, doomed *Suspension*, but for whatever reason, the movie was never made.

The first time Joss was hired to "doctor" a script, to add scenes or dialogue to punch it up, was for *Speed*—coincidentally, a movie that wags dubbed "*Die Hard* on a bus." Then, in the summer of 1994, Whedon became part of the adventure known as *Waterworld* when he was hired by Kevin Costner to work on the script. Joss should have known that any $100 million–plus movie that begins production without a finished script is not going to be a dream job.

The film was also marred by a bitter falling-out between director Kevin Reynolds and Costner, and although the two men blamed each other, an anecdote from Joss gives a good idea what the problem was. "I was on location in Hawaii for seven weeks and nearly every single idea I wrote down was thrown into the garbage by Kevin Costner. I became the world's highest-paid stenographer," says Whedon, who was not given any screenwriter credit.

In September 1994 Columbia Pictures paid a reported $1.5 million against $2 million for another spec script from Whedon, called *Afterlife*. The movie was a science-fiction love story, in which a scientist's mind is implanted into the body of a younger man so the scientist can continue his research project and get back with his loving wife. The catch is, the body belonged to a well-known serial killer. The studio announced it would immediately give the project a green light. And this time, they even had a star attached to it—Jean-Claude Van Damme. But a few months later, "the Muscles from Brussels" backed out of the project and the film was never made.

But Joss was still one of the more sought-after screenwriters in Hollywood and soon it seemed as if everyone was clamoring for his services.

Then came *Toy Story*, the animated movie that almost didn't get made after Disney executives were shown the first story reels. First of all, Disney was wary about the kind of computer animation being used, which was so different from classic Disney. But the biggest problem was that the two lead toy characters were sarcastic, antagonistic, and generally unappealing—particular the cowboy doll, Woody.

Joss explains, "Let's face it, Woody was a thundering asshole. So it was my job to make him somewhat likable." For his efforts, Whedon and the six other credited writers were nominated for an Oscar in the "Best Screenplay Written Directly for the Screen" category. The *Toy Story* group lost out to Christopher McQuarrie who wrote *The Usual Suspects*.

But the nomination had cemented Joss's reputation and put him in the upper echelon of script doctors who can command $100,000 a week for their services. That's what Whedon reportedly received for punching up the script for *Twister*, the 1996 film that starred Helen Hunt, Bill Paxton, and a lot of windblown animals, cars, and houses.

After executives at 20th Century Fox decided to revive one of their most successful film franchises, Joss got a call and the result was *Alien: Resurrection*, which took the original concept and turned it on its ear by combining the Ripley character (played by Sigourney Weaver) with the alien. Literally. In the process of resurrecting Ripley from some tissue and blood samples, her DNA mixes with the DNA of the alien creature she had been carrying inside her. The result is an incredibly strong Ripley who can spit acid. Audiences and critics were unimpressed, however, and the film is widely considered the least popular of the four.

After an executive from Sandollar, which co-produced the movie *Buffy the Vampire Slayer*, came to Joss with the idea of turning the film into a series, Whedon realized it was his chance to finally get his words right; he would finally get the chance to see his vision on film, which is the reason he started writing in the first place as a teenager. Perhaps that's why he named his production company Mutant Enemy. "Mutant Enemy was the name I gave to my very first typewriter," he explains. "I named it after a song by the group Yes, and that's why the company is called that."

Although Joss, who is now married to interior designer Kai Cole, who gave birth to their first child in January of 2003, says the workload of *Buffy* is more than he ever imagined it would be, he swears he has never been more satisfied in his professional life.

Buffy's success has guaranteed Joss the chance to tell even more stories. His Fox series *Firefly* was a sci-fi western hybrid adventure series set five hundred years in the future, after Earth has been destroyed and those who survived have colonized space. Despite his penchant for strange creatures,

there were not any aliens in the series. "I believe we are the only sentient beings in the universe, and five hundred years from now we will still be the only sentient beings around. This show is about people. It's just about life when it's hard. When I pitched the show, I said, 'This is about nine people looking into the blackness of space and seeing nine different things,'" Whedon explains. "What I'm looking for is people to go, 'These guys are me. I feel that.' They're going through the same struggle we are. They're trying to pay the rent, they're trying to buy gas, they're trying to get these things at the same time as, you know, with the gunfighting and all the stuff."

The series was much more *Gunsmoke* than *Star Trek*. Instead of laser guns, the *Firefly* characters carried six-shooters and rode horses when exploring planets. Whedon says he was inspired after reading Michael Shaara's Civil War book *The Killer Angels*, which recounts the Battle of Gettysburg. "I got obsessed with the minutiae of life way back then when things were not as convenient as they are now," says Whedon. "We wanted to do a show in the future that had a sense of history, that we don't solve all our problems and have impeccably clean spaceships."

Although *Firefly* was canceled after just a few episodes, Whedon's TV legacy is assured thanks to *Buffy* and the strong reaction it still elicits from fans. "It's really sweet when people react like that, and I love the praise, but to me, what they're getting emotional about is the show. And that's the best feeling in the world. There's nothing creepy about it. I feel like there's a religion in narrative, and I feel the same way they do. I feel like we're both paying homage to something else; they're not paying homage to me. I designed the show to create that strong reaction. I designed *Buffy* to be an icon, to be an emotional experience, to be loved in a way that other shows can't be loved."

THE CHARACTERS

Since her first days in Sunnydale, Buffy's core support group has remained unchanged. Willow and Xander, charter members of the Scooby Gang, and Giles, her Watcher, are the Slayer's comrades-in-arms and emotional touchstones. But in addition to that inner circle, many others have moved in and out of the gang and Buffy's life, all of whom have left indelible impressions, whether good or bad.

The Slayer

Buffy Summers (*Sarah Michelle Gellar*)

When we first met Buffy Summers, she was your typical sixteen-year-old girl-next-door—who just happened to be the latest in a long line of female Slayers fated to protect their generation from the powers of evil. During her high school years, she was an average student constantly under fire for not living up to her potential. But carrying out her Slayer responsibilities meant spending evenings using her superhuman strength battling vampires and other monsters, which left very little time for homework. Her strange behavior kept Buffy out of the "in" crowd she had been part of at her previous school. Instead she bonded with two fellow outsiders, Xander and Willow, who became her most loyal allies in the fight against the terrors of the Hellmouth.

Once she became an adult, Buffy still yearned for normalcy but accepted her fate and did her best to play the hand life dealt her—including having been brought back from the dead, and eternal peace in Heaven, to the Slayer hell that is Earth. Resuming her Slayer responsibilities forced Buffy to confront some personal demons of her own, in an often-dark journey of self-discovery that include a complicated affair with her onetime archnemesis, vampire Spike.

That relationship simply reinforced the sad fact that Buffy's love life has proven to be a minefield of pain and missed opportunities. Her first love was Angel, a vampire with a soul courtesy of an old Gypsy curse. Their star-crossed love affair eventually led Angel to leave Sunnydale so Buffy could move forward with her life. But finding someone who can both accept who she is and offer her the emotional release and support she needs, has so far been a painful and fruitless quest for the Slayer.

With her mother dead and her teenage years far behind her, Buffy must now balance the responsibilities of adulthood, such as earning a living and caring for her younger sister, with her Slaying duties. Looking back, the rigors of high school seem pale by comparison. However, life has a way of coming full circle, and Buffy finds herself reliving her high school years through her sister Dawn, now attending the rebuilt Sunnydale High, which still sits atop the Hellmouth.

The Watcher

Rupert Giles (*Anthony Stewart Head*)

There is a Watcher responsible for looking after every Slayer and Buffy's is Giles, who left a position at the British Museum to work as the Sunnydale

High School librarian in order to look after his charge. Giles himself came from a long line of Watchers—both his father and his father's mother were Watchers—and it is his job to help Buffy defeat whatever the Hellmouth spits out at her by interpreting otherworldly signs and prophecies, as well as guiding her through the realities of being both a Slayer and young woman.

Although he is educated and can speak five languages, Giles is not a didactic know-it-all and is often just as unsure and without answers as Buffy. He also follows his heart. While most Watchers would have refused to allow others into the Slayer's inner circle, Giles accepted Willow, Xander, and others without much fuss because his number one commitment is always to keep Buffy alive and he realized there was strength in numbers. So if that meant bending—or completely ignoring—the Slayer code of absolute secrecy, he was more than willing to do that.

Another reason Giles proved more flexible than Watchers of the past was because he related to the conflicts Buffy was going through as a young Slayer—if given the option, Giles would have been a pilot or a grocer or anything other than a Watcher. In fact, he was so resistant to his fate that during his college days he rebelled by falling in with a group who practiced black magic—a decision that has come back to haunt him on more than one occasion. But having had that alter ego, named Ripper, also gave Giles a unique perspective on the thin line between darkness and light.

While Giles's willingness to ignore the letter of the Watchers' Council law might have greatly extended Buffy's life expectancy, it hasn't been without personal cost, such as when he was temporarily replaced with a more by-the-book Watcher. But his affection for and loyalty to Buffy was unaffected because his relationship with her now goes far beyond mentor and father figure. As she has matured from teenager into young woman, they are now peers and confidants—which is not to say he still isn't her teacher as well. When he realized that Buffy needed to stand more on her own and not rely on him so much, Giles returned to England, forcing her to go through a painful but necessary period of personal growth. And while he may no longer involve himself in her day-to-day Slayer responsibilities, Giles remains a steadying force in Buffy's life and always shows up when he is most needed.

Current Main Characters

Alexander "Xander" Harris (*Nicholas Brendon*)

Too sensitive and sardonic to hang out with the jocks, and too cool to be a nerd, Xander is the kind of guy who got along better with the girls in high school than he did with the guys. He comes from a family of blue-collar workers, such as his uncle, who was a janitor at a local computer company that went belly-up. Like Willow and Buffy, he is an only child, and in many ways, the Scooby Gang has become his surrogate family and emotional foundation.

Although quick-witted and blessed with street smarts, Xander had neither the grades nor the funds to attend college. Instead, after a period of aimlessness and feeling alienated from his college-going friends, Xander has become a gainfully employed carpenter, although his true life's work remains helping Buffy save the world from the forces of the Hellmouth, a vocation both noble and bittersweet.

From the moment he first set eyes on her, Xander loved Buffy. Although Xander has had several relationships, first with high school princess Cordelia Chase, and then with the demon-turned-girl Anya, whom he almost married before bailing on the ceremony, a part of his heart will not-so-secretly always belong to Buffy. But he accepted early on that she would never love him with an equal passion, so rather than cut her out of his life in a snit of bruised ego, Xander became her most doggedly loyal friend and protector who willingly—and often recklessly—puts himself at risk to fight by her side.

Willow Rosenberg (*Alyson Hannigan*)

When Buffy first met her Willow was a shy computer whiz-kid; a gentle soul always willing to give others the benefit of the doubt even when reason screamed against it. Although wonderfully ironic in her observations of others, she was never mean-spirited and never went out of her way to insult or offend anyone even when reason screamed for it.

As Willow's academic prowess and hacking abilities became invaluable tools for the Scooby Gang, her self-confidence grew, and the once unassuming schoolgirl proved herself quite capable of taking charge, speaking her mind, and calling people on the carpet if the situation demanded it. Although confident in her intellectual abilities, for a long time Willow was stunted in the self-image area, in large part because of her unrequited pining for Xander, her best friend since childhood.

Willow eventually blossomed and experienced two meaningful relationships. The first was with Oz, a thoughtful, taciturn guitar-playing genius who also happened to be a werewolf. The other was with Tara, a soulful Wicca who opened an unexpected door to Willow's sexual passion. Openly declaring her love for Tara forced the rest of the Scooby Gang to reevaluate their own preconceived notions about Willow. After a few awkward moments, they accepted who she was and whom she loved.

But the most powerful force in Willow's life wasn't love, friendship, or sex. What began as a fascination with and affinity for witchcraft, slowly morphed into a dangerous and debilitating addiction. In the beginning, Willow only used her powers for the good of humanity and to protect those she loved. But over time, like a junkie needing a fix, it became impossible for her to get through the day without casting a spell. Willow rehabilitated herself for a while but then succumbed to the darkest powers of her magic while avenging Tara's death. Since attempting to bring about the end of the world, Willow has had to deal with the damage she caused to herself and everyone around her, and to try and find redemption in the aftermath.

Anya (*Emma Caufield*)

Born a regular girl sometime in the Middle Ages, Anyanka was transformed into a vengeance demon called the Patron Saint of Scorned Women after she herself was scorned by a lover. Through the power of the Wish, Anya gleefully avenged other wronged women for over twelve hundred years until one of her curses went very wrong and she found herself suddenly human—powerless, mortal, and trapped in the body of a teenage girl attending Sunnydale High. So Anya was forced to relearn being human again, and to interact with males without devising ways to torture, maim, or kill them.

Frequently confused about the host of human emotions suddenly filling her heart and head, Anya realized she was desperate to go to the senior prom and turned to the one guy who seemed least offensive—Xander. It was the beginning of an unexpected romance characterized by Anya breaking most social norms. Because she has none of the social constraints most people are taught growing up, Anya is bluntly direct. Her way of dealing with her sexual feelings was to drop her clothes and suggest to Xander they have sex right then and there.

But her twelve-hundred-year-old existence also gives Anya a unique perspective on both human behavior and Hellmouth happenings. For, as much as Anya is learning about how to fit into modern society, the Scooby Gang has benefited from her knowledge of the demon world, despite her inappropriate responses.

When Anya's romance with Xander came to a bad end, the trauma of it opened the door for her demonic vengeance tendencies to return. Only, she couldn't use any of her power on Xander because her gift is only to avenge others, not herself, so she had to learn to deal with the human pain of dashed dreams. And because Buffy and the others are the only friends she has, Anya must do it while still confronting Xander on a daily basis.

Dawn (*Michelle Trachtenberg*)

Dawn is the sister Buffy never had—literally. Although Dawn is now accepted and recognized as Buffy's kin, she started life as a mystical energy source, known as "the Key," hiding in human form. The Key is a portal to another dimension. A group of monks sent Dawn to Buffy to protect Dawn from the clutches of a god named Glory, who needed to use the Key's blood in a ritual to open the portal so Glory could return home to that other dimension. Two big problems here: First, once the portal opened, the barriers between *all* dimensions would break down, causing them to bleed together, and evil horrors of every type would feast on mankind in an all-you-can-eat frenzy, destroying the world. Second, Dawn would have to die in order to close the portal and prevent this from happening.

To keep Dawn's true identity a secret, those clever monks implanted false memories in everyone. Thus Buffy and all her friends have vivid memories of Dawn being there over the years, as does Dawn, even though she never really existed. For a while Dawn went through life cheerfully unaware of her true origins; her biggest traumas were being treated like a kid, and having to live in the shadow of a Slayer sister and her daily heroics. But every time Dawn would try and show just how grown-up she was, she would usually end up making a mess of things, which only made Buffy more exasperated with her.

Eventually Dawn learned the truth about who—or what—she really was. Since the threat of Glory has apparently passed, and Buffy has returned from the dead again, Dawn's life now is less about mystical energy and more about teenage angst. She is still beset by feelings of inadequacy, which is not helped by Buffy keeping Dawn on a very short leash, unaware that Dawn is picking up some of her sister's Slayer moves and isn't such a helpless little girl anymore.

Desperate for any attention, good or bad, Dawn began to steal and became an all-around pain in the butt. Buffy finally realized that her parenting skills needed a major readjustment and that her overprotective ways were stifling Dawn, not helping her. She promised Dawn that she will stop preventing her from living a full life by trying to shield her from its horrors, and instead will help her experience the beautiful things the world has to offer, Hellmouth be damned.

Spike (*James Marsters*)

Spike is a 130-year-old vampire who got his nickname from his penchant for torturing people with railroad spikes. Back when he was human, young William was a hopeless romantic. Raised in an upper-class London family, he dreamed of being a poet but his "bloody awful poetry" earned him the nickname William the Bloody. After being rejected by the girl of his dreams, Cecily, William was out wandering the streets in misery when he met up with Drusilla, who turned him into a vampire because she fancied him. Spike and Drusilla spent the next hundred years as a couple. He was completely devoted to her and they roamed the world, gleefully leaving drained corpses in their wake. But while together in Prague, Drusilla was injured by a mob and left weak and helpless, so Spike came to Sunnydale hoping the Hellmouth would provide a cure.

Never one to follow tradition, Spike has no time for most ancient prophecies and he doesn't suffer fools, be they human or undead. But if there's one thing Spike in particular *can't* stand, it is a Slayer. He's already killed two within the last hundred years—the first in China during the Boxer Rebellion and the second in a New York City subway—and has grand plans on making Buffy the next notch on his fangs. But Buffy isn't like any other Slayer he's encountered. For one thing, she has a support group who is always there to improve her odds.

And although he is loath to admit it, Spike respects Buffy and is more than a little intrigued with her. He sees a bit of himself in her—someone not afraid to buck the rules and chuck tradition in order to get results.

Although Spike left Sunnydale several times, swearing he'd never return, he always does. Broken up from Dru, who kept leaving him for demons, and incapable of hurting any human because of a chip implanted in his head, Spike turned to the Scooby Gang for companionship. In the process he fell in love with Buffy and doggedly devoted himself to protecting the Slayer and her family as a way to express his love.

Spike thought his dreams were coming true when he and Buffy has a passionate, raw affair. But when she ended it, his despair turned to rage and he once again left Sunnydale, taking off for Africa under the impression he could regain his capacity to kill by being "restored to his former self." But what he regained wasn't the ability to kill, it was his soul.

Recurring Characters

Harmony Kendall (*Mercedes McNab*)

In high school, Harmony was part of Cordelia Chase's popular "in"-crowd clique. Obnoxious and a complete wanna-be, Harmony did everything Cordelia did, but spent most of her time trashing anyone who wasn't one of their group. Xander was a favorite target of Harmony's barbs over the years.

But when the chips were down and Buffy's graduating class faced annihilation along with the rest of Sunnydale at the hands of a demon mayor, Harmony came through and helped Buffy and the Scoobies fight and defeat the mayor. Unfortunately, during the melee Harmony was attacked by a vampire, though in the confusion of battle, nobody realized her fate. The truth came out when Harmony returned to Sunnydale as Spike's new girlfriend. Their stormy relationship was powerfully sexual, but tinged with overt antagonism. Harmony didn't realize Spike's short temper was in part fueled by his growing desire for the Slayer.

Tired of playing second fiddle to others her entire living and undead life, Harmony made an attempt to establish herself as Sunnydale's next Big Bad evil by recruiting a handful of misfit minions on a mission to kill the Slayer and take over the town. Like most of Harmony's grand plans, this one backfired, too, and her minions ended up dust or making tracks out of Sunnydale. Foiled again, Harmony escaped, in part because Buffy let her.

Harmony came back to Sunnydale later, only to discover the shocking truth about Spike's love for the Slayer. That humiliation spurred Harmony to announce she was headed for Los Angeles but, having been born and raised in Sunnydale, it's quite possible she'll resurface sooner rather than later.

Ethan Rayne (*Robin Sachs*)

Ethan Rayne is that friend from your sordid past who keeps popping up as a reminder of times you'd rather forget. Back when Giles dabbled in the black arts, he befriended Ethan, a sorcerer. He is a consummate troublemaker who delights in causing as much misery as possible, particularly for Giles.

A malevolent prankster, Ethan first introduced himself to Buffy and her friends during high school, when he sold most of Sunnydale Halloween costumes that turned people into whatever character they were dressed as. The goal was to cause enough chaos that it would be easy for denizens of the Hellmouth to pick off victims at their leisure. Ethan eventually was caught by the Initiative, a shadowy government agency that hunts down vampires and demons and all other manner of evil creatures, and is now incarcerated in a secret location in Nevada.

Willy the Snitch (*Saverio Guerra*)

Willy is a local bartender who makes it his business to know what's going down in Sunnydale and is willing to share the information for a price—or even just to avoid a beating. Willy gets his info by befriending local demons and vampires who often hang out at his pub, and as a result, he often finds himself on the wrong side of Buffy's fist.

Amy Madison (*Elizabeth Ann Allen*)

Amy is the daughter of a witch who first met Buffy when her mom switched bodies with Amy to relive her high school cheerleader glory days. Buffy restored Amy back to her rightful body and trapped her mom in a cheerleading trophy so she couldn't hurt anyone again.

Xander was the first to discover that Amy had inherited her mom's witchy ways, and blackmailed her into performing a love spell in order to get Cordelia back. The spell went awry but under Giles's stern guidance Amy reversed the spell, though now the secret was out about her powers.

To avoid being burned at the stake during a demon-induced Sunnydale witch hunt, Amy turned herself into a rat. Willow tried repeatedly to undo the spell and change Amy back to human form but couldn't figure it out. So for the next three years Amy lived in a cage and amused herself on the exercise wheel until Willow was finally able to revert her. Once human again, Amy became obsessed with performing spells and turned into a very bad influence on Willow, introducing her to the dark side of magic, which led to tragic consequences.

Olivia (*Phina Oruche*)

Olivia is Giles's casual romantic interest from England. Although she seems to know Giles's background, she was somewhat of a disbeliever until she was frightened by the sight of demons called "the Gentlemen" floating past the window. Olivia hasn't been back to Sunnydale since.

Jonathan Levinson (*Danny Strong*)

Jonathan was a high school classmate of Buffy's, who always seemed to be in the wrong place at the wrong time. Frequently miserable and overwhelmed by feelings of inadequacy, Jonathan planned to kill himself until Buffy convinced him his life really was worth living.

But his insecurities remained a strong influence on Jonathan, and resulted in his dabbling in magic, including once casting a spell that made him a superhero in the eyes of everyone else. After Buffy discovered the ruse and broke the spell, Jonathan skulked off to plot revenge.

𝕲𝖔𝖓𝖊 𝕭𝖚𝖙 𝕹𝖔𝖙 𝕱𝖔𝖗𝖌𝖔𝖙𝖙𝖊𝖓

Angel (*David Boreanaz*)

Angel is an unusual vampire. Born in 1755 in Ireland and originally named Liam by his parents, he was "sired" by Darla when he was a young man. As Angelus, the vampire with the angelic face, he spent the next hundred or so years terrorizing people all across Europe—until he killed a Romanian Gypsy girl and her clan put a curse on him, restoring his soul, and with it, his conscience.

Overcome with guilt by the horror and carnage he had caused, Angel came to America and swore never to feed on a human again, surviving on the blood of rats. Rejecting his former "family," which included Darla, and the Master, the oldest-known vampire on record, Angel chose to live aboveground with humans and do whatever he could to atone for his evil deeds of the past. Even so, Angel was miserable and aimless, consumed by anguish, until a demon named Whistler gave him a new purpose by arranging for Angel to keep an eye on Buffy and help her battle the forces of evil.

In Buffy, Angel found redemption. He also unexpectedly found love and openly renounced his undead brethren, making him just as much of a marked man as Buffy is a marked woman. But their passion had an unexpected tragic consequence. The old Gypsy curse had a cruel, secret twist: Should Angel ever experience a moment of true happiness, he would lose his soul again. The night Angel finally made love with Buffy, he reverted back to Angelus and began a reign of terror, which included plans to end the world and stalking and tormenting Buffy in his spare time. Willow eventually succeeded in performing a spell that restored Angel's soul, but it was a moment too late. In order to prevent the end of the world, Buffy had to send him to Hell, which she did after a final kiss goodbye.

After suffering the torments of Hell, Angel was sent back and resumed his emotional relationship with Buffy although both knew they could never be intimate again. Realizing Buffy needed to have a full relationship, and that she wouldn't as long as he was there, Angel left Sunnydale for Los Angeles to find another path of redemption by setting up Angel Investigations, a detective agency dedicated to "helping the helpless."

Cordelia Chase (*Charisma Carpenter*)

In high school, Cordelia Chase was the unquestioned school diva. The most popular and prettiest girl in school—as well as the most completely self-absorbed and self-obsessed—Cordy had her choice of boyfriends, choosing to ignore their noticeably high mortality rate. Although she had an annoying tendency to act is if she were the center of the known universe, there was always more to her than meets the eye. She was well aware that in high school many of her so-called friends were only there to glow in her reflected light of popularity, but also was honest enough to admit it was better than being alone.

When Buffy first came to Sunnydale, Cordelia was one of the first students to extend a tentative hand of friendship. But after Buffy rejected Cordy's "in" group for the company of designated outsiders Willow and Xander, Cordelia bade her good riddance. Her opinion of Buffy plummeted even further when she always seemed to be around weird happenings, like students being killed and monsters taking over the local hangout.

But Cordy is a pragmatist, and when her own life was in danger she turned to Buffy for help, thereby opening the door to an edgy alliance. Over time Cordelia was reluctantly but steadily drawn into the fold, and learned the truth about Buffy being the Slayer. Although she really would have preferred to be out shopping for new designer fashions, Cordy proved she could be counted on to show up when needed—even though she complained endlessly about it afterward because she found blood and mayhem so . . . distasteful.

Cordy surprised everyone, herself included, when she started dating Xander. And she was devastated when she caught him making out with Willow. Even though both he and Willow swore it was just a case of raging hormones and not a commitment, Cordy broke it off with Xander for good and remained unattached romantically for the remainder of their senior year.

Shortly before high school graduation, Cordy's dad was convicted of income-tax evasion, losing all his assets, including the family home. With her parents suddenly broke, Cordy's plans to attend college were dashed. So instead she headed for Los Angeles to be an actress, but ended up working for Angel's detective agency.

Daniel "Oz" Osbourne (*Seth Green*)

Oz was born cool. A man of few words, he fell for Willow after seeing her dressed in an Eskimo costume during a "cultural dance" where his band, Dingoes Ate My Baby, was playing. Almost preternaturally patient, Oz delayed getting romantic with Willow, understanding she had issues to work out over her long-unrequited feelings for Xander.

After being bit by his cousin Jordy, Oz turned into a werewolf and discovered it runs in the family. To keep himself from hurting anyone, he locked himself up in a cage provided by Giles for the three nights of the full moon. He and Willow seemed completely compatible and Oz was thoroughly committed to her—until he met a female werewolf named Veruca who unleashed his animal lust and passion. Realizing it was a part of himself he couldn't control, Oz left Sunnydale to search for answers.

After a stint in the Himalayas, Oz learned to control the animal within, through meditation and herbs. Believing himself centered, he returned to Sunnydale to resume his relationship with Willow only to discover she was involved with Tara. After Willow explained that while she will always love him, she was in love with Tara, Oz accepted the truth of who Willow was and left Sunnydale in search of more answers.

Hank Summers (*Dean Butler*)

Buffy's father, who is divorced from her mom, lives in Los Angeles. During her high school years he was the ultimate weekend dad—seeing her only a few weekends every year. Because of the distance that separated them, both in miles and emotionally, and because of Buffy's tendency to withdraw into herself, Hank lost the ability to communicate with his daughter. Over time, Hank disappeared entirely from Buffy's life, too busy with his work and with his girlfriend.

Riley Finn (*Marc Blucas*)

Riley's first encounter with Buffy was jarring—she accidentally knocked some heavy textbooks onto his head her first week in college. Originally from Iowa, Riley was psychology Professor Walsh's teacher's aide, and at first he assumed

Buffy was just a normal girl. Buffy didn't know he was a member of a secret government agency called the Initiative, who trapped demons and conducted nefarious experiments on them, supervised by Professor Walsh.

Once they learned the truth about each other, their romance bloomed in earnest and he became Buffy's first serious, adult relationship. But Riley had issues with dating the Slayer, and constantly felt the need to try and live up to her near-superhuman abilities. After Professor Walsh's Initiative lab was disbanded, Riley lost his focus and became self-destructive when he felt Buffy was pushing him away, even though he always knew in his heart she didn't love him the way he loved her.

Knowing they were just treading water with their relationship, Riley accepted a new job hunting demons in Belize. After a year, Riley eventually got over Buffy and married a beautiful fellow demon-hunter named Sam.

Faith (*Eliza Dushku*)

Full of bravado and rage and possessing an overactive thrill-seeking gene, Faith was the Slayer sent to replace Kendra after Kendra was killed by Drusilla. Ever since the Master ever so briefly drowned the life out of Buffy there have been two Slayers, because a new Slayer is automatically called whenever the preceding one dies—even if she comes back to life.

From the beginning Faith was trouble—and troubled. Traumatized by seeing an ancient vampire named Kakistos torture and kill her Watcher, Faith takes too much pleasure in killing vampires. That's because for Faith, killing vamps is an erotic rush. After accidentally killing a human during a fight with vampires, she had trouble reconciling her guilt with her power. Believing herself to be above the law, the dark side of Faith's nature overwhelmed her and she turned into a rogue Slayer, aligning herself with the mayor as his right-hand muscle. During a confrontation, Buffy stabbed Faith and put her in a coma. When she woke up a year later, she was still out of control. On the verge of being shipped of to the Watchers' Council in London, she fled to Los Angeles where she tried to frame Angel for murder. Finally accepting Angel's help, Faith repented. She turned herself in and is currently in prison.

(Since the imprisonment happened on *Angel*, there's no telling how this will affect Faith's storyline on *Buffy*.)

Wesley Wyndam-Pryce (*Alexis Denisof*)

When Giles was relieved of his duties as Buffy's Watcher, he was replaced by Wesley. Although he was well intentioned, his by-the-book manner put him at immediate odds with Buffy and alienated him from Faith. In over his head, Wesley quickly lost control of the situation. As a fighter Wesley was also lacking and, more often than not, went down with the first blow while shrieking.

Unable to control either Slayer, the Watchers' Council fired Wesley. Rather than go back to England, he reassessed his life and moved to L.A. to become a rogue demon-hunter. Unfettered by the constraints of trying to follow the Watcher's code, Wesley finally loosened up. His skill at research and his good heart earned him a position at Angel's detective agency, and his story continues on *Angel*.

The Dearly Departed

Kendra (*Bianca Lawson*)

Kendra was called to be a Slayer after Buffy's brief death at the hands of the Master. Dedicated to a fault, Kendra prepared her entire life to be the Slayer, and had faithfully studied all the prophecies, demons, and vampires. However, her immersion in all things Slayer left her a little short-changed in the socialization and having-a-life departments.

When Kendra first showed up, Buffy was resentful and Kendra was appalled that a Slayer would be in love with a vampire, and in fact tried to kill Angel before she knew he had a soul. Kendra returned to Sunnydale later to help Buffy fight Acathla during the time Angel had re-lost his soul. While Buffy was off searching out Angel, Drusilla made a surprise attack on the library and slit Kendra's throat with the tip of a wickedly manicured finger.

Jenny Calendar (*Robia La Morte*)

A self-professed technopagan, Jenny combined old-fashioned mystical beliefs with Information Age technology to keep an eye on the forces of evil. In her spare time she read rune stones and attended pagan festivals for fun.

As Sunnydale High School's computer teacher, Jenny was often at odds with Giles over the value of cyberspace and Internet information; she saw it as the dawn of a new era, while to him it was temporary and elusive. Add to that Jenny's easy sensual aggression and Giles's shy eagerness, and it was a match made in Hellmouth heaven.

But as is often the case in Sunnydale, Jenny wasn't what she seemed. She was actually a member of the Kalderash Gypsies, the same clan that put the curse on Angel. Jenny had been sent to make sure he was suffering as the clan intended. When Angel re-lost his soul after making love with Buffy, Jenny re-created the long lost spell that gave Angel his soul. But before she could act on it, Angel tracked her down and broke her neck.

Joyce Summers (*Kristine Sutherland*)

After Buffy was kicked out of school for burning down the gym, her mom decided to leave Los Angeles and start a new life in Sunnydale. As a divorced single mom, Joyce was often too preoccupied getting her new business, an art gallery, off the ground to have time to pay close attention to exactly what her daughter was doing. She initially thought Giles was simply a concerned teacher trying to help her often academically-troubled daughter, and took Buffy's sometimes-moody behavior to be typical teenage angst, unaware her child faced life-threatening danger nightly.

But for all her worries, Joyce also ultimately had faith in Buffy and saw her daughter as self-reliant and someone not afraid to intervene on the behalf of others. When Buffy finally told her mother she had a Slayer for a daughter, Joyce was understandably shocked and incredulous and handled the news badly—so badly that Buffy ran away for several months before finally returning home. Through it all, Joyce remained Buffy's main source of emotional support. So when Joyce died of a brain aneurysm, Buffy didn't just lose her mom, but her very foundation.

Principal Flutie (*Ken Lerner*)

A kinder, gentler administrator, Mr. Flutie believed that even the most incorrigible students would come around, given enough support and understanding. He ultimately learned just how woefully wrong his philosophy was, when he was eaten by a pack of students possessed by the spirits of hyenas.

Principal Bob Snyder (*Armin Shimerman*)

Children, shmildren. This administrator could see his students for what they really were: horrible little troublemakers who would just as soon eat you as pick up a book and study. Sneaky, with a mysterious aura, Principal Snyder always seemed to know much more than he let on.

Or at least, he thought he did. He always considered Buffy one of the school's most troublesome students and would go out of his way to see she stayed on the straight and narrow by forcing her to participate in school activities she would otherwise spurn.

When the mayor turned graduation day into a potential teenage smorgasbord, Snyder stood his ground and demanded order—and for his bravery was eaten by the politico–turned–giant demon snake.

Professor Walsh (*Lindsay Crouse*)

No-nonsense and ever so vaguely menacing, Professor Walsh was the head of the Initiative who took a dislike to Buffy. Not only did she supervise the capture of and experimentation on demons and vampires, she also busied herself with a pet project—creating a super-solider she named Adam. But she suffered the same fate as Dr. Frankenstein and died at the hands of her creation-gone-bad.

Tara Maclay (*Amber Benson*)

Shy and unassuming, Tara was the daughter of a powerful witch who died young when Tara was 17. Not having a mother seriously impacted Tara, particularly in the self-worth department. Though sometimes stammering and unsure, Tara met Willow at a school Wicca meeting and the two immediately hit it off. Tara was attracted to Willow's intelligence and spirit while Willow found Tara's gentleness enchanting, and eventually they became lovers.

Although generally nonconfrontational, Tara could stand firm on a position she believed in. She temporarily broke up with Willow to show her disapproval over Willow's addiction to magic. Their reunion was tragically cut short after Tara was shot and killed by Warren, who was gunning after Buffy.

Ben (*Charlie Weber*)

Half the time Ben was a kind and gentle intern at Sunnydale General Hospital. The rest of the time he was Glory, the demon god pursuing the Key. That's because he shared the same body with Glory. When Glory's fellow Hell-gods expelled her, they imprisoned her in the body of a human infant boy. Once the baby grew old and died, so would Glory. Unfortunately for Ben, Glory was too powerful, and she was able to appear for stretches of time to cause havoc. In order to prevent Glory from returning, Giles suffocated Ben.

The Big Bads

SEASON ONE

The Master (*Mark Metcalf*)

The oldest vampire—and most powerful on record—the Master was a megalomaniac bent on destroying humankind and reclaiming the earth for "the old ones." After being trapped in a mystical portal beneath Sunnydale when his plan of opening the Hellmouth was interrupted by an earthquake, the Master spent his time plotting evil schemes and using ancient prophecies in hopes of being set free so he could begin his long anticipated extermination of man.

Buffy unwittingly set the Master free by going and confronting him, and in return he killed her—briefly. Xander was able to revive her using CPR. The experience left the Slayer stronger and she was able to finish off the Master by impaling him on a large shard of wood. Interestingly, though his flesh turned to dust, his bones stayed intact.

Darla (*Julie Benz*)

This four-hundred-year-old vampire had a penchant for dressing up in Catholic-school uniforms when she led young men expecting a good time to their unexpected deaths. When she was alive, Darla was a Virginia prostitute dying a slow and painful death of syphilis until she was turned into a vampire by the Master in 1609. She in turn sired Angel and together they roamed the streets of Europe, leaving death and horror in their wake. When Angel went over to the other side after regaining his soul, Darla was determined to win him back—or, failing that, kill him. But Angel turned the tables on her and killed his former lover.

Four years later, Darla was brought back as a human by an evil law firm in Los Angeles, but she never appeared in Sunnydale again.

The Anointed One (*Andrew J. Ferchland*)

The Anointed One was one of five people killed by vampires in order to fulfill an ancient prophecy. The twist was that the One chosen was a child, who was destined to help free the Master and sit at his right hand when Armageddon came. Although he still had the body of a child, the Anointed One's ruthlessness was second only to the Master's.

After Buffy killed the Master, the Anointed One persisted and conjured up a plan to resurrect him and fulfill Armageddon. But Spike, annoyed by taking orders from a whiny child, locked him in a cage and hoisted him into the sunlight and incinerated him.

SEASON TWO

Drusilla (*Juliet Landau*)

Not only is Drusilla a vampire, she's certifiable—as in nuts. She was driven to madness by Angel, who killed off her family one by one just for fun before turning her into a vampire and becoming her lover. Drusilla eventually turned her amorous attentions to Spike and they spent the next century happily causing mayhem.

But an attack by an angry mob in Prague nearly killed poor demented Drusilla so she and Spike headed for the Hellmouth. Using a ritual that included Angel's blood, Dru was cured, a terrifying situation because, while most vampires are simply evil, Dru is evil *and* insane.

Spike eventually made a deal with Buffy to help her prevent the end of the world in return for a free pass out of Sunnydale for himself and Dru. But Dru likes her men mean and she felt Spike had lost his edge so she dumped him for a series of demon lovers.

After a nasty run-in with Angel in Los Angeles in which he tried to torch her, Dru came looking to cry on Spike's shoulder. But instead of open arms Dru was greeted with manacles. She discovered to her horror that not only had Spike fallen in love with the Slayer, but he was willing to dust Drusilla to prove it. Dru fought her way out and hasn't been heard from since.

The Judge

The Judge was an ancient demon so powerful that "no weapon forged" could destroy him. After an epic battle that killed thousands, the Judge was cut into pieces which were buried in the four corners of the earth. In a moment of demented whimsy, Drusilla decided to reassemble the Judge and bring annihilation to all mankind.

Back in one piece, the Judge was a blue-colored demon with the power to burn anyone who carried even a trace of humanity in them. Interestingly, because they were capable of feeling emotion for one another, the Judge was disdainful even of Spike and Dru.

While no weapon forged hundreds of years ago could stop the Judge, a rocket launcher could. His shattered remains were boxed and scattered where he could never be reassembled again.

SEASON THREE

Mayor Richard Wilkins III (*Harry Groener*)

This is the politician of your worst nightmares. By all appearances he seemed like a dedicated, concerned public servant. He always had a word of encouragement and was a stickler for courtesy. But Mayor Wilkins had a much darker side. He was a sorcerer at least a hundred years old, who posed as both Richard Wilkins I and Richard Wilkins II.

Obsessed with power, and blindly ambitious, Mayor Wilkins made some unholy alliances to get to the top of Sunnydale's political heap, including a deal with a baby-eating demon named Lurconis. His ultimate goal was to become a full demon, with a very hearty appetite, through a transformation called the Ascension, scheduled to take place on the afternoon of Buffy's high school graduation. Making him even more dangerous, Wilkins enlisted the help of Faith, a Slayer-gone-bad, to be his muscle. Ironically, though, he genuinely cared for Faith and was very much a father figure to her. He was also the first to voice the doomed nature of Buffy's romance with Angel. If he hadn't been a power-hungry demon-to-be, the mayor actually would have been rather parental.

Recruiting her entire graduating class to help, Buffy was able to lure the demon mayor into the school library, which was rigged with dynamite, and killed him by blowing up the entire school.

Mr. Trick (*K. Todd Freeman*)

Mr. Trick was a thoroughly modern vamp recruited by the Mayor to head up his security team. A slick dresser, and lover of hi-tech gadgets, Mr. Trick ended up getting staked by Faith.

SEASON FOUR

Adam (*George Hertzberg*)

A modern-day Frankenstein's monster, Adam was the part-man/part-demon/part-machine creation of Dr. Walsh, meant to be the perfect soldier. But in a case of absolute power corrupting absolutely, Adam turned evil, killing his creator, and was bent on killing everything else he encountered by creating an army of others like him. A spell that combined the strength of all the Scoobies into one unleashed Buffy's primeval Slayer powers, handily enabling her to defeat and destroy Adam.

SEASON FIVE

Glorificus/Glory (*Clare Kramer*)

One of three gods who ruled a demonic dimension, Glory was unceremoniously booted out and trapped inside the body of a human baby boy in an attempt to kill her. Too powerful to be kept inside, Glory was able to emerge occasionally and when she did, she was hell on earth. Vain, whiny, and obsessed with her appearance, Glory was also driven insane by being trapped on earth. To cope, she needed to drain other people's sanity to maintain her own. When Giles killed Ben, Glory presumably died with him. But since gods are immortal . . .

The Trio (*Danny Strong, Adam Busch, Tom Lenk*)

Sometimes the most terrifying evil can be human. The Trio were three of Sunnydale's aimless Generation Y losers, who teamed up with aspirations of becoming the town's ultimate Big Bads. Warren, an electronics genius who once created a robot girlfriend for himself and later made a Buffy 'bot for Spike, was the ringleader. Warren recruited Andrew—whose brother Tucker once tried to ruin prom by unleashing hellhounds on his fellow students—and Jonathan, who Buffy had talked out of committing suicide during senior year, to form a gang.

Andrew's expertise was summoning demons. He was desperate for attention after having lived in the shadow of his brother, and saw the gang as a chance to make a name for himself. Jonathan dabbled in magic and also had an intense desire to be noticed.

At first Andrew and Jonathan treated the alliance as a game, but after Warren killed his ex-girlfriend, they both realized this was much more serious. Having tasted the dark power that comes from murder, Warren set his sights on the Slayer.

Jonathan wanted no part of hurting anyone, especially Buffy, since she had saved his life. But fear of Warren kept him from bolting. After Warren killed Tara in an attempt to shoot Buffy, Willow hunted him down and literally skinned him alive. Buffy was forced to protect Jonathan and Andrew from a Willow gone mad with grief. They went on the run, to avoid facing the consequences of their actions.

A BRIEF HISTORY
OF THE VAMPIRE

ythological versions of the creature we know today as the vampire—a reanimated corpse that rises from the grave to feed on the living by drinking their blood—have been around in many cultures, certainly since the time of the ancient Greeks and possibly even since the beginning of recorded time.

The Romans, and the Serbians of Eastern Europe, had specific names for these bloodsucking monsters—*sanguisuga* and *vukodlak*, respectively. Many scholars believe that the Slavic countries of Eastern Europe were the hot zone of early vampire belief from the Middle Ages on, and that our current perception of the vampire can be traced back to there.

Between 1600 and 1800, reports of suspected vampire cases reached epidemic proportions. Although it began in the Balkans region, the paranoia eventually spread west into Germany, France, Italy, Spain, and England. There were so many purported occurrences of vampire activity that writers of the time began to use the myth as the basis for literature.

The actual word *vampire* became part of the English language in 1732, when investigators for two English periodicals, *Gentleman's Magazine* and the *London Journal* reported on the chilling case of Arnold Paole, who was accused of killing people in the town of Meduegna, Yugoslavia, between 1727 and 1732.

At first nobody believed the ramblings of Paole, who while lying on his death bed, claimed that he was dying because he had been bitten by a vampire. But as soon as villagers started disappearing, people began to believe Paole *had* risen from the grave and was feeding on the locals. So a group of townsfolk dug up Paole's body and drove a stake through its heart. According to eyewitnesses, the body appeared unnaturally fresh for having been in the ground so long, and seemingly fresh blood squirted from the wound. On the heels of the Paole incident, more vampire attacks were reported in Serbia and subsequently, eight more "preserved" corpses were dug up and burned.

Another famous case of vampirism involved a seventeenth-century countess named Elizabeth Bathory, who belonged to one of the wealthiest and oldest families in Transylvania, an ancient area located in what is now Romania. Among her many powerful relatives were clergymen and political leaders, including a monarch—King Steven of Poland (1575–86).

Elizabeth married Count Ferencs Nasdasdy when she was just fifteen years old. As was typical in those days, he was away most of the time fighting one battle or another, so while Elizabeth sat at home she was introduced to the occult by one of her servants and briefly went off with a mysterious stranger, but eventually returned to the castle.

In 1600, her husband died and Elizabeth's behavior took a decided turn for the darker. According to the story, one day a servant girl accidentally pulled the countess's hair. Furious, Elizabeth hit her so hard she drew blood, a drop of which landed on her skin. Elizabeth was so taken by the effect of the girl's blood on her skin that she ordered the servant's blood be drained into a huge vat, which she then used as a beautifying bath treatment.

It took ten years for authorities to learn of the horrible atrocities occurring at Castle Csejthe. It eventually came out during the trial that nearly forty girls had been tortured and killed. The countess herself would often stab them with scissors, letting the blood drain out slowly. However, Elizabeth Bathory was never convicted. Even then, if you had enough wealth and power you could get away with murder. Instead she was literally walled up inside her bedroom and was found dead in 1614.

Interestingly, Elizabeth's family was connected to another family whose name would become synonymous with terror—and vampires. Back in 1476, Prince Steven Bathory helped a Romanian prince named Dracula regain his throne.

Although it has been the subject of great debate, the general consensus seems to be that Bram Stoker did indeed base his Count Dracula character on the real-life historical figure of Vlad III Dracula—also known as Vlad Tepes or Vlad the Impaler (the surname Tepes means "the Impaler" in the Romanian language).

Ironically, though, the historical Dracula—although it is acknowledged he committed atrocities against his own people—is remembered in Romania as a national hero who resisted the Turkish invaders from the east and maintained the national monarchy in the face of the powerful Hungarian empire.

Dracula was born in 1431, the son of Vlad II Dracul, who was the ruler of Wallachia, a Romanian province south of Transylvania, north of Bulgaria, and west of the Black Sea. At that time the area was in a constant state of political turmoil, with the Turks trying to invade on one side and Hungary trying to swallow up the other. After Vlad II was assassinated, Dracula (which means "son of Dracul") seized the Wallachian throne in 1448 with a little help from the Turks. He was forced off the throne two months later and fled the area.

He retook the throne in 1456 and ruled until 1462, and it was during this time he became known as "the Impaler" because of his torturous cruelty. Death by impalement, in which a stake was gradually forced through the body—often until it emerged from the mouth—was an unspeakably gruesome way to die. Often the victim would linger for days, sometimes hung upside down.

To amuse himself, Dracula often arranged the impaled bodies in geometric designs or set up rings of impaled victims outside the next town he intended to attack. The most shocking aspect of his pastime is that he also used impalement against his own people as a way to maintain authority. The elderly, the ailing, women and children, pregnant women—nobody was safe. He was known to impale thousands at a time—and then would sit eating dinner amid the carnage.

So, when Stoker needed a model for his vampire, no doubt Dracula seemed a perfect choice. Outside of Eastern Europe, Vlad the Impaler was an obscure historical figure, but those who did recognize the name would immediately associate it with horror and cruelty. One change Stoker did make was the locale—he moved Count Dracula's castle from Walachia to Transylvania, which during Stoker's time was an area that remained medieval in appearance and outlook.

Up until the seventeenth century, vampires were mostly an oral tradition, frightening tales passed down through generations as verbal remembrances. But as vampires became a staple of literature, the very mythology of the creature began to change until it became a reverse reflection of the societies from which the authors sprang. In ancient times vampires were evil creatures to be feared, avoided, and killed. But as they were analyzed through literature, they also became creatures to be understood, because, at their core, they represent mankind's deepest, darkest fears about death.

Vampire Mythology

Although Bram Stoker did not invent the vampire, his Count Dracula character certainly helped form the modern mythology of the vampire, which has changed drastically over the centuries. For example, early mythological vampires did not sleep in coffins—for very good reason. Up until the nineteenth century, only the very rich could afford coffins. So all a vampire needed to "rest" was a mound of native soil. Which is why, in Stoker's book, Dracula brings several crates of Transylvanian dirt with him. The only reason it became common to depict a vampire resting in a coffin is simply because in modern times we bury the dead in coffins.

Although Christians have long associated vampirism with satanic evil, it was not until Stoker's *Dracula* (published in 1897) that the crucifix was seen to wield supernatural power against the vampire. The crucifix, symbolic of goodness and holiness, became a mystical weapon to be used against the abject evil of the demon vampire. In the book *Dracula,* the crucifix could both weaken the vampire physically and burn its flesh.

Over the years, the powers attributed to the crucifix—a cross with the figure of Christ on it—was carried over to any cross. However, in recent years some writers, including Anne Rice, have broken with that tradition by depicting vampires who are immune to the effects of the cross and any other religious symbols. That's because these vampires are not associated specifically with Satan (consider them secular bloodsuckers) therefore religious artifacts have no effect. However, in the *Buffy* vampire mythology, crosses and holy water are still used to repel and ward off Sunnydale's brand of vampire.

But where the cross is falling out of favor in certain literary circles, garlic is making a leap in popularity. Since ancient times garlic has been used as both a food and as a healing agent, and in modern times is valued for it's ability to help strengthen the human immune system. As an aide against vampires in medieval times, garlic was either worn or hung outside a house to ward off vampires. Some cultures stuffed cloves of garlic in the mouth of a suspected vampire—after its head had been cut off the body.

It was also believed you could use garlic as a kind of vampire detector: If a guest in your house refused to eat the garlic, they could be a vampire. Again, the first literary reference to garlic was in Bram Stoker's novel *Dracula.* It happens when Van Helsing, the vampire hunter, puts it around Lucy's neck to keep Dracula away from her. Since then, garlic has become a major tool for vampire hunters everywhere, and even Buffy carries garlic cloves around in her Slayer satchel. However, being the rebel she is, Anne Rice tends to disregard its effectiveness in her Vampire Chronicles.

Rice does subscribe, however, to the long-standing belief that fire is a sure way to kill the undead. Culturally, it makes perfect sense because fire has been used since caveman days as a symbol of cleansing and purity. Ironically, *Dracula* is one of the few references—oral, literary, or cinematic—that *doesn't* make mention of fire. In Rice's Vampire Chronicles series, fire is the *only* way known to destroy a vampire.

Killing a vampire by stabbing it through the heart with a wooden stake has been the method of choice in vampire mythology for centuries. Initially, the stakes were used to literally spike a corpse to the earth, which would prevent the body from rising. But after coffins became a regular feature of burial, the stake became a way to actually kill the creature. However, there have been questions as to whether it was the actual puncturing of the heart that did the trick, or the wood itself that was necessary. In *Buffy*, as with most other depictions, it is necessary for wood to go through the heart. Anything else leaves a wound but the vampire keeps going. As a result certain woods were favored over others by vampire hunters, the most highly recommended being ash and juniper.

One of the aspects of vampire mythology that has changed drastically over the centuries is the effect of sunlight. Although most modern stories, including *Buffy*, hold that sunlight is absolutely lethal to vampires, that wasn't always the case. In medieval times, people believed that vampires walked around just as easily as humans do during daylight. But as the literary vampire developed, so did its aversion to the sun.

In *Dracula*, Stoker's vampires were able to be out during the day; the exposure to the sunlight, however made them considerably weaker. But since then, vampires have been portrayed as being lethally vulnerable to the sun's direct rays. In the television series *Forever Knight*, the cop/vampire can go out in during the day, but must avoid letting the light come in direct contact with his skin. However, like Dracula, just being in reflected light saps his strength. In the Vampire Chronicles, Anne Rice—ever the one to turn the mythology upside down—devised vampires that become immune to the sun's rays if they live long enough.

The idea that a vampire was able to alter its appearance, or shape-shift, has been part of the mythology for hundreds of years, but it was cemented by Stoker describing how the Count was able to turn into a bat or disappear in a spray of mist. However, that ability has frequently been discarded in

FANGS

Vampires haven't always had fangs and, in fact, European vampire lore does not list fangs among a vampire's definite traits. Historical accounts of vampires include blood in the coffin and blood on the mouth, but no fangs. Nor do any of the early works of fiction dealing with Vampires, such as Dr. John Polidori's *The Vampyre* (1819) speak of fangs.

The advancement of fangs corresponds to our scientific knowledge of animal physiology and biology. So it wasn't until the 1800s that vampires in liter-ature started being described as creatures with elongated canine teeth. Obviously this made it easier for the vampire to puncture the skin of the neck and the jugular vein while feeding.

It isn't until the first chapter of *Varney the Vampyre* (1840) that the idea of fangs appears. "With a plunge he seizes her neck in his fang-like teeth."

The movies jumped on this visual aid. However, in Bram Stoker's *Dracula*, published in 1897, all his vampires had sharpened incisors. But when the 1931 film version of Stoker's book was made, Bela Lugosi refused to wear any dental prosthetic and is noticeably missing anything resembling fangs. But in the classic *Nosferatu*, the vampire wore his fangs proudly.

Then, as special effects improved, vampires with retractable fangs began showing up. In Buffy, the vampires' teeth are normal until the demon face appears.

other literary and film depictions, including *Buffy*, where the closest thing to a disappearing act is the way Angel can leave a room without anyone hearing him.

The single aspect of vampire mythology that doesn't change regardless of the culture or era is the creature's need to drink blood in order to survive. Deprive a vampire of its blood supply and it will grow weak and eventually wither away. But when it comes to *why* exactly the vampire needs blood, there are varying interpretations. Like *Buffy*'s vampires, Anne Rice's undead in the Vampire Chronicles are inhabited by demons that make them lust for blood. In early literary works, it was inferred the vampire suffered from a sort of anemia, so he needed fresh blood to stay healthy and strong.

Another trait of vampirism that seems to hold true across the board is that once a person becomes a vampire, they stop aging. Hence the young girl in *Interview with the Vampire* remains a young girl throughout. It is also the reason why Whedon found it necessary to kill off the Anointed One, because the actor was visibly aging, plus the fact that Whedon found the character annoying.

As far as physical attributes go, it is generally agreed that vampires have good eyesight and excellent hearing, most likely because those are traits associated with other nocturnal creatures. A vamp's skin is usually pale, which makes sense if sunlight never touches skin. However, some literature indicates that a vampire will get a glow to his skin after feeding.

In *Buffy* and in many other depictions, the vampire possesses superhuman strength, but this wasn't always the case. Centuries ago, vampires were thought to attack only vulnerable victims, such as old people or children. But in more recent literature and film portrayals, vampires are powerful creatures with few weaknesses. That's what made *Buffy*'s Drusilla character unique—she was powerless and completely dependent on Spike, until revived through the ritual with Angel.

Now we come to the question many *Buffy* fans have no doubt wondered about: Can vampires have sex, either with each other or with humans? The answer is yes, on both counts. In some literature, vampires are simply not interested in sex, considering such carnal desires beneath them. But by and large, vampires have come to be seen as highly erotic, sensual creatures— although there are some definite drawbacks to becoming intimately involved with one.

The first problem is their skin temperature. Vampires are technically dead and therefore cold to the touch. All over. In some portrayals, vampires are shown as bloodless, with no circulation. But the *Buffy* vampires bleed when hurt, so Angel would have blood circulation, which for all males, even vampires, is important for a romantic interlude.

The biggest hurdle to overcome during physical intimacy with a vampire is the danger that the vampire will lose control and go into a feeding frenzy. If the point of the seduction is to feed and kill, then that's no problem; in the case of a long-term relationship, however, such a loss of control would be disastrous. The first time Angel kissed Buffy, the first thing that happened was his vampire face appeared. Some literature details how a vampire may feed just a little bit on a human lover, which enables the undead one to have normal sexual function. It's believed that true love tends to keep a vampire from going into a feeding frenzy during sex, which also means that one-night stands usually don't stand a chance.

And yes, vampires can have children. The offspring of a vampire and a human is called a *dhampir*. Traditionally, the father is a vampire and the mother human. And usually the baby is male. Because of their unique parentage, dhampirs are said to have the ability to ferret out vampires, and many, in fact, became vampire hunters. The dhampir's special sensory abilities can be passed down to his own children and are believed to last many generations. In fact, on *Angel*, *Buffy*'s spin-off, Darla and Angel conceived a child the "normal" way.

Vampires in Film and TV

Although the modern view of vampires has its roots in Bram Stoker's *Dracula*, the creature has been refined, and redefined, by other works of literature—most notably Anne Rice. But the art form most responsible for shaping the current view of the vampire is film.

The granddaddy of vampire movies has to be the 1931 Tod Browning film, *Dracula*, which starred Bela Lugosi. Lugosi's Dracula was a gothic figure, a man of the shadows. Because of his accent and foreign appearance, the film promoted the image of the alien vampire, the stranger who walks among us. Although by today's standards the film is pure camp, at the time women were passing out from fright in the aisles of theaters. It was also the genesis of the horror-film genre, which Universal Studios made into a cottage industry.

In a little-known bit of vampire movie trivia, studio executives believed *Dracula* would do very well in the overseas markets, so a second film was shot in Spanish, using the same sets, just days after *Dracula* wrapped. This version starred Carlos Villarias as Count Dracula and was directed by George Melford. Some film historians consider the Spanish version superior to the Browning version.

Although film vampires have tended to stay in the "tall, dark, handsome, and mysterious" vein, two distinct types of Hollywood vampires have emerged—the old-fashioned, courtly vampire who has an air of the Old

World about him, who tends to shy away from interacting much with humans; and the modern vampire, who often conceals his identity by hiding in plain sight, living among humans and interacting with them (aside from feeding on them).

Initially, all vampires were considered evil and better off dead. But as vampires have become ingrained in popular culture, that menace has become optional. On occasion, vampires have become lovable comic foils, as in the 1960s television series *The Munsters* and the films *Love at First Bite* and *Dracula: Dead and Loving It* (1995).

Buffy straddles both these approaches. Most of the vampires the Slayer encounters are soulless monsters out to hunt and feed on humans. But Angel is a vampire of a different sort because he's been cursed with a conscience, so he keeps the demon inside him in check and refrains from feeding on humans. He's got all the eroticism and power without the killer mentality.

No doubt much of the change in attitude toward vampires has to do with the times in which we live. During Victorian times, the qualities embodied by the vampire—the lusty, erotic, dangerous creature not bound by social convention—reflected the very aspects of man that era sought to repress. The sensibility of those times was incorporated both in 1992's *Bram Stoker's Dracula*, directed by Francis Ford Coppola, and in the 1994 film adaptation of Anne Rice's *Interview with the Vampire*, starring Tom Cruise.

While the majority of vampire portrayals maintain the convention that the undead are monsters who must be stopped, some opt for a more complex identity which in many ways reflects our own dual natures as creatures that can embody the greatest good and the worst evil. Now, vampires don't have to represent all that is evil.

Although vampires have populated close to a hundred films and have been the topics of literature for the past several centuries, television has been slower to jump on the vampire bandwagon. Part of that is the nature of series—how does one incorporate a vampire over an extended period of time? The easiest way is through comedy. In TV's *The Munsters*, Lily and Grandpa were vampires, but without any bite. And in the 1988 animated *Count Duckula*, a vegetarian duck battles against everyone's attempt to turn him to a bloodsucker.

Developing a dramatic series with a vampire as a lead character has proven to be a trickier matter, but in the right setting, vampires have shown they can be TV stars, too. In 1967, ABC introduced the gothic soap opera *Dark Shadows*, about two-hundred-year-old vampire named Barnabas Collins. Using soap conventions, *Dark Shadows* managed to milk the vampire myth for five seasons. Part of its success was due to the willingness of daytime viewers to accept the Gothic setting. Plus, daytime serials tend to move at a slower pace than prime-time shows, so it fit traditional vampire storytelling conventions.

The Night Stalker, one of the better scary television movies ever made, starred Darren McGavin as reporter Carl Kolchak, who investigates a series of gruesome murders in Las Vegas. But when ABC made the 1971 movie into a 1974 series, it proved impossible to sustain the story lines—which branched out beyond vampires into monsters of all kinds. The genuine fear-factor that had made the original telefilm so effective, mutated into toothless camp, and the show was canceled after a year. Years later, though, it served as one of the main inspirations for the much more popular nine-year series *The X-Files.*

The 1990s series *Forever Knight* and *Kindred: The Embraced* both took the "Vampires are people, too" approach. In *Forever Knight,* an eight-hundred-year-old vampire works as a Toronto homicide detective in an attempt to atone for his past sins and somehow regain his mortality. In *Kindred: The Embraced* a vampire named Luna is the prince of several clans of vampires—or Kindred—living in San Francisco. It's his job to maintain peace between the clans and enforce the Kindred rules against taking a human life or turning a human into a vampire against their wishes.

The lead characters of both series are reminiscent of *Buffy*'s Angel—vampires who have maintained some remnant of their humanity or are attempting to repent for atrocities they may have committed earlier during their lives as vampires. This trend of humanizing some vampires while acknowledging the overall evil of the species, seems to be the most successful way to portray vampires in series, because in television it's important for people to want to invite the show back into their homes week after week.

That's where *Buffy* has offered viewers the best of both worlds. Even villainous vampires, such as the pre-chip Spike, are portrayed as having the capacity to love, and as being loyal to their intimates. The lead character is a Slayer and the vampires she hunts are unequivocally evil, but the first love of her life was the only vampire who had a conscience, and was able to control the demon within—for the most part. Angel took the appeal of the tortured soul to a new level. By combining the traditional Gothic elements of vampire lore with the modern twist of redemption, *Buffy* has further developed the ongoing mythology of vampires.

While the classic elements of vampire mythology will undoubtedly endure in future films and series, as evidenced by *Buffy*, individual vampire characters will continue to diversify and grow in complexity because, at their core, they are simply a mirror into the dark side of our own hearts.

CAST BIOGRAPHIES

·✚·

As the series has evolved and matured, the characters populating Sunnydale have changed accordingly. Following are bios of the current main cast of characters.

Sarah Michelle Gellar

There's a stigma attached to being a kid actor. In order for preschool age children to succeed in such a highly competitive business, they must be precocious beyond their years, willing to please, possess a premature ambition, *and* be cute as a button to boot.

But the disapproval has less to do with the youngsters themselves than with the circumstances required for their having a career in the first place. All child actors must have at least one parent who at some point agrees to expose their son or daughter to the often ego-punishing world of show business. No matter how much a child maintains that they want to act, the fact is, unless the parent becomes part of the process, it simply won't happen. Many kids profess the desire to be in showbiz; however, the majority are gently told they can do whatever they want to—once they are old enough to get to auditions on their own.

The biggest criticism of child actors is what happens to them when they became adults. The film and television industries are littered with reminders—Dana Plato, River Phoenix, Todd Bridges, Danny Bonaduce, Corey Haim, to name just a few—of what can happen to young people subjected to the pressure of being the family's primary breadwinner . . . of juggling the angst of growing up with the responsibilities of an adult job . . . of not only achieving success, but maintaining it.

Some of the most vocal critics are former child stars themselves, such as *The Donna Reed Show*'s Paul Peterson—founder of A Minor Consideration (a group that advocates the rights of child performers)—who says the entertainment industry's tendency to view people as disposable goods sets young people up for a devastating fall once they (literally) grow out of their careers.

Of course, not all former child actors end up robbing dry-cleaners or overdosing on city sidewalks or marrying eight times and becoming a poster girl for the Betty Ford Clinic. Nor do all fail to make the transition to an adult career. Jodie Foster, Henry Thomas, Jerry O'Connell, and dozens of others are living proof that you can be a child actor, grow up into a relatively well balanced adult, and continue in your chosen profession. Sarah Michelle Gellar also can be added to that list of well-adjusted overachievers.

Gellar (pronounced GELL-are, not GELL-er) has been a professional actor since she was six years-old, and she is a bit weary of people making assumptions about former child actors. "I'm tired of people who say, 'Acting corrupts these young people,' " Gellar has said. "You know what? There are a lot of actors who have been working since a young age and they're just fine. I was not meant to be in Little League or the local ballet school.

"My mom was not living vicariously through me. It has always been my choice to act—and if my grades ever fell below an A, I had to stop working for a while. When I was old enough, it was my decision to go to college or pursue my career. If at any time I wanted to give it up, [my mother] would be behind me one hundred percent."

That said, it was actually an agent who first got the idea that Sarah had a face a camera could definitely love. Born April 14, 1977, in Manhattan, and raised on the Upper East Side, Sarah was discovered, in a Lana Turner moment, while eating lunch with her mother in a restaurant. "This woman walked up to me and asked if I'd like to be on television," Gellar says. "And I was like, 'Yeah, okay!' " Sarah was four years old and a would-be star was born.

A short time later, Sarah got her first national exposure when she was hired to play Valerie Harper's daughter in the CBS Movie of the Week, *An Invasion of Privacy*, which also starred Jeff Daniels. "The day I went in, I was supposed to read with Valerie but she'd already gone home," Sarah remembers. "But that was no problem; first I read my lines and then I read hers—in Valerie's voice. I was hired on the spot."

Although she went on to be cast as Burt Young's daughter in the 1983 feature *Over the Brooklyn Bridge*, and did a guest spot on the Tony Randall series *Love, Sidney*, Sarah worked mostly in commercials during those early years. She did over one hundred television spots, thirty of them for a long-running Burger King campaign.

At the tender age of five, Sarah learned just how cutthroat the entertainment business was, when she was named in a civil lawsuit filed by McDonald's against Burger King. Though a common practice now, the suit stemmed from Burger King openly daring to disparage rival McDonald's for their skimpy burger patties. "Well, McDonald's was very upset by this commercial," explains Gellar, "so they turned around and sued Burger King, J. Walker Thompson, the advertising company that came up with the idea for the spot, and me. I couldn't even say the word 'lawyer' and a few months later I was having to tell my friends, 'I can't play. I've got to give a deposition.' "

But Sarah says the lawsuit was the least of her concerns at that age. Worse was her truth-in-advertising contractual obligation to only publicly endorse Burger King. "When you're five, where do all of your friends have their birthday parties? Answer: McDonald's. So there I was, going to birthday parties wearing a big straw hat and sunglasses." The case, dubbed by the New York papers as "the Battle of the Burgers" was eventually settled out of court in 1982, and Sarah and her career sailed along untainted by the legal maneuvering.

By 1986, Sarah's career was gaining momentum. She played a little girl in the hospital on an episode of *Spenser: For Hire* ("Robert Urich was really wonderful to me") and made her Broadway debut in the drama *The Widow Claire*, which was staged at Circle in the Square. Sarah played the role of Molly opposite a still–up-and-coming Matthew Broderick.

"But then *Ferris Bueller* came out and Matthew left the show," Sarah recalled. "He was replaced by Eric Stoltz. Then Eric's film, *Some Kind of Wonderful*, came out and suddenly *he* was really big. And I became the most popular girl in school because I got to work with both of them."

But as positive and bright as her career was, Sarah's home life was decidedly darker. Her mother, Rosellen, then a nursery-school teacher, and her father Arthur, a salesman, were in the throes of a crumbling marriage. As an only child, Sarah had no sibling to turn to for comfort.

And although Sarah has steadfastly refused to discuss her parents' split, an interview given by Arthur in 1994 strongly indicates Rosellen's support and encouragement of her daughter's acting was at least one cause of friction.

Arthur, then an unemployed textile salesman, told *Star* magazine that he never wanted Sarah to go into show business because he worried about the effect it could have on her, having seen via some of his relatives what kinds of troubles life in the fast lane can bring. "I just wanted Sarah to have a normal life," he said. "Kids in the business grow up too fast."

After thirteen years of marriage, Arthur and Rosellen divorced in 1987. For a while, Arthur maintained contact with Sarah, but by 1990, when she was just twelve, all communication had been broken off. Even though they lived in the same city, Sarah wouldn't lay eyes on her father for many years to come.

As late as 1994, Sarah would respond coldly whenever asked about her father. "My parents divorced when I was very young and I don't see my real dad. We never got along, so when he left it was a much better environment. And he's out of the picture. My mom's fiancé is the one who sat in the front row at school recitals with the camera." She was even harsher in *TV Guide*: "He is not a person who exists in my life. Just because you donate sperm does not make you a father. I don't have a father. I would never give him the credit to acknowledge him as my father."

Despite his daughter's apparent anger and resentment, Arthur maintained he held no grudges. "I love Sarah very much. And even though I haven't seen her in years, there isn't a night that goes by that I don't think of her—but it's too painful to even watch her on TV."

Sarah refused to discuss her father publicly. For that matter, Gellar was also closemouthed when her mom came and lived with her for a while. A friend let slip that Gellar had quietly reestablished contact with Arthur, though there was no indication it was a full-fledged, open-armed reunion.

Whatever her relationship with her long-estranged father, it became moot in October 2001 when he was found dead in his Manhattan apartment, initially rumored to be a drug overdose. Police were called to the scene by a friend who'd reported that the sixty-year-old Gellar had been missing several days. They found him in bed with medication near his body. It was reported by friends that Arthur was undergoing cancer treatment and had suffered from depression, and it was determined he died from complications related to kidney cancer. Gellar steadfastly refused to make any public comment about her father's death and reportedly did not attend his funeral.

After her parents divorced, Sarah's resentment toward anyone who questioned or criticized her mother or herself over her acting career, would be a recurring theme for many years. But whatever emotional toll it took, it did nothing to slow Sarah down; if anything, she sped up. While attending the exclusive Columbia Grammar and Preparatory School, located at 5 West

93rd Street, across Central Park from where she lived, Sarah was a bundle of nonstop activity.

She was a competitive figure-skater for three years, ranking third in the New York State regional competition. "What was happening was, I was going to school, acting, skating, and taking Tae Kwon Do all at the same time. I would get up in the morning and head straight to the ice rink to practice. Then I'd go to school, then when school let out, I'd go on auditions, then take Tae Kwon Do classes in the evening."

Despite her amazing determination, stamina, ambition, and drive, Sarah eventually discovered she wasn't superhuman. "No human being can keep up that kind of schedule, and I was cracking," she admits. "So finally my mom stepped in. One day she sat me down and told me I could only do two things. One was school, so that left me the choice of picking the one thing that was my big love. And I chose acting."

Despite her talent, intelligence, and desire to fit in, Sarah was the class outcast during her junior-high years at Columbia Grammar and Preparatory School, surrounded by schoolmates under-enthused, and even more unimpressed—with her achievements as an actress, which by that time included parts in the features *Funny Farm* and *High Stakes*, where she played Sally Kirkland's daughter.

Sarah believes her professional achievements actually were resented by the other kids. "They were so hard on me. I never liked to talk about my acting because if I did, I was branded a snob. And if I didn't, I was still a snob"—which made her become secretive about her extracurricular activities. "In 1990, I had more absences in the first month than you're supposed to have in an entire year. I was telling them I had back problems and had to go to doctors all the time. I guess they believed me—until *A Woman Named Jackie* aired."

In that 1991 miniseries, Sarah played the young Jacqueline Bouvier. Besides being delirious at the opportunity to spend time away from the nightmare that was school, Gellar was excited to be involved in a project about the former First Lady. "I had always been fascinated by Jackie Kennedy, so to play her as a teenager was really a thrill," Sarah says.

The older Jackie was played by future *Touched by an Angel* star Roma Downey, to whom Sarah became instantly devoted. "I wanted to be just like Roma. Not just in the movie but in real life, too. If she sat down, so did I. If she walked, I walked. I tried to do *everything* she did. And fortunately, Roma was great about it. She didn't mind me becoming her little shadow at all."

Peer problems aside, Sarah's professional life was only getting better.

She was a cohost on the series *Girl Talk* and traveled to Europe to film the internationally syndicated series *The Legend of William Tell,* which in some areas was known as *Crossbow.* The 1991 series starred Will Lyman as William Tell, who was searching for his wife and son. Lyman was fresh off the short-lived 1990 series *Hull High,* NBC's failed attempt at a musical series.

The Legend of William Tell was not picked up for any additional episodes, but Sarah wasn't out of series work for long. In 1992, she appeared in Neil Simon's play *Jake's Women* at the Old Globe Theater in Boston. Next she was cast in *Swan's Crossing,* a much-hyped syndicated teen soap opera that was produced by WOR in New York. It was Sarah's first chance at ongoing national exposure and she went into the project with high hopes that it would be her breakout role.

Swan's Crossing debuted on June 29, 1992. According to the promotional material, the serial focused on the "lives, loves, and intrigues" of a dozen privileged New England teenagers and preteens, living in the fictitious coastal town of Swan's Crossing, who "stir up scandal and excitement in their small town."

Sarah played Sidney Rutledge, the mayor's scheming daughter. Among the other characters were the requisite woman-charmer, an evil ex-boyfriend, a former television star, and a young scientist working on formulating world's first self-perpetuating rocket fuel. Sarah's big chance didn't last long. After just three months on the air, *Swan's Crossing* ceased production on September 25, 1992. *TV Guide*'s soap columnist, Michael Logan, said bluntly. "Basically, it starred too many young people who couldn't act."

The original episodes were rerun over the next three months and then, despite a fervent outcry from the few but hardcore fans, the show faded way. After *Swan's Crossing* went off the air, Sarah shook off the disappointment and looked forward to her next chance at television notoriety, which came within a matter of months.

For a couple of years, the producers of *All My Children* had been thinking about introducing a new character as a foil for Erica Kane, played by daytime diva Susan Lucci, and were just waiting for the right moment. The time finally came in 1993, just as Erica was getting a little too comfortable settling into engaged bliss with her latest love Dimitri, played by Michael Nader. So the casting call went out for a young actress to play the part of Kendall Hart, Erica's long-lost daughter.

The soap's producers were determined to keep the shocking story line a secret, so during the casting process the actresses were told that Kendall would be Erica's new assistant. "I didn't know when I auditioned for Kendall that she would turn out to be who she is," Sarah says. "I had heard rumors, but everybody was denying it. Besides, I was scared enough at the thought of working with Susan."

Practically every teenage actor in New York auditioned for the plum role, which eventually went to Sarah. Besides bearing a resemblance to Lucci, Sarah had the acting chops and the forceful personality needed to go up against Susan. After all, this daughter was supposed to be a chip off the Kane block.

"When they told me I would be playing her daughter, I was like, 'What!? Daughter? Me?' 'I remember on my first day when I walked into the rehearsal hall, Susan and Michael were rehearsing a scene. I was very nervous. I kept thinking, 'What if I'm really bad and they fire me?' I just snuck in the back and tried to blend in with the coffee machine, when all of a sudden, Susan said, 'Hold it, we need to stop for a minute.'

"Then she walked over to me and said, 'Congratulations! I'm very glad you're here.' She put her arm around me and said, 'Don't worry, nobody bites.' And then she introduced me to everyone who was there. She really did help me and always made sure I was okay during my first couple of weeks when I was still unsettled. Both Susan and Michael made me feel comfortable."

But it wasn't a complete set of strangers. Also there to hold her hand was actress Lindsay Price, who played the character An Li Chen and who also happened to be an old school friend of Sarah's.

Kendall was introduced on February 24, 1993, to an unsuspecting audience as Erica's new twenty-two-year-old assistant. Eventually the truth was revealed: Kendall was Erica's long-lost daughter. She was also mad as hell for being abandoned at birth—even though the pregnancy had resulted from a rape—and determined to exact revenge against Erica as payback.

Although Gellar cheerfully admits Kendall was the most terrible daughter on daytime during her reign (during her first week on the show she locked her little half-sister in a crypt and tried to seduce her stepfather Dimitri—and when he turned her down, slept with the stable boy, after which she cried rape and then went to jail), she refuses to admit the character was evil: "I chose to see Kendall as misunderstood, which was how as an actress I justified her actions. It was amazing, though, playing a psycho-looney."

As Kendall became more central to the story line, Gellar's workload increased, making her school obligations that much more difficult to meet. This time, however, there was no talk of Sarah having to sacrifice work for grades. "In the beginning of high school, I had the typical high school experience," she says. "But it became incredibly difficult because of my work schedule. Then, after I started working on *All My Children*, where we were shooting five episodes a week, it became impossible. I had to transfer to a school specifically for children with different schedules. It was called Professional Children's School and it was for musicians, ballerinas, writers—just the most talented group of young people. Kids from all over the country, as well as from all over the world, go there."

Finally Sarah had found an environment where she could flourish without feeling guilty about her career or having to compromise her ambitions. "I thank God for that place. It's an amazing place because all of the kids who go there are very talented. And it's a place where your talent is special, but it doesn't affect your schoolwork. Everyone there had a talent and everyone there was respected for that talent. If someone didn't like you, they simply didn't talk to you. They didn't make fun of what you did or punish you for it. When I enrolled, I felt amazingly untalented. But they gave me a chance to find myself." Gellar eventually graduated two years early with a 4.0 GPA.

All My Children proved to be a gold mine for Sarah. Longtime fans of the soap saw Sarah as the second coming of Erica. The more Sarah showed she could handle the work, the more the writers showcased her. Gellar's social life became a whirl of soap-related activity and, for the first time in her career, she became a household name, at least to the legions of faithful daytime viewers. Fans wrote to tell her she reminded them of Natalie Wood and people stopped her in the street. Sarah recalls the time she got in a cab to be greeted by name by the driver. "I had no idea who this guy was. It turns out his son was the doorman at my apartment building."

In addition to the adoration of fans, Sarah was also initiated to the perks of celebrity. And she quickly realized it was a lifestyle she could easily get used to. While buying a ticket to see the movie *Guilty as Sin*, Sarah was recognized by the theater manager, who was so excited to have her there that he treated Sarah to a free movie and complimentary concessions. It was a memorable day because, as Sarah said later, "It was the first time anyone had gone out of their way like that for me."

But it would not be the last. During an affiliates' event in West Virginia, Gellar and co-star Eva LaRue were given the royal treatment at the resort where they stayed. After mentioning they were hungry, the chef came out and personally took their order and when the actresses asked if they could go swimming, the resort opened the closed pool area just for them.

Although she was still in school, *All My Children* had become the center of Sarah's life. She became friends with several co-stars, including Kelly Ripa and Eva LaRue. LaRue, who had joined the soap around the same time Sarah had, and who was ten years her senior, became Sarah's best friend, especially after Lindsay Price left the soap. (Price later appeared on *The Bold and the Beautiful* and *Beverly Hills 90210*.)

In 1994, Sarah proved that not only was she a fan favorite, but a respected member of the acting community as well, when she was nominated for a Daytime Emmy in the Outstanding Younger Actress category for the 1993–94 season. Gellar was asked by *Entertainment Tonight* to be a guest correspondent for the awards and to provide a behind-the-scenes look at the Daytime Emmys. She exuded an easy charm and affability that once again belied her years.

Although she lost, Gellar wasn't disappointed. She had come a long way in a short time and knew she was only going to get better. But life can be a lot like a soap opera at times. While Gellar's working relationship with Susan Lucci had begun cordially enough, over time it subtly, then blatantly, began to deteriorate. The year of Sarah's discontent had begun.

✦ It wasn't long before the rumors started. Some reports insinuated that Lucci, who for years had made a cottage industry out of not winning an Emmy, was miffed that Sarah was nominated her first year out—the same year Lucci failed to earn a nomination of her own.

"The truth is," says a show associate, "Susan was against the idea of the Kendall story line to begin with, because she didn't really want Erica to be seen as the mother of a daughter in her twenties. Ironically, one of the ways the producers convinced Susan to accept the plot was to convince her that this was the story line that would finally win her the Emmy." It didn't. (Lucci would finally win the Emmy for Outstanding Lead Actress in 1999.)

Soon Sarah began spending a lot of time denying the rumors of tension. But according to a source on the show, who requested anonymity, their personality clash actually began shortly after Sarah's arrival.

"Susan actually made Sarah's life hell from the beginning by doing things to undermine her. For example, she would play a scene one way during rehearsal then abruptly change it when the cameras were rolling. Then, when Sarah would stop short, confused, Susan would chastise her, telling her she should really be more professional and learn her lines before shooting a scene. Susan would also make cutting little remarks about Sarah's acting, and a few times Sarah was reduced to tears. The rest of the cast thought Susan's behavior was appalling and that's when the first stories began leaking about Susan being a bitch."

But another person familiar with the conflict says—contrary to the perception at the time—it wasn't just Susan contributing to the tension: "In many ways, Sarah was just as guilty, although it wasn't as obvious as Susan's snits. Sarah was, and is, intelligent and aware and she knew how to push Susan's buttons. She just did it subtly and with a smile. Lucci is an old pro and has long had a reputation for being a generous performer. But then along came Sarah, who makes sly jokes about Susan's age and pushes other hot emotional buttons, and before you know it, the set becomes thick with tension. They were just a bad mix.

"Plus, Sarah loved being the center of attention and she wasn't shy about how her career was heating up," says a former soap employee, who claims the situation between Gellar and Lucci deteriorated to the point where they simply stopped talking. "They would be professional and perform their scenes together, then leave and not say a word once the cameras stopped rolling."

It also didn't help that Sarah was frequently referred to as "the baby Erica" and was being groomed to be the next major leading-lady in daytime—and had made it clear she was up to the challenge.

In fact, by the end of 1994 Sarah had developed a different attitude toward her acting. Instead of just being something she did for fun, it became a more serious pursuit. "If you train when you're young, I think it ruins your spontaneity," Gellar explains. "Kids have a natural honesty that no adult really can, and at some point, you lose it. It wasn't until I got *All My Children* that I started to study and see it as a craft."

In a 1994 interview, Gellar responded sharply when asked if she didn't sometimes wish she could have enjoyed a traditional high school experience. "I don't feel like I'm missing out on anything," she said. "Your childhood is what you make it. I do all the normal things that most teenage girls do, like go to the movies, hang out with friends and go on dates. At the Professional School, I get to have it all. I go to proms and I go to formal dances, and you know what? I yawn."

Now, looking back she says, "I had the same kind of decisions Buffy did: Do I go to a school dance or slumber party, or do I go to an audition? But I don't have any regrets. I've done a tremendous amount of traveling and it's given me the opportunity to see all the different things that are out there in the world.

But in 1995, Sarah was too busy to spend much time on philosophical reflection. She was preparing to graduate from high school and for the second year in a row she had been nominated for a Daytime Emmy. As luck would have it, the awards ceremony fell at the same time her prom was scheduled, but there was never a question which event would win out, especially since Sarah was considered the odds-on favorite to win the Outstanding Younger Actress Emmy.

But what only a handful of people knew as the Emmys approached was that, win or lose, this would be Sarah's soap swan-song. She had asked to be released early from her contract, which wasn't officially up until February 1996. "I had decided not to renew my contract some time before, and told the show very far in advance, because I felt that was fair. Then, when my story line slowed to one day a week, I asked to be released even earlier." Besides the inactivity, her contract—and the show's unwillingness to accommodate her—was preventing Sarah from pursuing other opportunities. "I was offered two other projects, which I was not released to do," she says pointedly. "And to be honest, I was a little bitter about that."

The producers reluctantly agreed to release her but the network insisted she keep the departure a secret until after they made the official announcement—after the Emmys. Sarah agreed, although the decision would later come back to haunt her when it put her in a bad light with fans of the show. "The timing was terrible because it made me look incredibly bad."

As expected, Gellar won the Emmy. Also as expected, Lucci *didn't* win in her own category. So when news broke the following week that Gellar was leaving the show, one of two assumptions was made: The first was that Lucci was so beside herself over Sarah's Emmy win that Gellar had been practically forced out of the soap. The other was that Sarah was so full of herself, she abruptly decided to quit and go Hollywood.

The charges stung and Gellar felt compelled to confront the rumors. "Contrary to what one newspaper reported, I was *not* fired because I won the Emmy and Susan Lucci didn't," Sarah said. "Nor, as another one claimed, did I win the award on a Friday night and quit the following Monday morning because I got 'too big for my britches.' "

Gellar's last day on *All My Children* was July 3, 1995. Although she continued to downplay the acrimony between her and Susan Lucci for a while, these days Sarah can speak about the situation with the dispassion of distance:

"It wasn't an easy time in my life. Susan and I didn't have the most amazing relationship; we were not best friends and we're never going to be. I denied it for a long time because that's what you're supposed to do, but it also wasn't as bad as people made it out to be. The thing I said to her—that I was not competing against her—was the truth. She was in the 'Leading Actress' category and I was in the 'Younger Actress' category. And let's be honest: 'Leading Actress' is a much more difficult category. And you don't work alone—I won for scenes submitted with her, for work we did together.

"We worked very well together, but it wasn't the easiest working relationship. Basically, the best I can say is that we worked together, on top of each other for so long, that problems were inevitable. But would I do it all over again? Absolutely. Being on a soap is the best training in the world because, technically, it's a very difficult medium to work in. I feel that if you can do daytime, you can do anything."

After leaving the soap, Sarah prepared to make her next big career move—relocating to California. In an interview given shortly before her move to Hollywood, Gellar expressed her determination to be picky about the work she took. "The most important thing for me is to do work I enjoy— that I'm proud of and respect. If it takes me time to find work, then it will, but I'm not going to jump on the first things that have been offered, because they're not what I'm interested in. And if I wanted to do another soap, there'd be no reason for me to leave *All My Children*. It was an amazing two years, but I wanted to spread my wings and do other things, something totally different."

Gellar technically moved to L.A. in August, but resisted putting down roots—a common syndrome that afflicts many New Yorkers when they first relocate to the West Coast. Despite being fresh from an Emmy win, the door of Hollywood didn't exactly spring open for Sarah. She auditioned for, and lost, several high-profile parts—including *Romeo and Juliet* to Claire Danes.

"I had a lot of offers for movies-of-the-week, disease-of-the-week, this girl in peril, that girl in jeopardy, and I turned them down. I was really waiting for the role that was going to be special—the role that could establish me more seriously. I had to wait about a year and a half before I started working again."

Apparently temporarily putting aside her desire to be taken seriously, Sarah appeared in the ABC telefilm *Beverly Hills Family Robinson*, opposite Martin Mull and Dyan Cannon, which was filmed in 1996. Then she was sent another script, and immediately sensed this was the role she'd been waiting for. Gellar just knew she was perfect for the part of Buffy. Unfortunately, though, she had been asked to read for the part of Cordelia, the school's most popular—and most annoying—girl.

When Sarah requested to read for Buffy, she was politely but firmly turned down. Repeatedly. But she hadn't moved cross-country to let a golden opportunity slip by, so she fought to change the producers' mind: "I really wanted Buffy, but when they were auditioning, I had long dark hair and very light skin. I kept trying to convince people to let me read for Buffy. They kept saying, 'You're not Buffy.' And I kept saying, 'I can be Buffy.' "

Her persistence—and her offer to dye her hair blonde so that Buffy would remain a quintessential-looking California girl—eventually wore down creator Joss Whedon, and Sarah got to read for Buffy. Then she got to read again and Whedon was convinced he had found his Buffy, except for one last detail: "For both auditions, I wore this ankle-length dress with sneakers and they were afraid I was trying to hide a really ugly pair of legs," Gellar laughs.

Sarah and her co-stars shot a two-hour pilot then she went back to New York for six months. After the WB gave the series the go-ahead as a midseason replacement and scheduled it for a January 1997 debut, the cast reassembled and filmed ten additional episodes.

Buffy debuted on March 10, 1997, to rave critical response, and quickly generated a host of Web pages devoted to the series and its stars, especially Sarah. However, she wasn't around to see it because she had just landed her most important film role to date, in *I Know What You Did Last Summer*, which co-starred *Party of Five*'s Jennifer Love-Hewitt, and Ryan Phillippe and Freddie Prinze Jr.

"It was about two weeks before *Buffy* was scheduled to go on the air. I was on a press junket for the show when I heard about the movie, and I went and auditioned. Screaming was my entire screen test for the movie. I just stood there and screamed for about five minutes. Gut-wrenching. Love-Hewitt has this really pretty, high melodic scream, while mine sounds like a cat in heat.

"I got *I Know What You Did Last Summer* the week *Buffy* first aired," Gellar explains, "so I was off to North Carolina. We were filming in this very small town in Sonoma County that only got *Buffy* on a little cable station. And believe me, most people there didn't have cable. So for two and a half months I was spared from it. I never heard about the Web sites and didn't see any of the billboards that WB put up all over the place. So I had two months to prepare for it."

The last of the four main characters to be cast in *Last Summer*, Gellar admits she was still carrying around Buffy's attitude when she first started filming. "In the beginning, the director would have to tell me that I wasn't running a triathlon: 'You can't kick the guy.' It was also hard just because of my training and what I had gotten used to on a day-to-day basis. I'm so used to being the aggressor in a fight."

She's not kidding. Once, while visiting Knott's Berry Farm, an L.A.-area amusement park that hosts annual Halloween "Fright Nights," Sarah punched a park employee/vampire who jumped out of the shadows to scare her. "Yeah, the guy grabbed me and I hit him," Sarah says, chagrined. "It was just an instinctive reaction."

The day production wrapped on *I Know What You Did Last Summer* in June, Sarah flew to Atlanta to begin work on *Scream 2*, in which she plays one of Neve Campbell's sorority sisters. She had got the movie by pure coincidence. Although she'd already been cast in *I Know What You Did Last Summer*, writer Kevin Williamson had never met her. After running into her on a plane, Williamson, who also wrote *Scream 2*, was professionally smitten, and recommended Sarah to director Wes Craven for the part of Cici, a character who doesn't make it to the end of the film.

"I didn't have to push very hard because Wes fell in love with her, too," Williamson says. "It's a juicy little part, and she's rocking! I want her in every one of my movies because you know when you hire her to do a job she's not going to be in the trailer complaining about everything. She's going to be right out there giving you the tenth take in the freezing cold."

For all of Williamson's high praise, Gellar was a basket case when she got to the location. "I got down there and was so intimidated and in awe, that the day before we finished the read-through I literally called my manager and said, 'I'm going to pack my bags. I'm going to be fired. I'm coming home.' Actually, I do that at every job after a read-through. I did that at the first read-through for the first season of *Buffy*—and after the second season I *still* thought I was going to be fired." It was an actor's version of buyer's anxiety. "This is what I've waited for my whole life. But I'm worried that something's going to go wrong. I keep thinking I'm going to mess it up somehow."

Scream 2 was still in production when it was time to report back to *Buffy*. Unlike the *All My Children* producers, who had prevented Sarah from doing outside projects, Whedon and the other executives worked around Sarah's movie schedule. "Basically, I'd work on *Buffy* Monday through Thursday, then I'd start *Scream* on Friday, wouldn't finish until Sunday, and just basically go straight to *Buffy*, shower and start work there.

And as Sarah can attest, filming *Buffy* is exhausting enough by itself. "It's a real difficult show to shoot, and I never have a day off. Sometimes they don't finish shooting until two A.M. and I have to be there at five some mornings. So there were times when I did feel as if I was in over my head. One day I was driving to work. I had the top down and I noticed people were looking at me. I look down and realize I'm only wearing a slip because I had forgotten to put my dress on. But I've learned I can juggle things."

During each of her *Buffy* hiatuses, Gellar has continued to make films. During 1998 she filmed two movies which were released in 1999. The first was the romantic comedy *Simply Irresistible*, opposite Sean Patrick Flannery, playing a mediocre chef on the verge of losing the restaurant she inherited, whose life is transformed by a mysterious seafood salesman. He gives her a magical crab and suddenly she is able to concoct delicious desserts that act as culinary aphrodisiacs, enabling her to save her restaurant and find true love. A soufflé of a film, critics uniformly dismissed *Simply Irresistible* as very resistible, but the unflattering reviews didn't hurt Gellar's cinematic bankability.

That same year she once again teamed up with Ryan Phillippe in *Cruel Intentions*, based on Choderlos de Laclos' classic French novel, *Les Liaisons Dangereuses*. This time around, the film is set in an upper-crust Manhattan prep school, with Gellar and Phillippe as stepsiblings Kathryn Merteuil and Sebastian Valmont, who wager a bet on whether or not he can take the virginity of the pure Annette Hargrove, played by Phillippe's real-life wife, Reese Witherspoon. If he loses, Merteuil gets his classic 1956 Jaguar; if he wins, he gets to have his way with his stepsister, who brazenly tells him, "You can put it anywhere you like." Clearly Sarah was looking to remind her fans that there's more to her professionally than just the upright and honorable Buffy. "It was important to prove I can do other things," Sarah explains. "*Buffy* is only one step in my career."

Tom Gliatto of *People* called it "a brainless good time for the WB set." *Entertainment Weekly*'s Troy Patterson noted: "Here is the fourth screen adaptation of a novel derided centuries ago as 'a picture of the most odious immorality.' Director Roger Kumble is less concerned with exploring the souls of cynical libertines than with plumbing the nuances of teenage lesbian tongue-kissing. The picture is odious, sure, but its first hour is so zippily titillating as to make for tasty trash."

Critical notices notwithstanding one of the best parts of *Cruel Intentions* for Sarah was winning the Best Screen Kiss at that year's MTV Movie Awards—for a kiss with Selma Blair. "That was the coolest thing," she says.

Although Gellar took a break from acting during her hiatus in 1999, she was hardly idle. In between traveling to Europe to promote *Cruel Intentions*, Sarah donated a week of her time to Habitat for Humanity in the Dominican Republic where she helped build a house for a homeless family. "I made a very good windowsill until someone stepped on it, and then I had to redo it because it wasn't dry," she recalls. "I learned how to lay floor. I mixed a ton of cement. I've never had calluses like that on my hands. And my fingers were just bloody. I guess I've never done an honest day's labor in my life, apparently."

In the summer of 2002 Gellar appeared as Daphne in the film version of the classic cartoon *Scooby-Doo*. Whereas Daphne was the damsel in distress in the original series, Gellar gave her a new-millennium makeover in assertiveness. "It upset me that Daphne was always getting captured, so when the script had her being proactive and strong I immediately wanted to do it," says Gellar, who admits she wanted to do the film because she had grown up watching the cartoon series. "I loved that Scooby wasn't gender-specific. Cartoons like *G.I. Joe* and *Transformers* were for boys, while *My Little Pony* and *Strawberry Shortcake* were for girls. Scooby had something for everyone and I knew the movie would, too."

The film, which co-starred Freddie Prinze Jr. as Fred, Linda Cardellini as Velma, Matthew Lillard as Shaggy, and a computer-generated Scooby-Doo surprised Hollywood by raking in $54 million at the box office its opening weekend, making it Gellar's first bona-fide film hit.

"There are certain movies in Hollywood that have a buzz about them, and this was one of them," Sarah told Desmond Sampson in *Crème*. "But because I work nine months a year on *Buffy*, for me to take my three-month hiatus and do a movie, it has to be something that I really want to do, something I really want to be a part of, something that's worth sacrificing my time for. *Scooby-Doo* was."

But working on the film meant double-duty for Gellar, who spent most of the fifth season of *Buffy* commuting back and forth from Australia. "I would spend two weeks shooting *Buffy* in L.A. and then fly down to Australia for two weeks to shoot *Scooby-Doo*." By that time Gellar and Prinze were openly living together, and rented a beach home in Queensland during filming. "Freddie and I stayed in a solar-powered house in Tanglaoma, which is a really great idea in theory, except it was winter and the house was in the trees," she recalled to *Crème*'s Sampson. "There was sunlight four hours a day. Forget doing laundry, we couldn't get enough hot water to take a bath."

Director Raja Gosnell says the fans went crazy whenever Sarah was in the country. "Sarah is the preeminent teen star in Australia as well as America. There were these Japanese tour boats that would drive past their house so people could take pictures even if they weren't there. We needed added security for our group whenever they came out with us at night."

Gellar says one of the best things about *Scooby-Doo* was her belief that she was going to make MTV awards history. At one point in the film, after Daphne switches bodies with Fred, Sarah has a scene where she kisses co-star Linda Cardellini. "The whole time I was making this movie—and I don't really care about awards, but this award I care about—I was literally thinking, 'I'm gonna win this twice. I wonder if there's even been a two-time 'Best Kiss' winner?' And then they cut it out of the movie and I watched my chances of a second 'Best Kiss' prize—of possibly being the only one to win that twice— just disappear. I was crushed."

Next up for Gellar will be the *Scooby-Doo* sequel and the comedy *A Semester Abroad,* for Deep River Productions, about a tough girl from Queens who earns a scholarship to study in a highly regarded but somewhat stuffy British school where her street edge grates her decidedly more refined schoolmates.

Sarah steadfastly maintains that her silence about her personal life is simply a way to protect her own personal space in a business where loss of anonymity is an accepted price to pay for fabulous wealth and fame. Her desire to be in control is most noticeably reflected in her jealously guarded privacy. "Here's my thing: I made a rule way back when I was on *All My Children* that there would be a part of me I put out to the public and a part I keep to myself. This has caused me problems. It has caused me to lose interviews. But I need a life

to go home to that only my close friends know about. I am *sooo* proud of my house, but you will never see it in *InStyle*. I don't think people should know what my bedroom looks like. We give away too much information.

"I have to have a life outside my career. I have to have things that are sacred to me. My fans have *Buffy* and they have my films. I think they respect that I need to have some privacy."

For a long time, Gellar kept mostly mum on the subject of her relationship with Freddie Prinze Jr., though their romance might have been one of Hollywood's worst-kept secrets. Her first acknowledgment that he was perhaps more than just a buddy came when she admitted in an interview that Prinze worried whether she was wasting away. "During the time I was promoting *Scream 2*, I was really stressed out and exhausted and just not eating. One night I got home to find Freddie and several of his friends in my kitchen cooking up a feast. Then they wrapped up the leftovers to make sure I would have plenty of food in the refrigerator," she related, adding, "Freddie's my baby."

Although Sarah won't comment on specific romances she has had in the past, she will talk about her philosophy on relationships in general: "I do think you have to have some compromise to make a relationship work but I would never change drastically. You have to be true to yourself and I think if you're not happy with what you're doing, you've crossed the line. You shouldn't be going out with someone just to say you're going out with them. You're going out with them, hopefully, because you enjoy who they are and they enjoy who you are."

When Sarah was still on *All My Children*, there was a curious incident involving co-star Windsor Harmon. Once during an interview, Harmon announced that he and Sarah were dating and a romantic item.

"Sarah was outraged," says an acquaintance. "But whether she was outraged because it was not true, or because he had let the cat out of the bag, nobody was completely sure. In the end, most people figured that Windsor was just trying to up his profile by attaching himself to Sarah. As it happened, he left the show shortly after that, moved to California, joined *The Bold and the Beautiful*, and is now married with a family."

Sarah was once quoted as saying, "Right now, because all I do is work, the only people you meet are actors, and I'd rather not date actors." Apparently she changed her mind because, after months of discreet dating, Freddie Prinze moved into Sarah's house in 2000. "I met him first as an actor and I respected his work—and then it went from there."

One thing anyone involved with an actor must endure is seeing their partner in cinematic love scenes, such as Buffy's erotic escapades with Spike. Gellar says it's not so easy being in the scenes, either. "To be honest, it is truly the unsexiest thing in the world. David Boreanaz [who played Angel] and I were the worst. We would do horrible things to each other. Like eat tuna fish and pickle before we kissed. If he had to unbutton my shirt or my trousers I would pin them or sew them together to make it as hard as I could." Not surprisingly, Prinze prefers not to watch, although Gellar adds dryly, "Oddly enough, he liked my girl-on-girl scenes from *Cruel Intentions*."

Gellar and Freddie were married on September 1, 2002. She admits that many of her friends are starting families. "It does make you think about it," she told Desmond in *Crème*. "Ultimately, I think everyone's dream is to be happy, be fulfilled, get married, and have kids. Having kids is such a huge step in your life, though. We both want children. It has to be at the right time, when both people are ready for it. So, when we're both ready, we will. Would I stop working? I don't know. I mean, obviously, I think it depends on what I was doing and where I was in my life."

Gellar is aware of the chord *Buffy* has struck with the audience, especially females. "Everyone says it's such a burden to be a role model. But they're looking at it the wrong way. It's an honor. The only thing is, it's important that there's a certain line of separation where I'm seen as Sarah and not Buffy.

"I know when I was growing up how important certain teen icons were to me. They respond to Buffy because for years we didn't have a character young girls could look up to," she explained during a *TV Guide* interview. "Mallory on *Family Ties* was an idiot. Carol on *Growing Pains* wasn't happy being smart; she wanted to be popular. Those were not role models. And then you have the actresses who are so physically perfect you can never be like them. Buffy is not the smartest or the most beautiful. She's kind of awkward, but she is okay with who she is. The most important lesson we need to learn in our formative years is that it's okay to be an individual. It's okay to be you. And the guys see Buffy as a take-charge, kick-ass girl who has never lost her femininity. The ones who are threatened by that don't watch our show."

Gellar is not only a role model on-screen, but off-screen as well. "I don't drink, I don't smoke, and I've never done drugs," she said in a *Bliss* interview. Which is not to say she isn't adventurous in her own way, with piercings, in each ear and a pierced belly-button. She's also fond of tattoos. "I have a Chinese symbol for integrity on my back, and one on my ankle, which is a heart and a knife. I find tattoos addictive. I'm not worried about scarring my body; if I don't like them when I'm older I'll just get rid of them."

Ultimately she believes the reason for the show's longevity is that its audience continues to relate to it as the characters age and mature. "I think this is very important for keeping the show alive, and our audience has grown with us. I'm very pleased that Buffy's progression is so clearly charted on the show. We've seen her go from a high school student, to her first love, to college, and now she's a single mother who has to get a job. The things she is doing now—finding yourself and confronting your inner demons—are the things most people do in their mid-twenties."

There are still many professional challenges Sarah looks forward to. "I want to do period pieces; I want to be in a *Die Hard*–type movie; I want to do comedy. But mainly I just want to do good work."

Anthony Stewart Head

When *Buffy* first premiered in 1997, Anthony Stewart Head was best known for a series of coffee commercials, in which he played a smitten java-lover who woos his equally caffeine-driven neighbor. What a difference a hit series makes. Now Head is indelibly identified with Giles, Buffy's father-figure Watcher. "It is always nice being recognized for whatever reason, but *Buffy* is very different from anything I've done before, so it's been really cool."

Born in the Camdentown area of North London, Head grew up in nearby Hampton and trained for the theater at the London Academy of Dramatic Arts. His first role after leaving school was as Jesus in the national tour of *Godspell,* and over the years Tony has maintained his ties to the theater, appearing in *Yonadab* at the Royal National Theater in London, *Chess, Lady Windermere's Fan, Rope,* and *The Heiress.* He also donned fishnets and a dress to play Dr. Frank N. Furter in a West End revival of *The Rocky Horror Picture Show.* His brother, Murray Head, is also a well-known British actor, best known for originating the role of Judas in *Jesus Christ Superstar.*

In addition to his theater work, Tony has worked steadily in television, amassing a resumé full of credits, including the British series *Enemy at the Door, The Detectives, Ghostbusters of East Finchley,* and *Jonathan Creek.* On the big screen, Tony has appeared in *A Prayer for the Dying,* the 1987 drama that starred Mickey Rourke as an IRA bomber, and 1991's *Lady Chatterley's Lover,* starring Sylvia Kristal, who is best known for her soft-porn *Emmanuelle* movies.

Even though Head has appeared in his fair share of American series, including guest spots on *NYPD Blue* and *Highlander,* and as a regular on Fox's 1995 sci-fi series *VR.5,* it was his commercial work for Taster's Choice that made Tony a household face.

The budding romance that began in a 1990 commercial featuring Head and actress Sharon Maughan evolved over thirteen different spots that eventually included the woman's son and ex-husband. Because of the spots' popularity, there was actually talk of turning the commercials into a television series. Head said scripts were written, but in the end, "the bottom line is, it's all kind of said in a fifty-second commercial, you know? Unless the scripts that came to us were radically different or somehow managed to expand the characters, there was never really any point in doing it." Finally Anthony told the producers, "Enough is enough."

Starring in the commercials was a double-edged blessing. Financially it was a boon. "While Taster's Choice didn't make me wealthy for life, the commercials did give me the money to have a very nice house, a very nice lifestyle," he acknowledges. "The money has also put me in the position that actors dream about, which is the luxury of picking and choosing jobs. I don't have to take a job just to make the rent or feed the kids. And that's quite nice."

Professionally, however, it loomed as a potential obstacle. In England, he says, "the commercial limited people's perceptions of me in terms of what I could do. One of the reasons I chose to do Giles, apart from it being an astonishing script and wanting to do it, was that it was a character role. It wasn't leading man. It wasn't leading *young* man, for sure. It was a character part, and I had a feeling that after the commercial people tended to view me as a lightweight. I wanted them to see that I had range.

"But at the same time it opened up horizons" in the U.S., says Tony. He credits his longtime partner, animal trainer Sarah Fisher, with convincing him to take advantage of the commercials' popularity in America by coming to Los Angeles during pilot season. "When I first arrived, I was sitting on my ass for two months, waiting to hear if Fox was going to pick up this pilot I had done and biting my nails. I said, *'It's driving me mad, why am I here? I want to go home.'* And Sarah said, *'Do something while you're out there—go take classes or something; learn how they do it.'* So I did. And the day I signed on at class I got the Fox show called *VR.5.*"

Studying with drama coach Milton Katselas helped give Anthony a fresh perspective. "He's this wonderfully intuitive teacher and his premise is basically: The only real barriers are the ones we put in front of ourselves. If you say, *'My character wouldn't do that'*—bullocks! Ultimately it's you who wouldn't say that. Who knows what your character might do?"

VR.5 starred Lori Singer as telephone technician Sydney Bloom, who accidentally hacks into a fifth level of virtual reality that lets her access the subconscious minds of whomever she dials up on her modem line. She can also bring other people into VR.5 and create the setting—but has no control over the outcome. When she tries to use the technology to uncover the truth about her father's suspicious death, she is introduced to the mysterious Committee, a shadow government agency that wants to own access to VR.5.

When asked if it's just coincidence that he seems to get cast frequently in science-fiction and fantasy roles, Head admits it's a genre he particularly likes: "Yes, I do seem to gravitate toward science fiction and fantasy and I do love it. I used to be a serious fan of Ray Bradbury when I was young. It is wonderful stuff and I've always been attracted to it. But more than that, as an actor, I'm attracted to good roles. *Highlander* was a wonderful opportunity and *VR.5* was a great series; it was sad that it didn't go a second season. I think it might have been just a little ahead of its time."

VR.5 only lasted two months, going off the air in May 1995. Once the series was canceled, Tony headed back to England, where he worked in theater and did a couple of television productions. Then he was sent two scripts for a new television series.

"Joss sent me scripts for the first two episodes of *Buffy* and they were seriously special," Tony says. "The timing was wonderful because I had been asked if I wanted to do the series *Poltergeist: The Legacy* and, to be perfectly honest, I thought it was too dark. I was close to doing it and then *Buffy* came along, which I much preferred because it had a lighthearted side to it. It just seemed to come from a lighter place, although Joss also told us from the beginning that we were going to be serious about the dark, scary stuff—that it would be real, with no gags. Which I thought was important because I do believe there is a dark side, a black side."

Tony believes the secret of the series' success is its ability to incorporate several different genres into one. "Joss has proved that you can have real horror, real suspense, real situations, and yet have real humor. I think it's amazing that Americans have this unique ability to switch abruptly between emotions. I used to marvel at the fact that one moment you can have a complete farce and then the next moment it turns into a real weeper, and American audiences are right there. It's something the English have never been very good at doing. Joss has just taken that a step further by adding suspense."

Although Head is the senior member of the cast by a significant number of years, he says there is no generation gap off-camera. "You always hear actors saying, *'Oh, we're like family,'* but in this case, it really is true. We tend to gravitate to each other's trailers and hang out."

Joss also hosted get-togethers, where Tony and other cast members read Shakespeare: "Then we'd have a few tequilas, sit around the piano and sing." In fact, it was one of these sessions that first inspired Whedon to write the sixth season's musical episode. "This bunch is really, really talented, and dedicated and nice people," Head says. "I've been very lucky, because in the twenty-one years I've been working, I've rarely come across egos that have gotten in the way of stuff. I've been really lucky with the people I've worked with, and this is no exception."

Which is not to say there haven't been occasional creative disagreements. "We're very faithful to the scripts," notes Head. "I see a gag and I'll try and play it, and Joss says, 'No, there's a time and a place for a gag and this is not it.' We've had our run-ins, but invariably he's right. I think Giles's journey has been fascinating. I think that's what made it such a joy to play. The character was never static; you never knew what his deal was. And you still don't know what his deal is. The conflicts I was given to play are not soapy; they're not silly things or huge story arcs."

Despite the affection he feels for the cast and his enjoyment of playing Giles, Tony was getting tired. "There's a slight feeling when you're doing twenty-two episodes back-to-back of, *'Heads down, see you at the end.'* There is a point two-thirds the way through, when everybody's kind of got a sick smile on their face because they're just shattered because once it's up and running it's unstoppable." He was also homesick.

He and Sarah have two daughters, Emily and Daisy, and working on *Buffy* meant he only spent four months a year with them. Ironically, it was his kids who had second thoughts about his leaving the show. "It's always been a family decision as to how long I'd be out there, so when I first asked them what they thought of me leaving, they said, 'Please don't. It's a really cool show and we like you in it.' When we eventually agreed that I'd become a recurring regular rather than a series regular, Emily found it especially difficult to come to terms with the fact I wasn't in the opening credits anymore."

Whedon was equally distressed when Tony told him he needed out. "At the time he went, 'Oh my god, where the hell does that leave me?' " Head recalls. But in fact, Giles's departure actually propelled the series forward, forcing Buffy and the rest of the gang to become more self-reliant, just as when Seth Green opted out in order to pursue film work and Joss took the opportunity to explore Willow's sexuality. The result, Head says, is that the sixth season is "definitely about taking responsibility."

Since moving back to England, Head has co-starred in the BBC2 series *Manchild*, opposite Don Warrington, Ray Burdis and Nigel Havers. In it, he plays one of four middle-aged male friends who spend their days living out their fantasies. "He is a millionaire, he's divorced from his wife and left his children, and he can't get it up," Tony says of his character. "Basically, we have all the toys that men apparently think they want, and this is the lifestyle that they would like to pursue. And ultimately, the success of the series is the fact that you see the life we're crowing about, this misogynistic, hedonistic wild time, you learn quite quickly that it's a very, very hollow life indeed.

These guys have the cars, the babes, and the money, but what's missing from all their lives is reality. They don't have their feet on the ground and they don't know who they are."

Also in the works is the long-planned *Buffy* spin-off called *Ripper*, which would be a collaboration between Whedon and the BBC. Like *Manchild*, *Ripper* would be a typical "short-order" British series of eight episodes. Head describes the drama series as "*Cracker* with ghosts." Tony is hoping it will be filmed in the West Country "because it's where I live and because it's steeped in myth and tradition." In the meantime, Head will appear in BBC1's drama, *Spooks*.

In the seventh season of *Buffy*, Giles is more a part of the Slayer's life again, with Head appearing in at least ten episodes. Having managed to find the right balance in his life, Head says he feels as if he's got the best of both worlds and that his life, both personally and professionally, is on a steady course. "There's nothing I can think of that isn't already under way or in hand."

Nicholas Brendon

Like a surprising number of actors, such as Jack Wagner and Dean Cain, Nicholas Brendon actually started out wanting to be a professional athlete.

Nicholas—called Nicky by friends and family—grew up dreaming of being a baseball player. His goal was to play ball in college and, hopefully, get signed with a big-league team.

But first he had to get through high school. Nicholas and his identical twin brother Kelly were born April 12, 1971, in Los Angeles. They have two younger brothers, Christian and Kyle. Unlike co-star Sarah Michelle Gellar, Nicholas did not attend private school. Instead he was educated at public schools.

"I went to L.A. Unified, which was a very scary experience," Brendon says, referring to the notoriously troubled Los Angeles school district. "I learned a lot of lessons but it was a horrible experience. High school isn't really great to many people. It's like a mandatory prison sentence. In Israel they make you join the army, in America we go to high school."

The normally traumatic high school experience wasn't made any easier by Nicholas's introverted tendencies and a terrible stutter that plagued him throughout his youth. "The sad thing is, there is no cure for it. I will always have a stutter. In fact, it still comes up to this day, when I am at auditions or speaking in front of a group of people. I just hide it better now. But rehearsing and practice definitely changed it. I feel really fortunate. I think having a stutter is one of the most devastating things that can happen to a young kid. I was very shy in high school. I wouldn't even talk to people."

The experience remains a vivid one for Nicky, which is why he has spent time volunteering for the Stuttering Foundation of America. "We've gotten a lot of letters," Brendon said on the WB.com Web site. "I guess it reached out and touched a lot of people."

Because he was so shy, Nicholas says, "One of the scariest things about going to high school was dealing with girls. My first kiss happened in eighth grade but it was awful because our friends were spying on us. I was so embarrassed at being caught that I had to break up with the girl and that started a long dry spell."

Once he was through with high school, Nicholas went on to college, but his plans for a baseball career ended abruptly after he broke his elbow while playing. Adding to that disappointment were problems at home.

"I went through a rough time back in my early twenties," he explains. "My parents were going through a divorce. I felt really lost. One night I went to the backyard, and I was talking to God, asking for direction, and acting was the answer I got. That was pretty terrifying, because I was not a confident kid. I had a stutter. I had ears that stuck out, and acne. I was definitely not cut out for acting. The thing is, even though I was shy in school, with my family I was the entertainer and I loved making everyone laugh so I decided to chance it. So I just talked to God because talking in front of one person, much less thousands of people, terrified me. But I just decided to take the challenge."

Acting was a family business, of sorts—his mom is an agent. "My mom sent me out on stuff, so that was a help. My first job was in a Clearasil commercial."

Although he appeared in the play *Out of Gas on Lovers' Leap* at the Pasadena Playhouse in 1991, he still needed to scramble to support himself.

So while he waited to get back in front of the cameras, Nicholas worked behind the scenes, which ultimately led to his first break in prime time.

"What happened was, I was a production assistant on the sitcom *Dave's World* and they allowed me to audition for a guest spot—and I got it. After I taped the episode, they fired me as a PA, but told me they really liked my acting and that I should pursue it full-time. That was pretty much where it started."

Other small parts in television and movies followed, such as being cast as "Basketball Player 1" in the 1994 feature-film gorefest *Children of the Corn III*, and making appearances on *The Young and the Restless* and *Married . . . With Children*. Nicholas continued to be active in theater and starred in Los Angeles productions of *The Further Adventures of Tom Sawyer* and *My Own Private Hollywood*, both Equity Waiver productions, in which the theater is required to have ninety-nine seats or less, and paying the actors is optional.

But an odd job here and there, especially in small theater productions, is not enough to pay the bills. At this point Brendon really was just acting for the love of it. His first big chance to break through came when he was cast in the television pilot *Secret Lives*, but the show—which presented dramatizations of real-life marriages—was not picked up as a series. "I also turned down a part because of nudity once," he says. "It was one of the *Friday the 13th* movies, something like part eight or nine. That was a line I wouldn't cross."

Although acting had become Nicholas's passion, he also realized he couldn't stay an unemployed actor forever. "There was a time in my life when I almost gave up acting completely," Nicholas admits. "I gave myself one year and told my family that if my career still hadn't gone anywhere, I would quit and go back to college and study medicine."

The year had almost gone by and Nicholas was still praying for his big break while waiting tables at Kate Mantilini restaurant, a longtime celebrity hangout known for its mashed potatoes, located on the edge of Beverly Hills. Then his agent set up an audition for a series being cast at the WB called *Buffy the Vampire Slayer*.

"I was surprised they were making the movie into a show," Brendon admits, "and then pleasantly surprised when I read the script. The writing was so intelligent. I really have to thank Joss for hiring me because I don't know where I'd be if he hadn't."

After filming the episodes, Nicholas—now more financially stable—went home to the Hollywood Hills home he shared with his brother, and waited for the series to air. He passed the time going to auditions, reading, and playing his guitar while sitting on the balcony in his rocking chair. Then, once *Buffy* debuted to rave critical reviews, Nicholas soon found himself a new TV heartthrob. At fan events, girls and women lined up to flirt and it made him a little uneasy. "It's weird to hear myself referred to as being hot or cute because I don't see myself that way. It makes me feel really shy."

But Nicholas seems to genuinely enjoy interacting with fans. At one fan-fest gathering during the first season, Nicky even treated the cheering crowd to an impromptu exhibition of Xander's gyrating dance moves. Overall, except for the time he was groped by an overzealous fan, Brendon enjoys interacting with *Buffy* fans. "Fans are the main reason I do what I do," he told WB.com. "I have been given this opportunity to reach out to a lot of people. And I love being able to entertain somebody, even if it's only for a few minutes; someone who otherwise might be having a really bad day."

The first few seasons the show was on the air, Kelly Brendon says he was frequently mistaken for his brother. "As we get older, we're starting to look different. Even our faces are changing a little bit. But people still mistake me for Nick. If a little kid comes up, I say, 'Yeah.' But if an adult comes up and asks me if I'm the guy on *Buffy*, then I say, 'No, we're twins,' although once people threw French fries and napkins at me when they didn't believe me." Kelly has appeared in *Buffy* as the confident half of Xander's personality in "The Replacement" and has also worked as his lighting double.

Unlike Xander, who left Anya at the altar, Nicky has no fear of long-term commitment. On September 1, 2001, he married actress Tressa DiFiglia at her parents' ranch in Carlsbad, California, in front of three hundred guests. "It was just an awesome wedding. I can't describe how great it is, how I wasn't even alive before I met her."

Unlike his co-stars, Brendon hasn't made the jump into much film work. *Psycho Beach Party* was a film-festival favorite but earned less than $2 million at the box office. Nicky and Tressa spent a month during the summer before the wedding in Europe, rather than on a set. "I like my sanity so I'd rather not sit in a trailer for three months during my time off," Nicky says. "But I would love to get my hands on a decent script sometime soon. It's tough, but they are out there. Ultimately I would like to do a dramatic, emotional film. I have a lot of that inside if me, and that would be a great way to get it out."

He's also thankful that *Buffy* came along when it did, because he's the first to admit that even had he gone back to college to pursue a different career, his heart would have been elsewhere. "If I wasn't acting, I'd be wishing I was acting. What I've learned is that if you want to do something, do it. The last thing you want is to be forty and be saying, 'I *wish* I had done that.' To me, acting is a blessing and I hope to be able to entertain people for as long as I possibly can."

Alyson Hannigan

Sometimes it's hard for fans to separate the actor from the character. While Willow may prefer to spend her time behind a computer or trying to expand herself spiritually—especially since flaying a human alive—Alyson Hannigan is much more of an earthy spitfire.

Case in point: During the filming of *American Pie 2*, she was annoyed to find out the male actors were spending much of their off-time at local exotic-dancer clubs without asking the girls to join in the fun. "The boys are the boys and they really have their little group and they didn't invite the girls to the strip club, so I was in my trailer reading," she recalls. "I like going to strip clubs. They're fun. I think most of my birthday parties have been at a strip club. They have the best music there."

Part of the appeal of the *American Pie* movies—in which Hannigan played the surprisingly sexual "Band Camp Girl," Michelle—was to shed some of Willow's "good girl–next–door" persona. "There's the sweet-little-ol'-playing-with-the-band side," says Alyson. "And then there's the no-holds-barred–sex side. She's definitely not shy when it comes to bedroom issues."

Neither is Hannigan. In an interview with *Playboy*, Alyson answered a series of probing questions about her sex life with good-natured directness. Among the revelations were that she's had sex while driving, prefers being on the giving end of oral sex, has never had a one-night stand, and likes porn. "Just give me the porn. I don't need a plot."

Ironically, when *Buffy* first aired, the intense media interest in the show caught her off-guard and admittedly rendered her mute. The first time the cast met en masse with assembled television critics from all over the country in January 1997, Hannigan was so intimidated that she literally only uttered a sentence or two—and that was under duress.

But since then, Alyson's comfort level and confidence has grown. Now, during interviews or in front of fans at sci-fi conventions and other *Buffy*-related events, she's positively outgoing and gregarious, displaying a quick wit and charming personality.

Like co-star Sarah Michelle Gellar, Alyson Hannigan has been acting almost as long as she has been talking. Born Allison Lee on March 24, 1974, in Washington, D.C., her parents divorced when she was two. The family moved south to Georgia and, just like Gellar, Alyson started working when she was four years old. "I started out by doing commercials in Atlanta," says Alyson. "I had always wanted to act and I loved it. But at the same time, I don't really consider myself 'an actor' because it's not necessarily who I am, it's just what I do."

Although she was the only one with acting aspirations in her family, Alyson's family moved to Los Angeles in 1985 so she could try to break into films and television. Her first break came when she was cast in the 1988 sci-fi spoof, *My Stepmother Is an Alien,* which starred Dan Ackroyd, Kim Basinger, and Seth Green, who played her boyfriend. In 1990 she appeared on an episode of *Roseanne,* playing a friend of the eldest daughter, Becky.

From there Alyson was hired on her first series, the short-lived *Free Spirit,* which ran on ABC from September 1989 to January 1990. The show was an updated takeoff on *Nanny and the Professor,* in which a widower with three children hires a housekeeper named Winnie—who is actually a witch dispatched by her elders—to help a human family. Alyson played thirteen-year-old Jesse Harper, the lone daughter.

Alyson's next movie was the TV movie *Switched at Birth,* based on the real-life story of Kimberly Mays, who was switched at birth with another child, Arlena Twigg, who later died. Alyson played Arlena's sister Gina, at ages thirteen through sixteen. Bonnie Bedelia played her mother.

As a student at North Hollywood High in California, Hannigan says she was more of a Goth geek than computer whiz like Willow. "I dressed in black and dyed my hair black. I wanted to fit in, and this was the crowd that accepted me," she says. "My theory on high school was, 'Get in, get out and hopefully I won't get hurt.' Basically, it's a miserable experience, because you're a walking hormone in a place that is just so cruel. There were times that were okay, but it's not the little myth that 'High school is the best years of your life'—no way."

According to Alyson, not only were the other kids mean, some were just plain strange. "There was this one guy who went to a dentist and had his teeth sharpened into fangs. It was so insane. I mean, how would you even find a dentist who would do that?"

Alyson graduated in 1992, and a year later made two guest appearances on NBC's *Almost Home*, which was a reworked version of *The Torkelsons*, about a single mom raising her five children. In the episodes, originally aired April 17, 1993, and June 5, 1993, Alyson played a tomboy named Sam.

After appearances on *Picket Fences* and *Touched by an Angel*, the last job she had pre-*Buffy* was the ABC television movie *The Stranger Beside Me*. In this woman-in-peril thriller, Tiffani-Amber Thiessen, who had just made a splash as the new girl on *Beverly Hills 90210*, played a recovering rape victim who is swept away by a seemingly perfect guy, played by Eric Close, who is actually a Peeping Tom.

Then came *Buffy*. Other than the prospect of getting another series, Alyson had another reason to be thrilled about the audition: "Even before I met Joss, *Toy Story* was my favorite movie. I'm actually slightly obsessed with that film because when I was a kid, I would spend countless hours trying to sneak up on my toys because I *knew* they had secret lives. I was determined to catch them in the act, but I, uh, never did."

The casting process was a long, drawn-out affair that tested Hannigan's nerves. "I auditioned way too many times and finally they couldn't find anyone else who looked as young and acted as immature, so I got the job," jokes the still-babyfaced actress.

Although she had worked steadily, *Buffy* was the first time Alyson has starred in a project that had such high visibility and such intense fan interest. A cybernut in real life, Alyson often communicated with fans over the Internet via posting boards and became the object of many adoring Web sites devoted to all things Alyson. And since her character became involved with another woman, she's become a gay icon.

"I've had a really positive response from the people that I've spoken with, and it's just so rewarding," she told Kenneth Hubbard of *SFX* magazine. "And it's just so nice, and it's so wonderful to meet people that actually have been affected by it personally. It really makes a difference in their lives. I mean, who can ask for anything more than that?"

But Alyson viewed the relationship between the now-deceased Tara and Willow not so much in terms of being same-sex, but in terms of emotional connection. "I don't really treat Tara any differently than I treated Oz," she told slayage.com. "Okay, she has bumps on top and she's softer to kiss, but it's

not like, 'Ooh, ah, same sex, oh dear, I've got to really work into this!' It's not something I ever experienced, but then, I've never had to experience bringing back my friends from the dead, either."

Hannigan says that although she has always loved the environment of television and movie sets, there is something special about working on *Buffy*. "I love everything about this show, even doing the stunts, although after some of the actions scenes you definitely get bruised up. And the people on *Buffy* are wonderful. I love them very much and everyone has become like family. And the show itself is a lot of fun to work on."

When asked to share some of the raucous good times she's had while working on *Buffy*, Hannigan is aware some of the hilarity might be lost in the translation. "Most of the stories are of the 'You had to be there,' variety. Like the time I 'pantsed' Nick. Sarah is the one who told me to do it because she wouldn't—she chickened out. So I did and accidentally pulled his pants all the way down.

"Another time, I had these really stale animal crackers that I had given to Joss's assistant, George. He tried to be polite and eat them but they were just so stale. Then Nick comes along and starts eating them and didn't notice they were stale. I was crying I was laughing so hard."

But it wasn't always fun and games. During the first season Alyson had some problems with castmate Julie Benz, who played Darla. "She was very mean to me," Hannigan said in an interview. "She was, like, the meanest person ever to me. I didn't like her. That was the first season and I still have that grudge. I was on a brand-new show and so excited, and to have someone be so mean to me, I just wanted to cry. Actually, I think I did."

Alyson's first high-profile romance was with Marilyn Manson drummer Ginger Fish, whose real name is Frank Kenny Wilson. But even then there was a connection between her and former *Buffy* co-star Alexis Denisof, who currently plays Wesley on *Angel*.

"I had the 'I will not date actors' philosophy and so did Alexis at the time," Alyson explained to slayage.com. "So it was one of those flirtatious friendships. Then I started dating somebody else, and Alexis didn't like that. When that wasn't working out, it was like, 'Oh, we're still friends, and we're going to date now.' "

Hannigan and Denisof have discovered there are advantages of dating a fellow actor. "We understand the difficulties, and not even just as an actor understanding another actor's difficulties," says Denisof. "We know the specifics of the two shows because we've both been on them. So when Alyson tells me whoever's bugging her that day, I know who she means, and the same for me."

Although she's not yet looking past *Buffy*, Alyson says she hopes that one day she'll be established enough to be able to pick and choose the scripts she'd like to work on, rather than audition out of necessity. Other than that, her needs and wants are simple. "You have to go for the good things, like world peace, a cure for everything—and a really cool house."

James Marsters

Had things gone according to his original plan, James Wesley Marsters would be performing Shakespeare in London's West End. The Bard-loving actor never dreamed his ticket to fame would be a vampire with a killer wit.

Marsters was born in the northern California town of Greenville but grew up in Modesto, a small city of under 200,000 residents located ninety miles east of San Francisco. Modesto was founded in 1870 when the Central Pacific Railroad chose the barren wind- and sand-swept local to be the end of its line.

The youngest of three children, James came from a religious family—his dad was a minister and his mom is a social worker who once considered becoming a nun. After making his stage debut in a fourth-grade production of *Winnie-the-Pooh*, playing Eeyore, the mournful donkey, James knew that was what he wanted to do the rest of his life. Unfortunately, it made the rest of his schooling seem unimportant, and his grades were affected accordingly.

"To do well in school, my mother had to convince me that it somehow related to acting, like chemistry and higher math, and that was hard to rationalize," he told Rupert Laight in *Starburst*. James was further isolated from the usual school interactions after seriously injuring his leg on a sprinkler head. "My leg slid down my bone like a sock," he says. He had to undergo skin grafts to repair the damage and was laid up for almost a year.

By the time he reached Davis High School, Marsters admitted in an alloy.com interview, he was "a total outcast and had *no* interest in being popular. I ran with the group of punk-rock punks. We did not want to be liked; we did not want to fit in. We had a rock-and-roll band and the irony was that we became enormously popular because we just didn't care. We threw the most enormous parties in the town and sought subtle revenge on all the big kids who abused us in junior high. We made sure they didn't get any when they came to our parties. Yes, we would crush their self-esteem. I don't like mean kids." Thinking back, James admits, "The only thing that kept me out of serious trouble over the years is that, ultimately, I love acting more than anything."

Hearing his siren song, James headed to New York where he attended the famed Juilliard School, appearing in productions of *Twelfth Night* and *Troilus and Cressida*. To support himself, James worked a number of jobs, from waiting tables and telemarketing to working in a hospital and bartending. It was during his stint as a bartender in New York that he was the victim of an attempted mugging, which resulted in the scar on his left eyebrow.

"I worked like ninety hours a week to put myself through Juilliard—so they could tell me I was a horrible, useless actor," Marsters revealed in an interview on his Web site, jamesmarsters.com. He says he had such a bad experience at the school that it made him leery of all acting teachers. "I would really pity the acting teacher that tried to tell me what to do. They might have a perfectly valid thing, but in my mind, the audience tells me when it's working, when it's not working. If you're lucky and wise enough to surround yourself with people who are competent enough to figure out why it's not working, then you can fix it. It's kind of like a car."

Still pursuing theater, James spent time in Chicago where he made his professional debut in Shakespeare's *The Tempest* at the Goodman Theatre, then moved to Seattle in 1990, where he appeared in John Pielmeier's *Voices in the Dark*, playing a killer. For the role, he gained thirty-five pounds. "I was two hundred pounds, so I was hulky."

Marsters told ET Online that finding good theater became increasingly difficult. "It got its legs taken out during the eighties. A friend of mine, a great actor, decided to come to L.A. because he couldn't get his car fixed. I figured he couldn't get enough money to keep a new car and was going out to L.A., then I was going out."

But James knew the bulked-up bruiser look he had adopted for the play might not fly in L.A. "I looked at television and noticed that all the guys have these celery-stalk thighs," he recalled on his Web site. "So I lost fifty pounds before I ever even came down here. It's all about molding your body. Really, it's about keeping your body so that you're not too big or too small, so you can kind of change quickly. But you never want to do anything that'll give you a long-term problem, like gaining a lot of fat. I really wouldn't want to do that, because cellulite doesn't go away."

Marsters's first television role was in 1992 as a bellhop in *Northern Exposure*. "It was absolutely terrifying. I had five lines, and they were each monosyllabic." Those hoping to catch a glimpse of James will be hard-pressed since only the back of his head and profile made it into the shot. "Thank God—I couldn't have handled more. I was absolutely petrified. If I had been made to do more, I might have been scared away from the whole thing. But as it was, it came out well"—well enough that he was hired again the following season to play a minister. "It was weird. My learning curve was pretty steep. That was my second role, and I just kind of banged it out in one take."

James continued to dabble in theater and music between occasional guest roles. Then, in 1997, he auditioned for the role of Spike. "The casting director asked me to do it in both a Southern accent and in an English one. It's kind of weird; it's almost inexplicable when something clicks in you, and you just have an instinct toward a role. I was able to just kind let go and have fun with it, and the usual thoughts of how well I did were just kind of erased. I just had a fun time."

James got a callback and was asked to read with Juliet Landau. He didn't realize she had already been cast as Drusilla. "We went in and read for all the producers and Joss, and we just kind leapt straight into it. What was really cool about that is they were looking for a punk, rough-around-the-edges character. I've had a lot of rough chapters in my past, but I've kinda cleaned up, and so I didn't come in with anything pierced or anything. They trusted that they had the facilities to create the visual impression, and that the internal reality of the character was most important. That's pretty rare in Hollywood."

Marsters went into it assuming it was a temporary job. "I was told very bluntly that I'm not going to be here very long." He recalls Joss Whedon telling him, "Dude, you're going to die, you're cannon fodder."

James didn't care. He was thrilled to join the cast and even happier playing an evil character. "I love scary movies. I love being scared and I love scaring people. Most people are into vampires. The vampire myth is more powerful than Frankenstein or the Werewolf or the Mummy. Vampires rock."

Producers decided to go with an English accent for Spike instead of a

Southern drawl. Marsters credits his obsession with *Monty Python* and a fortu-itous theater production with helping him prepare. "I was doing a produc-tion of *The Tempest* at the Shakespeare Festival in L.A., and there was a guy from North London playing one of the roles. So I kinda pulled him aside and asked him for some help."

After his original story arc in the second season ended, Whedon brought James back for the eighth episode in Season Three. "I thought, 'Well, maybe I'll get one this year, maybe I'll get one next year.' " Instead Marsters was hired on as a regular for the fourth season, despite Juliet Landau's decision not to return full-time as Drusilla.

"We knew that James was great from day one," Whedon says. "The only question was, how much of the show would he become?" Whedon decided to explore Spike without Dru.

The only downside to playing Spike full-time was having to peroxide his hair twice a month—although he says adding Sweet 'n Low to the dyeing solution helped alleviate the burning—and maintaining his pallid complex-ion. So although he lives at the beach, James stocks up on strong sunblock. And being the resident stud-pony, Marsters takes great care to keep in shape. He Rollerblades, does countless stomach crunches, and works out with free weights, but not to bulk up. "I do a lot of repetition with low weights because I want definition. It's your product; you want to make it ready."

James also makes a point of keeping his weight down to the point of dis-comfort. He told Richard Harrington of the *Washington Post*, "I've been after a body type since I got on the show. Playing a vampire for six years, it's hard to be hungry, but I'm a metaphor for hunger, psychological and sexual. And I noticed that the only vampires to really hit the American consciousness and stay there were almost unhealthily thin, with the one exception of the origi-nal, Bela Lugosi."

After moving to UPN, the theme explored in the *Buffy* episodes grew noticeably darker, which Marsters found invigorating: "It's an interesting synergy. It seems that Joss's crucible of experience, the thing that he draws from, is his adolescence, and Buffy is no longer an adolescent." James told the *Washington Post* he believes it was the perfect time for Marti Noxon to take over the day-to-day running of the show. "Marti's crucible seems to have been in her mid-twenties and it's just perfect; now we have someone who wants to explore herself with this metaphor. So we get a new head writer and a new network, all of which facilitates exploring Buffy as a young adult."

As the show has evolved, so has Spike, who, Marsters notes, "has been used in different ways—as disposable villain, hapless wreck for comedic purposes, wacky neighbor by design, and then love interest." One of the more difficult transformations for Spike was to would-be rapist. After Buffy breaks off her relationship with Spike, his desperation leads him to try to take her by brute force on her bathroom floor. Marsters told about.com he can't watch the scene even now. "I can't even watch a movie where that's in there. I get up and want to kill the guy. It's my personal issue. I told Joss, 'You cut right to the bone, dude. This is not a safe show.'

"That was one of the hardest things I've ever done in my life. I went home shattered after that. I still don't think I've picked up the pieces of that one. Sometimes the work gets real tough, I've got to say. When the writing is that good it can surprise you sometimes how it can rock you."

Much easier for James are the love scenes and the fighting sequences. "More and more, the choreography is stuff that I can do well enough that we don't have to cut to a stunt double, which doesn't really make Steve Tartalia [his stunt double] very happy. He gets very bored. I've always wanted the fighting to be more street-fighting moves, which is stuff that I'm more used to, as opposed to sophisticated martial-arts stuff."

During Spike's first love scene with Buffy, James was nude—and very carefully filmed—but he shrugged it off, since he also appeared nude in his first professional play. Nor does he think the sometimes-graphic sexual content of the show is over-the-top. "All the sexuality is implied, we're not doing anything graphic, or that hasn't been done elsewhere on TV," he told *Starburst*'s Rupert Laight. "I also think it's a responsible exploration of a young person's sexuality. It's not just titillation."

Because of his hair and his physique, James is frequently recognized by fans, but says celebrity has not been an obstacle, although it sometimes makes for strange experiences, such as the one Halloween when he was approached by a fan dressed as Spike. "This guy walked up to me dressed as me, and he asked his friend to take a picture of me," Marsters told about.com. "The friend was dressed as Darth Maul, and he was getting a piece of pizza. So I had to sit and wait for Darth Maul to get his pizza. It was very surreal, but mostly the fans are great."

Being on *Buffy* has allowed James to pursue other interests. His band, Ghost of the Robot, has released a CD and he provides the voice of Spike for the animated series as well as the *Buffy the Vampire Slayer* X-Box video game from Fox Interactive. As far as where Spike's road will lead, Marsters isn't sure. The only think he does know is that "nothing ever stays the same season to season—nothing."

Michelle Trachtenberg

It's hard being the new kid on the block, or for that matter, the new actor on an established series, especially when the cast is very close knit. But in Michelle Trachtenberg's case, joining *Buffy* was almost like coming home. Because not only had Michelle been a die-hard Slayer fan since the show started, but she was also an old friend of Sarah Michelle Gellar's. The two worked together on *All My Children* in 1994–95 when Gellar was playing Susan Lucci's daughter and Trachtenberg was cast as Lily Benton Montgomery.

The two kept in touch over the years, so when Gellar invited Michelle to visit the *Buffy* set, Trachtenberg was thrilled. Little did she know Sarah had an ulterior motive. "I went when they were shooting the fourth-season finale," Michelle recalls. "While I was there I met Joss; then, a couple of weeks later, I got a call to read for 'Dawn.' " Whedon had already seen a number of actresses for the new character and it was at Gellar's urging that he called in Michelle. "I pushed really hard for her," Sarah acknowledges. In the end,

Whedon agreed and Michelle was hired to play Buffy's out-of-the-blue sister.

Typically, Joss kept Trachtenberg guessing as to what exactly was in store for her character. "My first creative meeting with Joss was rather short. 'Hi, welcome to the show, you're a teenager, you have a secret—you're a Key but we really don't know what that is yet. Have fun.' But it was a little nerve-wracking because they'd all been together so long and were a well-oiled mix. I was worried, but on my first day I was welcomed with open arms and they really accepted me and made me feel at home, like I'd been there for four years along with everybody else. I blended right in. It helped that I was a huge fan of the show." So much so, Michelle calls herself "a little walking *Buffy* encyclopedia."

Despite her youth, Trachtenberg is a seasoned veteran. Born in Brooklyn on October 11, 1985, she decided she wanted to act when she was all of three years old. "I was watching a little girl braiding Barbie's hair in a commercial and I thought I could do it just as well. So I announced I wanted to be on TV and wouldn't move until I was told I could be."

Trachtenberg's parents, Russian émigrés Lana and Michael, decided to let Michelle give acting a try. Lana found an agent in New York who sent Michelle on her first commercial audition for Wisk detergent and by the time she was ten, she had been in more than a hundred commercials. In 1993 she was cast in the Nickelodeon series *The Adventures of Pete and Pete*. A year later she joined *All My Children*, playing an autistic character. "On the set, Sarah was like a big sister," Trachtenberg told Serena Kappes in a People.com interview. "She would take me into her dressing room and we would play around between scenes. We would find a way to sneak around and have fun."

Her breakout role was the feature film *Harriet the Spy* in 1996, co-starring Rosie O'Donnell and based on Louise Fitzhugh's 1964 novel. Three years later, she appeared in *Inspector Gadget* opposite Matthew Broderick. Through it all, Michelle took the accolades and critical raves in stride. "Hopefully I'll never ever go on an ego trip," Trachtenberg says. Her mom Lana, who also acts as her manager, does her part to make sure her daughter keeps every-thing in perspective by making Michelle toe the line like any other teenager. "I have to do my chores and the whole thing," Trachtenberg admits. "I get grounded if I don't clean my room."

In 1997, Michelle was cast in the short-lived series *Meego*. She and her mom moved to Los Angeles but her father, a phone installer in New York, stayed on the East Coast. Two years later, Lana and Michael Trachtenberg divorced. Currently Michelle lives with her mom and older sister Irene, an agent. During hiatus, she attends private school, but when filming has a tutor on the set and maintains a straight-A average. "While we're all eating cake, she has to take a trig test," noted Gellar to *People*. "She handles it with ease."

That's because to Trachtenberg, her studies are just as important as her job. "I think education is one of the most important things offered in the world," she says, and muses about attending college one day and studying theater in England. "I try to set my goals high and I work hard to reach them."

She told TeenHollywood.com that she's also thinking about getting an education in life as well as academia. "I know what to do before the cameras. Now I want to learn what to do behind them. I'm even thinking of taking a year off after I graduate high school and maybe making a movie in a place like Italy—that would give me a chance to travel and work at the same time. Education is important to me. So is work. But the most important thing in my life is my family."

The upside of being a celebrity is that it gives Trachtenberg the chance to influence and help others. Being a role model is also a priority for Michelle, who is active in several anti-drug causes. "If I can stop one kid from doing drugs, then I've really accomplished something," she says earnestly. The downside of fame is the loss of anonymity, says Michelle, such as "when you just want to go out with your friends to the mall, or you're having a bad hair day, you're not looking forward to someone stopping you and recognizing you." On the other hand, she says fans are uniformly gracious, so "the truth of the matter is, it's always flattering when it happens."

Despite her youth, Trachtenberg has some sage advice for others who want to follow her example and act: "I always like to say that even though you may be attracted by the more glamorous aspects of Hollywood, it doesn't happen overnight," she told *SFX* magazine. "There's a lot of hard work that goes into being a good actress. People do not just wake up and think, 'I want to be on TV today.' You have to truly believe in your goals, and really fight for what you love."

Emma Caulfield

In some ways, being a successful actor for Emma Caulfield has been a case of 'Be careful what you wish for, you just might get it.' Although Caulfield says starring in a hit series is a dream come true on one hand, on the other, she sometimes feels there's something lacking in her life. She admits the entertainment industry as a whole doesn't "feed my soul. For a while now I've had this feeling that there's something else that I'm supposed to be doing, like I've missed my calling somehow."

While in Australia filming the horror film *The Tooth Fairy*, scheduled for a January 2003 release, Caulfield said she finally made peace with her angst. "I had this awakening there of what I'm supposed to do. I made peace with the fact that this business is not what I'm supposed to do. It's really a stepping stone for other projects," she said. "I think it probably has something to do with animals, because I'm very passionate about animals."

However, Caulfield doesn't want to sound ungrateful: "I really love what I do, and I have since I was a kid. I was always the little drama queen. But I've said it before: I don't know that I'll be doing it in ten years. I mean, I love the process of acting, but not the masochism. No matter how successful you get in Hollywood, you cannot rest. Your new movie doesn't open well, they're looking for the next person to replace you; it's always something. You never have true peace."

Caulfield was born Emma Chukker April 8, 1973, in Greenville, California, near San Diego, and began studying drama as a teenager at the La Jolla Playhouse and the famed Old Globe Theater. After high school, she enrolled at UCLA as a psych major but ended up dropping out after being stopped on the street by an agent who offered to represent her. "I had only been in Los Angeles for a couple of weeks. It was just that random. And you have a choice. Are you going to pursue it or what? This was too random for me to just turn my back on it. And so I started auditioning and started working, but school was always something I wanted to finish. I really liked school and really liked psychology."

While waiting for her break, Emma earned money by working at a number of odd jobs. "I had so many retail jobs growing up and starting out, when I moved here to L.A.," she recalls. "I worked for Nordstroms, in the hosiery department, which was the one retail experience I had that was actually enjoyable, because the company was really cool. I remember thinking when I first started auditioning, 'Oh, I don't want to do this, I'll just work in Nordstrom. I don't care, I'll just have a normal life.'

"I had a bunch of different waitress jobs, too, but I was a horrible waitress. I remember being a cocktail waitress at a bar here in L.A. and they had horrible food, so when customers asked what would I recommend to eat, I would just say, 'The food here is horrible, you don't want to eat this . . . but, you know, our melon-ball shots are great and our beer on tap is fantastic!' So instead of eating, they'd drink and drink and I ended up getting big tips. Had the management known, I would have been fired earlier than I was; it was the only time I was ever fired, but it was because I was so bad."

Emma worked sporadically the first few years, appearing in a handful of television guest roles, including *Silk Stalkings, Renegade, Burke's Law,* and *Saved by the Bell: The New Class,* which Emma says was one of the best experiences of her career. But Caulfield's days as a waitress finally came to an end in 1990 when she was cast on *Beverly Hills 90210,* as Brandon's college girlfriend Susan during the 1995–96 season. After a small role on *General Hospital* as Nurse Lorraine Miller, Caulfield abruptly decided she wanted to go back to school, and enrolled at San Francisco State University. "I do love psychology. I think people are just fascinating."

However, the reality of paying bills intruded on Caulfield's sabbatical. "I needed to make some quick cash," she told *SFX* magazine. "I still knew people, like the casting director for *Buffy*. He contacted my agent and told him they were looking for someone to play a female demon. I immediately agreed to meet Joss Whedon, because I already knew the show very well, and really enjoyed it. Shortly after doing my reading, I learned that I had the part. It was just supposed to be a onetime thing, but sometimes Joss likes what he sees and something happens."

Caulfield thinks Anya struck a chord because her attempts to understand human idiosyncrasies reflect very basic insecurities. "She still doesn't get it quite right and that's something we can all relate to—the idea of not being able to get something right, no matter how hard you try." Caulfield credits Whedon for developing such a character. "He's very much in tune with what the response of the audience will be. So here I am, acting now. But I could have easily been a psychiatrist, and happy with it."

Caulfield has found it difficult to simply be a celebrity. She told *Buffy the Vampire Slayer Magazine*, "I really do hate it but I'm trying to learn how to view it differently. I hated it so much for such a long time that I avoided anything at all. I just went to work and that was it. I had to shut it off. But I realized that is as big a part as anything else in this business, to be seen outside of who you are on the show, and let people get to know you a little bit."

Although Caulfield has been linked romantically to actor Andrew Woodworth, there are no wedding plans in her immediate future. Nor is Emma sure she will return to *Buffy* after the seventh season, even if the series is renewed. "But then, what I'm thinking now, I might not feel six months from now." Even so, the idea of working in films increasingly appeals to her. "I don't think I'd want to do another hourlong series right away. In films, you're only booked for three months and then you're back to square one again. Whereas with a hit show you know it's going to run for a few years. It's been nice having that consistency with *Buffy*, but I think I'm ready to move on now and venture out."

THE EPISODES

or the *Buffy*-obsessed, there's probably very little anybody could say about the episodes that would be a revelation after having watched each one countless times until every frame is seared into memory. But there is more to a series companion book than mere production facts and continuity bloopers. Hopefully, the episode guide will offer even the most knowledgeable *BtVS* fan not only a complete reference source, but food for thought as well, by taking a look at the series from several different points of view.

Each episode listing includes a brief plot summary; anecdotal and production information, including names of the regular cast, recurring cast, and guest stars; any obvious bloopers; some noteworthy facts about the episode or some related aspect of the series; plus commentary and observation on the characters' development. The subtext of each episode will also be analyzed in order to explore the ongoing theme of the series—that the horrors of life, both emotional and personal, rival any found in the movies. One aspect of the series' overall theme—that life in high school, in college, and in general, is a real-life horror film—will be discussed in detail.

Production Information

Executive producers: Joss Whedon, Sandy Gallin, Gail Berman, Fran Rubel Kuzui, Kaz Kuzui
Produced by: Mutant Enemy, Inc., and Kuzui/Sandollar in association with 20th Century–Fox Television
Created by: Joss Whedon
Theme music: Performed by Nerf Herder

SEASON ONE

Sarah Michelle Gellar (*Buffy Summers*)
Nicholas Brendon (*Xander Harris*)
Alyson Hannigan (*Willow Rosenberg*)
Charisma Carpenter (*Cordelia Chase*)
Anthony Stewart Head (*Rupert Giles*)

1. and 2. "Welcome to the Hellmouth"
(MARCH 10, 1997)

Director: Charles Martin Smith ("Welcome to the Hellmouth") and John Kretchmer ("The Harvest")

Teleplay: Joss Whedon

Recurring cast: Julie Benz (Darla); David Boreanaz (Angel); Ken Lerner (Principal Flutie); Mark Metcalf (the Master); Kristine Sutherland (Joyce Summers)

Guest cast: Eric Balfour (Jesse); J. Patrick Lawlor (Thomas); Mercedes McNab (Harmony); Jeffrey Steven Smith (student); Natalie Strauss (teacher); Brian Thompson (Luke); Teddy Lane Jr. (club bouncer); Deborah Brown (girl); Amy Chance (girl); Tupelo Jereme (girl); Persia White (girl)

Music: "Saturated" (during scene where Buffy is debating outfits); "Believe" (played onstage when Buffy arrives at the Bronze); "Things Are Changing" (as Buffy leaves the Bronze to look for Willow); and "Right My Wrong" (Buffy's confrontation with Flutie at the school gate)—by Sprung Monkey, from *Swirl*; "Wearing Me

Down" (the song Cordelia says she loves) and "Ballad for Dead Friends" (as vampires descend on the Bronze), by the Dashboard Prophets, from *Burning Out the Inside*

Plot: *While trying to settle into her new surroundings in Sunnydale, California Buffy must come to grips with the realization that it is her destiny to be the Slayer—whether she wants to be or not.*

THIS WEEK'S PROPHECY: On the night of the Harvest, the Master Vampire can draw power from one of his minions while it feeds. This means that once he's gathered enough strength, the Master Vampire will be able to break through the mystical barrier and come aboveground. If he succeeds, his plan is to begin the annihilation of humans so "the old ones" can regain control of the earth.

INTRODUCING: The first episode introduces the main cast of characters—Buffy Summers, Willow Rosenberg, Xander Harris, Rupert Giles, Cordelia Chase, and the mysterious Angel, who warns Buffy to beware of the Harvest when presenting her with a silver cross.

THE BIG BAD: The Master—the oldest, most powerful vampire who has been trapped beneath Sunnydale for years after getting stuck in a mystic portal while attempting to open the Hellmouth. The Master's attempts to gain his freedom is the overriding story arc of the first season's twelve episodes. Among his many minions is Darla, who uses her schoolgirl look to lead unsuspecting young men to a grisly end.

As it happens, a lot of the Master's plans eventually involve the Bronze, Sunnydale's only nightspot open to the high school set. When not beset by vampires looking for sacrifices to bring to the Master, the Bronze offers the town's teens soft drinks, bands, and overfed cockroaches.

ANALYSIS: The first episode picks up by retroactively revising the end of the feature film version of *Buffy the Vampire Slayer*. Instead of the ending of the movie, we are now informed that Buffy wiped out the horde of vampires by trapping them inside her school gymnasium, then setting it on fire. Los Angeles school authorities were not amused and summarily expelled Buffy, so she and her mom are hoping to make a fresh start in Sunnydale, California.

The film was more campy than creepy, but when Buffy, on her way to rendezvous with Willow and Xander, hears footsteps behind her, it's established early on that the series won't be afraid to evoke palpable unease in its viewers. Buffy's stalker is the enigmatic Angel, whom Buffy finds both intriguing and off-putting. As many women can attest, there's something dreadfully attractive when a handsome face is combined with a whiff of danger.

The pilot effectively establishes the relationships between Buffy, her Watcher Giles, and her new friends Xander and Willow, who will become the Slayer's inner circle. Xander represents the "everyman" nonbeliever who is forced to believe, against all logic or reason, in all sorts of creatures that do a lot more than just go bump in the night. Complementing Xander is Willow, the whiz kid who faces the unbelievable with more amazement than doubt. Giles, whose British countenance should not be mistaken for meekness, assumes the role of mentor/father figure to Buffy's rebellious but well-intentioned nature. While many teenagers go through a period of resisting the responsibilities that come with pending adulthood, Buffy has a better reason than most, to want to remain carefree—she'd like to live long enough to *become* an adult.

One of Buffy's primary character traits is her unwillingness to leave people behind, even if it means putting herself in jeopardy. She might be fighting an unending internal struggle over her role as the Slayer, but when someone is threatened, she has no choice but to go save them. This is one of her great human strengths, but also an Achilles' heel the Master and others to come will use against her.

The pilot also establishes that Buffy is not invincible. She feels every punch and kick doled out by her Hellmouth adversaries. This vulnerability will prove to be a crucial aspect of the series—while she may possess superhuman strengths and abilities, Buffy is no Superwoman. The high mortality rate of previous Slayers is what propels Giles to push Buffy so hard. The secret to her longevity will ultimately prove to be her loyal, if not exactly fearless, support group, who will come to call themselves "the Scooby Gang." Buffy does more than just "get by" with a little help with her friends—she lives to Slay another day.

THE REAL HORROR: Enrolling at a school after everybody else has already formed well-defined cliques. Anybody who's ever been "the new kid" can empathize with Buffy's nervousness at walking into an unfamiliar situation, whether it be a new job, a new neighborhood, or, especially, a new school. Nothing is so nausea-inspiring as having to decipher a high school's preordained popularity pecking-order and going through the agony of finding where you fit in—which is not necessarily where you'd like to be.

Although she'd like to be as popular as Cordelia, the queen of the "in" crowd, Buffy is drawn to Willow and Xander, who represent the vast majority of students who pass through high school just *this much* on the outside: They're close enough to see in but seldom get invited to join the party.

Xander's buddy Jesse reflects another common adolescent occurrence: A friend you've known all your life suddenly turns into not just a stranger, but an absolute monster. It's "hanging out with the wrong crowd" taken to a horrific extreme. But even though Jesse has become a vampire, he still looks like the same person he used to be, so it's difficult for Xander to accept the change. He's hoping that something will restore Jesse to the guy he was before. Fortunately for Xander, while his intellect and emotions are battling it out, Jesse is pushed onto the wooden stake Xander's clutching, causing Jesse to disintegrate in a puff of ash.

BLOOPERS: In the scene where Giles is piling ancient tomes in Buffy's arms, the bindings first face Buffy; then in the next shot, face Giles; then, finally, face Buffy again.

OF SPECIAL NOTE: "Welcome to the Hellmouth" was originally filmed as two separate episodes: "Welcome to the Hellmouth," and "The Harvest," which was to be the second episode. The two episodes were combined and presented as a two-hour pilot. But for this episode guide, the two-hour movie will be counted as Episodes 1 and 2.

Sunnydale High is actually Torrance High School, which was also used in *Beverly Hills 90210.*

Although most Buffy fans may be too young to remember, Charles Martin Smith, who directed the first hour of the pilot, was once best known as an actor, having gotten his big break in *American Graffiti*—along with Richard Dreyfuss, Harrison Ford, and Suzanne Somers.

MUSICAL NOTE: The band that performs the theme song, Nerf Herder, took their name from a bit of *The Empire Strikes Back* dialogue, when Princess Leia referred to Han Solo as a "scruffy nerf herder." And no, she was not being complimentary at the time.

3. "The Witch"
(MARCH 17, 1997)

Director: Stephen Cragg

Teleplay: Dana Reston

Recurring cast: Kristine Sutherland (Joyce Summers); William Monaghan (Dr. Gregory)

Guest cast: Elizabeth Anne Allen (Amy); Jim Doughan (Mr. Pole); Nicole Prescott (Lishanne); Robin Riker (Catherine); Amanda Wilmshurst (head cheerleader)

Music: "Twilight Zone," by 2 Unlimited

Plot: A girl's obsession with becoming a cheerleader is suspected of being the evil force behind a series of witchcraft-like spells spontaneously combusting, blinding, and otherwise maiming other members of the squad. When the student witch realizes Buffy knows her secret, she puts Buffy under a deadly spell that will kill her, unless Giles can locate her book of Magic and reverse the spells.

THIS WEEK'S EVIL CREATURE: A very powerful witch trying to hold on to her youth.

INTRODUCING: Science teacher Dr. Gregory is introduced, as is Cordelia's frightening lack of driving skills. Also, "The Witch" represents the first non-vampire story line.

ANALYSIS: Buffy's desire to try out for the squad reflects the dichotomy of Buffy. She doesn't conform to the will of the Cordelias of the world in order to gain acceptance, and yet she wants to be accepted enough that being a cheerleader really matters to her—even though she'd never admit just how much it matters. For, as much as high school life has changed over the last half century in America, there remain a few constants—the jocks and the cheerleaders are still considered to be near the top of the high school food-chain hierarchy; they are the golden children secretly envied and openly resented.

If anyone doubts the lengths some girls—and mothers, on their behalf— will go to win a spot on the sidelines, consider the real-life incident that occurred in Texas in 1991, where an overzealous mother was convicted of

WITCHES

The word *witch* is derived from the German *wic*, which means "to bend or turn." Historically, witches are women who use supernatural powers, in the form of black magic, for evil purposes to "bend" or "change" events or people. Male witches are called warlocks. They can either be possessed by evil spirits, or under the guidance of some mystical power or deity. Because of their association with magic, the term *sorcery* has long been synonymous with witchcraft in the English-speaking world. (However, neo-pagan witches hold a deep and abiding respect for the freewill of all living creatures and abide by the motto, "Do what you will, but harm no one.")

Records reveal that belief in witchcraft dates back to prehistoric times. There are several references to sorcerers in the Old Testament, and the Greek writer Homer makes references to witch-craft. Among the Germanic peoples, belief in and fear of witches was widespread.

Witch mythology varies from country to country. For example, while in many cultures witches have been historically depicted as ugly old women, a more modern view of witches tends to cast them as ordinary or beautiful women who just happen to have the power to cast spells.

In Europe witches are often portrayed as thin and gaunt, much like the Wicked Witch of the West as she appears in the *The Wizard of Oz*, but in Central Africa witches are thought of as being fat from eating human flesh. The notion of witches buzzing around on brooms actually came from a long-standing European tradition which has become part of American pop culture thanks to Halloween. Sometimes witches use animals either to help them carry out their evil deeds or as protectors. In Europe they use cats, dogs, or weasels; in Japan, hyenas or owls; in Africa, baboons. Some witches can even take animal forms.

From the mid-fifteenth to the-eighteenth century—during what's been referred to as Europe's "witchcraft craze"—witches were accused of having special links to the Devil. Thousands of people were convicted of witchcraft and executed. The most notable American example was the Salem witch trials of 1692, during which nineteen people were hanged.

In the early years of the witch hunts, the accused were mostly women. One interesting study concluded that women who were economically independent made up 89 percent of women executed for witchcraft in New England. Scholars believe that was no coincidence. In *Mystic Cats*, author Roni Jay explains:

"In the thirteenth century, people were becoming disillusioned with the Church and the whole structure of society. The Church needed a scapegoat, and it picked on witchcraft—after all, old women were less likely than anyone to put up a serious defense. Over the next few centuries, thousands of women throughout Europe were executed for witchcraft—and many cats were condemned along with them."

Poor kitties.

plotting to murder one of her daughter's competitors for a spot on the cheerleading squad. The surreal situation was the basis for the Emmy-winning HBO movie *The Positively True Adventures of the Alleged Texas Cheerleader-Murdering Mom.* So, by comparison, using witchcraft to make the squad doesn't seem all that unbelievable.

The major revelation of the episode—that Amy's mother has literally stolen her daughter's youth by switching their bodies—provides a shocking plot twist that is indicative of *Buffy*'s storytelling conventions: Just when viewers think they have things figured out, the story often takes a creative and surprising turn.

IT'S A MYSTERY: How and when did Amy steal Buffy's bracelet? We see how Buffy makes off with a lock of Amy/Catherine's hair—but whatever scene showed Amy lifting the bracelet must have been left on the cutting-room floor.

THE REAL HORROR: Trying to live up to your parents' sometimes unreasonable expectations.

In this episode, both Buffy and Amy are confronted with the reality that they haven't always lived up to what their parents had hoped, either in achievement or in character. In Buffy's case, her secret exploits have resulted in a complete family upheaval but she's unable to explain to her mother why "Life with Buffy" is so difficult. It's not that she wants it to be a problem but she can't help it—what teenager can?

When Joyce suggests that Buffy work on the yearbook committee—an activity on the low end of the 1990s school social scene—she's projecting her own past glories onto Buffy without taking into account that her daughter is a very different person than she was, and that projecting interests onto a child usually just sets the stage for hurt feelings: The child's belief that the parent doesn't have a clue is reinforced and the parent is injured because something that was once so important to them is summarily blown off, which is often interpreted as a personal rejection.

In Amy's case, her mother so desperately wants to relive her youth through her daughter, she casts a spell enabling her to switch bodies. What Catherine "the Great" does isn't all that much more horrific than parents who drive their children into careers or activities in an effort to live vicariously through them. Catherine is *Gypsy*'s Mama Rose with a spellbook. The biggest irony of the episode is that after Catherine has switched bodies and is finally poised for her moment of triumph, she discovers that no matter how much she practices, no matter how strong her desire, Catherine as Amy simply doesn't have the innate skills to be great again. She failed to learn one of the most important lessons of parenting: Your child's destiny is their own, and trying to live vicariously through them by re-creating your youth through them can only lead to tragedy . . . or being trapped in a trophy case for eternity.

FORMER SERIES CO-PRODUCER DAVID GREENWALT ADDS: "What I love about what Joss has done with the show is, he can take the psychological truth behind the true story of the mother who had her daughter's rival killed because she didn't make the cheerleading squad, and turn it into a story of a mother who takes her daughter's body so she can relive her glory days as a cheerleader. I like that he takes very real issues and then magnifies them. It's fun doing that."

BLOOPERS: In the gymnasium, a sign reads: "1996 CHEERLEADING TRY-OUTS." It didn't read "1997" because the series was originally supposed to debut at the beginning of the 1996 season that autumn, but was pushed back because of production problems.

OF SPECIAL NOTE: Robin Riker, who played Catherine the Great, is no stranger to witches, having guest-starred in 1996 on *Sabrina the Teenage Witch.*

4. "Teacher's Pet"
(MARCH 25, 1997)

Director: Bruce Seth Green

Teleplay: David Greenwalt

Recurring cast: David Boreanaz (Angel); Ken Lerner (Principal Flutie); William Monaghan (Dr. Gregory)

Guest cast: Jean Speegle Howard (Natalie French); Jackson Price (Blayne); Musetta Vander (She-Mantis)

Music: "Already Met You" (music in Xander's dream) and "Stoner Love" (at the end when Xander chops up the eggs), by Superfine, from the *Stoner Love 7* vinyl release.

Plot: After the gruesome death of science teacher Dr. Gregory, Xander falls for the flirtatious charms of the new substitute, who brings new meaning to the term "man-eater."

THIS WEEK'S PHENOMENON: Metamorphosis, which is a very ancient belief that certain people have the magical ability to change themselves and others at will into other life forms, such as other human beings, animals, birds, and insects. In this episode, the animal of choice is a She-Mantis, who can only maintain her human form by mating with, and then devouring, virginal young men.

INTRODUCING: The first death of a recurring character. In this case, science teacher Dr. Gregory, who is dragged off by a creature just minutes after giving Buffy a supportive pep talk. The character of Dr. Gregory is the first recurring character introduced on the series who will later be killed off. Breaking the long-standing tradition of only killing off guest stars, having recurring characters regularly die will become a hallmark of the show.

Also new to the scene is the mutual sexual attraction sparking between Angel and Buffy. Up until this episode, Buffy has been wary of and annoyed with her mysterious shadow. But her initial distrust is being replaced by flirtatious banter and bedroom-eyes glances.

ANALYSIS: Poor Xander. Not only is his sexual prowess repeatedly challenged by self-proclaimed womanizer Blayne, now he discovers that Buffy's mystery man, Angel, looks like he stepped straight out of a *GQ* ad. Meeting Angel for the first time, Xander obviously feels threatened on an "attractability" scale.

The episode is a showcase for Xander, as his creepy-crawly encounters with the She-Mantis take center stage. But while the story allows Nicholas Brendon to display his acting range, his alter ego wished some things had been left unrevealed—like the fact that the creature only goes after virgins, which the others are all too aware of. Xander takes out his frustration over the revelation of his virginity on a sac of mantis eggs, which he chops apart with a machete.

THE REAL HORROR: Learning how to cope with adult feelings of sexual desire while still an emotionally immature teenager. Among high school boys, it expresses itself as verbal sexual competition.

Xander represents the average teenage boy who feels compelled to play along with the game rather than admit sexual innocence and risk eternal ridicule from their more sexually mature peers. But even worse than being ridiculed by the guys, is having the object of your fantasies and passion find out you're not sexually experienced. There's a reason why so many high school girls date older guys.

THE MORAL OF THIS STORY: Although hormones will be hormones, in this age of deadly sexually transmitted diseases—and evil creatures who are drawn to Sunnydale like ants to blood—uninformed sex with a stranger can kill.

BLOOPERS: When the substitute teacher is first seen sitting at her desk preparing her sandwich, her sleeves are pushed up to her elbows. But during the close-up of her hands dumping the crickets on the bread, the sleeves of her sweater are clearly visible. Then, in the very next shot of her taking a bite of the sandwich, the sleeves are pushed back up.

OF SPECIAL NOTE: The director of this episode, Bruce Seth Green, has some experience with television action heroes, having also directed episodes of *Hercules* and *Xena*. And his horror credentials include a stint on *Airwolf*, the onetime Jan-Michael Vincent vehicle.

Jean Speegle Howard, the actress who plays the "real" Natalie French, was the mother of actor-turned-director Ron "Opie" Howard (she died in 2000).

5. "Never Kill a Boy on the First Date"
(MARCH 31, 1997)

Director: David Semel
Teleplay: Rob Des Hotel and Dean Batali
Recurring cast: David Boreanaz (Angel); Andrew J. Ferchland (Colin, the boy in the bus); Mark Metcalf (the Master)
Guest cast: Geoff Meed (bus passenger); Robert Mont (bus driver); Christopher Wiehl (Owen);
Music: "Strong" (first song Buffy and Owen dance to) and "Treason" (next song they dance to), by Velvet Chain, from the *Groovy Side*, "Let the Sun Fall Down" (when Buffy tells Owen they should just be friends), by Kim Richey, from *Kim Richey*.

Plot: Buffy develops a crush on sensitive, poetry-loving Owen, who asks her out on her first date since moving to Sunnydale. But her night of hoped-for romance is interrupted by a new prophesy the Master is bent on seeing fulfilled in order to gain his freedom.

THIS WEEK'S PROPHECY: A great warrior vampire will "be born" and become the Master's secret weapon against the Slayer and ultimately lead her to doom, although exactly how he's supposed to do that remains a mystery at this point.

INTRODUCING: The Anointed One. Through this vampire, the Master plans on both killing Buffy and gaining his freedom so the "old ones" can once again rule Earth. The twist here is that instead of being one of the more violent, nastier-looking adult vampires, the Anointed One is a little boy, someone Buffy would never suspect of being an evil creature intent on seeing her dead—until it's too late. The Anointed One's role in this episode is limited to a surprise introduction at the end but the character becomes the focal point of the story line in the season finale, "Prophecy Girl" (Episode 12).

ANALYSIS: Buffy is going through some typical adolescent growing pains in this episode, complicated by her secret life as the Slayer. Still holding on to the hope of being able to resume a fairly normal social life, Buffy is thrilled when Sunnydale's resident brooding, sensitive, poetry-loving hunk takes an interest in her. So what if some apocalyptic prophecy is about to be set into motion? She'd rather go on a date.

The only reason Giles is doing what is actually Buffy's job, is his guilt over her destiny, which is more evident here than in past episodes. Rather than pull Watcher rank and insist she do her Slayerly duties, he relents because he empathizes with her longing to be free from—at least for a night—the weight of being the world's savior—just as he once longed to live the life of a grocer, blissfully ignorant of all the evil lurking in the shadows of the Watcher's world.

Buffy's sense of duty finally kicks in, but her lapse in responsibility may have disastrous consequences. Although she saved Giles and the others by incinerating the vampire believed to be the Anointed One, she is too distracted to consider the possibility he wasn't the Anointed One after all—a fact that will come back to haunt her in Episode 12, "Prophecy Girl."

THE REAL HORROR: Responsibility and sacrifice. One of the more sobering passages into maturity—except for those suffering from permanent arrested development—is the realization we won't always be able to follow our heart's fondest desire. Sometimes we either have to choose responsibility over selfish indulgence, or sacrifice our personal needs and wants for the greater good. It can be a really depressing revelation, especially when it involves a potential love interest.

Just as some of life's greatest romances are ultimately unable to overcome fundamental obstacles such as religious differences, political beliefs, or even jobs that cause long separations, Buffy is forced to acknowledge that being the Slayer puts a serious but necessary damper on your social and love life. While most teens simply incur heartbreak or angry parents when they make irresponsible choices, Buffy's margin of error is much less and with much greater consequences. It would not only be irresponsible on Buffy's part to knowingly put Owen at risk, but pursuing a relationship of any kind with someone outside the inner Slayer circle could put Xander, Willow, and Giles at risk as well.

Just like the overextended parent who fleetingly wonders what it would be like to have absolutely nobody to care for but themselves, or the executive who daydreams of leaving behind the stress and pressure of corporate America for a simpler, downsized way of life, Buffy learns that at the end of the day, being an adult—or being a Slayer—means having to take into consideration how our actions affect the people around us. We might be answerable only to ourselves, but we are responsible to everyone we make a part of our lives.

BLOOPERS: When the shuttle bus is first seen from far away, all of the lights inside the bus are on and brightly lit. But when the camera cuts to an interior shot of the bus and its passengers, all the lights are off.

OF SPECIAL NOTE: Because he's under his vampire makeup, viewers may not recognize Mark Metcalf, who appeared on *Seinfeld* in the recurring part of "the Maestro." But Metcalf's signature role is still as Douglas C. Neidermeyer in *National Lampoon's Animal House*.

MUSICAL NOTE: The group performing during Owen and Buffy's date at the Bronze is Velvet Chain.

6. "The Pack"
(APRIL 7, 1997)

Director: Bruce Seth Green
Teleplay: Matt Kiene and Joe Rinkmeyer
Recurring cast: Ken Lerner (Principal Flutie)
Guest cast: David Brisbin (Mr. Anderson); Jeff Maynard (Lance); Justin Jon Ross (Joey); Jeffrey Steven Smith (Adam); James Stephens (zookeeper); Barbara Whinnery (Mrs. Anderson); Gregory White (Coach Herrold); Eion Bailey, Michael McRaine, Brian Gross, and Jennifer Sky (the Pack)
Music: "All You Want" (when Xander joins Buffy and Willow at the Bronze), by Dashboard Prophets, from *Burning Out the Inside*; "Reluctant Man" (as the Pack enters the Bronze), by Sprung Monkey from *Swirl*; "Job's Eyes" (as the Pack prowls among the students in slow-mo), by Far, from *Tin Cans and Strings for You*

Plot: During a field trip to the zoo, Xander and a gang of four school bullies become possessed by the spirit of a vicious hyena. With Xander as pack leader, they start a reign of terror at Sunnydale High. Buffy and Giles need to figure out how to exorcise the evil spirit before it permanently takes over Xander's soul.

THIS WEEK'S EVIL: Transpossession—which is when a person becomes possessed by the spirit of an animal, most often a predator of some kind. Certain tribes, including the Maasai in Africa, believe an animal spirit can inhabit the body of a human, thereby elevating the person to a higher, purer spiritual plane.

INTRODUCING: The primal side of Xander. After he's taken over by the hyena spirit, Xander's more "basic instinct" side emerges, where hedonistic desires flourish without any tempering codes of social conduct. Normally his love for Buffy, combined with common courtesy and manners, would prevent him from going after her like an animal in heat, but as hyena-boy, he just follows his urges.

ANALYSIS: If there was any doubt left about Willow's feelings for Xander, or his attraction to Buffy, it's completely dispelled in this episode. It's also clear that the thing Willow finds most attractive about him in a romantic sense—and Buffy, on a friendship level—is Xander's good-natured personality, because when he comes into the Bronze after the field trip and starts acting in a more "male animal" fashion, both Willow and Buffy are instinctively put off by him.

When Xander nearly rapes Buffy, his claim that he's only being what Buffy finds attractive—dark and dangerous à la Angel—strikes at the heart of the *Men Are from Mars, Women Are from Venus*–type misunderstanding between the sexes. While Buffy does find Angel's sexiness and attractiveness heightened by his mysterious aura, in her fantasies about him she's not in any kind of real jeopardy because *she's* the one controlling the situation. But as soon as Xander pins her against the wall, their encounter automatically becomes about power, not attraction—which is why she then hits him with a desk.

The episode takes a sharp turn to the dark side, first with Xander and his group eating Herbert the pig, Sunnydale's mascot, followed by the cannibalistic murder of Principal Flutie by the other members of the Pack, minus Xander. Whether intended or not, Flutie's death at the hands of his students can be seen as a symbolic morality play about the alarming escalation of juvenile crime that is just as much of a problem in the suburbs as in the inner city.

While the events of this episode threatened to destroy their friendship forever, in the end, after the hyena spirit is released from Xander, the bond between Buffy, Willow, and Xander is strengthened by the girls' ability to forgive, and Xander's pretense of forgetting what happened.

THE REAL HORROR: Predators, sexual or social. The modern extreme is gangs, but less dramatic examples can be found in every school where packs of students, both male and female, are on the prowl. In this episode, Xander and his hyena-possessed crew represent the primal behavior that teenagers can fall into when in groups. Case in point—Spring Break in Fort Lauderdale, or Palm Springs, or any place where hordes of hormonally charged teenagers and young adults gather. Xander's overt sexual aggression toward Buffy reflects the kind of disparity there can be between male and female sexuality during the teen years, and serves as a powerful analogy for the intense drive young men experience as their hormones go into overdrive. In fact, Xander and the Pack's behavior is so typical of many teenagers, especially boys, that Giles dismisses Buffy's concern.

BLOOPERS: When Willow is in the library supposedly watching a clip about hyenas that is playing on the computer, the animals shown with the white fluffy tails are not hyenas, but a type of wild dog.

OF SPECIAL NOTE: The actor who plays Dr. Anderson, the father of the family in the van, played Mr. Ernst on Nickelodeon's *Hey, Dude.* Eion Bailey was one of the stars of *Significant Others,* the short-lived Fox series by the creators of *Party of Five.*

7. "Angel"
(APRIL 14, 1997)

Director: Scott Brazil
Teleplay: David Greenwalt
Recurring cast: Julie Benz (Darla); David Boreanaz (Angel); Andrew J. Ferchland (Colin/the Anointed One); Mark Metcalf (the Master); Kristine Sutherland (Joyce Sutherland)
Guest cast: Charles Wesley (Lead Vampire of the Three)
Music: The song playing over the final scene between Buffy and Angel in the Bronze is "I'll Remember You," by Sophie Zelmani.

Plot: It's the best of times and the worst of times for Buffy. The good news: Angel loves her. The bad news: He's a 240-year-old vampire.

THIS WEEK'S KILLER VAMPIRES: Tired of Buffy killing off his family, the Master calls upon warrior vampires—the Three—to kill her. When they fail, Darla, the vampire who dresses like a schoolgirl, takes it upon herself to get rid of Buffy.

INTRODUCING: Angel's history and Xander's dancing. In the opening scene, Willow looks on lovingly as Xander jerks and gyrates his way across the dance floor. Due to the response of fans, more of Xander's inimitable style will be seen in future episodes. More seriously, both the dark and sensitive sides of Angel are revealed as the truth about his past is uncovered.

ANALYSIS: Buffy is both surprised and thrilled to discover that Angel returns her romantic feelings. But this is a horror series and nothing will be easy, especially love. Just as it seems Buffy's deepest desire may come true and she may experience her sensual awakening with the man she loves, Angel shows his true face and it's not a pretty sight.

Trust is a major theme of this episode, with Buffy ultimately trusting her instinct that Angel is not a monster—even though she makes a halfhearted attempt to kill him when she is under the mistaken belief, courtesy of Darla, that he attacked her mother Joyce.

Joyce Summers's character is also fleshed out further in this episode. For, whatever traumas caused them to leave Los Angeles, mother and daughter are shown to have a close, respectful relationship. Despite all the problems her daughter has experienced, in and out of school, Joyce is surprisingly trusting of Buffy, especially when finding Buffy at home with an obviously older man.

Angel offers proof of his love for Buffy by killing Darla, the vampire who "made" him, knowing that her death will forever brand him an outcast among his people. This sacrifice helped cement Angel as one of the contemporary television's most romantic characters.

THE REAL HORROR: The realization that love isn't always enough to overcome every obstacle facing a relationship—that there are circumstances beyond the couple's control that will ultimately determine its success or failure. This never seems as true as it is for teenagers.

And the impact of unrequited, unrealized passion is magnified in youth. First loves are so intense and the emotions behind them so exposed and raw because teens haven't yet learned to protect themselves; they haven't formed the emotional calluses that come with age, experience, and previous loss. Buffy and Angel's apparent hopeless, *Romeo and Juliet* situation represents any relationship conspired against by culture, parental disapproval, age, or circumstances.

IT'S A MYSTERY: When did Buffy call Giles and tell him about being attacked by three vampires? All we see is Buffy taking Angel home, encountering her surprised mom, then going upstairs to go to sleep.

BLOOPERS: When Buffy is walking home early in the episode, she walks past a store window lit in a greenish hue. After walking several steps, she hears a sound, stops a moment, then keeps walking—right past the exact same green-lit window.

When Buffy is training with Giles in the library, she is wearing pants and a blue T-shirt. In the very next scene, she walks into her bedroom, says hi to Angel and offers him some food while dressed in a white dress.

During Buffy's confrontation with Angel in the Bronze, she puts down her crossbow, walks three or four steps to stand next to him, and dares him to kill her. But when Darla appears, Buffy—who is still next to Angel—is able to just flip the crossbow up into her hand because it is suddenly right next to her foot. Also, how come Darla never has to reload her guns?

OF SPECIAL NOTE: Kristine Sutherland, who plays Buffy's mom, is married to former *Mad About You* co-star John Pankow.

8. "𝕴, 𝕽𝖔𝖇𝖔𝖙—𝖄𝖔𝖚, 𝕵𝖆𝖓𝖊"
(APRIL 28, 1997)

Director: Stephen Posey
Teleplay: Ashley Gable and Thomas A. Swyden
Recurring cast: Robia La Morte (Ms. Calendar)
Guest cast: Mark Deakins (voice of Moloch); Edith Fields (nurse); Chad Lindberg (Fritz); Pierrino Mascarino (Thelonius); Jamison Ryan (Dave)

MOLOCH

There really is a record of a demon named Moloch. He was a Canaanite deity associated with human sacrifices, primarily sacrifices of children. In areas where he was worshipped, a bronze statue with the head of an ox and body of a man would be erected and infants would be placed in it to burn to death. He is usually depicted as an old man with ram's horns, holding a scythe. For the literary-minded, Moloch is mentioned in Milton's *Paradise Lost*, in book 6, line 365:

"Touch of Evil"

Touch of evil
On the faithful bestowed
Burn for Moloch
Sacrificial inferno
Submitting the offspring
Swallowed in flames
Baptismal immolation
Another soul claimed
Hell on earth
The pagan returns
To please the deity
Children shall burn
Your children are mine
Placate me with them
You worshipped before
You will kneel again
As the young are scorched
We welcome the end
The lord of the altar of incense unleashed
Apocalypse begins.

Plot: Willow accidentally scans a demon trapped in an ancient book into the school computer. Once free to roam through the world's computers via telecommunication lines, Moloch has some cyberfollowers build him a robot body. His plan is to first kill Willow, Buffy, and Xander then wreak havoc and destruction on the world—unless Giles and Ms. Calendar, the computer-science teacher, can find a way to stop him.

THIS WEEK'S DEMON: Moloch the Corruptor, whose specialty was seducing the young and innocent into doing his evil bidding. He was only stopped after his soul was imprisoned by medieval monks in an ancient tome, where he was destined to remain until the words of the book were read aloud. Apparently, scanning served the same purpose.

INTRODUCING: Ms. Jenny Calendar, computer-science teacher and self-described technopagan. A child of the Information Age, Ms. Calendar butts heads, taunts, and openly flirts with computerphobic, bibliophilic Giles. When Giles needs help to rid the Internet of Moloch, it's Jenny who arranges for an online circle to exorcise the demon from cyberspace. She points out to Giles that the mystical world isn't limited to ancient texts and relics—that the divine also exists in cyberspace. Jenny's knowledge of and belief in prophecies and other mystical events and creatures foreshadows her future inclusion in the Slayer's inner circle.

ANALYSIS: This time it is Willow's turn to try her hand at Hellmouth romance. But even though Willow is smitten with her wooing suitor, she's not one to completely lose her senses. When Malcolm slips up and reveals that he's been checking up on Buffy, Willow grows leery. She is obviously more loyal to proven friend Buffy than to an unknown would-be boyfriend. Willow might be lonely and desperate for some romantic attention, but she's not going to lose her head—at least not figuratively.

In an evocative scene, Willow goes after Moloch, venting her hurt feelings and frustration at being lied to and manipulated, revealing just how much of an Achilles' heel her loneliness is. After Buffy tricks Moloch into short-circuiting himself, Buffy, Willow, and Xander compare their unlucky-in-love track records, and like many teenagers who remain out of the dating loop, come to the conclusion they will never find a relationship the way other people do.

THE REAL HORROR: The dangers of Internet intimacy. This episode is almost of the ripped-from-the-headlines variety. Willow establishes a "relationship" with an unknown, unseen stranger by chatting on the computer. With the recent flurry of reported crimes being committed by people who were first "met" on the Internet, the presence of a demon inside the modem is already a perceived reality to some technophobes.

IT'S A MYSTERY: How did Buffy, on foot, manage to follow Dave, who was driving a car, to the computer research facility?

BLOOPERS: When Moloch is hacking into the school computer to see Buffy's school record, her birthdate changes from "10/24/80" the first time we see the computer screen, to "5/6/79," and her grade changes from "sophomore" to "senior."

OF SPECIAL NOTE: The director of this episode, Stephen Posey, who also works as a cinematographer, began his directing career working on a number of horror films, including *Slumber Party Massacre*, which had the distinction of being banned from movie theaters in Germany.

The voice of Moloch/Malcolm is supplied by Mark Deakins, who was a popular daytime star on *The City*, playing Kevin Larkin.

The voice heard while Giles is listening to the radio is that of series creator Joss Whedon.

9. "The Puppet Show"
(MAY 5, 1997)

Director: Ellen Pressman
Teleplay: Dean Batali and Rob Des Hotel
Recurring cast: Armin Shimerman (Principal Snyder); Kristine Sutherland (Joyce Summers)
Guest cast: Krissy Carlson (Emily); Chasen Hampton (Elliot); Lenora May (Mrs. Jackson); Natasha Pearce (Lisa); Burke Roberts (Marc); Richard Werner (Morgan); Tom Wyner (voice of Sid)

Plot: The Sunnydale High School talent show turns sinister when one of the featured students, a ventriloquist with a eerily real dummy, is suspected by Buffy and the gang in the gruesome murder of another student, who had her heart cut out.

THIS WEEK'S EVIL CREATURE: A demon who, in order to retain its human form, must eat a human heart and brain every seven years. This demon is the last of a group of seven demons, the others having been killed by Sid, the demon hunter. Unfortunately for Sid, he's the victim of a curse that left him a wooden dummy: Think Pinocchio with hormones and an attitude. In order to be freed from the curse, Sid must kill the last of the demons, hopefully before it finds a suitable brain to eat.

INTRODUCING: Principal Snyder, who is determined to restore order to Sunnydale High. He feels his predecessor Mr. Flutie, who was eaten by a pack of hyena-possessed students in Episode 5, was too soft on the students. The new principal's hard-line motto is that children should be disciplined and controlled; trying to understand them will only lead to an out-of-control school and a limited mortality.

Snyder seems to have focused his attention on Buffy and her cohorts because, he says, they seem to be the school's bad element. He keeps appearing out of nowhere and his too-close-for-comfort, invading-her-personal-space interest in Buffy begins to take on a skin-crawling quality. Is he just an overzealous authoritarian, or something more sinister, possibly even demonic?

Also introduced is Willow's stage fright, which will play a major role in Episode 10, "Nightmares," and Episode 78, "Restless."

ANALYSIS: As the reluctant director of the talent show, Giles's antisocial personality is fleshed out. His discomfort at having to deal with hordes of students is palpable and is reflected by how disheveled he looks whenever he interacts with the participants. He isn't kidding when he tells the new principal that the reason he became a librarian in the first place was to minimize contact with the students.

Through Sid, there is more sexual innuendo than in previous episodes. When everyone still thinks it's Morgan providing the voice of the dummy and Sid says, "Once you've had wood, nothing else is as good," Buffy deals with the sexual connotation by confronting Morgan in a mature, calm manner. Considering creator Whedon stated that at this point Buffy is definitely a virgin, she's an *aware* virgin at ease with sexuality.

At the end, when Giles is locked in a real guillotine, it's the first time the Watcher needs to be saved from imminent death. Although Buffy readily puts herself at risk to save anyone, she seems particularly panicked when she realizes that the demon will go after Giles because he's the smartest person around. Although she herself might not yet realize it, Buffy has started to see Giles as a surrogate father figure.

THE REAL HORROR: Mandatory participation in a high school talent show and the ensuing public humiliation for the artistically impaired. Nothing is quite so sadistic as forcing students, or anyone else for that matter, to get up in front of a roomful of people and perform. While some people, like the Cordelias of the world, have no shame or sense of embarrassment about themselves and are happy to get up on a stage and sing off-key just to be in the limelight, others, like Buffy, Xander, and Willow, find the experience degrading. Ironically, the people with the worst self-image problems are the ones most damaged by this barbaric school ritual. Buffy sums up the prevailing attitude of most students when she tells her mother, "If you really want to support me, you'll stay far, far away."

A second, and more serious issue is raised by Morgan's illness. The monster of this episode, a demon who coldly robs people of their lives for its own insidious gain, could be seen as the fictional embodiment of his terminal brain cancer, a disease that literally eats away at bodies to keep itself going. For anyone there are few horrors so great as the thought of dying a slow, painful death from disease, but it is especially so for a young person. Debilitating illnesses are not supposed to afflict children, but do—and anyone who has ever had a classmate die from disease knows the difficult realization that there are no guarantees that we will all enjoy a long, aged life.

BLOOPERS: Sid kills the demon by stabbing it through the heart with a jumbo-sized kitchen knife. But in the next shot, when Buffy is carrying the lifeless dummy away, there is no knife in the demon's chest.

OF SPECIAL NOTE: Principal Snyder is played by Armin Shimerman, who is known to *Star Trek: The Next Generation* fans as Quark. According to Whedon, the casting was simply lucky. "Armin came in to read because I guess he had some free time, and he was hilarious."

Lenora May, who plays Mrs. Jackson, appeared in the classic 1979 horror film *When a Stranger Calls.*

The voice of Sid is supplied by Tom Wyner, who produced, directed, story-edited, and narrated the animated series *Techman.*

The scene Buffy, Willow, and Xander perform for the talent show at the end of the episode is from *Oedipus Rex.*

10. "𝕹ightmares"

(MAY 12, 1997)

Director: Bruce Seth Green

Teleplay: David Greenwalt

Story by: Joss Whedon

Recurring cast: Dean Butler (Hank Summers); Andrew J. Ferchland (Colin/the Anointed One); Mark Metcalf (the Master); Kristine Sutherland (Joyce Summers)

Guest cast: Jeremy Foley (Billy Palmer); Scott Harlan (Aldo Gianfranco); Tom Magwili (Billy's doctor); J. Robin Miler (Laura); Sean Moran (stage manager); Brian Pietro (Billy's coach); Justin Urich (Wendell)

Plot: An attack on a young boy leaves him comatose, and his wandering spirit unleashes everyone's worst nightmares, making them come true. While battling her own REM. demons, Buffy races the clock to uncover the identity of the boy's attacker before reality folds completely.

THIS WEEK'S MYSTICAL PHENOMENON: Astral projection—the belief that while the physical body is unconscious, the astral body is able to navigate freely through dimensions of time and space.

INTRODUCING: Dean Butler, who plays Buffy's dad, Hank Summers. Hank still lives in Los Angeles and only comes to visit Buffy on occasional weekends. The depth of Buffy's emotional reaction to her parents' divorce is delved into, as well as her worry that she may have in some way contributed to their growing apart because of the havoc wreaked by her secret life as the Slayer.

ANALYSIS: The opening dream sequence in which Buffy confronts the Master and is terrified into paralysis as he leans in for the kill, is a clear indication that Buffy's unspoken fear of the Master's power is growing—a nice foreshadowing of the season finale.

Suddenly life at Sunnydale High begins to take on a surreal, dreamlike quality when nightmarish events become daytime realities. In one of the more upsetting scenes, Buffy's father tells her he left because he couldn't stand living in the same house with her—she's too much trouble and an overall disappointment, and he really has no interest in maintaining a facade of a relationship. The girl who has faced down death on a weekly basis crumbles under the emotional barrage, revealing her true Achilles' heel.

The bizarre happenings are related to Billy Palmer, a boy who lies comatose in the hospital after a brutal attack. The nightmares Billy's astral body has brought with him from his comatose state are enveloping reality. Buffy's worst nightmare—that she'll become a vampire—comes true, but in a dramatic dénouement, Giles figures out how to reverse the nightmares, and restores reality.

THE REAL HORROR: This prickly episode touches on our secret fear of public humiliation: nightmares of standing naked in front of class; being onstage and not knowing your lines; getting lost in a familiar place; being chased by malevolent clowns; becoming physically disabled or mentally incapacitated—all are common dream manifestations of universal anxieties. But concerns of ostracism are probably never as intense as during the unforgiving high school years, when the smallest social misstep can become a permanent red-letter identification.

Series creator Joss Whedon, who came up with the story idea for the "Nightmares" teleplay, accentuates the power of these fears by resurrecting them out of sleep and giving them flesh. To Whedon, true terror is found in the mundane, not the fantastic. While a vampire may give us the creeps, a family member we thought we knew, turning monstrous, is far more frightening. When Hank Summers tells Buffy that the family fell apart because she wasn't worth loving, Whedon taps into the overriding fear harbored by most children of divorce.

BLOOPERS: In the opening scene, when Buffy is talking about her parents' divorce, Willow turns her back to the camera and slides her backpack off her shoulder. Quick cut to Willow's face, and the backpack is still on her shoulder.

OF SPECIAL NOTE: Take a close look when Willow opens her locker and you'll see a Nerf Herder bumper sticker on the inside of the door—an homage to the band that plays the show's theme song over the show's opening credits.

Dean Butler, who plays Buffy's dad, starred on *Little House on the Prairie* for five years as Almanzo Wilder, who married Melissa Gilbert's character, Laura.

11. "Invisible Girl"
(MAY 19, 1997)

Director: Reza Badiyi
Teleplay: Ashley Gable and Thomas A. Swyden
Story by: Joss Whedon
Recurring cast: David Boreanaz (Angel); Armin Shimerman (Principal Snyder)
Guest cast: Ryan Bittle (Mitch); Denise Dowse (Ms. Miller); Clea DuVall (Marcie Ross); Julie Fulton (FBI teacher); Mercedes McNab (Harmony); Mark Phelan (Agent Doyle); Skip Stellrecht (Agent Manetti)

Plot: After her boyfriend, best friend, and teacher are all attacked by an unseen assailant, Cordelia—who has just been voted May Queen—pleads with Buffy for help. The problem is, the assailant is a former classmate who is now invisible and bent on exacting revenge, with Cordelia as her primary target.

THIS WEEK'S PHENOMENON: Invisibility. According to a basic tenet of quantum physics, reality can be shaped and created by our perceptions of the world and of the people around us. In the case of Marcie, the invisible girl, she literally faded away because she didn't exist in the eyes of others.

INTRODUCING: A kinder, gentler Cordelia. Sort of. When Cordelia realizes she's actually the one who Marcie is after, she comes begging for Buffy's help, making it clear she does not have the ability or wherewithal to fight an invisible opponent. It's a new vulnerability for Cordelia, albeit laced with the same self-serving pragmatism.

The first season's story arc involving the Master is pushed along by the appearance of the Codex, courtesy of Angel. The Codex is a book of prophecies concerning the Slayer that Giles had believed was lost. Its appearance sets the stage for the season finale.

ANALYSIS: Once again Buffy's good heart is emphasized by her inability to refuse Cordelia's plea for help. Even though the look on her face says she would really love to see Cordelia squirm, she can't. She is, after all, the Slayer, and evil is evil, and Marcie, who has gotten increasingly violent, needs to be stopped.

It's also interesting to note that while Buffy often seems harried and at loose ends whenever she runs into Cordelia and her entourage in the hallways, Buffy is in her element in the library and all it represents. Her body language—languidly sitting back in the chair while listening to Cordelia—speaks volumes about Buffy's double life. Out in the scary, sociopolitical world of high school, she's just as insecure as anyone, but in her Slayer's lair, she's confident and in command.

This episode marks the beginning of a sea change in Cordelia's relationship with Buffy and company. Cordelia's admission to Buffy that being the school's most popular girl isn't all it's cracked up to be, is a surprising show of vulnerability. Appearances are still everything, but Cordelia has begun to show that there's something else, too, underneath her haughty exterior. Cordelia is not a bad person, nor is she stupid; she is simply a prisoner of her own inverted social standards.

Angel also is slowly becoming a more accepted presence. Giles starts to look at him the way a father scrutinizes his daughter's new boyfriend. Giles immediately picks up on the fact that Angel is in love with the Slayer, and his response that the situation is poetic, "in a maudlin sort of way," shows both his sensitivity to emotion as well as his concern that such a pairing will probably only bring Buffy heartbreak. He is now not only concerned with her physical safety, but her emotional well-being as well.

Angel's role as protector is further cemented when he turns up in the nick of time to save Giles, Xander, and Willow after they are locked in the school basement by Marcie, who has jammed open a gas valve. Up to now his interaction has largely been confined to Buffy; with this episode he shows that his concern extends to her friends as well.

THE REAL HORROR: Unpopularity and exclusion. At some point or another, nearly everyone during their high school career feels left out of the loop, but for some students, it's a full-time position. Marcie represents all the kids who somehow manage to pass through school nearly totally anonymous. Not only are they not included by their classmates, but even teachers tend to overlook them. These kids aren't the nerds, who tend to hang with each other, and thereby have their own clique. The Marcies of the world are teenagers who don't seem to fit in anywhere and spend most of their time completely alone.

BLOOPERS: In the scene where Buffy and Cordelia are being held captive, Buffy frees herself and manages to untie Cordelia's left hand before getting punched by Marcie. In the very next shot, the hand is still tightly tied to the chair.

OF SPECIAL NOTE: This episode was originally titled "Out of Mind, Out of Sight."

Denise Dowse, who plays the teacher, Ms. Miller, appeared for two years on *Beverly Hills 90210* as Mrs. Teasley, the headmaster.

Clea Du Vall, who plays Marcie, has had practice playing the supernatural. She co-starred in *Little Witches*, a poor man's takeoff on *The Craft*, in which four girls at a Catholic boarding school delve into the occult.

12. "𝕻𝖗𝖔𝖕𝖍𝖊𝖈𝖞 𝕲𝖎𝖗𝖑"
(JUNE 2, 1997)

Director: Joss Whedon
Teleplay: Joss Whedon
Recurring cast: David Boreanaz (Angel); Andrew J. Ferchland (Colin/the Anointed One); Mark Metcalf (the Master); Robia La Morte (Ms. Calendar); Kristine Sutherland (Joyce Summers)
Guest cast: Scott Gurney (Kevin)
Music: "I Fall to Pieces" (while Xander is lying on the bed, depressed) by Patsy Cline; "Inconsolable" (while Buffy morbidly looks at the photo album), by Jonatha Brooke, from *Plumb*

Plot: The Codex, the book of Slayer prophecy given to Giles by Angel, tells of a great battle between Buffy and the Master, which will result in her death and the opening of the Hellmouth. When Buffy discovers her foretold death, she initially bolts, but eventually returns to face the Master and her destiny.

THIS WEEK'S PROPHECY: According to the Codex, the Slayer will face the Master—and be defeated by him. Once freed, will open the mouth of Hell and release an apocalypse of demons onto the Earth which will result in the annihilation of humankind.

INTRODUCING: Cordelia and Ms. Calendar's full initiation into the Slayer's inner circle, when they help fight the Master's minions and witness the opening of the Hellmouth.

ANALYSIS: All the primary players go through a transition or a coming to terms with emotions as the first season's story arc ends. Xander has to come to grips with the reality that Buffy will never love him the way she loves Angel. After Buffy turns down Xander's invitation to the dance and rejects his romantic overtures, Willow provides a double whammy by also refusing Xander's suggestion that the two of them go to the dance as buddies, making it clear her feelings about him prevent her from being his platonic date.

Buffy's impending battle with the Master brings out Xander's mettle as a friend and once again emphasizes his dogged loyalty. Despite being romantically rejected by Buffy, he's still willing to risk his life to save her—so much so, he swallows his pride and enlists the help of Angel to find Buffy. But it ends up being Xander, not Angel, who brings Buffy back from the dead by resuscitating her after she is drowned at the hands of the Master.

Cordelia and Jenny Calendar's presence when the Hellmouth opens after the Master is released—and Angel's decision to help Xander—is a precursor to the increased involvement they will have with Buffy in the second season.

THE REAL HORROR: Premature death. In fact the concept is so unnatural that most people, much less teenagers, have a mental block when it comes to mortality. Dying in the prime of youth just doesn't compute, so it is rejected out of hand by most teens.

When Buffy is confronted with the knowledge that her life will be ended sooner rather than later, her basic reaction is to go through the famous steps laid out by thanatologist Elizabeth Kubla-Ross, M.D. First she denies her destiny; if she simply walks away from her role as the Chosen One, she can beat death. Then she gets angry that she should have to sacrifice so much: she didn't ask to be the Slayer! Then, she is overcome with sadness at everything she will never experience—represented by the dress her mom surprises her with, which she wears to go face the Master, and her fate, when she finally accepts her situation.

IT'S A MYSTERY: How does Xander know where Angel lives, since it's never been revealed to the audience? When did Giles get his phone number and what last name does Angel give to the phone company?

BLOOPERS: When the Master pushes Buffy into the pool of water after biting her, she lands facedown with her arms under her body. But when Xander and Angel show up, her arms are floating straight out from her body.

OF SPECIAL NOTE: This is the first episode to be rated "TV-14."

Joss Whedon says that even though he was confident the series would be picked up for a second season, he opted against a season-ending cliffhanger: "And I'll continue to do that every season, because I hate loose ends. Like when *My So-called Life* left me hanging just when Brian revealed he had written Jordan's letters for him."

WHAT THE CRITICS SAY: "The clever season finale takes place on prom night, giving new meaning to the phrase 'high school Hell.' Buffy and company don't make it to the dance; they're too busy keeping the mouth of Hell from spilling its contents into Sunnydale High. Bloodsucking brutes aside, the series' real delight is watching these appealing teens balance school, home, and the saving-the-world thing." (*TV Guide*).

SEASON TWO

SEASON TWO REGULAR CAST

Sarah Michelle Gellar (*Buffy Summers*)
Nicholas Brendon (*Xander Harris*)
Alyson Hannigan (*Willow Rosenberg*)
Charisma Carpenter (*Cordelia Chase*)
Anthony Stewart Head (*Rupert Giles*)
David Boreanaz (*Angel*)

✦

13. "When She Was Bad"
(SEPTEMBER 15, 1997)

Director: Joss Whedon
Teleplay: Joss Whedon
Recurring cast: Dean Butler (Hank Summers); Andrew J. Ferchland
(Colin/the Anointed One); Robia La Morte (Jenny Calendar);
Armin Shimerman (Principal Snyder); Kristine Sutherland (Joyce)
Guest cast: Tamara Braun (Tara); Brent Jennings (Absalom)
Music: "It Doesn't Matter" (during drive to school with Joyce), by Ali-
son Krauss and Union Station, from *So Long So Wrong*; "Spoon"
(as Buffy first enters the Bronze) and "Super Relax" (during the
dance) by Cibo Matto, from *Viva! la Woman*

*Plot: Buffy's back from spending the summer with her father in Los Angeles
but something is not quite right. She's acting bitchy and cruel and seems
bent on driving everyone away. She almost succeeds when her behavior ultimately puts the lives of her friends in danger.*

THIS WEEK'S EVIL PLAN: Resurrection. If the Anointed One can get back the bones and perform a ritual using the blood of the people who were present in the library at his death—Jenny, Giles, Willow, and Cordelia—then he will be able to revivify the Master.

INTRODUCING: A new season, a new vampire population, including a preacher-type called Absalom. Gone are the Master's minions, and in their place are the Anointed One's followers, who have come to Sunnydale to do his bidding. Also gone is the Anointed One's reverberating voice from Season One.

Buffy returns to Sunnydale sporting a shorter, Jennifer Anistonequse hairstyle, and Xander has lost the bangs and gone for a shorter, more mature look. A new school lounge. This season Buffy and her friends relax in a bilevel campus lounge, complete with couches and a soda machine.

ANALYSIS: Buffy may have physically survived her encounter with the Master, but she hasn't gotten over it. Her uncharacteristically bitchy attitude is driving a wedge between her and the people she loves most. But it isn't until she's confronted with the cold reality that her actions have put her friends' lives in danger that she finally starts to snap out of her emotional straitjacket. She goes on a vampire-killing spree, which ends with her weeping on Angel's shoulder. The tears signal the return of the old Buffy, minus a big chunk of invincibility and her former Slayer innocence.

While her basic self-involvement remains the same, Cordelia's character has softened around the edges, making her more dimension and less of a caricature. The question of whether Cordelia knows Buffy is the Slayer is answered when Cordelia comes up to ask if Buffy fought any demons over the summer.

Also for the first time, we see Buffy's parents together and hear their mutual concern for their daughter. It's revealing to see they both feel incapable of communicating with her, and are powerless to help Buffy through whatever is troubling her.

THE REAL HORROR: Realizing how much your best school friend has changed over summer vacation. The distance between Buffy and her friends is an extreme example of classmates who grow apart over the course of a summer because they don't have the common denominator of school. But in her case, the time spent away from Sunnydale has exacerbated the unresolved issues brought about by her confrontation with the Master. For most teens, it's simply that without the forced bonding of school, many otherwise close-seeming friendships drift apart.

BLOOPERS: When Buffy is in the car with her mother on the way to school, she is wearing a pink top. But in the next scene at school, she's wearing a white tank top. The pink top shows up again later, in what is supposed to be the next day.

OF SPECIAL NOTE: David Boreanaz is now a series regular. Brent Jennings, who plays the vampire preacher, has had some previous experience with creepy kids, having co-starred in the movie *Children of the Corn*.

Nicholas Brendon is more noticeably bulked-up at the start of the second season. Part of the reason for so many new looks is that the original half-season was filmed and completed toward the end of 1996, and the new episodes for the second season didn't begin shooting until the summer of 1997.

WHAT THE CRITICS SAY: "This is a thoroughly entertaining season-opener that has humor, wit, and style. The performances are stellar. Sarah Michelle Gellar is wonderful in the lead, displaying the full 12–20 range of adolescent angst. All of the regular players . . . are well cast and believable in their roles" (*Hollywood Reporter*).

14. "Some Assembly Required"
(SEPTEMBER 22, 1997)

Director: Bruce Seth Green
Teleplay: Ty King
Recurring cast: Robia La Morte (Jenny Calendar)
Guest cast: Michael Bacall (Chris); Melanie MacQueen (Mrs. Epps); Ingo Neuhaus (Daryl); Angelo Spizzirri (Eric); Amanda Wilmshurst (cheerleader)

Plot: The bodies of three high school girls are dug up from their graves by two would-be Dr. Frankensteins. But their creation is more than a science experiment—it's a literal labor of love.

THIS WEEK'S MONSTERS: A quite literally "born-again" high school jock and his ghoul brother. After getting killed in a rock-climbing accident, Daryl Epps is brought back to life by his genius brother Chris, but Daryl's libido has gone berserk for female companionship.

INTRODUCING: Giles and Jenny Calendar's budding romance. The flirtation finally graduates into a real date: take-out followed by a night out at the Sunnydale High School football game. Angel's jealousy over Buffy's friendship with Xander also surfaces.

ANALYSIS: After Buffy's emotional catharsis of the previous episode, things between her, Willow, and Xander appear to be back on an even keel, though they are still adjusting to the new dynamic brought about by Xander's revealing his feelings for Buffy in the first-season finale, "Prophecy Girl".

This season Giles will also be seen outside the context of just being a Watcher and surrogate parent. His attraction to Ms. Calendar forces Giles out of the library and into the world, which he finds almost as frightening as the monsters Buffy fights—and a lot less familiar.

If Giles is a father figure for Buffy, then he's Willow's and Xander's favorite uncle. Intentional or not, it's an interesting commentary on the rootlessness of teenagers today that neither Willow nor Xander ever seems to have any family commitments. And they seem freer to come and go than Buffy, who often has to sneak out her window to go patrolling for vampires. In Buffy's case, her mom is a single parent trying to run a new business. But both Willow's and Xander's parents are still married, and yet seem to have even less interaction with them than Buffy's mom does with her.

THE REAL HORROR: Losing a family member who dies. While in Sunnydale, death is sometimes just the beginning; in the real world death is permanent. It leaves in its wake guilt, depression, fear, and loss. Supposedly the only animal aware of its own mortality, man must somehow confront on a daily basis the knowledge that he and everyone he loves will die someday. Considering the powerful emotions caused by the death of a loved one, it's easy to see why the *Frankenstein* story has remained so compelling, pertinent, and timeless. Being able to overcome death, whether through magic, religion, or science, reflects a primal human desire.

IT'S A MYSTERY: If the surface of the main story line about human reanimation is scratched ever so slightly, it exposes more glaring plot loopholes in this episode than in any other. First of all, when and how exactly did Chris manage to steal the body of his brother? If, as Willow points out, formaldehyde destroys the brain tissue, Chris would have had to steal the body before it was preserved . . . And nobody noticed the body was missing? And Daryl is so concerned with a few facial scars that he prefers to live in a basement? Has he never heard of plastic surgery and intensive therapy?

BLOOPERS: The pictures that Eric takes of Buffy, Willow, and Cordelia could not have been the same photos he took earlier at school because none of the poses match what was seen onscreen.

OF SPECIAL NOTE: Although Sarah Michelle Gellar performs quite a bit of her own fighting, she does use stunt doubles for the more acrobatic moves. Her stunt double for the first three seasons was Sophia Crawford, who can be seen, minus the Buffy wig, as "Katya Steadman" in the "Dragonswing II" episode of *Kung Fu: The Legend Continues.*

Anthony Stewart Head now provides the narration for the brief series prologue, which also has a new score.

15. "School Hard"
(SEPTEMBER 29, 1997)

Director: John T. Kretchmer
Teleplay: David Greenwalt
Story by: Joss Whedon and David Greenwalt
Recurring cast: Andrew J. Ferchland (Colin/the Anointed One); James Marsters (Spike); Robia La Morte (Jenny Calendar); Juliet Landau (Drusilla); Armin Shimerman (Principal Snyder); Kristine Sutherland (Joyce)
Guest cast: Alan Abelew (Brian Kerch); Alexandra Johnes (Sheila)
Music: "1000 Nights" (Willow and Buffy doing homework) and "Stupid Thing" (Spike watching Buffy at the Bronze), by Nickel, from *Stupid Thing*

Plot: Not only does Buffy have to organize Parent-Teacher Night under the critical eye of Principal Snyder, she also has to contend with a new vampire in town, who is planning to make the Night of St. Vigius the Slayer's last.

THIS WEEK'S UNHOLY HOLIDAY: The Night of St. Vigius in honor of a crusading vampire who slaughtered his way across Eastern Europe and into Asia. On that night, the vampires' strength is at their greatest, and they plan to flex their momentary muscle by killing the Slayer.

INTRODUCING: "Vampires, a Love Story"—starring Buffy's new nemeses, Spike and Drusilla. Spike was known as "William the Bloody," but earned his current nickname because of his penchant for torturing victims with railroad spikes. She is emotionally and physically fragile and totally dependent on Spike. Relocating to Sunnydale from their previous home in Prague, Spike hopes the mystical energy of the Hellmouth will act as a curative and restore Drusilla's fragile health. Together they bring a sort of Goth/punk quality to the show.

ANALYSIS: the introduction of Spike and Drusilla sets up a new series arc. Although he may not be as powerful as the Master, Spike seems more dangerous because he's not as bound by tradition as the Master was. An unpredictable vampire offers a whole new set of potential risks for Buffy. Spike refers to Angel as his "sire" and "mentor," which sets the stage for later revelations about their history together—including that it was Drusilla, and not Angel, who made Spike into a vampire.

When Spike and his horde crash Parent-Teacher Night, the ensuing showdown between Buffy and Principal Snyder is powerful and revealing. Buffy is no longer the nervous student trying to appease the disapproving principal. She's his equal and then some. It's an eye-opener for Buffy's mom who like most parents, tends to see her child in the context of the family dynamic—not in how she relates as an individual to others out in the world.

Finally, the question of just who Principal Snyder is becomes even more mysterious when it's revealed that he knows the attack was by vampires and not PCP-addled gang members but conspires with the police detective to cover up the truth. Again.

THE REAL HORROR: Parent-Teacher Night. It's always just a little unnerving to have your parents meeting face-to-face with teachers who aren't terribly enamored with you. There's nothing like getting the parental "Wait until we get home" glare. Part of the uneasiness of parent-teacher conferences is that it's the collision of two worlds teenagers instinctively try to keep separate, just as many adults tend not to completely share their life at work with their spouse at home.

BLOOPERS: When Buffy takes a break to go dance, she leaves her notebook open on the table where she and Willow were studying. But when Xander returns to get Buffy a stake, the books are gone and only her bag remains.

OF SPECIAL NOTE: Mrs. Summers's name, Joyce, is spoken for the first time. Principal Snyder's first name is also mentioned for the first time—when the detective, at the end, calls him Bob.

Joss Whedon has said the decision to fry the "Annoying One" was made because a person is supposed to stop aging when they become a vampire and Andrew Ferchland was getting noticeable older and bigger.

Making their debut on *BtVS* is the band Nickel, who performs "I Did a Stupid Thing Last Night" as Spike cases the Bronze.

Throughout the first season, Buffy burning down her previous school's gym was mentioned repeatedly. But in this episode, when talking to biker-girl Sheila, Buffy indicates she has actually burned down more than one building.

16. "Inca Mummy Girl"
(OCTOBER 6, 1997)

Director: Ellen Pressman
Teleplay: Matt Kiene and Joe Reinkmeyer
Recurring cast: Seth Green (Oz); Jason Hall (Devon); Kristine Sutherland (Joyce)
Guest cast: Gil Birmingham (Inca guard); Ara Celi (Inca princess); Joey Crawford (Rodney); Samuel Jacobs (the real Ampata); Henrik Rosvall (Sven); Danny Strong (Jonathan); Kristen Winnicki (Gwen)

Plot: A mystical seal is broken, enabling a five-hundred-year-old mummified Inca princess to come to life as a beautiful sixteen-year-old. The only catch is, to stay alive she has to literally suck the life out of others. Naturally Xander falls for her, unaware of her deadly secret.

THIS WEEK'S THREAT: An Incan princess bent on reliving her lost youth. Sacrificed to a mountain god when she was just sixteen, the princess has been entrapped in her mummified form by a holy seal. Once freed, she is intent on making up for lost time—even if it means killing innocent people to keep herself from reverting to mummy form.

INTRODUCING: Oz—Sunnydale High School student by day, guitarist in a band by night. Unlike most of the boys in school, he seems singularly unimpressed with Cordelia but becomes instantly smitten with Willow when he sees her dressed as an Aleut at the Bronze's cultural-diversity dance.

ANALYSIS: Other than pouting because she has to try and find a murderous mummy instead of going to a dance honoring Sunnydale's exchange students, Buffy seems more like herself than she did in the previous Season Two episodes, although she's still prone to sudden spells of mortality-related brooding and self-pity.

More emphasis is placed on the characters' romantic lives—or lack thereof—this season, so teenage angst is more on display than it was in the first season. Not only is the group having to come to terms with the ramifications of Buffy's near-death, they are also coping with changing interpersonal dynamics caused by the tangled romantic webs they're all weaving.

Although Xander is clearly still in love with Buffy, he's also open to looking for love elsewhere. So when Ampata shows interest in him, he's thrilled; she'll never be Buffy, but she could be his. Unlike his lustful crush on Ms. French—the preying mantis of Episode 3—his feelings for Ampata are romantic and soulful, which makes the revelation that she's really a murderous five-hundred-year-old Incan princess that much more tragic.

THE REAL HORROR: Having chronically rotten taste in the opposite sex. Xander's recurring tendency to fall for the wrong girl continues with a flourish, but his plight is nothing new. Like a lot of teenagers—and adults, for that matter—he can't have who he really wants, and doesn't want who he could have, so he ends up with someone he shouldn't. He's so anxious to find someone, he rushes in without knowing who the person really is. Of course, in the world of the Slayer, this is not only emotionally frustrating, but potentially fatal as well. Once again, Whedon is heightening reality to a horrific level.

IT'S A MYSTERY: How do they explain to Ampata's family in Peru and the local authorities that she's dead and in a trunk in Buffy's room?

BLOOPERS: When the mummy's guard attacks Xander and the fake Ampata on the bleachers, her bag is kicked away during the struggle. But when she stands up to run, it's back right in front of her.

Right before killing the mummy's guard, the faux Ampata was standing at the mirror in the bathroom putting on lipstick, but later that same night she tells Buffy she has no lipstick.

The first time Buffy opens the trunk, the real Ampata's mummified head is laying on Buffy's right side. When she opens it the second time with Giles, it's on her left side.

Finally, Ampata sneaks up on Giles and grabs the seal before he's had a chance to glue the last piece of the seal back. But in the next shot, as Ampata raises the seal then throws it to the ground, it's quite clearly in one whole piece.

OF SPECIAL NOTE: Seth Green, who plays the recurring character Oz, has been acting since he was ten years old. Green's highest-profile role, to date, is as Scott Evil, the son of Austin Powers' nemesis, Dr. Evil. By the way, Seth Green is *not* related to director Bruce Seth Green.

The band that Oz and Devon belong to—Dingoes Ate My Baby—is fictional. The music they play is actually by the group Four Star Mary.

Xander apparently got his license over the summer because, for the first time, he offers to drive the gang to the Bronze.

17. "Reptile Boy"
(OCTOBER 13, 1997)

Director: David Greenwalt
Teleplay: David Greenwalt
Recurring cast: David Boreanaz (Angel)
Guest cast: Todd Babcock (Tom); Greg Vaughan (Richard); Jordana Spiro (Callie)
Music: "Bring Me On," by Act of Faith; "She," by Louie Says

Plot: Angry that Giles has become a relentless taskmaster, and hurt over Angel's reluctance to give in to his feelings for her, Buffy rebels by going to a fraternity party with Cordelia. But her attempt at retaliation backfires when she and Cordelia are drugged so they can be sacrificed to a reptile-like demon.

THIS WEEK'S RITUAL: For fifty years, a demon-worshiping fraternity annually sacrifices three girls, on the tenth day of the tenth month, to a lizard-skinned creature—in exchange for power, wealth, and professional success.

INTRODUCING: "Cordy." In the first season, Cordelia was only ever referred to as "Cordelia," but in the second season she has picked up the diminutive "Cordy," which serves two purposes: The first is to give her character more familiarity, and the other is to show her acceptance by and for Buffy and the gang. Although she is still fighting it, Cordelia now shares a bond with them, and in her own way has come to recognize their value as people and—though not exactly as *friends*—at least as partners in horror.

ANALYSIS: In the past, Buffy has pouted. She's been snappish and moody and whiny about having to go trolling for vampires instead of going out with her friends, and she's had irrational temper tantrums as a result of the post-traumatic stress of her up-close and personal encounter with the Master. But she's never pulled a bona-fide teenage rebellion before. Her insubordination provides the catalyst for growth in her relationship with Giles. The scene in which Buffy admits her deception to Giles emphasizes how their relationship has taken on a parent-child aspect: her unhappiness at disappointing him, and his admission that he pushes her because, in essence, she's so important to him and he dreads the thought of something happening to her. The episode ends with Giles protectively holding her arm as they walk up the stairs from the frat-house dungeon/basement—one of the first times they make any sustained physical contact that isn't fight-related.

"Reptile Boy" also unveils the evolution of Angel's character. When he joins forces with Giles, Willow, and Xander to save Buffy, Angel's full acceptance by the others is confirmed. But he's still keeping his emotional distance. When Buffy finally confronts him about it, he tells her he's afraid to lose control. Her line about wanting to die when he kisses her has been interpreted to mean: (1) she wants to die from ecstasy; (2) she wants to die from sadness, knowing they can't ever be together; (3) she wants to literally die and join him as his eternal mate; or (4) a combination of all of the above. Whatever the correct answer, the bottom line is, she's got it bad and that ain't good.

THE REAL HORROR: Getting caught in a *really* big lie. There are few things more mortifying than having a carefully crafted lie blow up in your face. There is nowhere to hide, and anything you say just makes matters worse, because it is indefensible. Most teenagers lie to go somewhere, see someone, or do something they know—because it's either dangerous, or has been, or would be—is forbidden. So, when caught, the crime isn't just the lie, but the irresponsibility of putting oneself in an unwarranted situation. In the real world, that might end with a girl being drugged and getting date-raped. But in Sunnydale, the consequences can be decidedly more fatal.

OF SPECIAL NOTE: Greg Vaughan, who plays creepy frat-boy Richard, co-starred with Charisma Carpenter on the series *Malibu Shores*, as her romantic interest on the show.

18. "Halloween"
(OCTOBER 28, 1997)

Director: Bruce Seth Green
Teleplay: Carl Ellsworth
Recurring cast: Seth Green (Oz); Juliet Landau (Drusilla); James Marsters (Spike)
Guest cast: Robin Sachs (Ethan Rayne); Larry (Larry Bagby III)
Music: "Shy," by Epperley; "How She Died," Treble Charger

Plot: Halloween takes a terrifying new twist when make-believe becomes reality. This is particularly bad news for Buffy, who is suddenly a defenseless eighteenth-century noblewoman: an opportunistic event not lost on Spike, who sets out to kill the powerless—not to mention clueless—Slayer.

THIS WEEK'S SPELL: A black-magic incantation made to the spirit of Janus turns everyone into the real-life incarnation of their Halloween costume. Janus is the two-faced Roman deity that represents opposites such as good and evil.

INTRODUCING: Ethan Rayne, a shopkeeper who shares a mysterious connection to Giles that dates back to his pre-Sunnydale days.

ANALYSIS: This episode inventively incorporates a holiday into a story line that actually maintains the character and context of the series. When

Ethan casts a spell through the two-faced deity Janus, he's releasing the inner fantasies of those who bought costumes in his shop. Xander, who feels emasculated after Buffy saves him from being punched out by a bully, dresses up as a commando. Buffy, on the other hand, dreams of being someone whose biggest worries are cosmetic and not supernatural, so she pretends to be a noblewoman from the 1700s.

Buffy's tendency to use brute force over diplomacy is highlighted when she smashes Larry, the bully bothering Xander, into the soda machine. Buffy tends not to be conflicted about the use of force; in fact it's become second nature to her, which is good when patrolling for vampires in the dead of night, but not always appropriate for social situations.

The biggest surprise of the episode comes courtesy of the "B" story line, when Giles confronts Ethan and it's revealed they know each other from the past. The final shot of Giles in the now-empty costume shop, reading a note left by Ethan that indicates he'll be back, is the precursor for a future revelation about Giles's past.

THE REAL HORROR: Getting what you wish for. It's better to play the hand you're dealt, because along with granted wishes usually come unexpected consequences. Beyond that, it's depressing to discover that living out a situation we've fantasized about for a long time seldom lives up to our expectations.

For Buffy, the irony is that her wish—to be an eighteenth-century girl whose sole job is to be dainty and pretty—actually turns out to be a turnoff for Angel because that's exactly the kind of girl Angel *isn't* attracted to.

BLOOPERS: When they are reading the Watcher's diary, Willow mentions that the excerpt is from when Angel is eighteen years old. Since we know he is now 241, that means he was born in 1756. So he would have been eighteen in 1774. However, when she becomes the noblewoman, Buffy says the year is 1775. Since one must assume that in her fantasy she was the noblewoman from the diary, she's off by a year—but who's counting?

And, if vampires can only enter a home when invited, why was a vampire able to sneak into Buffy's house through the kitchen door?

OF SPECIAL NOTE: Robin Sachs, who plays the up-to-no-good Ethan, is known to *Babylon 5* fans for two separate roles—Hedron and Na'Kal. And who can forget his performance in the movie *Vampire Circus?*

This episode set the stage for a future romantic liaison between Cordy and Xander. Creator Whedon admits that the idea of pairing up Xander and Cordy as a Sunnydale "odd couple" had been discussed for this episode but, since the potential plot twist was leaked by *TV Guide*, it was delayed.

19. "𝕷𝖎𝖊 𝖙𝖔 𝕸𝖊"
(NOVEMBER 3, 1997)

Director: Joss Whedon
Teleplay: Joss Whedon
Recurring cast: Robia La Morte (Jenny Calendar); Juliet Landau
   (Drusilla); James Marsters (Spike)
Guest cast: Jason Behr (Billy "Ford" Fordham); Julia Lee
   (Chantarelle); Jarrad Paul (Marvin); Will Rothhaar (James)

Plot: A onetime classmate—and object of Buffy's fifth-grade desire—shows up unexpectedly in Sunnydale. But it turns out his visit is neither social nor neighborly. Instead he's in town to trade Buffy's life for vampirish immortality.

THIS WEEK'S ANTAGONIST: The past. Buffy lets her affection for an old school crush blind her to his sinister motives. And one of Angel's cruelest deeds is finally coming back to haunt him—and puts Buffy at risk.

INTRODUCING: The darkest side of Angel's dark days as a vampire. It turns out that Angel isn't only personally acquainted with Spike, but he also has a history with the childlike Drusilla. Well, "childlike" if it's the child from *The Bad Seed.*

ANALYSIS: Everybody seems to be having trust issues in this episode. When Billy "Ford" Fordham shows up unexpectedly in Sunnydale, Xander finds someone else to be threatened by, while Angel instinctively doesn't trust him. Of course Buffy is too busy catching up with her old friend Ford, and using him to make Angel jealous, to notice something isn't quite right.

When Buffy discovers Ford's murderous motives, her moral indignation is briefly tempered by his reason for doing it: Rather than die an excruciating death from brain cancer, he would rather sell his soul and stay alive. But Ford still brings Buffy up short. Up until the moment Ford told her he was dying, she had gone around killing vampires without a moment of internal conflict. But Ford is no demon—at least not yet. He is scared and angry and desperate; not too dissimilar from Buffy when she thought she was going to die at the hands of the Master. Even though she's right that we always have a choice, sometimes both options suck.

The final scene between Buffy and Giles—where he tells her that life only ever gets more complicated and less uncertain—establishes that the Watcher is now as much a confidant as he is Slayer coach. He's the one adult Buffy can turn to for guidance, a role her parents simply can't fill.

THE REAL HORROR: Discovery of the gray zone. At some point we are all introduced to the reality that most of life plays itself out in shades of gray, and not absolutes, and that situations don't always have a happy ending. Children who grow up in poverty or in deteriorating inner cities tend to lose their innocence at such a tender age, that permanent hopelessness settles into the gaping void left by premature disillusionment. But for others, the jolting realization that life is a lot more complex and ambiguous than was previously thought, usually occurs during the teen years.

Teenagers tend to think that once they become adults, most of the troubles they face will automatically be solved. The law says adults can drive, drink, smoke, have sex, stay out all night, wear what they want, eat what they want—all without parental permission. But what never seems to be explained, or perhaps understood, is that passing through childhood into adulthood simply means exchanging one set of problems and obstacles for another, and the adult version is a much harder game to play. While there's nobody telling us what to do, there's also nobody to really fall back on. We're stuck with the consequences of our own choices, which are made all the harder because—the more life we experience, the more we realize that right and wrong, honestly and deceit, moral certitude and ambivalence, love and infidelity, good and evil, can co-exist and often do—it all comes down to a matter of degree.

Charting our individual moral grounds, and establishing our requirements of others, is part of life. But the disturbing part is knowing that no choice comes with a guarantee that what we're doing is absolutely the right thing.

BLOOPERS: When Buffy is fighting the vampire in the alley, the length of her hair changes noticeably from one shot to the next. Perhaps this isn't exactly a blooper, but it wasn't fine filmmaking, either. While it's a given that Buffy possesses supernatural physical agility and strength, she's never been

LESSER-KNOWN EVIL CREATURES

When you live on a Hellmouth, all sorts of uninvited guests tend to pop into town. Below are some of the less commonly known monsters who may show up someday in Sunnydale.

An *Alp* is a German demon that can take the form of cats, dogs, birds, and even pigs. Whatever its appearance, it always wears a hat and drinks blood from a person's nipples.

Ashtaroth is usually depicted as an ugly demon riding a dragon and carrying a viper in his left hand. In addition to being the treasurer of Hell, he was also the Grand Duke of its western regions. He encouraged sloth and idleness.

Asmodeus kept very busy as the demon of lust. He has three heads—a bull's, a ram's, and a man's. Not coincidentally, these three creatures were considered to be the most sexually lecherous creatures in the animal kingdom. Using the same line of thinking, he had the feet of a rooster.

A *bajang* takes the appearance of a cat and threatens children. However, a bajang can be captured and turned into a demon-servant and kept in the family for generation after generation.

The *Baobhan Sith* is an evil Scottish fairy, who appears as a beautiful woman and dances with men until they are totally exhausted, and then eats them.

Beelzebub is one of the powerful seraphim—the highest order of angels—first recruited by Satan. Once he switched sides, his specialty was tempting people with pride. He became associated with flies because he sent a plague of them to Canaan.

Belial is the demon of lies and is also immortalized in Milton's *Paradise Lost*.

Bruxsas are Portuguese demons that have characteristics of both a vampire and a werewolf.

Cambions are the offspring of incubi and succubi.

An *incubus* is the male version of a succubus.

Mephistopheles is famous as the demon summoned by Faust, who wanted to be granted immense power. Mephistopheles fulfilled all of Faust's desires on the con- dition that at some point, Faust would owe him one. When payback time came, all that was left of Faust was his torn and blood- ied corpse, his soul having gone to Mephistopheles in Hell.

A *rakshasa* is an Indian vampire, which appears human with animal fea- tures, usually those of a tiger. In addition to drinking the blood of their victims, they also eat the flesh.

Strigoiuls are a kind of vampire that likes to hunt in groups.

Succubi are interesting vampirelike creatures. Female, the succubus usually subsists by having sex with the victim until he's exhausted, then feeding on the energy released during the erotic encounter. They can enter homes uninvited and can take on the appearance of other persons. And they will often visit the same victim repeatedly with the victim experiencing the visits as dreams, like an alien abduction.

able to defy gravity before so noticeably. At the Sunset Club, as the vampires are beginning their feast, Buffy jumps from the ground floor to the balcony like a chop-socky Michael Jordan. The feat is so implausible, and the wirework so obvious, that it detracts from the drama of the moment.

OF SPECIAL NOTE: Juliet Landau, who plays Drusilla, is the daughter of *Mission Impossible* star Martin Landau, who won an Oscar for playing Bela Lugosi, the original Dracula, in Tim Burton's film, *Ed Wood*.

The actor portraying Dracula in the movie playing at the Sunset Club is Jack Palance, who would go on to win an Oscar for *City Slickers*.

20. "The Dark Age"
(NOVEMBER 10, 1997)

Director: Bruce Seth Green
Teleplay: Dean Batali and Rob Des Hotel
Recurring cast: Robia La Morte (Jenny Calendar)
Guest cast: Carlease Burke (Detective Winslow); Stuart McLean (Philip Henry); Robin Sachs (Ethan Rayne); Wendy Way (Dierdre)

Plot: As a rebellious youth in London, Giles and a group of friends dabbled in black magic. Now their old demon playmate is in Sunnydale looking to kill the last two survivors of the group—and is using Ms. Calendar's body to do it.

THIS WEEK'S DEMON: Eyghon—a demon of Estruscan origin, it is also called "the sleepwalker" because it can only exist on Earth by possessing someone who is unconscious or dead.

INTRODUCING: Giles's demons—inner *and* outer.

ANALYSIS: Up to now, the only inner demons Buffy has fought have been her own. But in order to defeat Eyghon, she also has to battle Giles's guilt and self-recrimination over bringing the demon into Earth's realm, through his experimentation with black magic twenty years earlier.

Their conversation at the end brings a momentary role reversal—Buffy acting as Giles's confidante and offering understanding solace, while Giles bares his soul and acknowledges his regret over not being able to live up to Buffy's expectations. Of all the consequences of Giles's youthful stupidity— his friends' deaths; Ms. Calendar being possessed by a pointy-eared demon; Ethan endowing Buffy with the lethal mark of Eyghon and the complete trashing of his apartment—the thing that seems to weigh on him most heavily is the overall sense of letting Buffy down, both as a Watcher and in a parental sense.

Buffy, however, has learned a few lessons of her own. She hasn't always made the best choices, or been the standard-bearer of model behavior, and in the process has put those closest to her at mortal risk. But just as Xander and Willow forgave her at the end of "When She Was Bad" (Episode 13), tacitly letting her know that real friends allow room for error, Buffy reassures Giles that the lowering of his pedestal a notch has actually strengthened their bond and made her feel that much closer to him.

THE REAL HORROR: Realizing adults don't have a clue, either. When you're little, the adults you hold in the greatest esteem seem to have all the answers. And if there's something they don't know—like how a caterpillar turns into a butterfly—they can go look up the answer in a book.

Then comes the inevitable moment when you find out that not only have they done some pretty stupid things in their life and that if they don't have the answers for their own lives they're certainly not going to have them for you. And these are the people running the world!

Buffy's momentary disillusionment with Giles, his shame over what he's done, and his remorse over the sense he's been lessened in Buffy's eyes, is a scenario that plays out in real life on a daily basis. The ramifications of such a fall from grace can range from mild recrimination to a permanent rift. But usually people accept such revelations first with disappointment, followed by a period of awkwardness, then, finally, reluctant acceptance of the fact that even those we look up to most, can be just as unsure and imperfect as we are.

BLOOPERS: It's amazing Cordelia was able to tell the others that the police were talking to Giles about a homicide, since that fact was never mentioned in Cordelia's presence. She entered the library after Detective Winslow told Giles about the death.

OF SPECIAL NOTE: We now know Giles is forty-one. He has said several times he's known Ethan for twenty years, and told the police he knew the dead guy twenty years ago. Confessing his past to Buffy, he told her he was twenty-one when he encountered Eyghon.

21. "What's My Line? (Part I)"

(NOVEMBER 17, 1997)

Director: David Solomon
Teleplay: Howard Gordon and Marti Noxon
Recurring cast: Seth Green (Oz); Juliet Landau (Drusilla); James
    Marsters (Spike); Armin Shimerman (Principal Snyder)
Guest cast: Kelly Connell (Norman Pfister); Saverio Guerra (Willy);
    Bianca Lawson (Kendra); Eric Saiet (Dalton);

*Plot: Tired of Buffy's meddling, Spike contacts a sect of bounty hunters to
kill her once and for all. But in addition to the Slayer hit men, there's also a
new girl in town, who claims that she, too, is a Slayer.*

THIS WEEK'S EVIL CLAN: Three members of the Order of Taraka, a
group of human and nonhuman bounty hunters who continue to send members until their quarry is dead. Apparently these killers are so fearsome, even
vampires fear them.

INTRODUCING: Kendra, the *other* vampire Slayer.
Oz finally gets introduced to his "mystery girl" when they are the only two
students at Sunnydale High interviewed by the world's largest software company as part of Career Week.

ANALYSIS: For the most part, Buffy's angst over her lot in life, and the
occasional broody or self-pitying anger it ignites, has fit in the given context
in which it was displayed. However, in this episode, it seems as if the petu-
lance is being forced, which results in Buffy coming across as if in the throes
of a particularly bad case of PMS. "Moody and broody" is more in keeping
with Buffy's character as developed than bitchiness is, which is exactly why
her 'tude in "When She Was Bad" (Episode 13) is so effective.
Using the plot point of the school's Career Week as the reason for her
churlish behavior seems incongruous, especially since, last we saw Buffy and
Giles together, she was comforting him over his Eyghon experience. The
unevenness of the characterization seems more related to direction than the
actual written dialogue.
This episode features a Kodak *"Beauty and the Beast"* moment for star-

crossed lovers Buffy and Angel. After he is injured helping stave off the first bounty hunter, Angel tells Buffy he's uncomfortable having her touch him when he's vamped out. She says she didn't even notice, leading to a passionate Slayer-vampire kissfest.

Watching this intimate moment is a mystery girl, who later announces she's Kendra the vampire Slayer and the stage is set for Buffy to have a full-blown identity crisis.

THE REAL HORROR: Realizing you're not just paranoid—everybody really *is* out to get you. In Slayerdom, that means bounty hunters and terminal consequences; but in the heightened reality that is high school, with its insular social community, the effect can sometimes feel just as deadly. Like that numbing moment when you realize a former friend is spreading vicious stories about you—especially if they're true—or when you fall out of favor with a certain clique and become the object of their contempt.

Adults can also readily empathize with Buffy's feeling of isolation and persecution. Ex-spouses sometimes discover that once the marriage is over, people they had thought were friends, have taken sides in the breakup and turned against them. And in the back-stabbing corporate world, workers who steal credit for others' work in hopes of leapfrogging past them on the promotion ladder are as plentiful as members of Sunnydale's vampire community.

While the problem sometimes resolves itself, more often than not it requires confrontation, which is an entirely different horror.

IT'S A MYSTERY: How did Kendra know where Angel lives? And how was Willow able to stay out all night, if her parents are so strict that she's not even allowed to have male friends in her bedroom?

BLOOPERS: When the door of the bus carrying one of the bounty hunters opens, the camera zooms in on the steps, which are initially white but then suddenly turn maroon as the bounty hunter's foot comes into frame.

OF SPECIAL NOTE: Bianca Lawson, who plays Slayer number two, has co-starred on two series—*Goode Behavior* with Sherman Hemsley, and as Megan Jones on *Saved by the Bell: The New Class.*

22. "What's My Line? (Part II)"
(NOVEMBER 24, 1997)

Director: David Semel
Teleplay: Marti Noxon
Recurring cast: Seth Green (Oz); Juliet Landau (Drusilla); James
    Marsters (Spike)
Guest cast: Kelly Connell (Norman Pfister); Saverio Guerra (Willy);
    Bianca Lawson (Kendra); Danny Strong (Jonathan, student held
    hostage by assassin)

*Plot: Buffy must save herself from the Order of Taraka assassins, and save
Angel from Spike, who is planning to kill Angel during a ceremony that will
give back Drusilla her strength. Complicating matters is the second Slayer,
who goes strictly by the rules, which includes killing vampires, not saving—
or dating—them.*

THIS WEEK'S EVIL CEREMONY: An ailing vampire can be restored to
health by performing the ritual the night of the first moon which requires
killing the sick vamp's sire.

INTRODUCING: Xander and Cordelia's first kiss; Willow's and Giles's
first kills; Drusilla's first moment back at full vampire strength; the Slayer's
Handbook.

ANALYSIS: This episode took a giant leap in character development,
beginning with Buffy's new appreciation for her role as the Slayer. Ever since
she arrived in Sunnydale, Buffy has moaned and groaned how being a Slayer
has put a crimp in her other life. But when the prospect of not being the
Slayer arises, Buffy suddenly realizes it's not a job she can just walk away
from—it's part of who she is, for better or worse.

Kendra, the Slayer-in-waiting, makes Buffy realize that her calling is an
honor, not a sentence of drudgery. Compared to Kendra—who was given up
by her parents as a young child so she could train full-time to be a Slayer,
without the distractions of family or school—Buffy has a well-rounded life.
Through Kendra's eyes, Buffy finally sees the glass as half full: She's got

devoted friends who offer her companionship and support—and who have saved her life on many occasions.

While Kendra and Buffy were coming to terms, Xander and Cordelia were going through some changes of their own. After a close encounter of the "yuck" kind with a gruesome grub monster, Cordy and Xander's customary bickering leads to an unexpected but very passionate kiss. Believing they were just carried away by the stress and terror of the moment, they sweep the incident aside—although it's apparent this love connection will be continued in future episodes.

During the final confrontation in the church with Spike and the assassins, the killing isn't left only to Buffy this time. Although Xander accidentally killed a vampire in the past (his friend Jesse in the second half of Episode 1, "Welcome to the Hellmouth"), most of the killing has been at the hands of Buffy. But in the church, Xander, Cordelia, Giles, and Willow all participate in the Slayage.

THE REAL HORROR: Being replaced. Nobody likes feeling dispensable. For adults, the most glaring example is in the workplace, where employees who suddenly lose their jobs often fall into deep depressions spurred by feelings of worthlessness.

In high school, emotions are much more fragile and the slightest slight can result in a traumatic crisis. Kids who suddenly fall out of a group's favor slink around, social pariahs, their confidence and self-worth dramatically shaken. And nearly everybody has experienced the nauseating pain of being dumped by a boyfriend or girlfriend in favor of someone else. When we are replaced, whether it be in a job, as a friend, as a lover, or even as teacher's pet, the message is clear: We don't matter enough; we're not worth the care.

In Buffy's case, the prospect of being replaced as the Slayer goes to her fundamental, care being. It's not just what she does, it's a integral part of what makes her Buffy. Without that center, her purpose and direction in life would suddenly be uprooted.

IT'S A MYSTERY: How did Kendra's parents *know* their daughter was a Slayer-in-waiting? Are there other Slayer schools elsewhere in the world? And why did Kendra's accent, presumed to be Caribbean, occasionally sound Irish?

BLOOPERS: Early in the episode, Spike talks about how the ceremony has to take place the night of the full moon. But later Giles says the ceremony takes places on the night of the new moon. A new moon and full moon are not the same thing—and happen on different days of the month.

OF SPECIAL NOTE: Buffy's crack to Kendra about making sure not to watch the in-air movie if it stars Chevy Chase is amusing, considering Sarah made a brief appearance in Chase's dreadful 1988 film *Funny Farm*, playing one of many students in a classroom.

23. "Ted"
(DECEMBER 8, 1997)

Director: Bruce Seth Green
Teleplay: David Greenwalt and Joss Whedon
Recurring cast: Robia La Morte (Jenny Calendar); Kristine Sutherland (Joyce Summers)
Guest cast: Jeff Langton (vampire #2); Jeff Pruitt (vampire #1); James G. MacDonald (Detective Stein) John Ritter (Ted Buchanan) Ken Thorley (Neal)

Plot: Buffy's mother has a new beau, Ted. Although to everyone else he's Mr. Wonderful, Buffy's Slayer sense tells her there's something very wrong about Ted—but nobody will believe her. So when an altercation with Ted leads to tragedy, Buffy becomes an outcast even among her family and friends.

THIS WEEK'S ANTAGONIST: The perfect man. He's a gourmet cook, he washes dishes, he's attentive, he's romantic, he's gainfully employed, he's committed . . . In other words, he's just *way* too good to be true. And because he's everything to everyone, he's a far more insidious adversary than any of the monsters or undead creatures Buffy has previously encountered.

INTRODUCING: Joyce Summers as a sexual being. Up until now, Buffy's mom has been presented as a harried, mostly absent single parent whose chief function is to remind Buffy that if she screws up in Sunnydale, there won't be another chance. But with the introduction of a love interest, Joyce's character becomes more complex as she is torn between the desire for a relationship with Ted, and love and loyalty to her daughter.

ANALYSIS: Although they don't realize it, Joyce and Buffy have a lot more in common than is first apparent. Both of them are lonely and yearn for romance in their life. Buffy doesn't think she'll ever get it because of her life as the Slayer, and because the only guy she's interested in happens to be a vampire. Joyce worries that she may never experience love again because of age, work obligations, and being a single parent.

The final scene between Buffy and her mom reveals a new understanding between them, as if Joyce suddenly sees her daughter as an insightful person whose intuition shouldn't be so quickly dismissed. And Buffy appreciates the fact that her mother is also a woman who can make bad decisions out of a desire to have some romance in her life—something Buffy can relate to.

The rekindling of the romance between Giles and Jenny is a nice counterpoint to Joyce's bad choice in androids. Unlike the perfect Ted, Giles often falls short, but it's his genuineness that ultimately brings Ms. Calendar back around.

THE REAL HORROR: The prospect of stepparents. Even in the most stable households, family dynamics are a tricky and fragile thing. But when a single parent introduces a new person into the equation in the form of a lover or spouse, it can turn into an explosive situation as everybody tries to figure out the new parameters such an arrangement brings.

In Buffy's case, it's not just that the unspoken desire to see her parents back together is made less likely by the appearance of her mother's new boyfriend; it's that the whole hierarchy of her home life is being turned upside down. Instead of being answerable to just her mother and father, she's being put in the position of having to be accountable to a virtual stranger. It's an invasion and a threat. By usurping Joyce's parental authority, Ted is also creating a wedge between mother and daughter as part of a divide-and-conquer strategy.

While younger children may adjust more easily to a new authority figure in the house, teenagers, who are in the midst of striving for independence as it is, are more likely to resist a situation where they suddenly have one more person telling them what to do. Their predicament is often made worse by the natural parent being reluctant to cause any tension in the new relationship, just as Joyce defers to Ted when it comes to Buffy.

The episode also touches, very lightly, on the reality of abuse by stepparents or live-in lovers. Again, out of a desire not to lose the relationship, some parents—especially women who need the financial support of their partners—may turn a blind eye to physical or emotional abuse against their children, rationalizing it as "discipline." However, in Buffy's case, she was able to turn the tables on Ted, and turn him into a pile of short-circuitry.

IT'S A MYSTERY: When did Sunnydale build a miniature golf course? During Season Two's first episode, "When She Was Bad" (Episode 13), Willow comments that there's not even a miniature golf course in town.

BLOOPERS: During the first confrontation in Buffy's bedroom with Ted, after she smacks him back, her diary is laying on the floor in the middle of the doorway in one shot, but disappears in the next.

OF SPECIAL NOTE: After Buffy first meets Ted, she vents her anger on the next vampire she encounters in the cemetery by beating him senseless before staking him. This vampire was played by Jeff Pruitt, who suffered an injured hand after Sarah whacked him with the lid the of the garbage can.

24. "Bad Eggs"
(JANUARY 12, 1998)

Director: David Greenwalt
Teleplay: Marti Noxon
Recurring cast: Kristine Sutherland (Joyce Summers); Jonathan (Danny Strong)
Guest cast: Brie McCaddin (girl at mall); James Parks (Tector Gorch); Jeremy Ratchford (Lyle Gorch); Eric Whitmore (school security guy); Rick Zieff (Mr. Whitmore)

Plot: As if it's not bad enough that there's two new cowboy vampires in town, Buffy has to play single mother to an egg as part of an class assignment on responsibility. But when the eggs turn out to be from a Hellmouth creature, Buffy suddenly finds herself facing an opponent even scarier than vampires—and a lot more gross.

THIS WEEK'S ADVERSARIES: In addition to the Gorch brothers, Lyle and Tector, two low-rent cowboy vampires who were into massacring Mexican villagers even before they were undead, the Hellmouth has belched up the *bazor*, a prehistoric demon parasite that uses its larva to possess its human host.

INTRODUCING: The brighter side of Angel. Compared to his somber mood of the past, Angel is positively giddy in this episode. Ah, young love . . . relatively speaking. The only moment Angel turns somber is when the topic of Buffy one day wanting children is brought up. But other than that, he's like a 241-year-old teenager in love.

ANALYSIS: "Bad Eggs" is mostly a poor man's homage to the classic science-fiction film *Invasion of the Body Snatchers*. In that film, a man discovers that something from inside what looks like giant pea pods is taking over people's bodies and minds. The possessed person becomes devoid of emotion and follows the command of an unseen force.

This episode is merely a Hellmouth version of the same story, but has a much happier ending than any of the film versions. In those films, it appears there's no way to stop the loss of our humanity, whereas in this episode Buffy manages to kill the bazor and restore everyone's personalities and selves.

In a way, this episode may have been much stronger had it concentrated on the loss-of-self aspect, with those closest to Buffy turning into deadly strangers, rather than diluting it with the rather weak story line involving the Gorches, who appeared to be there mostly for comic relief. For a series that has horror at its core, neither element was developed for enough to generate any real sense of threat or danger and all the characters seemed to be merely going through the motions.

THE REAL HORROR: Responsibility, and all it entails. The irony of Buffy being saddled with an egg-baby is that she's already assuming the ultimate responsibility for keeping the world safe from vampires, specifically, and evil in general. However, the eggs are used as a metaphor for all the types of responsibilities teenagers must assume as they make the transition into adults. For Buffy, it means juggling her mother's expectations with her secret life as the Slayer, as well as not completely losing her head over Angel.

IT'S A MYSTERY: When Buffy and Angel are talking about children, he tells her he can't have kids. She responds by noting there are probably lots of things a vampire can't do. However, as noted previously in this book (see Chapter 3), according to vampire mythology, vampires can indeed have children. The offspring of a vampire and a human is called a *dhampir*. Traditionally, the father is a vampire and the mother human and the child is usually male. So either the writer made a glaring vampire-lore error, or it was intended to mean that Angel in particular can't have children, or that he doesn't *think* he can. He finds out later he can, after he sires a child with Darla on the spin-off series *Angel*.

BLOOPERS: When the girl in the mall is playing pinball in the closed arcade, her handbag moves up and down her arm from shot to shot.

OF SPECIAL NOTE: The names of the characters Tector and Lyle Gorch were taken from characters in Sam Peckinpah's film, *The Wild Bunch*.

25. "Surprise"
(JANUARY 19, 1998)

Director: Michael Lange
Teleplay: Marti Noxon
Recurring cast: Seth Green (Oz); Robia La Morte (Jenny); Kristine Sutherland (Joyce Summers)
Guest cast: Juliet Landau (Drusilla); James Marsters (Spike); Eric Saiet (Dalton); Vincent Schiavelli (Gypsy uncle); Brian Thompson (the Judge)
Music: "Anything" by Cari Howe; "Transylvanian Concubine," by Rasputina

Plot: It's Buffy's birthday and everyone seems to have a surprise for her. Angel professes his love, the gang throws her a surprise party, and Drusilla is back with a vengeance—and an itch to annihilate the world.

THIS WEEK'S HORROR: A revitalized Drusilla. In honor of her reacquired health, Dru is planning a coming-out party that will wreak horror and destruction on the world.

INTRODUCING: Jenny Calendar's true identity. She is Jana, a member of the Gypsy tribe who put the curse on Angel that restored his soul, after he killed their most beloved daughter.

ANALYSIS: The series takes a giant dark turn beginning with this episode. Up until this point in the season, the overall tenor of *Buffy* has been relatively light, once Buffy was able to put her trauma over the Master to rest. But her suddenly disturbing dreams, in which she sees Drusilla killing Angel, are portents of an end to the relative calm that had been hovering over Sunnydale.

In a surprising revelation, Jenny Calendar turns out to be much more than she seems, and is not in Sunnydale by accident. Originally sent to keep an eye on Angel, Jenny now finds herself torn between what her people expect of her, and what in her heart she knows to be true. Her Gypsy uncle is unmoved by Jenny's pleas on Angel's behalf—he objects that to honor the girl Angel killed, even one moment of happiness for him is too much.

That moment happens after Buffy and Angel narrowly escape being charbroiled. Their brush with death emboldens Buffy, and she and Angel make love. The final scene, where Buffy is sleeping in pure contentment while Angel is propelled out into the street in searing agony, sets the stage for the next phase of their relationship.

THE REAL HORROR: Juggling fear of loss with sexual responsibility. Now that Buffy has found the person she believes to be her true love, she lives in terror of losing Angel because, like any teenager experiencing their first true romantic love, she can't imagine ever feeling this way again about someone. In Buffy's case, there's the added element that the future, and whether she'll even have one, is a huge unknown. Although she doesn't *want* to be careless or irresponsible, she also knows that as the Slayer, she truly might not live to see another day.

In her dreams she sees Angel killed, and so the fear uppermost in her mind is his loss of existence. It doesn't occur to her that Angel could be lost to her in another way: that the person she has fallen in love with—the *soul* she has fallen in love with—could change.

IT'S A MYSTERY: Since when is Sunnydale a port city with cargo ships sailing in and out?

What exactly does "one moment of true happiness" mean? This has been hotly debated, but the initial assumption that the phrase was euphemistic for "orgasm" was dispelled by David Greenwalt in an interview, who explained that Angel could have sex, but it was only by making love with his true love and soul mate—Buffy—that Angel would to lose his soul. Which is why Angel could sleep with Darla on *Angel* and retain his soul.

BLOOPERS: In the dream sequence, the monkey switches directions as the scenes cut back and forth between Willow and Buffy.

OF SPECIAL NOTE: Although Mercedes McNab, who plays Cordelia's snotty friend Harmony, is listed in the opening credits, she doesn't appear in this episode because her scene was cut. According to Joss Whedon, "Mercedes was in a scene where Cordy and Xander try to broach the idea of dating to their friends. Cordy mentions him to Harmony, who looks and sees him dancing like a fool for Willow. We were running long, it's gone, but Mercedes is back soon."

Joss Whedon's name is now "above the title" during on-air promotions: *Joss Whedon's Buffy the Vampire Slayer.*

26. "Innocence"
(JANUARY 20, 1998)

Director: Joss Whedon
Teleplay: Joss Whedon
Recurring cast: Seth Green (Oz); Robia La Morte (Jenny Calendar); Kristine Sutherland (Joyce Summers)
Guest cast: Ryan Francis (soldier); Juliet Landau (Drusilla); James Lurie (teacher); Carla Madden (woman); James Marsters (Spike); Vincent Schiavelli (Gypsy uncle); Parry Shen (student); Brian Thompson (the Judge)

Plot: Angel and Buffy consummate their relationship, but the joy Angel experiences has disastrous consequences. Willow discovers the truth about Xander's relationship with Cordelia. Jenny and Giles become estranged after he learns her true identity.

THIS WEEK'S NEMESIS: The Judge, an ancient demon who had been conjured "to rid the earth of the plague of humanity," as the vampires like to say. The Judge was so powerful, he could not be killed. An army eventually subdued him and dismembered him, burying his different parts in various far reaches of the world.

INTRODUCING: Angelus—you've heard about him! Now meet the vampire evil enough to have sat at the right hand of the Master, who makes even Spike look like a good-natured evil being. Also, Oz joins the inner circle.

ANALYSIS: When things go bad in Sunnydale, they *really* go bad. First, Angel has reverted to Angelus after experiencing a "moment of true happiness" while making love to Buffy. Then Willow discovers Xander and Cordelia's clandestine romance, which brings unexpressed feelings to the surface and marks an irrevocable change in their friendship.

Most of the episode deals with Buffy's confusion over Angel's sudden disappearance after their night of passion. As confident as she is about her Slayer skills, she wears her insecurities about her sexual inexperience on her sleeve. She needs to be reassured by Angel, and when she can't find him, she becomes increasingly vulnerable emotionally. When she finally tracks down Angel at his apartment, she finds him cool and aloof—and cruel. The encounter leaves Buffy the lowest she's ever been, more demoralized even than when she was targeted by the Master.

Buffy's realization that she is the one responsible for "killing" Angel— and her inability to really kill him when she has the chance—will have painful consequences in episodes to come. When, later, her mother brings out a cupcake with a birthday candle on it, all Buffy can do is watch it burn down: all her wishes now gone the way of Angel's soul.

THE REAL HORROR: Loss of your first true love. In real life this happens whenever what was thought to be eternal love, turns out not to be— maybe because the couple grows apart, or one person loses interest and wants to move on. Few things are more demoralizing for teenage girls than to have their first sexual experience, only to find out the boy she gave her heart and body to, didn't really love her the way she thought he did. But in Buffy's world, Angel hasn't changed simply because he's looking for more wild oats to sow, but because he's lost his soul.

Now Buffy has to deal with two painful truths: the man she loves has literally been extinguished, and she's in part responsible for the transformation.

IT'S A MYSTERY: Does Oz have his van painted regularly or does he own a fleet of them? In the "Halloween" episode, his van was black-and-white-striped but now it's a solid color.

Just how big *is* Sunnydale? Not only is it a port city, as revealed in the previous episode, but it's also the home of a fully equipped army base.

BLOOPERS: The final shot of the previous episode had Angel kneeling in pouring rain calling for Buffy in a *Streetcar Named Desire* sort of way (reminiscent of Marlon Brando's character standing at the window screaming, "Stellaaaa!") However, at the beginning of this episode, which picks right up where the previous episode, "Surprise," left off, there's no rain to be seen. Even Angel looks dry.

Possibly the most notable blooper of the entire series takes place in this episode, the result of a major continuity gaffe. The sequence occurs this way:

After Buffy runs out of the library in despair, Xander tells the group he has a plan that requires Cordelia's help. They agree to meet at Willow's house in a half hour, where they will hook up with Oz and his van.

Cut to Buffy's bedroom. She lies on her bed and cries herself to sleep, where she dreams about seeing Angel and Jenny at a funeral and Angel saying, "You can't see what you don't know."

Next scene shows Buffy storming into Ms. Calendar's room and throttling her, demanding Jenny tell her what she knows. Buffy learns about the curse.

Then, immediately after this, comes the scene where Xander and Cordelia are at the army base stealing a missile launcher—an event supposed to have occurred the night before.

When asked about the error, Whedon owned up: "I was watching the final mix before air when I caught that *huge mistake.* No one else caught it but since I *caused* it, I get only tiny shriveled kudos. So my theory now is that he was having her come over to [Willow's house] to *practice* being a trashy army girlfriend. We'll just run with that, okay?"

OF SPECIAL NOTE: Brian Thompson, who plays the Judge, appeared in the series pilot, "Welcome to the Hellmouth," as Luke, the Master's right-hand vamp who Buffy reduced to dust during the final fight scene in the Bronze.

In a bit of synergy and advance promotion, one of the movie theaters at the mall is playing *Quest for Camelot*, which happens to be the name of an animated feature from Warner Bros. not due for release until May 1998.

The movie Buffy is watching at the end of the episode is *Stowaway*, starring Shirley Temple.

27. "Phases"
(JANUARY 27, 1998)

Director: Bruce Seth Green
Teleplay: Rob Des Hotel and Dean Batali
Recurring cast: Seth Green (Oz)
Guest cast: Larry Bagby III (Larry); Keith Campbell (werewolf); Jack

Conley (Cain); Camilla Griggs (gym teacher); Megahn Perry
(Theresa Klusmeyer)
Music: "Blind For Now," by Lotion

*Plot: A werewolf is prowling Sunnydale and Buffy needs to capture the crea-
ture and find out who it is, before the bounty hunter in town who is out gunning for it. Xander unwittingly learns a fellow student's secret. Willow is
growing impatient with Oz, who's being a bit too gentlemanly for her tastes.*

THIS WEEK'S NEMESIS: A werewolf. According to Giles's research, a
person inflicted with the curse transforms three nights a month—the night
before the full moon, the night of the full moon, and the night after the full
moon.

INTRODUCING: Willow's and Cordelia's acceptance of each other. After
weeks of tension caused by Willow's discovery of Cordelia and Xander's
romance, Willow has accepted the relationship enough to where she feels
comfortable talking to Cordelia about her frustration with Oz's apparent
reluctance to get physical.

ANALYSIS: This episode has several story-line threads running through
it. In a nice change of pace, the primary focus is on Willow and Oz, instead
of Buffy's trauma over the loss of Angel's soul and his transformation back
into Angelus, alleviating some of the intensity of the two previous episodes.

This installment makes clear how much Willow's character has grown
since the series' inception. She takes the initiative to confront Oz about why
he's hesitating with her. A year earlier, Willow never would have dreamed of
being so bold, but her association with the Slayer has given her self-
confidence. Ironically, though Oz turns out to be a werewolf, it appears Willow is going to be the more assertive partner in their relationship.

THE REAL HORROR: Teenage mood swings. It's not too far a stretch to
see Oz's transformation to a werewolf as being symbolic of the emotional ups
and downs experienced by practically all teenagers as their bodies and psy-
ches go through throes of growth that will eventually lead to adulthood. Oz,
in fact, has no more control over the change in his appearance and character
than does the teenager who one moment is a silly school kid and the next, an
angst-filled pre-adult.

Just as Oz can do nothing about his transformation except recognize the problem and learn to cope with it, teenagers can only ride the hormonal wave until it settles back down to a more manageable level.

IT'S A MYSTERY: Why Oz waited until after his second transformation to call his aunt to see if Jordy was a werewolf. Didn't he realize something was up the morning before, when he woke up somewhere outside, naked?

BLOOPERS: While trapped in Cain's net, Buffy's flashlight goes on and off throughout the scene. After Willow falls in the woods, her clothes have visible dirt stains. But when she comes into the library in the very next scene, her clothes are completely clean. Giles' glasses appear, then disappear, throughout the scene when he's preparing the tranquilizer gun.

OF SPECIAL NOTE: According to Alyson Hannigan, a scene was shot for this episode—which was later cut—where Cordelia and Willow get into a verbal catfight before turning their mutual aggression onto Xander, at which point they both hit him and knock him down. By the scene's end, Cordelia and Willow have become more bonded, which explains why Willow and Cordelia are seen commiserating in the Bronze about their respective men.

28. "Bewitched, Bothered, and Bewildered"
(FEBRUARY 10, 1998)

Director: James A. Contner
Teleplay: Marti Noxon
Recurring cast: Elizabeth Anne Allen (Amy); Seth Green (Oz); Robia La Morte (Jenny Calendar); Juliet Landau (Drusilla); James Marsters (Spike); Mercedes McNab (Harmony); Kristine Sutherland (Joyce Summers)
Guest cast: Tamara Braun (student); Jennie Chester (Kate); Jason Hall (Devon); Scott Hamm (student); Kristen Winnicki (Cordette)
Music: "Pain," by Four Star Mary; "Drift Away," by Naked; "Got the Love," by the Average White Band

Plot: After being rejected by Cordelia on Valentine's Day, Xander plots revenge. He turns to witchcraft, but his plan to make Cordelia pine after him backfires, with potentially deadly consequences.

THIS WEEK'S PREDICAMENT: Love potions—as explained by Giles, they are the most unpredictable of spells because when someone under the spell is rejected, their hurt can turn violent.

INTRODUCING: Cordelia and Xander as an official couple, and Amy (first seen in Episode 2, "The Witch") as a practicing witch.

ANALYSIS: In this episode Xander and Cordelia finally must come to grips with their feelings for each other. After dumping him to remain cool in their friends' estimation, Cordelia realizes that she's become a follower, a sheep—and being a sheep is not cool. Even though Cordelia retains some of her superficiality, she also has shown enough growth to where she is more comfortable being her own person regardless of what others think. And Xander's willingness to take on Cordelia's image-conscious baggage shows his growth, to be able to follow his heart as well.

THE REAL HORROR: Being the unwanted object of someone's desire. Although not as poignant as unrequited love, unwanted crushes can be just as difficult to deal with. How does one make it clear in a nice way that someone's romantic desire is not returned? Especially, as in the case of Xander and Willow, when the person happens to be a friend?

The case of Buffy and Angel is a darker example of unrequited obsession, with Angel in essence stalking Buffy, determined to kill her so he can have her with him forever, in the same way a jilted lover turns violent when rejected. It's hard enough for adults to deal rationally with rejected desire, but it's especially difficult for teenagers, whose emotions are heightened to begin with. Recent real-life events in which spurned students have gone on shooting rampages at their schools reflects the depth and intensity youthful obsession can reach. The love potion Xander has Amy cast is symbolic of this occasionally out-of-control hormonal state that afflicts nearly all high schoolers.

BLOOPERS: The board Xander nails onto the basement doorjamb appears to move from one shot to the next.

29. "Passion"
(FEBRUARY 24, 1998)

Director: Michael E. Gershman

Teleplay: Ty King

Recurring cast: Juliet Landau (Drusilla); Robia La Morte (Ms. Calendar); James Marsters (Spike); Kristine Sutherland (Joyce Summers)

Guest cast: Richard Assad (shop owner); Richard Hoyt Miller (policeman); Danny Strong (Jonathan)

Music: "Never an Easy Way," by Morcheeba

Plot: Angel's obsession with Buffy takes a dark and deadly turn, putting everyone around her at risk.

THIS WEEK'S ANGUISH: Regret.

INTRODUCING: The darkest side of Angel.

ANALYSIS: Of all the episodes, "Passion" is probably the most viscerally disturbing, because of the unexpected death of Jenny Calendar. Even though by now everyone knows that creator Joss Whedon has no qualms about killing off recurring characters, never before has such a *regularly* recurring character died. And seldom has a death been as upsetting, because of the prolonged chase, with Jenny running for her life from Angel.

Viewers have gotten used to seeing Buffy, Willow, Giles, Xander, and Cordelia in life-threatening situations, only to be saved at the last minute. But there will be no last-second reprieve for Jenny this time. And what makes her demise all the more poignant is that she has just begun to mend bridges with Buffy and Giles. The scene in which Giles comes home in anticipation of a romantic evening with Jenny, to find her dead body in his bed, is especially disturbing.

The shot of Angel peeking through the window, smiling at the pain he's caused, reinforces his title as "television's most evil villain."

THE REAL HORROR: Realization of mortality. Even though Buffy and her friends have seen more death than any big-city homicide detective, for the most part they were all able to maintain enough emotional distance to keep it from paralyzing them. But Jenny's death is extremely personal, especially for Buffy, who must live with the knowledge that Jenny would be alive if Buffy had followed her duty and killed Angel when she had the chance.

The permanence of death and the void left by it, is reinforced for the gang daily because suddenly Jenny isn't at her computer and can't be found walking the halls anymore. Where Jenny once *was*, now she *isn't*. And there's no bringing her back. It's similar to what happens when a class suffers the lost of a student. The empty desk serves as a reminder that the absence is forever, a concept almost innately alien to the teenage mind. However, once it does sink in, the effect can be profound because it comes with the realization that we are all subject to the whimsy of fate.

IT'S A MYSTERY: Why didn't Jenny have a cross handy to ward off Angel, knowing he could come into the school anytime he wanted?

OF SPECIAL NOTE: The singer heard during the graveyard scene is Anthony Stewart Head.

When Giles comes home and finds Jenny, Puccini is playing on the stereo.

30. "𝕶illed by 𝕯eath"
(MARCH 3, 1998)

Director: Deran Sarafian
Teleplay: Rob Des Hotel and Dean Batali
Recurring cast: Kristine Sutherland (Joyce Summers)
Guest cast: James Jude Courtney (*Der Kindestod*); Andrew Ducote (Ryan); Willie Garson (security guard); Richard Herd (Dr. Backer); Juanita Jennings (Dr. Wilkinson); Denise Johnson (Celia); Robert Munic (intern); Mimi Paley (little Buffy)

Plot: While in the hospital battle a debilitating flu and high fever, Buffy suspects a demon is killing children.

THIS WEEK'S EVIL CREATURE: *Der Kindestod*, a demon usually invisible to adults, who kills children by straddling them and literally sucking the life-breath out of them.

INTRODUCING: The budding friendship between Giles and Joyce Summers.

ANALYSIS: This episode also reinforces Xander's new role as Buffy's primary protector. Previously it was Angel who would stay behind and watch her back, but now that Angel is the enemy, Xander has filled the void.

Xander's devotion to Buffy creates conflicting emotions in Cordelia, who on one hand does care for Buffy but, on the other, doesn't like playing second fiddle to anyone. Her growth as a character—without losing that "I should be the center of the universe" Cordelia uniqueness, is particularly evident in this episode. Even though she still shows flashes of her self-centered superficiality, she also now shows that it's balanced by a sweet, caring side, enabling the viewer to understand why Xander is attracted to her.

THE REAL HORROR: Childhood illness. While unexpected, youthful death is a horror unto itself, prolonged illness is a special kind of horror because it robs a youth of the very vigor and vitality that marks childhood and the teen years. While part of Buffy's fear of the hospital was the repressed memory of seeing Celia killed, she was also reacting to the idea of being ill and not having all of her faculties to rely on. Although losing one's physical strength and capabilities would be particularly wrenching for a Slayer, it is just as frightening a thought for any flesh-and-blood teenager who inherently believes himself to be healthy and not subject to the ravages of illness.

IT'S A MYSTERY: Why is the access door to the basement located in the middle of a children's ward?

BLOOPERS: On the door to the basement, a sign reading BASEMENT ACCESS suddenly appears from one scene to the next.

In the scene in Buffy's hospital room when she sees *Der Kindestod*, the clock first reads 2:27, but later in the same scene it reads 2:15.

OF SPECIAL NOTE: James Jude Courtney, who plays the evil *Kindestod*, is also a professional stuntman. Roughly translated, *Der Kindestod* means "kid killer."

31. "I Only Have Eyes for You"
(APRIL 28, 1998)

Director: James Whitmore Jr.

Teleplay: Marti Noxon

Recurring cast: Juliet Landau (Drusilla); James Marsters (Spike); Armin Shimerman (Principal Snyder)

Guest cast: Meredith Salinger (Grace Newman); Christopher Gorham (James Stanley); John Hawkes (George); Miriam Flynn (Ms. Frank); Brian Reddy (police chief Bob); Brian Poth (fighting boy); Sarah Bibb (fighting girl); James Lurie (Mr. Miller); Ryan Taszreak (Ben); Anna Coman-Hidy (girl #1); Vanessa Bednar (girl #2).

Music: "Charge," by Splendid; "I Only Have Eyes For You," by the Flamingos

Plot: The spirit of a young man who killed his lover in a fit of passion years ago, forces Buffy to confront her guilt over the loss of Angel's soul.

THIS WEEK'S SPIRIT: A poltergeist. These spirits are frequently considered harmless ghosts who cause mischief but no real harm because they are generally believed to be the spirits of young people. There have also been reports of malevolent poltergeists. However, according to Giles, a poltergeist is someone who died with unresolved issues, too, and the only way to make the ghost go away is to resolve those issues.

INTRODUCING: The official cover-up of the Hellmouth, when it's revealed Principal Snyder and the police chief are aware of its existence. Although it was intimated in Episode 14, "School Hard," that he knew more than he was letting on, it's now clear that Snyder is fully aware of Sunnydale's evil underbelly.

Also, new digs for Dru, Spike, and Angel, since their old warehouse burned down after Giles firebombed it at the end of "Surprise" (Episode 25).

ANALYSIS: Although at first it seems this episode will simply be a ghost story, it uses the story of the student who killed his teacher/lover as a treatise on forgiveness. It also offers some intriguing parallels between Buffy and Angel and the earlier ill-fated lovers.

In an interesting twist, the ghost of the student takes over Buffy and the ghost of the teacher briefly possesses Angel. Their reenactment of the tragedy of James (in Buffy's body) and Grace (in Angel's) finally brings resolution, enabling the spirits of James and Grace to leave in peace. In a particularly touching scene, Grace/Angel tells James/Buffy that they are forgiven, and that they loved them with their dying breath. For the first time since Angel's transformation, we sense that Buffy might be ready to start forgiving herself for what happened.

The other brief story line in the episode has Dru, Angel, and Spike moving to a new residence, complete with garden. The tension between Angel and Spike is palpable. After Dru and Angel go off to feed, Spike gets up out of his wheelchair, signifying that a showdown with Angel is now inevitable.

THE REAL HORROR: Guilt. While guilt is an emotion that never dulls with age, like all passions, it seems to be felt more keenly among the uncallused hearts of teenagers. Through the story of James, Buffy finally openly confronts her guilt over having destroyed the person she loved most. Initially she is resistant to the idea that James deserves forgiveness, because Buffy doesn't feel she does.

IT'S A MYSTERY: How is it possible that Willow has been browsing Ms. Calendar's computer, when Angel smashed and burned it in Episode 29, "Passion"?

BLOOPERS: In the scene showing James prior to killing himself, he's listening to a version of "I Only Have Eyes for You" by the Flamingos, which wasn't released until 1959.

32. "Go Fish"

(MAY 5, 1998)

Director: David Semel
Teleplay: David Fury and Elin Hampton
Recurring cast: Armin Shimerman (Principal Snyder)
Guest cast: Charles Cyphers (Coach Marin); Jeremy Garrett (Cameron Walker); Wentworth Miller (Gage Petronzi); Conchata Ferrell (Nurse Greenleigh); Danny Strong (Jonathan); Shane West (Sean); Jake Patellis (Dodd McAlvy)

Plot: Buffy suspects the Sunnydale swim team is being filleted by a mysterious sea creature.

THIS WEEK'S DANGER: Better living through chemicals. An overzealous coach exposes his athletes to an experimental inhalant in hopes of improving their performance—and succeeds *too* well.

INTRODUCING: Xander as jock. In order to keep an eye on the school's quickly disappearing swimmers, Xander tries out for, and makes, the team.

ANALYSIS: One of the more lighthearted episodes, comparatively speaking. "Go Fish" doesn't do much to advance the characters or second-season story arc, but reestablishes Buffy and her gang as some of the more quick-witted high school students around. After spending most of the Season Two in a state of perpetual angst, it's nice to see Buffy back in the guise of frustrated high school student.

Buffy and the gang believe that a fishlike monster is killing off members of the swim team. But in an inventive plot twist, it turns out the boys haven't been killed by a monster, they are turning into monsters—a fact Buffy comes to understand after watching one swimmer rip open his skin to reveal a fish-man—actually, a fish-boy—underneath. She manages to escape Gage and other fish-men with the help of Coach Marin, who later claims ignorance when questioned by Giles.

This particular scene was very out of character for the series. Even though *Buffy* deals with vampires and monsters, the characters have always come across as real and their reactions to their situations have always rung true. First, the fact that the coach would be so unrattled by the discovery that his swimmers were turning into fish-boys seems incongruous. Although Giles and Buffy dwell in a world of monsters, presumably the majority of people at the school live in blissful ignorance. So the coach should have been in a state of shock or at least severe disbelief. On the other hand, his blasé reaction to the turn of events should have then immediately caused Giles to suspect Marin was in some way involved in whatever was going on.

THE REAL HORROR: A win-at-all-costs attitude. Anybody who has ever so much as attended a high school sporting event knows that pressure to win. For coaches, it may mean keeping their jobs or not. For the athletes, it's either a matter of ego, or their ticket to college. And for the school, winning means prestige and—though boosters and game attendance—money.

Although the pressure is often greatest at the collegiate level, high school athletes also can feel the heat.

Stories of performance-enhancing drugs are commonplace, so this episode merely heightens a prevalent reality of modern-day athletics.

IT'S A MYSTERY: How exactly did the coach use *steam* to impart fish DNA the athletes? And how did he have the knowledge to do so?

Since when does Sunnydale High have such direct access to the city's sewer tunnels, which apparently run directly under the school?

33. "Becoming" (Part I)
(MAY 12, 1998)

Director: Joss Whedon

Teleplay: Joss Whedon

Recurring cast: Seth Green (Oz); Juliet Landau (Drusilla); Bianca Lawson (Kendra); James Marsters (Spike); Armin Shimerman (Principal Snyder)

Guest cast: Julie Benz (Darla); Nina Gervitz (teacher); Zitto Kazann (Gypsy man); Jack McGee (Doug Perren); Max Perlich (Whistler); Richard Riehle (L.A. Watcher); Shannon Welles (Gypsy woman); Ginger Williams (girl)

Plot: The story of Angel "becoming" a vampire at the hands of Darla. Also how, as Angelus, he waged a reign of evil and terror, and how the vengeful Gypsy reinstated his soul so Angel would suffer eternal torment for his deeds, is interwoven with Buffy's determination to kill Angel once and for all.

THIS WEEK'S DEMON: Acathla, an ancient demon capable of opening up a whirlpool that draws everything in this world into the demonic reality beyond, where all nondemon life would suffer eternal torment.

INTRODUCING: Angel's biography.

ANALYSIS: By presenting Angel's full, two-hundred-years–plus story, series creator Joss Whedon is able to show Angel as both victim and criminal. Just as Buffy is conflicted in her emotions, loving the Angel that was and despising what he has now become makes for some serious dramatic conflict.

The fact that Angel eventually loses his soul because of the love he and Buffy share, makes his transformation back to Angelus a tragedy of Greek proportions. And it makes their final confrontation inevitable. There is no way Angelus can let Buffy go. They both cannot live—one must die.

Since the time of Angel's transformation, Buffy often has been portrayed as more preoccupied and less quick-witted than she was previously. The result has been to put herself and others in danger over the course of the second half of the season. But in this episode, her preoccupation and obsession with Angel finally proves fatal.

Using Angel as a decoy she knows Buffy can't resist, Drusilla ambushes the library. Xander and Willow are injured, Giles is kidnapped, and Kendra is killed by Dru, leaving Buffy to wallow in a sea of regret and guilt.

THE REAL HORROR: Not being able to turn back the hands of time. Everyone has regrets, but errors in judgment made as a teenager seem to resonate more and take on greater importance. In the world of the Slayer, errors in judgment can prove fatal, as demonstrated by Buffy's relationship with Angel.

If Buffy had it to do all over again, she wouldn't. But she can't, so now she's left to deal with the fallout of her misbegotten passion for Angel, the guy from the ultimate wrong side of the Hellmouth tracks.

IT'S A MYSTERY: All right, just how old *is* Angel? In Episode 14, "Some Assembly Required," Angel stated that he was 241 years old. And according to the Watcher diary in Episode 18, "Halloween," Angel was eighteen years old in 1775—*prior* to becoming a vampire—which means he was born around 1756. However, in this episode Angel was bitten by Darla in 1753, years before his previously established birth.

Beyond that, in Episode 7, "Angel," it was established that Angel's soul had been restored sometime in the twentieth century, circa the 1920s. However, in this episode it's revealed to have taken place in 1898.

BLOOPERS: During the scene in which he's killed by Drusilla, Doug's hand moves on and off the statue from one shot to the next.

OF SPECIAL NOTE: Julie Benz reprises her role as Darla for the first time since the "Angel" episode.

The building used for Hemery High in the flashback to 1996 is the same one used for the Hill Valley Clock Tower in the first two *Back to the Future* films.

34. "Becoming (Part II)"
(MAY 19, 1998)

Director: Joss Whedon
Teleplay: Joss Whedon
Recurring cast: Seth Green (Oz); James Marsters (Spike); Robia La
Morte (Ms. Calendar); Juliet Landau (Drusilla); Armin Shimerman
(Principal Snyder); Kristine Sutherland (Joyce Summers)
Guest cast: Max Perlich (Whistler)
Music: "Full of Grace," by Sarah McLachlan

*Plot: As Angel feverishly tries to unleash Acathla on the world, Spike reveals
a few plans of his own as he teams up with Buffy to stop world annihilation.
Meanwhile, Willow tries again to restore Angel's soul using the spell left
behind by Jenny Calendar.*

THIS WEEK'S THREAT TO HUMANITY: Angel as the instrument for
Acathla.

INTRODUCING: Joyce Summers, to the world of the Slayer. When
attacked by one of Drusilla's vamp-goons in front of her mother, while on the
run from the police who suspect her in Kendra's death, Buffy is forced to
stake the vampire and finally reveals to Joyce her real identity as the Slayer.

REINTRODUCING: Angel with soul. Briefly.

ANALYSIS: One of the biggest dramatic questions of the Season Two
was how to restore Angel's soul and maintain the integrity of the series. Considering all he had done since losing it, not the least of which was killing
Jenny Calendar, it seemed as if the series had backed itself into corner.
  If Angel had anguished over what he had done to strangers the first time
his soul was restored, how would he ever be able to face Buffy and the others,
especially Giles, now? And even if everyone could get over that hurdle, how
could Angel and Buffy ever pick up where they left off, knowing that it was
their love that had unleashed the demon inside him in the first place?
  Talk about no-win situations! Whereas the first season's villain, the Master, was someone everyone could agree on hating, this season was more com-

plex. Even though Drusilla is bad to the bone, she was made insane by Angel. Although Spike had no loyalties but to himself and Drusilla, it turns out he had no more desire to end humanity than your next average-Joe vampire. And the greatest villain was also Buffy's great love. There would be no easy answers to end this season's story arc.

With the final episode, the series took some major turns, and some major risks. The first was the revelation to Joyce that her daughter was the Slayer. In many regards, this opened up the series and created many new story possibilities for the seasons ahead.

It also gives the Joyce Summers character a chance to grow and get out of the "She must be dumb as a post" category, to not notice something strange is going on with her daughter. Now she can be the voice of informed concern and it opens up the possibility of a relationship with Giles, who has become Buffy's well-defined father figure anyway.

Although we've learned that in Sunnydale few things are as they seem, the decision to cast Angel into Hell with Acathla—and, presumably, out of the series, at least for a while—was, in the end, the only logical way out of the "Angel as evil" story line.

With the season finale ending with Buffy on a bus out of town, Whedon sets up the third season to be a different kind of journey for Buffy. In Season One, she had to face her own mortality and come to terms with her destiny. In Season Two she has had to learn sacrifice and what it's like to love. In the third season, Buffy will have to deal with issues closer to home, such as her mother, and with a hostile principal who obviously knows her identity. In other words, Season Three will see Buffy graduate not only from high school, but from adolescent to full-fledged adult.

THE REAL HORROR: The greater good. In life there are occasions when it's necessary to do what's right, as opposed to what would best serve our own interests. It's never easy and many people simply cannot do it. But in Sunnydale those occurrences take on cataclysmic importance, so Buffy has no choice but to sacrifice Angel and her own happiness for the sake of others.

A sword-wound cannot kill a vampire, so she doesn't kill Angel. She banishes him to an existence of eternal torment because if she doesn't, the world would come to an end. Instead, her world does. Sending Angel to the agonies of Hell just as his soul is returned to him, is a loss she may never get over.

The biggest irony is that many of the people she is suffering for, have no appreciation of her sacrifice. Her mother wants her daughter to have a different fate and to ignore her calling. The school principal is looking to keep a lid on the local troubles. Even Xander is more interested in seeing Angel suffer than in what it will cost Buffy emotionally.

IT'S A MYSTERY: Was the spell Willow used to restore Angel's soul the exact same one the Gypsies first used, which came with the caveat that Angel would lose his soul if he experienced "one moment of true happiness," or did it restore his soul with no strings attached?

Also, does Kendra's death mean that another Slayer will be called?

How does Buffy know it was Drusilla who killed Kendra?

BLOOPERS: During the final fight scene with Angel, Buffy's hair goes back and forth, from loose to pulled back, from shot to shot.

OF SPECIAL NOTE: The week this episode aired, the WB announced that they were spinning off a series to star David Boreanaz as Angel for the 1999–2000 season.

Third-year overview: Now a senior in high school, Buffy will spend the next year better embracing her destiny as the Slayer. Along the way she is surprised by a second chance, threatened by an unexpected enemy, and forced to rely on the help of others to stop her most powerful opponent yet.

SEASON THREE REGULAR CAST

Sarah Michelle Gellar (*Buffy Summers*)
Nicholas Brendon (*Xander Harris*)
Alyson Hannigan (*Willow Rosenberg*)
Charisma Carpenter (*Cordelia Chase*)
David Boreanaz (*Angel*)
Seth Green (*Oz*)
Anthony Stewart Head (*Rupert Giles*)

⁜

35. "Anne"
(SEPTEMBER 29, 1998)

Director: Joss Whedon
Writer: Joss Whedon
Recurring cast: Kristine Sutherland (Joyce Summers)
Guest cast: Julia Lee (Lily); Carlos Jacott (Ken); Mary-Pat Green (blood-bank nurse); Chad Todhunter (Rickie)
Music: "Back to Freedom" (during Xander, Willow, and Oz's conversation about Slaying), by Bellylove

***Plot:** After having spent the summer hiding out in Los Angeles, still reeling from having "killed" Angel, Buffy is forced to confront who she really is when local street kids start dying mysteriously.*

THIS WEEK'S DEMON IN DISGUISE: Ken, a seemingly kind social worker who is really a demon that kidnaps runaways and literally works them to death in a Hell dimension.

INTRODUCING: A new opening-credits montage, Seth Green as a cast regular, and a new shoulder-length hairdo for Willow.

REINTRODUCING: Chantarelle, from "Lie to Me," who has now renamed herself Lily.

ANALYSIS: While time may be the great healer, three months after having left Sunnydale, Buffy is still clearly numbed by the trauma of having banished Angel to an eternity in Hell. Her efforts to kill the pain by erasing her previous identity—adopting the name Anne and taking a mundane job as a waitress—haven't done much to improve Buffy's overall outlook on life. Morose and solitary, Buffy is empty because in a fit of understandable but unwise self-pity, she left behind the very people who could have helped her through her grief. As the weeks and months pass, it becomes ever harder to reach out because she herself has created a distance that is as much emotional as it is geographical.

So when Buffy happens to run into an acquaintance from Sunnydale who seeks her help, Buffy's reaction is to push the girl away. Not only does she not want to be reminded of the legacy that comes with a frequently deadly cost, but it is also a painful reminder that she no longer has her support group to lean on. She tells Lily she doesn't want to get involved because getting involved means caring, and caring only leads to pain and loss.

But being the Slayer isn't just what Buffy does, it's who she is. So when she discovers Lily's boyfriend Rickie in a lifeless heap looking like a very old man, Buffy's innate compassion and hibernating sense of duty emerge, albeit against her will. Buffy's will to live and survival instincts kick into high gear when she is dragged into a Hell dimension, where street kids are being worked to death in a demonic factory. Rather than let herself and the others perish, Buffy releases the Slayer within and in so doing, not only defeats the demons, but comes to the realization that she can't run from herself any longer.

THE REAL HORROR: Coping with loss. The pain of losing Angel was so intense, topped by the perceived loss of her mother's love, Buffy chose to leave Sunnydale. But in trying to reinvent herself, Buffy came to see that while you might be able to run, you really can't hide from who you are.

There comes a time for everyone when the realization sinks in that, for better or worse, we are who we are. In Buffy's case, being the Chosen One means a significant part of her life in inherently out of her control. But what she *can* control is how she responds to what fate hands her. Returning to Sunnydale to face her pain head-on is the first step in what will prove to be a long healing process.

BLOOPERS: While in the Hell dimension, Buffy's shoes change noticeably from when she is climbing the rope to when she opens the portal so the others can escape.

OF SPECIAL NOTE: Anne is Buffy's middle name.

Gone is Anthony Stewart Head's voice-over narration from the opening credits.

The sickle-like weapon that Buffy uses is an African throwing ax called a "nunga-munga."

The location for the Hell dimension was the old *Los Angeles Herald Tribune* newspaper building. The crew was warned that if they spilled any water on the floor, which was still covered with seeped-in ink, the water and chemicals in the ink would combine to create toxic fumes. Joss Whedon says they had about 60,000 gallons of water in the barrels for the shoot, but managed to film the episode without poisoning anyone.

MUSICAL NOTE: Nerf Herder's opening title theme for *Buffy* has been rerecorded.

36. "Dead Man's Party"
(OCTOBER 6, 1998)

Director: James Whitmore Jr.
Teleplay: Mari Noxon
Recurring cast: Kristine Sutherland (Joyce Summers); Armin
  Shimerman (Principal Snyder)

Guest cast: Nancy Lenehan (Pat); Danny Strong (Jonathan); Jason Hall (Devon); Paul Morgan Stetler (young doctor); Chris Garnant (stoner #1)

Music: "Never Mind" (Oz's band plays the song at the party), by Four Star Mary, from *Thrown to the Wolves*

Plot: While Buffy deals with the adjustment of being back in Sunnydale and the consequences of her actions, a mysterious force raises the local dead.

THIS WEEK'S EVIL ACCESSORY: A Nigerian tribal mask will turn any zombie who wears it into a powerful demon, Ovu Mobani (which is the Nigerian phrase for "evil eye").

INTRODUCING: Willow's open pursuit of learning witchcraft. A new Sunnydale hot spot—a corner plaza with an espresso bar called the Espresso Pump.

ANALYSIS: Being back in Sunnydale isn't the happy reunion Buffy had anticipated. After expressing their initial relief and happiness at having her back, her mother and friends also have justified feelings of anger over Buffy's summer disappearing act. Buffy realizes it's going to take awhile before she completely regains her mother's trust but she is taken aback by the undercurrent of resentment coming from Giles, Willow, and Xander. On the one hand, Buffy is still wallowing in self-pity. She feels unfairly punished by Snyder—who refuses to reverse her expulsion—and that she's not getting the sympathy she deserves considering what she went through. What doesn't seem to sink in is that Buffy put her mother and friends through a similar torment when she left.

Although Buffy's life came to a kind of emotional halt during her absence, those left behind struggled to move on. At every turn, Buffy feels alienated, even in her own house. Her mom's new friend Pat seems more at home there than Buffy does. Her friends seem to be avoiding her, and the general unspoken undercurrent is giving her an itch to bolt again. It's almost a welcome distraction when a dead cat mysteriously comes back to life.

During a planned "Welcome Home" dinner that morphs into an impromptu party, Buffy is stung to hear her mother talking about how hard it is, adjusting to Buffy being back home. The hurt and humiliation is too much and Buffy prepares to take off again, which leads to a confrontation between her and Willow, during which all their unexpressed feelings are voiced and Buffy finally begins to accept the enormity of her actions.

THE REAL HORROR: Facing consequences. When Buffy boarded the bus out of town, she never considered what the consequences of her actions would or could be, down the road.

CIVILIAN FATALITY: Joyce's friend Pat, who turns into a zombie demon. Her power is short-lived, as Buffy drives a shovel into her head.

LITERARY REFERENCE: During Buffy's absence, Joyce read *The Deep End of the Ocean,* a 1996 novel by Jacquelyn Mitchard about a family whose youngest son is kidnapped.

MUSICAL NOTE: The title of this episode, "Dead Man's Party," is also the name of a 1985 Oingo Boingo song.

37. "Faith, Hope, and Trick"
(OCTOBER 13, 1998)

Director: James A. Contner
Teleplay: David Greenwalt
Recurring cast: Kristine Sutherland (Joyce Summers); Fab Filippo (Scott Hope); K. Todd Freeman (Mr. Trick); Eliza Dushku (Faith); Armin Shimerman (Principal Snyder)
Guest cast: Jeremy Roberts (Kakistos); John Ennis (manager)
Music: "Going to Hell" (while Willow and Oz are outside the high school), by the Brian Jonestown Massacre, from *Strung Out in Heaven*; "The Background" (during Buffy's dream), by Third Eye Blind from *Third Eye Blind*; "Cure" (at the Bronze), by Darling Violetta, from the *Kill You* EP; "Blue Sun" (at the Bronze), by Darling Violetta, from *Bath Water Flowers*

Plot: There's a new Slayer in town who arrives with secrets, issues, and an agenda to make Sunnydale "her" town.

THIS WEEK'S ANCIENT VAMPIRE MENACE: Kakistos, a vampire so old his hands and feet are cloven, who is on a mission to kill the new Slayer.

According to Whedon, "The idea is that the older vampires get, the more ani-malistic they get. They devolve. That's my theory."

INTRODUCING: Faith, a street-tough Slayer with an attitude—and a dangerous edge; Mr. Trick, a dapper African-American vampire; the Watch-ers' Council, a Britain-based authoritarian organization that oversees Slayer activities; Scott Hope, a potential love interest for Buffy.

ANALYSIS: Buffy is slowly picking up the pieces of her life, despite being haunted by dreams of Angel. After the school board forces Snyder to readmit her, Buffy is finally starting to feel more surefooted so the last thing she really needed was to have a new Slayer breeze into town. Called as Kendra's replacement, Faith is nothing like Kendra. Where Kendra was ded-icated and saw her duty as Slayer in almost reverential terms, for Faith it's all about power and kicking ass.

Her lighthearted take on slaying charms the gang and Buffy finds herself feeling like a stick-in-the-mud by comparison. Buffy is a bit chagrined that Faith seems to have no issues or personal torments and finds herself feeling *thismuch* threatened at how her friends are welcoming Faith with open arms. Despite whatever conflicts she has about being the Slayer, she's not too keen on someone coming in and trying to step right into her life.

But Faith isn't all she seems; beneath her "life as Slayer is a daily party" demeanor, Buffy senses a darkness that she can't quite interpret, but she goes with the flow and tries to welcome Faith by inviting her to dinner. Later, on patrol, Buffy's instincts prove right when it becomes clear Faith isn't just into killing vamps, but is into causing them pain.

After Giles learns Faith's Watcher isn't at a retreat but has been killed by Kakistos, who now is after Faith, Buffy confronts Faith and tries to tell her nothing is solved by running, a lesson Buffy herself has recently learned the hard way. It becomes a moot point when Kakistos shows up and Faith dusts him with a makeshift stake the size of a small pole.

Although Buffy can't help but feel compassion for Faith—who was ordered to stay in Sunnydale by the Watchers' Council pending further orders—it's clear she still senses that Faith is seriously troubled—and poten-tial trouble.

THE REAL HORROR: Being compared to others. Beset with angst from having killed Angel and enduring her friends' anger over leaving town, Buffy knows she hasn't been a bundle of laughs lately. So when Faith shows up, telling funny Slayer stories and seemingly without a care in the world, Buffy really feels like a walking black cloud.

For a moment, Buffy tries to be more Faithlike by telling her own Slayer war stories, but it simply isn't who Buffy is. In the end, she learns that it's much better to just be yourself because others aren't always whom they may seem to be.

OF SPECIAL NOTE: Joss Whedon gives some Watcher background: "There are Watchers all over the world because although there are potential Slayers all over the world, it is never known until the last one dies which one will be called. Sometimes a Watcher can find a potential and train her, sometimes they cannot interfere in her life, and sometimes they don't find them, until after the other has died"—which was the case with Buffy.

Kakistos is Greek for "the worst of the worst."

MUSICAL NOTE: Darling Violetta performs the song onstage at the Bronze.

38. "All Men Are Beasts"
(OCTOBER 20, 1998)

Director: James Whitmore Jr.
Teleplay: Marti Noxon
Recurring cast: Eliza Dushku (Faith); Fab Filippo (Scott Hope)
Guest cast: John Patrick White (Pete); Danielle Weeks (Debbie); Phill Lewis (Mr. Platt)
Music: "Teenage Hate Machine" (playing on Faith's Walkman), by Marc Ferrari, from *Grunge/Punk (MSVOL23)*

Plot: Oz is suspected of committing a brutal murder while transformed, but Buffy fears the real killer may be Angel, who has returned from Hell more animal than human.

THIS WEEK'S HORROR: Pete, who alternates between loving boyfriend and abusive monster.

REINTRODUCING: A tormented Angel.

ANALYSIS: The question of how well we really know even those closest to us is a recurring theme in this episode. Although Oz the person would never harm anyone, Oz the werewolf isn't in control of what he does and, in fact, doesn't even remember his transformed state. Could he really be responsible for the gruesome killing?

Or is it possible that Angel, having suffered the agonies of Hell for hundreds of years—because time in Hell dimensions slows down so that one day on earth is equal to a year in Hell—has gone mad and lost all traces of humanity, his reinstated soul notwithstanding? Buffy wishes her life could be as uncomplicated as Pete and Debbie's. To all outward appearances they are ideal sweethearts.

But beneath the surface, rage roils inside Pete. At first his fury, and the strength and power that goes with it, was chemically induced through a liquid concoction. But soon he is able to turn into a monster at will—and at the slightest provocation. He hides this side of himself from everyone, except Debbie, who despite being hit is all too willing to believe the good side will win out.

Afraid of what Angel has possibly become, and afraid to tell the others he's alive because of the pain he caused those around her after losing his soul, Buffy is also having to put on a false face. Like Debbie, she has a secret she can't share, and feels helpless. Although Buffy is relieved when she realizes that Pete, and not Angel, is responsible for the killings, she is horrified that Debbie would allow herself to be abused.

As Pete increasingly gives in to the power of rage, Angel fights back to regain his humanity, as it were, and their final confrontation is symbolic of the struggle between the beast and angel within all of us.

THE REAL HORROR: Abuse. The terror Debbie feels at seeing the boy she loves turn into an abusive monster is unfortunately too common an occurrence in our society. The episode clearly pinpoints the root of abuse, jealousy, and insecurity, and vividly shows the emotional and physical damage created when rage is allowed to take control.

LITERARY REFERENCE: The voice-over that Sarah Michelle Gellar does at the beginning and end of this episode is from the book *Call of the Wild*, by Jack London, which Willow mentions reading to the werewolf/Oz, to calm him.

OF SPECIAL NOTE: John Patrick White, who plays Peter, co-starred with Seth Green in the 1998 movie *Can't Hardly Wait.*

39. "𝕳omecoming"
(NOVEMBER 3, 1998)

Director: David Greenwalt

Teleplay: David Greenwalt

Recurring cast: K. Todd Freeman (Mr. Trick); Fab Filippo (Scott Hope); Harry Groener (Mayor Richard Wilkins III); Eliza Dushku (Faith)

Guest cast: Jeremy Ratchford (Lyle Gorch); Ian Abercrombie (Germans' boss); Danny Strong (Jonathan); Jason Hall (Devon); Jack Plotnick (deputy mayor); Billy Maddox (Frawley); Joseph Daube (Hans); Jermyn Daube (Frederick); Lee Everett (Candy Gorch); Tori McPetrie (Michelle); Chad Stahelski (Kulak)

Music: "Fell Into the Loneliness" (at the Bronze), by Lori Carson, from *Where It Goes*; "Jodi Foster," (during yearbook picture–taking), by the Pinehurst Kids, from *Minnesota*; "How" (while Xander and Willow get ready for the dance), by Lisa Loeb, from *Firecracker*, "Fire Escape" (during Homecoming Queen campaigning), by Fastbal, from *All the Pain Money Can Buy*; "She Knows" (played by Oz's band during dance), by Four Star Mary from *Thrown to the Wolves*

Plot: Buffy competes with Cordelia for Homecoming Queen, while Willow and Xander's relationship takes an unexpected turn.

THIS WEEK'S NEFARIOUS PLOT: Slayerfest '98. Mr. Trick invites a motley crew of would-be assassins—two Germans, vampires Lyle and Candy Gorch, and the demon Kulak—to hunt down both Slayers.

INTRODUCING: Xander and Willow's budding sexual attraction to each other; deputy mayor Allan Finch.

THE BIG BAD: Mayor Richard Wilkins III. For the rest of the season, Mayor Wilkins's evil designs on Sunnydale will become the overriding story arc.

ANALYSIS: After facing apocalypse, being killed by the Master, and sending her lover to Hell, you'd think Buffy would have some serious life perspective. However, the teenage girl within rears her wanna-be tiaraed head, and even though it shouldn't be, being Homecoming Queen suddenly is the most important thing to Buffy. Had Buffy never been called as the Slayer, and had she been able to finish high school in Los Angeles, she probably *would* have been Homecoming Queen. So, taking home the crown would make up in a big way for all she's sacrificed over the past few years. To have a glimpse, however fleeting and fanciful, of what her life might have been like had not duty called, is a fantasy Buffy wants—and she wants it bad.

Her dream of having one memory of high school that doesn't in some way involve Slaying is typically shattered as Buffy finds herself battling the assassins with Cordelia in tow. For, as much as Buffy might have wanted to beat Cordelia as Homecoming Queen, when put to the test she would also give her life to protect Cordelia. Once again, battling evil has the effect of putting life into perspective for Buffy, so when it turns out that neither Buffy nor Cordelia wins, there's a certain poetic Hellmouth justice.

THE REAL HORROR: Competition. As if adolescence isn't ego-busting enough, with hormones churning up a smorgasbord of insecurities and angst, the institution of Homecoming Queen merely creates one more opportunity for most high school girls to feel inadequate.

Buffy seems almost insulted that nobody can envision her as Homecoming Queen. If she is good enough to save the world, repeatedly, why isn't she good enough to wear a tiara? At the same time, though, unlike many teenage girls who are still searching for an identity, Buffy already has been endowed with a sense of self, so in the end, while she would have liked to be queen for just a day, her self-worth will remain intact regardless of the outcome of the voting.

OF SPECIAL NOTE: Chad Stahelski, who played spiny-headed demon Kulak in this episode, was David Boreanaz's regular stunt double.

While filming this episode, Sarah cracked a bone in her left hand. The bandaged hand is visible in the scene where Buffy is standing in front of the white board in the library.

This episode marks the second appearance of Jeremy Ratchford as Lyle Gorch. He was first seen in "Bad Eggs," Episode 24, from Season Two.

40. "𝕭and 𝕮andy"
(NOVEMBER 10, 1998)

Director: Michael Lange

Teleplay: Jane Espenson

Recurring cast: Kristine Sutherland (Joyce Summers); K. Todd Freeman (Mr. Trick); Robin Sachs (Ethan Rayne); Harry Groener (Mayor Richard Wilkins III); Armin Shimerman (Principal Snyder)

Guest cast: Jason Hall (Devon); Peg Stewart (Ms. Barton)

Music: "Blasé" (while talking about the SATs), by Mad Cow, from *Eureka*; "Tales of Brave Ulysses" (while Joyce and Giles are in his apartment), by Cream, from *Very Best of Cream*; "Violent" (played by Oz's band at the Bronze), by Four Star Mary, from *Thrown to the Wolves*; "Slip Jimmy" (at the Bronze), by Every Bit of Nothing, from *Austamosta*.

Plot: Something is causing the adults of Sunnydale to regress.

THIS WEEK'S MIND-ALTERING TREAT: Chocolate bars that turn adults into their teenage alter egos as part of Mr. Trick's plot to feed Lurconis—a sewer-dwelling demon—a sacrifice of human babies.

ANALYSIS: When Buffy suddenly finds herself in the unlikely and uncomfortable role of being one of the most mature people in Sunnydale, the safety net of having someone tell her what to do is suddenly gone. Seeing all her authority figures suddenly acting more like her classmates, is initially disorienting. However, seeing her mother and Giles—who is in full Ripper mode—in a hormone-driven clinch is downright disturbing and makes Buffy even more determined to return things back to normal. When she discovers Ethan Rayne is behind the spiked candy bars, she takes her frustration out on him, in part because he deserves it and in part because she's still appalled at the unseemly sight of adults acting like such juveniles.

Not having Giles to spearhead the research, Buffy has to wear both Watcher and Slayer hats. In a telling display of her growing maturity, although she's not happy about having to do it, Buffy ably takes command, directing Willow and the others to their tasks, all while keeping her mother and Giles at arm's length.

THE REAL HORROR: Realizing your parents are just grown-up teenagers. Although it's a teenagers rite of passage to rebel against authority on the way to becoming an adult, there's a certain security in having parents to fall back on. But parents have another side of their lives that children either don't see or choose not to think about. Seeing her mother and Giles behaving impulsively, not to mention sexually, was a rude reminder to Buffy that fun and desire isn't exclusive property of the young.

IT'S A MYSTERY: How does Buffy know who Mr. Trick is?

OF SPECIAL NOTE: Angel is seen practicing T'ai Chi Ch'uan, an ancient Chinese martial art.

Lurconis, the name of This Week's Demon, means "glutton."

41. "Revelations"
(NOVEMBER 17, 1998)

Director: James A. Contner
Teleplay: Douglas Petrie
Recurring cast: Eliza Dushku (Faith)
Guest cast: Serena Scott Thomas (Gwendolyn Post); Jason Hall (Devon); Kate Rodger (Paramedic)
Music: "Run" (performed by Oz's band), by Four Star Mary, from *Thrown to the Wolves*; "West of Here" (at the Bronze), by Lotion, from *The Telephone Album*; "Silver Dollar" (at end of the episode), by Man of the Year, from *The Future Is Not Now*

Plot: Buffy faces the consequences of hiding Angel. Faith's new Watcher has a secret past.

THIS WEEK'S WATCHER-GONE-BAD: Power-mad Gwendolyn Post hopes to take over the world by finding the Glove of Mynhegon.

ANALYSIS: While the mind might say one thing, frequently the heart says another. As Angel recuperates from his torturous time in Hell, Buffy realizes that her feelings for him are as powerful as ever. She has backed herself into a corner by keeping his return a secret from the others for so long, and knows the longer she goes without being honest, the worse the repercussions will be. But she puts off the inevitable, afraid what the outcome will be. However, Buffy's not the only one harboring a secret. Both Willow and Xander are guilt-ridden over a number of shared passionate kisses, which they can't seem to control even though both are involved with others.

Buffy's obvious distraction is chalked up to Slayer moodiness, which isn't helped by the arrival of Faith's new Watcher, the incredibly prim and proper Gwen Post. When Xander stumbles across Buffy and Angel sharing a kiss, the secret is out and Buffy must face the gang's anger and sense of betrayal. But the confrontation makes her belief in Angel even more resolute, and in the end, he proves himself to be the Angel of old by protecting Willow from Gwen Post after she dons the Glove of Mynhegon.

Buffy is more worried about Faith than herself. After seeing her first Watcher killed by a vamp and now discovering Gwen Post was excommunicated from the Watchers' Council for being partial to evil magic, Faith seems disillusioned and angry and responds by pushing others away and building up a wall that buries her emotions ever deeper. Faith feels that it's her against the world, and it's clear the chip on her shoulder will soon propel her over the edge.

THE REAL HORROR: Disillusionment. Being disappointed by those we either care about or want to look up to is painful, and Giles especially feels the hurt of Buffy not being honest about Angel's return. Even though intellectually Giles knows Angel was a different being without his soul, he can't forget that Jenny was taken from him.

Although Faith had no real emotional connection to Gwen Post, she felt played for a fool by the ex-Watcher, which stirred up her deep-seated feelings of inadequacy. For all her bravado, Faith yearns for acceptance and approval and when she doesn't get it, it reinforces her justification of blaming the world. Her resentment of Buffy is beginning to show. Even when Buffy screws up, she's still respected and looked up to. Faith feels she's not getting similar respect or benefit of the doubt, and that resentment will prompt Faith to become even more reckless.

BLOOPERS: During the scene where Buffy says, "Faith, we can work this out," a boom mic can be seen above Gellar.

OF SPECIAL NOTE: It's revealed that Sunnydale has twelve cemeteries.
Guest star Serena Scott Thomas is the sister of Kristin Scott Thomas, best known for her Academy Award–nominated role in *The English Patient.*

42. "Lovers' Walk"
(NOVEMBER 24, 1998)

Director: David Semel
Teleplay: Dan Vebber
Recurring cast: Kristine Sutherland (Joyce Summers); Harry Groener
  (Mayor Richard Wilkins III); James Marsters (Spike)
Guest cast: Jack Plotnick (deputy mayor); Marc Burnham (Lenny);
  Suzanne Krull (clerk)
Music: "My Way," performed by Gary Oldman, from the *Sid and Nancy*
  soundtrack

*Plot: Distraught over being dumped by Drusilla, Spike returns to Sunnydale
with a plan to win back his lady vamp's love, while Willow and Xander pay
the price for their lack of control.*

THIS WEEK'S UNDOING: Love.

REINTRODUCING: Spike, Sunnydale's newest resident vamp.

ANALYSIS: For the Slayer, life tends to be lived very much in the
moment because the threat of death is so ever-present. But after Buffy scores
unexpectedly high on her SAT, the possibility of having a future beyond Sunnydale and the Hellmouth leaves her a bit unsettled. While fighting evil has
its own terrors, they are familiar fears. An unknown future away from her
identity as Slayer is emotionally scarier than facing vampires.

Her reluctance to leave home is complicated. In part, being the Slayer so
informs her identity, that giving it up and handing the job over to Faith
would feel like losing a part of herself. Nor does she want to leave Angel
behind, now she's gotten him back. She's so conflicted that when she hears
others encouraging her to leave, it almost feels like rejection.

Buffy's not the only one at a crossroads. Spike feels directionless since
being dumped and decides to have Willow use a love spell to get Dru back.
Willow and Xander are trying to ignore their attraction to each other but the
danger of it seems to act as an aphrodisiac. Nobody seems comfortable with
their life, nor do they seem sure of where they are going. Ironically, the two
who seem most confident that all is well with their worlds, Oz and Cordelia,

will be the ones whose lives will be most turned upside down by Xander and Willow's indiscretions.

In the end, nobody has what or who they want—some by choice, some by fate, and some by the consequence of their own actions.

THE REAL HORROR: Betrayal. The symbolism of Cordelia being impaled after walking in on Xander and Willow says it all—such a breach of trust is like a knife through the heart. And while some might eventually be able to forgive, it's a wound that never fully heals.

LITERARY ALLUSION: The book Angel is reading, *La Nausée* (*Nausea*), was published in 1938, the first novel by noted French writer and existentialist philosopher Jean-Paul Sartre.

OF SPECIAL NOTE: According to the WELCOME TO SUNNYDALE sign demolished by Spike's car, the population of Sunnydale is 38,500, which is roughly the size of Palm Springs, California.

Drusilla was supposed to appear in this episode but she had to be written out because of Juliet Landau's schedule conflicts.

43. "The Wish"
(DECEMBER 8, 1998)

Director: David Greenwalt

Teleplay: Marti Noxon

Recurring cast: Mark Metcalf (the Master); Emma Caulfield (Anya/Anyanka); Mercedes McNab (Harmony); Danny Strong (Jonathan)

Guest Cast: Larry Bagby III (Larry); Nicole Bilderback (Cordette #1); Nathan Anderson (John Lee); Mariah O'Brien (Nancy); Gary Imhoff (teacher); Robert Covarrubias (caretaker)

Music: "Tired of Being Alone" (in Bronze), by the Spies, from *Toy Surprise Inside*; "Dedicated to Pain" (when Willow and Xander visit the Master), by Plastic; "Slayer's Elegy" (during slow motion sequence), by Christophe Beck with Bobbi Page; "Never Noticed" (end of episode), by Gingersol, from *Extended Play*.

Plot: *A demon grants Cordelia's wish that Buffy had never come to Sunny-dale, resulting in an alternative world in which vampires rule.*

THIS WEEK'S DEMON: Anyanka, the vengeance demon.

INTRODUCING: Willow and Xander as vampires; and Anya, who in human form will become a regular character.

ANALYSIS: At some point everyone wonders, "What if?" How different would one's life be different if one particular incident had not happened? When living on a Hellmouth, the answer to such musings can be dangerous.

Psychologists tell us we are a product of our genes, our hormones, and our environment. But while we are influenced by external factors, we possess a certain core personality. Thrust Buffy into the hard streets of Cleveland and the sunny, California aspect of the Slayer we know might be replaced by an urban edge, but her basic character traits, such as responsibility to duty, would remain.

Likewise, in the alternative universe Cordelia wishes for, everyone is different, but at the same time hauntingly familiar. Giles still relies on intellect and Oz offers quiet support, but their lives are consumed by trying to simply survive every night after sundown.

The episode also touches upon the question of fate. Since Buffy never came to Sunnydale, the Master has risen and made Hell on Earth. But just as Giles destroys Anyanka's necklace and returns reality, the Master breaks Buffy's neck. Regardless of the alternative universe in which they reside, Buffy appears destined to die at the hands of the Master. However, there's no CPR that will cure a broken neck.

The most significant difference is that Willow and Xander have become vampires and Giles was never her Watcher, leaving Buffy more vulnerable than we've ever known her. It reinforces the fact that beyond her own grow-ing abilities, what makes Buffy such a formidable Slayer is her support group. In this reality, without them to give her emotional strength and practical help, death seems more inevitable for Buffy.

THE REAL HORROR: Getting what you wish for. Like many people who are in emotional pain, Cordelia looks for somebody to blame. She not only lashes out at Xander, the appropriate target, but at Buffy. The way Cordelia sees it, had Buffy never moved to Sunnydale, Cordelia never would have been drawn into the Scooby Gang, never would have had reason to get to know Xander, and therefore never would have had her heart broken.

But while this particular hurt may never have happened, Cordelia fails to think through what events might take its place. This episode takes the common human tendency of fervently wishing for something only to have it fail to meet expectations, to its most horrific level.

LITERARY ALLUSION: When Anya comments, "I had no idea her wish would be so exciting. Brave new world," she's referring to the classic novel *Brave New World* by Aldous Huxley. Set in the twenty-sixth century, the book describes a man-made utopia that isn't as wonderful as it appears at first glance. The origin of the phrase "brave new world," however, comes from Shakespeare's *The Tempest*, when the character Miranda says:

> *"O, wonder!*
> *How many goodly creatures are there here!*
> *How beauteous mankind is! O brave new world,*
> *That has such people in't!"*

OF SPECIAL NOTE: Nicole Bilderback, who guest-stars as Cordette #1, appeared with Seth Green in the 1998 movie *Can't Hardly Wait.*

44. "Amends"
(DECEMBER 15, 1998)

Director: Joss Whedon
Teleplay: Joss Whedon
Recurring cast: Kristine Sutherland (Joyce Summers); Robia La Morte (Jenny Calendar); Saverio Guerra (Willy); Eliza Dushku (Faith)
Guest cast: Shane Barach (Daniel); Edward Edwards (male ghost); Cornelia Hayes O'Herlihy (Margaret); Mark Kriski (weatherman); Tom Michael Bailey (tree seller)
Music: "Can't Get Enough of Your Love, Babe" (when Willow tries to seduce Oz), by Barry White, from *All Time Greatest Hits*

Plot: Haunted by the evil deeds of his past, Angel decides the only way to end his pain is through suicide, Christmas notwithstanding.

THIS WEEK'S APPARITION: The essence of absolute evil known as "the First," which is summoned by eyeless priests called the Bringers, or Harbingers, and takes the form of Jenny Calendar.

ANALYSIS: While typically broody about his past evil deeds, Angel's angst is ratcheted up even more than usual in this episode, to the point of emotional implosion. He's so pathetic than even Giles feels compassion for him and agrees to help Buffy try to figure out what is driving him to the brink of madness. Instead of seeing his return to earth as a second chance, to Angel, he's still in Hell.

The theme of second chances runs through the episode, with Oz forgiving Willow for her indiscretion with Xander because the alternative, of not having her in his life, is unacceptable. It's equally unacceptable for Buffy to allow Angel to end his life. Tormented by the First, in the guise of Jenny Calendar, Angel is so vulnerable, disjointed, and haunted by the people he has killed, he believes it when the First says the only way to keep Buffy safe from himself is to die. But a miracle snowfall that blocks the sun keeps him from turning into a pile of smoldering ashes, proves that Angel's second chance on Earth was not by accident, and that redemption is possible through acts of love.

THE REAL HORROR: Remorse—wishing we could undo the past is something everyone can relate to. Self-loathing often goes hand in hand with remorse, and Angel's got it in spades in this episode. He doesn't feel worthy of redemption until he gets a message from the heavens, literally, that if life is so precious he mourns those lives he took, then the only way to redeem himself is to keep living and try to put good back into the world.

IT'S A MYSTERY: Although a major plot point was that Sunnydale was experiencing a heat wave, most of the people were dressed for much cooler weather.

OF SPECIAL NOTE: The weatherman seen in the episode, Mark Kriski, is the real-life morning news weatherman for Los Angeles WB affiliate KTLA.

While thrilled to reprise the role of Jenny, Robia La Morte was reportedly disappointed that the character was an evil spirit.

45. "𝔊ingerbread"

(JANUARY 12, 1999)

Director: James Whitmore Jr.

Teleplay: Jane Espenson

Recurring cast: Kristine Sutherland (Joyce Summers); Harry Groener (Mayor Richard Wilkins III); Armin Shimerman (Principal Snyder); Elizabeth Anne Allen (Amy Madison); Jordan Baker (Sheila Rosenberg)

Guest cast: Lindsay Taylor (little girl); Shawn Pyfrom (little boy); Blake Swendson (Michael); Grant Garrison (Roy); Roger Morrissey (demon); Daniel Tamm (monster)

Plot: Joyce becomes an activist to rid Sunnydale of evil—even if it means killing her own daughter to do it.

THIS WEEK'S BRATS: A demon hiding in the guise of two helpless children, Hans and Greta Strauss.

INTRODUCING: Willow's mom, Sheila Rosenberg.

ANALYSIS: This week's demon is different in that it lets people do its dirty work. By simply invoking fear, the darker side of our human nature takes over and the result is persecution of innocents.

Joyce's desire to better understand her daughter's life as the Slayer is understandable but, just as most teens prefer to keep parts of their lives private from their parents, Buffy isn't sure she wants her mom to become a member of the Scooby Gang. Not only would Buffy worry about Joyce's safety, but her mom isn't a hardened veteran of the Hellmouth wars the way Buffy, Willow, Xander, Cordelia, and Giles are. Because of all they've been through together, they share a tacit understanding of the ways of evil that Joyce and the other parents couldn't begin to appreciate.

The scene where Joyce and Sheila Rosenberg stand ready to burn their daughters at the stake is the ultimate in lack of communication between parent and child. By criticizing Buffy's effectiveness as the Slayer, she undermines her daughter's self-confidence. Like most teens, Buffy wants her mother's approval, especially in this case, since Slaying isn't just a pastime but a noble calling.

While Joyce's heart starts out in the right place, she plays into the demon's hands by allowing her emotions to take the lead. In the end, when confronted with the evil humans can inflict on one another, the horror of the near-fatal consequences of her actions causes Joyce to go into denial and pretend none of it ever happened, another typical human response that is the basis for the adage: "Those who forget history are doomed to repeat it."

THE REAL HORROR: The mob mentality. The events in this episode are obviously meant to reference the Salem witch trials of 1692, an incident in American history that demonstrates the dangers of fear, magnified by a crowd feeding on the emotions of one other. The normally rational people of Sunnydale are turned into vigilantes who justify their actions in the name of "good." It's sobering how quickly human beings succumb to mob rule, proving that, for all our civilization, we are still not far removed from our primitive ancestors.

IT'S A MYSTERY: Why doesn't Willow ask Giles to help her turn Amy back into a human? Wouldn't he remember how Amy turned Buffy back from a rat in Episode 28, "Bewitched, Bothered, and Bewildered"?

OF SPECIAL NOTE: Jordan Baker appeared with Alyson Hannigan in an episode of *Picket Fences*, called "To Forgive Is Divine."

In the spell Amy uses to turn herself into a rat and escape being burned at the stake, she calls on Hecate, the Greek "Goddess of the Dark of the Moon," who was also the patron of magic. Hecate, whose name means "influence from afar" has three forms that allow her to be all-seeing and all-knowing.

46. "Helpless"
(JANUARY 19, 1999)

Director: James Contner
Teleplay: David Fury
Recurring cast: Kristine Sutherland (Joyce Summers)
Guest cast: Jeff Kober (Zackary Kralik); Harris Yulin (Quentin Travers) Dominic Keating (Blair); David Haydn-Jones (Hobson); Nick Cornish (guy); Don Dowe (construction worker)

Plot: *Buffy gets an unwelcome surprise for her eighteenth birthday, courtesy of the Watchers' Council.*

THIS WEEK'S PSYCHOTIC VAMPIRE: Zachary Kralik, a criminally insane serial killer—and that was *before* he became a vampire.

INTRODUCING: The Cruciamentum, an age-old Slayer rite of passage that tests a Slayer's resilience and resourcefulness. After using drugs to sap all her powers, the Slayer is locked in a house with a vampire. She either survives by her wits and training—or dies.

INTRODUCING: Quentin Travers, head of the Watchers' Council

ANALYSIS: To paraphrase: Those who can, Slay; those who can't, work for the Watchers' Council. Although the Council is in charge of maintaining the Slayer legacy, their old-school ways seem harshly out-of-step with the front-line evil-fighting that happens in Sunnydale. Buffy displays her abilities and resourcefulness on a daily basis so it seems patently absurd that she would be forced to prove herself in a barbaric ritual overseen by stuffed shirts who may have never dusted a vampire in their lives. But what makes it particularly appalling is that Giles is forced to participate in the deception by secretly drugging Buffy to dull her powers.

Although Buffy has never been one to immerse herself in Slayer lore or demonology the way Kendra did, she more than makes up for her lack of academic interest with her instincts. So even though she has lost the strength she has come to depend on, is no longer as impervious to pain, and her reflexes have been downgraded to those of a mere mortal, Buffy still has her wiles and instincts, which ultimately come through and prove to be her most formidable weapon, even when facing a homicidal maniac like Kralik.

The father-daughter aspect of Giles and Buffy's relationship is once again explored. But in this case, he is just as disappointing as her real father, who suddenly is too busy to see Buffy even for her birthday. While Giles may have failed Buffy through his deception, in the end he proves he would give his life for her. Although he may not share her blood, he proves that the ultimate measure of a parent is being there when you're needed the most. The Council might be able to fire Giles for having become too emotionally attached to Buffy, but they can't come between them.

THE REAL HORROR: Betrayal. Because of the trust Buffy places in Giles and his role in her life as father figure, his deception is more painful than when Buffy's real dad is a no-show for her birthday. Not to mention potentially fatal.

Even though Giles redeems himself by admitting the truth to Buffy after Kralik escapes, and by putting his own life and job on the line to dust a vampire about to pounce on her and Joyce, there is a sense that it will take awhile for the damage to their relationship to mend completely.

BLOOPERS: The boom microphone is visible in the top left-hand corner of the screen as Buffy is fighting the vamp in the episode's first scene.

LITERARY ALLUSION: The book Angel gives Buffy, *Sonnets from the Portuguese* by Elizabeth Barrett Browning, was originally published in 1850 and contains the famous poem "How do I love thee? Let me count the ways."

OF SPECIAL NOTE: Dominic Keating, who guest-stars as Blair, is best known as Lieutenant Reed on *Enterprise*.

Jeff Kober, who plays Kralik, also played Daedalus, head of the Nosferatu clan of vampires in the 1996 television series *Kindred: The Embraced*.

Cruciamentum means "torture" or "torment" in Latin.

47. "The Zeppo"
(JANUARY 26, 1999)

Director: James Whitmore Jr.
Teleplay: Dan Vebber
Recurring cast: Eliza Dushku (Faith); Saverio Guerra (Willy)
Guest cast: Channon Roe (Jack); Michael Cudlitz (Bob); Darin Heames (Parker); Scott Torrence (Dickie); Whitney Dylan (Lysette); Vaughn Armstrong (cop)
Music: "Dodgems" (as Xander drives up in his uncle's car), by Sound Stage, Ltd., from *Alternative Volume 1*; "G-Song" (at the Bronze), by Supergrass, from *In It for the Money*; "Easy" (while Xander is in the car with zombies), by Tricky Woo, from *The Enemy Is Real*.

Plot: Xander's desire to be considered cool leads him down a path littered with cars, women, and zombies.

THIS WEEK'S DEADLY CULT: The Sisterhood of Jhe, a demon cult on a mission to open the Hellmouth and end the world.

ANALYSIS: The latest apocalypse takes a backseat to Xander's crisis of confidence in this episode. At the same time Buffy and the others are forced to fight an epic battle with a demon and walked away victorious, Xander is left to battle his personal demons. The Hellmouth throws so many world-threatening evils at Buffy and her friends that it's easy to forget that in addition saving the world, these teenagers are also trying to figure out who they are and what their ultimate place in the grand scheme of things will be. Xander's insecurities make him worry that he's a hanger-on around Buffy when compared to Willow, Angel, and Giles, and his confidence is further eroded when he feels intimidated by a surly classmate, Jack.

Preoccupied with his image and desperate bid to amp up his cool factor, Xander seeks acceptance from Jack, who turns out to be the ringleader of a gang of high school jock zombies whose idea of a fun night is to blow up Sunnydale High. So while Buffy and the others are trying to avert the end of the world—again—Xander is left to prevent their destruction at the hands of the bomb-happy zombies. Left to his own devices, without Buffy or anyone else there to help or save him, Xander's innate courage and heroism, which are frequently obscured behind his self-deprecation and insecurities, are on full display when he stares down Jack and practically wills him to disarm the bomb.

It seems fitting that on the same night Xander finds his sense of self-worth, he also loses his virginity. Even though sex with Faith is a far cry from his romantic fantasies about making love to Buffy, it takes him one more step away from being a teenage boy, to becoming a confident young man.

This episode is a sly satire of several now-established aspects of *Buffy*, especially the frequent attempts by various villains to bring about the apocalypse, and the intensity of the Buffy-Angel relationship.

THE REAL HORROR: Feeling inconsequential. Because the sum of the gang's collective strong points is so great, Xander loses perspective of his individual contribution. He has to literally stare down death before he realizes that true courage is having the strength of your own convictions.

OF SPECIAL NOTE: Channon Roe appeared with Seth Green in the 1998 movie *Can't Hardly Wait* and with Nicholas Brendon in the 2000 film *Psycho Beach Party*.

Xander is driving a 1957 Chevrolet Bel Air.

48. "Bad Girls"

(FEBRUARY 9, 1999)

Director: Michael Lange

Teleplay: Douglas Petrie

Recurring cast: Kristine Sutherland (Joyce Summers); Eliza Dushku (Faith); K. Todd Freeman (Mr. Trick); Harry Groener (Mayor Richard Wilkins III); Alexis Denisof (Wesley Wyndam-Pryce)

Guest cast: Jack Plotnick (Allan Finch, deputy mayor); Christian Clemenson (Balthazar); Alex Skuby (Vincent); Wendy Clifford (Mrs. Taggert)

Music: "Chinese Burn" (while Buffy and Faith dance), by Curve, from *Come Clean*

Plot: Buffy takes a walk on the wild side, but Faith's recklessness has tragic consequences.

THIS WEEK'S ADIPOSE-CHALLENGED NEMESIS: Balthazar, an obese demon who sends his minions—the sword-wielding El Eliminati—to find an amulet that will restore his strength.

INTRODUCING: Buffy's new Watcher, Wesley Wyndam-Pryce; Willow referring to herself as a Wicca for the first time; Oz with black hair.

THE BIG BAD: Mayor Wilkins and his pending "ascension."

ANALYSIS: Having carried the fate of the world on her shoulders for so long, part of Buffy envies Faith's lack of angst and sheer enjoyment of Slaying. She tries on Faith's attitude, like a pair of new shoes, and decides she likes the fit. It's like getting to be someone else for a change: a new Buffy who isn't weighed down by concerns of school tests or following laws—or being responsible to loyal friends.

Faith believes Slayers are above "normal" people and encourages Buffy to join her and embrace their power. And at first the view from atop Faith's world leaves Buffy exhilarated and energized. The false sense of freedom is addictive and Buffy is seduced by it. The cold slap of reality quickly brings Buffy back down to earth after Faith accidentally kills the deputy mayor.

The guilt Buffy feels over the death makes her see the danger in getting caught up in the frenzy of the kill. She also realizes she and Faith aren't alike at all. Faith Slays for the excitement but Slaying isn't supposed to be sport; it's a sacred responsibility and commitment.

It's as if Faith intentionally tries to lead Buffy down a path of recklessness precisely because she knows Buffy's motives are pure; Buffy selflessly accepts her calling in order to save and protect others. In her heart, Faith knows that she will never be as respected as Buffy because she will never have the strength of character Buffy possesses. Had Faith been able to make Buffy over in her own likeness, it would have made them equals, but as it stands, Faith is merely a shadow of a Slayer when compared to Buffy.

THE REAL HORROR: Hanging out with the wrong crowd. Why is it the bad kids often seem like they are having more fun? The idea of having nobody to answer to sounds ideal, but Buffy quickly learns that a lack of personal responsibility leads to emotional chaos. Because Faith has no commitment to anyone other than herself, she also has no anchor or steadying influence in her life. The downside of setting oneself apart from others is that when you fall, there's nobody there to catch you.

IT'S A MYSTERY: Although the audience doesn't know what he's talking about, Balthazar alludes to the mayor's planned "Ascension." Is this common knowledge among Sunnydale demons or does Balthazar have insider information?

OF SPECIAL NOTE: Both Anthony Stewart Head and Alexis Denisof guest-starred on the series *Highlander*.

Among the schools Willow applies to is Wesleyan College in Connecticut, Joss Whedon's alma mater.

49. "Consequences"
(FEBRUARY 16, 1999)

Director: Michael Gershman
Teleplay: Marti Noxon
Recurring cast: Eliza Dushku (Faith); Kristine Sutherland (Joyce Summers); K. Todd Freeman (Mr. Trick); Harry Groener (Mayor Richard Wilkins III); Alexis Denisof (Wesley Wyndam-Pryce)

Guest cast: Jack Plotnick (Allan Finch, Deputy Mayor); James G. Mac-Donald (Detective Stein); Amy Powell (TV news reporter); Patricia Place (woman in alley)

Music: "Wish We Never Met" (while Willow is crying in the bathroom), by Kathleen Wilhoite, from *Pitch Like a Girl.*

Plot: While Buffy faces the emotional consequences of her walk on the wild side, Faith joins the forces of evil.

THIS WEEK'S UNEXPECTED ADVERSARY: Faith, as a Slayer-gone-bad.

ANALYSIS: Although Buffy didn't wield the stake that took the life of the Deputy Mayor, part of her feels responsible. Had she been paying better attention, or been quicker, she might have prevented his death. The weight of being involved in any way with the taking of a human life overwhelms Buffy. Plus she feels ashamed at the way she let herself follow Faith's reckless lead, hurting her friends' feelings in the process.

Buffy's seemingly endless well of compassion is once again on display. Rather than turn her back on Faith, Buffy feels even more compelled to reach out. So does Angel, who can relate to the conflicts raging within Faith. He knows the seductive power that taking a life engenders. He knows intimately the dark places within the soul, and his voice of experience begins to breaks down Faith's emotional walls. She's put up so many barriers to keep people from being able to hurt her, that she's lost the ability to feel compassion or remorse.

But whatever chance Angel had to reach Faith is destroyed when the Council takes matters into its own hands through Wesley's attempt to kidnap Faith and send her back to England for incarceration. Once again the Watchers' Council's by-the-book mentality fails because Faith has no respect for the system. Not only does she escape, but, by establishing itself as her enemy, the Council in essence frees Faith to go over to the dark side and offer her services to Mayor Wilkins. Once the Council turns its back on Faith, she takes the attitude that if they think she's so bad that she needs to be locked up, she'll show them just how bad she can be.

THE REAL HORROR: Helplessness—no matter how desperately Buffy wants to save Faith from herself, she can't. It's the same helplessness many teens and young adults feel when they see former friends making choices that will only lead to a bad end.

OF SPECIAL NOTE: Originally Wesley was supposed to have been killed by Faith during her escape from the Council's custody.

MUSICAL NOTE: The featured song in this episode is sung by actress Kathleen Wilhoite, best known for playing Chloe Lewis on *ER*.

50. "𝕯𝖔𝖕𝖕𝖊𝖑𝖌𝖆̈𝖓𝖌𝖑𝖆𝖓𝖉"
(FEBRUARY 23, 1999)

Director: Joss Whedon
Teleplay: Joss Whedon
Recurring cast: Eliza Dushku (Faith); Harry Groener (Mayor Richard Wilkins III); Alexis Denisof (Wesley Wyndam-Pryce); Emma Caulfield (Anya); Armin Shimerman (Principal Snyder)
Guest cast: Jason Hall (Devon); Ethan Erickson (Percy West); Andy Umberger (D'Hoffryn); Corey Michael Blake (bartender); Megan Gray (Sandy); Michael Nagy (Alfonse); Norma Michael (older woman); Jennifer Nicole (Willow's body double)
Music: "Virgin State of Mind" (when vampire Willow goes to the Bronze), by k's Choice, from *Buffy the Vampire Slayer* soundtrack; "Priced 2 Move" (at the Bronze), by Spectator Pump, from *Styrofoam Archives*

Plot: While unwittingly helping former vengeance demon Anya regain her powers, Willow accidentally summons her vampire alter ego from Cordelia's alternate, "without Buffy" universe.

THIS WEEK'S EVIL TWIN: Vampire Willow.

INTRODUCING: Percy West, a jock whom Willow tutors.

ANALYSIS: Whether intentional or not, this episode lays the groundwork for Willow's later exploration of her sexual identity. It comes as a shock to Willow to notice that her vampire self is overtly sexual and seems to have lesbian leanings—in part because up to this point, Willow's sexuality has been confined to schoolgirl crushes and romantic fantasies, as opposed to the physical and emotional realities of sexual activity. While Oz, with his wolfian interior, is all guy, he is also a very safe, romanticized boyfriend who exhibits traditionally female traits. He's artistic, sensitive, in tune with Willow's emotions, and isn't controlled by his hormones: Even when Willow offers herself up to him sexually, he turns her down because he doesn't feel she's doing it for the right reasons.

There are other aspects that seem to intrigue Willow, such as the vampire Willow's confidence and how she uses fear to engender respect from others. Surprised by her realization, and perhaps a little troubled that she could possess tendencies she hasn't noticed, meeting her vampire self seems to open the door of future possibilities for Willow to ponder.

THE REAL HORROR: Confronting your dark side. It's not uncommon for people to muse about the darker side of their natures. By conjuring up her vampire alter ego, Willow is confronted with the living embodiment of what she would be like, devoid of conscience and social convention. It's a sobering realization that all of us harbor the potential of evil, given the right circumstances.

OF SPECIAL NOTE: D'Hoffryn, Anya's demon boss, was called "Mr. Hodgepodge" by the makeup people because they used pieces from the Judge, a demon of Jhe, and the Rage Monster to create his look.

According to *Webster's*, a *doppelgänger* is "a ghostly counterpart of a living person."

MUSICAL NOTE: k's Choice is performing onstage during the scene where vampire Willow goes to the Bronze.

51. "Enemies"
(MARCH 16, 1999)

Director: David Grossman
Teleplay: Douglas Petrie
Recurring cast: Kristine Sutherland (Joyce Summers); Eliza Dushku (Faith); Harry Groener (Mayor Richard Wilkins III); Alexis Denisof (Wesley Wyndam-Pryce)
Guest cast: Michael Manasseri (horned demon); Gary Bullock (shrouded sorcerer)

Plot: The mayor and Faith's plot to steal Angel's soul and turn him against Buffy backfires in a big way.

THIS WEEK'S MYSTICAL PRIZE: The Books of Ascension, which the mayor needs to complete his transformation to pure evil.

INTRODUCING: Oz with light hair. Again.

ANALYSIS: Buffy's instincts take center stage again in this episode. Even though the Council has been convinced to allow Faith to go back on the streets as a Slayer, Buffy senses something is amiss. Faith might be going through the right motions, but there's a darkness surrounding Faith that Buffy can sense, and although she doesn't let on to Faith, Buffy sets a trap.

Typically, Angel finds himself caught in a no-win situation. He agrees to pretend to lose his soul to trick Faith into revealing what she knows about the mayor. As part of the act, he causes Buffy pain when she assumes he has had to "get physical" with Faith.

Buffy's sense of loss at the end of the episode is twofold. First, she is pained that she wasn't able to help Faith. Now that it's out in the open that Faith has aligned herself with the mayor, she turns into a completely rogue Slayer and throws down the gauntlet to Buffy, indicating they are now enemies. Even though Buffy refuses to give up on Faith completely just yet, she knows she now has two formidable opponents to contend with. Added to that is her uncertain future with Angel, a subject they both studiously avoid confronting head-on. Just as Faith's fall from grace seems inevitable, the hard truth about Buffy's future with Angel seem just as inescapable, so she avoids it as for long as possible.

THE REAL HORROR: Being right. Many times our instincts tell us one thing but our hearts try to ignore the evidence staring us in the face. Buffy suspected that Faith was up to no good but it depresses her to learn just how right she was.

BLOOPERS: While he's in the mayor's office, Angel's hand can be seen reflected in the mayor's nameplate.

LITERARY ALLUSION: The line, "The girl makes Godot look punctual," refers to the Samuel Beckett play *Waiting for Godot,* about two men who spend the entire play waiting for Godot, who never shows up.

52. "Earshot"

(SEPTEMBER 21, 1999)

Director: Regis Kimble
Teleplay: Jane Espenson
Recurring cast: Kristine Sutherland (Joyce Summers); Alexis Denisof (Wesley Wyndam-Pryce); Danny Strong (Jonathan)
Guest cast: Lauren Roman (Nancy); Ethan Erickson (Percy); Larry Bagby III (Larry); Justin Doran (Hogan); Wendy Worthington (lunch lady); Karem Malicki-Sánchez (Freddy Iverson); Robert Arce (Mr. Beach); Molly Bryant (Ms. Murray); Rich Muller (student); Jay Michael Ferguson (student)

Plot: Buffy is infected by demon blood which gives her the ability to hear people's thoughts. Buffy psychically overhears someone planning mass murder at Sunnydale High.

THIS WEEK'S PARANORMAL AFFLICTION: Mind-reading—an aspect of the demon that infected Buffy. These demons must communicate telepathically because they have no mouths.

ANALYSIS: Ever since coming to Sunnydale, Buffy has fought feelings of alienation. Being the Slayer makes her frequently feel apart from her peers, and she is occasionally overwhelmed by the enormity of the pressure she is under. It becomes clear to her, however, by listening to the thoughts of others, that it's all relative. While other kids in her class may not be saving the world, they are consumed by their own feelings of insecurity, loneliness, and alienation. Most people—with the telling exception of Cordelia—harbor dark inner thoughts but keep their feelings to themselves, either out of fear of ridicule or because they don't think anyone would understand. The intensity of the unspoken emotions enveloping Buffy becomes a din and threatens to literally drive her mad.

But amid the noise, Buffy's instincts single out a more menacing thought—from someone planning to commit mass murder. Because of the comtemporary rash of real-life school shootings, Buffy assumes it's a student and has the gang try to ferret out the potential killer by interviewing targeted suspects. But, as Buffy has learned, people very seldom say exactly what it is they are thinking. The only way to truly know what is going on in someone else's mind is to be able to "read" it.

After Angel cures Buffy with a demon-heart–based antidote, she has a new perspective and greater compassion for the pain that is part of the human condition. That compassion stops short, though, with the cafeteria lady, who had finally snapped from having to deal with one too many moody teenagers—and planned to wipe out the entire school with rat poison.

Buffy's reaction to hearing her mother thinking about the time Joyce and Giles had sex on a police car while under the influence of Ethan Rayne's spiked candy bars was also telling. Clearly, Buffy's view of Giles as a father figure extends to her reluctance to know any details about his sex life, especially as it pertains to her mother.

THE REAL HORROR: The honest truth. Although we all say we want to know the truth, in reality it would be very hard to deal with the brutal truth of what people around us are thinking. Private, uncensored thoughts can be hurtful and upsetting, and if our friends and family told us everything they were thinking we'd be on sensory overload and, like Buffy, overwhelmed.

Jonathan was also overwhelmed—but by feelings of inadequacy. His inner voices were making him so miserable the only way to turn them off seemed to be suicide. Like Buffy, he never stopped to consider that others share similar feelings, and it wasn't until Buffy talked to him that he realized he wasn't so different from anyone else.

BLOOPERS: The time on the watchtower clock changes repeatedly as Buffy looks for Jonathan.

OF SPECIAL NOTE: The broadcast of this episode, along with Episode 56, "Graduation Day (Part II)" was delayed because of the Columbine High School shootings, which occurred the week before "Earshot" was scheduled to air.

Jonathan's selection to present Buffy with the "Class Protector" award at the prom made much more sense in light of the events in "Earshot."

Lauren E. Roman previously worked with Sarah Michelle Gellar on *All My Children*, where Lauren played Laura Kirk English.

53. "Choices"
(MAY 4, 1999)

Director: James A. Contner
Teleplay: David Fury
Recurring cast: Kristine Sutherland (Joyce Summers); Eliza Dushku (Faith); Harry Groener (Mayor Richard Wilkins III); Alexis Denisof (Wesley Wyndam-Pryce); Armin Shimerman (Principal Snyder)
Guest cast: Keith Brunsmann (vamp lackey); Jimmie F. Skaggs (courier); Jason Reed (guard); Bonita Friedericy (manager); Michael Schoenfeld (security guard #1); Seth Coltan (security guard #2); Brett Moses (student)

Plot: Buffy and her friends find themselves pondering their futures. The mayor's powers continue to increase.

THIS WEEK'S EVIL CRITTERS: The Box of Gavrok contains killer spiderlike bugs which, when eaten, give the mayor a megadose of demon energy.

ANALYSIS: Just as Buffy looks to Giles as her mentor and father figure, Faith has been taken under the wing of the mayor, who showers her with genuine affection and concern. Faith probably has never had anyone make her feel so special and, even if he's about to turn into evil incarnate, her loyalty to Wilkins is absolute.

Buffy finds herself in her typical quandary of trying to juggle saving the world with making college plans. To the surprise of just about everyone, her high SAT scores have gotten her admitted to prestigious Northwestern University in Illinois. Her mother is thrilled but Buffy is subdued. Again, although a part of her dreams of leaving the Hellmouth behind and building a normal life for herself, so much of her identity is integrated with her life as Slayer, leaving Sunnydale would be like leaving part of herself behind. Nor does she want to leave Angel.

But during a showdown with the mayor, Wilkins gives Buffy and Angel an honest vision of how doomed their love is. Speaking like a stern parent, the mayor chastises them for being so shortsighted, and makes it clear he thinks that weakness is another reason they will not be able to defeat him.

Although the mayor could have killed Willow after capturing her during the break-in attempt, he is one to look at the big picture. Methodical and organized, it's more important to stay on the Ascension schedule than to be distracted by extraneous killings. In his mind, he'll be killing everyone soon anyway, so what's the rush?

This episode more clearly defines the crossroads at which the characters find themselves, and sets the stage for some painful decisions to come.

THE REAL HORROR: Making hard decisions. Buffy is at a point where all teenagers eventually find themselves: She has to figure out what she really wants to do with her life and what path she will take to get there. Although everyone around her has an opinion, it's ultimately a decision Buffy must make on her own because it's now her life to lead.

Buffy's afraid of change. But as high school draws to a close, she knows her life will be changing whether she wants it to or not.

OF SPECIAL NOTE: The knife used by Faith is called a Gil Hibben Jackal, and is available for public purchase.

54. "The Prom"
(MAY 11, 1999)

Director: David Solomon

Teleplay: Marti Noxon

Recurring cast: Kristine Sutherland (Joyce Summers); Alexis Denisof (Wesley Wyndam-Pryce); Emma Caulfield (Anya); Danny Strong (Jonathan)

Guest cast: Brad Kane (Tucker); Andrea E. Taylor (salesgirl); Mike Kimmel (Butcher); Bonita Friedericy (Mrs. Finkle); Joe Howard (priest); Tove Kingsbury (boy in tuxedo); Michael Zlabinger (student); Damien Eckhardt (Jack Mayhew); Monica Serene Garnich (girl); Stephanie Denise Griffin (girl in store)

Music: "Praise You" (playing in first shot of the prom), by Fatboy Slim, from *You've Come Along Way, Baby*; "Celebration" (song playing as hellhounds approach school), by Kool & the Gang, from *All-Time Greatest Hits*; "The Good Life" (as Buffy enters the gym), by

Cracker, from *Gentleman's Blues*; "El Rey" (while Giles and Wesley talk about Cordelia), by the Lassie Foundation, from *Pacifico*; "Wild Horses" (as Buffy and Angel dance), by the Sundays, from *Blind*.

Plot: A bitter student tries to ruin prom night. Angel comes to a painful conclusion. Buffy is surprised by her classmates.

THIS WEEK'S DEMON PETS: Hellhounds.

INTRODUCING: Anya and Xander as prom couple.

ANALYSIS: Buffy should know better by now than to look forward to anything, especially a high school fantasy night like prom. The episode begins with Buffy and Angel snuggling together after a night of patrolling. She is still deluding herself into believing they can share an exquisite love that doesn't involve physical intimacy, and is looking forward to a romantic evening at the prom.

HELLHOUNDS

Not exactly "man's best friends," hellhounds are large, demonic canines that look like mastiffs, with black teeth and eyes that glow either red or yellow. They can also breathe fire, especially when stalking victims.

Originally from a demon plane, on Earth hellhounds travel and hunt in packs. Possessing a cruel temperament, they have been known to torture their victims before the final kill.

Different cultures have various names for hellhounds. In England, they are called "Barghest," and according to local legend, anyone who sees the hound in clear view will die shortly thereafter. In Wales, hellhounds are called "Gwyllgi," and on the Isle of Man they are called "Mauthe Doog."

But an honest conversation with Joyce convinces Angel that Buffy will never move forward with her life if he's still in it. And, if he can't give her a full life, then the next best thing he can do is give her a future, even if it means he can't be in it. He decides to leave Sunnydale—if they survive the Ascension. Although his timing leaves a lot to be desired, in her heart Buffy knows Angel is right, but that doesn't make the devastation she feels any easier to bear.

Almost against her will, Buffy is being forced to grow up. She's not the only one learning to deal with life's harsh realities: Cordelia is ashamed at having to take a part-time job to support herself after the IRS nails her father for tax fraud. But rather than kicking her when she's down, Xander shows compassion—and the care he really feels for her—by paying for the prom dress she can't afford. However, Xander has agreed to be the date of the former vengeance demon, Anya, who has been stuck in the body of a teenager since Giles destroyed the source of her power in order to reverse the effects of Cordelia's wish. They have all come to see that life is a series of choices and compromises.

The one constant Buffy can depend on is her work. She channels her pain and frustration into tracking down the pesky hellhounds who have been trained to attack anyone in formalwear, then goes to the prom, determined to at least see the experience even if she can't share in it. When Angel surprises her by showing up and asking for a dance, it's clear this is his way of starting to say goodbye.

THE REAL HORROR: Having your heart broken. It's a well-worn cliché that you never love again the way you do the first time you fall in love but it's based on the truth of experience. When Buffy fell in love for Angel, there was no hesitation. Now that she is losing Angel, she will probably never love as freely because she will remember the pain that came when she lost that love and had her heart broken. Even when she falls in love again, she will never be able to recapture the innocence of first love.

BLOOPERS At the prom, the color of Wesley's napkins changes from red to yellow.

OF SPECIAL NOTE: The wedding dress Buffy wears in Angel's dream was designed by Vera Wang, who also made Sarah Michelle Gellar's real-life wedding gown over three years later.

55. "Graduation Day (Part I)"
(MAY 18, 1999)

Director: Joss Whedon

Teleplay: Joss Whedon

Recurring cast: Kristine Sutherland (Joyce Summers); Eliza Dushku (Faith); Harry Groener (Mayor Richard Wilkins III); Alexis Denisof (Wesley Wyndam-Pryce); Armin Shimerman (Principal Snyder); Emma Caulfield (Anya); Mercedes McNab (Harmony)

Guest cast: Ethan Erickson (Percy West); James Lurie (Mr. Miller); Hal Robinson (Professor Lester Worth); John Rosenfeld (vamp); Adrian Neil (vamp)

Music: "Sunday Mail" (as Buffy enters Faith's apartment), by Spectator Pump, from *Styrofoam Archives*

Plot: Faith shoots Angel with a poison arrow. Anya sheds light on the Ascension.

THIS WEEK'S POISON: The Killer of the Dead, which is fatal to vampires. The only antidote is for the afflicted vamp to drain a Slayer of her blood.

ANALYSIS: Once Anya explains exactly what the Ascension is—a human transforming into a pure demon, which is much bigger and more powerful than the human/demon hybrids they have encountered up until now—the enormity of their situation finally sinks in. But just when the group, and the world, needs Buffy to be at her most focused, Faith knows exactly how to distract her: shooting Angel with a slow-acting poison. Faith doesn't want merely to distract Buffy, she wants her to suffer.

The heightened emotions of the pending Ascension bring a different response from everyone. Anya's "fight or flight" mechanism kicks in and she chooses the latter option. Oz and Willow find sexual comfort in one another. Giles asserts himself again as Watcher figure. And Buffy cuts off all ties with the Council, realizing she needs to take charge herself. She already possesses all the skills she needs to defeat the mayor; she just has to listen to her instincts and draw strength from the people around her.

THE REAL HORROR: Being reduced to the other person's level. Faith always taunted Buffy about burying her Slayer killer instinct beneath talk of nobility and duty. Buffy finally lets out her own dark side when confronted with the possibility of Angel's death. Although Buffy seems incapable of taking a human life, she seems willing to make an exception with Faith. When Xander says he's afraid of losing Buffy, he's not so much worried that Buffy will be killed, but that a part of her soul will be lost if she crosses that line. Fortunately for Buffy, although she seriously wounds Faith, she is saved from having to make the ultimate choice of taking a life. She's left with one chance to save Angel and it's clear she's willing to make the ultimate sacrifice to do so.

IT'S A MYSTERY: How does Buffy know Faith's new address?

BLOOPERS: During their fight, Faith tumbles into some debris and her backside gets covered in white dust. A few moments later the dust has disappeared.

OF SPECIAL NOTE: When describing the Ascension she witnessed, Anya talks about the demon Lohesh, which in demon lore is a four-winged soul-killer.

Angel can enter the professor's house uninvited because once the owner is dead, the invitation requirement no longer exists.

56. "Graduation Day (Part II)"
(JULY 13, 1999)

Director: Joss Whedon
Teleplay: Joss Whedon
Recurring cast: Eliza Dushku (Faith); Harry Groener (Mayor Richard Wilkins III); Alexis Denisof (Wesley Wyndam-Pryce); Armin Shimerman (Principal Snyder); Danny Strong (Jonathan); Mercedes McNab (Harmony)
Guest cast: Larry Bagby III (Larry); Ethan Erickson (Percy); Paulo Andres (Dr. Powell); Susan Chuang (nurse); Tom Bellin (Dr. Gold); Samuel Bliss Cooper (vamp Lakey)

Plot: After saving Angel's life, Buffy devises an unconventional plan to defeat the mayor.

THIS WEEK'S TRANSFORMATION: The Ascended mayor as a giant—and very hungry—serpent.

ANALYSIS: High school is an evil that one must vanquish on the way to adulthood. This premise is presented with an exclamation point in this episode. Because it so envelops us during perhaps the most socially formative years of our lives, and because high school is such a self-contained experience and environment, the idea of life beyond those academic walls sometimes seems as if it will always remain out of reach. In the case of Buffy and her friends, just making it to see tomorrow seems iffy as they prepare for the mayor's Ascension.

Although Buffy is numbed by the prospect of Angel leaving, watching him die is simply out of the question. The depth of her commitment to and love for Angel leaves no other option but to offer her own blood to save him, trusting him to stop in time to keep her from dying. He does, and now—even if their lives will be spent apart—they are bound by ties that transcend any force of nature.

For the past three years Buffy has been diligently, if sometimes crankily, saving as many of her classmates as possible from the variety of horrors thrown their way by the Hellmouth. Now, in order to fight the mayor, Buffy has to ask their help in return, and all give it willingly. Better to die on the offensive than wait to be a demon snack. And Faith reveals the key to defeating the mayor to Buffy—when they invade each other's dreams—an ironic twist indicating it is possible that Faith isn't beyond redemption just yet.

Another clever irony is that, while love and loyalty prove to be the mayor's weakness (after Buffy shows the transformed Wilkins the knife she stabbed Faith with, he follows her into the booby-trapped library), those same traits are also the greatest source of human strength.

THE REAL HORROR: Saying goodbye. They say the devil you know is better than the devil you don't. As they walk away from high school to face a an uncertain future, Buffy and her friends are also saying goodbye to their childhoods. While they have gained wisdom and strength, they have also lost their innocence—in more ways than one. While their optimism remains, it is tempered by the knowledge that, as young adults, we are not in control of our destiny as much as we once thought we were.

As the smoke clears, Buffy is still numb, and has yet to absorb all that has happened. But cutting through the haze is her last vision of Angel, staring silently through the haze, his silence a deafening profession of undying love.

While she survives the day, a part of her heart dies as he turns and walks out of her life.

IT'S A MYSTERY: What exactly "counting down from seven-three-oh" means. The same phrase is referred to in Season Four, in "Restless" (Episode 78). Some fans have suggested it pertains to the fact that in two years (730 days), Buffy will die in the "The Gift" (Episode 100).

BLOOPERS: When Angel is talking on the pay phone, you can see the reflection of his fingers in the phone handle, and, later, when he grabs the mayor in the hospital, Angel's reflection is seen briefly in the glass of the room's door.

OF SPECIAL NOTE: Not only was the broadcast of this episode delayed out of deference to the Columbine shooting, but the ending was rewritten. Originally, as they walk away at the end, Xander had lines expressing the thrill of having blown up the school. Those were cut out and the episode ends in a much more thoughtful note.

✦ SEASON FOUR ✦

Fourth-year overview: Just when Buffy was getting the hang of high school, she now finds herself having to start school over again. While Willow and Oz easily adapt to the transition to college, Buffy feels disjointed and out of place. Xander also has to adjust to being odd man out, since his school days are officially over and he faces uncertain job prospects. The one constant is the Hellmouth, but this year Buffy will learn that even people with the best of intentions can unwittingly release evil on the world.

SEASON FOUR REGULAR CAST

Sarah Michelle Gellar (*Buffy Summers*)
Nicholas Brendon (*Xander Harris*)
Alyson Hannigan (*Willow Rosenberg*)
Seth Green (*Oz*)
James Marsters (*Spike*)
Marc Blucas (*Riley Finn*)
Anthony Stewart Head (*Rupert Giles*)

✦

57. "The Freshman"
(OCTOBER 5, 1999)

Director: Joss Whedon
Teleplay: Joss Whedon
Recurring cast: Kristine Sutherland (Joyce Summers); Marc Blucas (Riley Finn); Phina Oruche (Olivia); Lindsay Crouse (Professor Maggie Walsh)

Guest cast: Dagney Kerr (Kathy Newman); Pedro Balmaceda (Eddie); Katharine Towne (Sunday); Mike Rad (rookie); Shannon Hillary (Dav); Mace Lombard (Tom); Robert Catrini (Professor Riegert); Scott Rinker (R.A.); Denice J. Sealy (student volunteer); Evie Peck (angry girl); Jason Christopher (guy); Jane Silvia (conservative woman); Mark Silverberg (passing student); Walt Borchert (new vampire)

Music: "Universe" (as Buffy walks on campus), by Stretch Princess, from *Stretch Princess*; "Freaky Soul" (as Buffy walks into the dorm), by Paul Riordan, from *Alternative Volume 1*; "I Wish that I Could Be You" (as vamps talk), by the Muffs, from *Alert Today, Alive Tomorrow*; "Memory of a Free Festival" (as Buffy walks into Giles's apartment), by David Bowie, from *Space Oddity*; "You and Me" (at the Bronze), by Splendid, from *Have You Got a Name*

Plot: Buffy is overwhelmed by the adjustment to college life, and it begins to affect her self-confidence—and her Slayer duties.

THIS WEEK'S BIG BAD ON CAMPUS: A vampire named Sunday, who preys on college kids.

INTRODUCING: An unemployed Giles and his new girlfriend, Olivia; Buffy's dorm roommate, Kathy; psychology professor Walsh; Riley Finn, Walsh's teacher's aide.

ANALYSIS: Buffy is lost, literally and figuratively. Instead of being an exciting adventure, her first day on campus feels like a test that she's failing miserably. All around her are enthusiastic faces, including Willow's, but Buffy feels overwhelmed and out of place.

Typically, the one potential new friend she meets, disappears under mysterious circumstances. Making her feel even more adrift is Giles's apparent emotional distance and his disinterest in the turn of events. Part of the reason is that he has company from England—a new squeeze named Olivia—and then there's the fact that Giles has been unemployed since they blew up the school in order to kill the mayor.

Buffy's encounter with a street-tough vamp named Sunday—who goes after kids who aren't adapting well to college life, leaving fake suicide notes and stealing all their belongings—goes badly, leaving Buffy humiliated on top of everything else. Sunday's m.o. strikes a nerve in Buffy because, of course, *she's* not adapting quickly to college.

Xander's pep talk reminds Buffy that she's not as alone as her self-pity was making her feel and it's a reinvigorated Slayer who goes out to dust some vampire butt. When Giles runs in—albeit after the fight is over—guilt-ridden over not having paid more attention to Buffy, it emphasizes that the ties binding Buffy and her friends remain strong regardless of what environment they find themselves in.

THE REAL HORROR: Change. For all her complaints about high school, at least it was familiar and offered a sense of structure for Buffy. Back when she first came to Sunnydale, Buffy was more outgoing and, in fact, established the foundation for her friendship with Willow and Xander the first day of school. It wasn't until she started Slaying that she felt like an outcast. Walking around the large campus, unsure where to go, and feeling like a jerk for not enjoying the college experience as much as she thinks she's supposed to, Buffy seems dwarfed.

IT'S A MYSTERY: How were Sunday and her minions able to enter Buffy's dorm room uninvited? Are we to assume that Kathy invited them and didn't intervene when they stripped Buffy's side of the room bare?

BLOOPERS: When the vamps clean out Eddie's room, you can see a couple of them in the mirror above the sink.

OF SPECIAL NOTE: The "University of Sunnydale" is actually UCLA.
Katharine Towne, who plays Sunday, previously worked with Sarah Michelle Gellar in the 1999 movie *She's All That*.

58. "Living Conditions"
(OCTOBER 12, 1999)

Director: David Grossman
Teleplay: Marti Noxon
Guest cast: Dagney Kerr (Kathy Newman); Adam Kaufman (Parker Abrams); Paige Moss (Veruca); Clayton Barber (demon #1); Walt Borchert (demon #2); Roger Morrissey (Tapparich); David Tuckman (freshman)

Music: "Believe" (played several times by Buffy's roommate Kathy), by Cher, from *Believe*; "Pain" (as Willows hangs a poster of Oz's band), by Four Star Mary

Plot: Nobody believes Buffy when she says there's something very wrong with her roommate.

THIS WEEK'S DEMON TRANSFER STUDENT: Kathy, a Mok'tagar demon disguised as a college student, who tries to rob Buffy of her soul to prevent her family from finding her and taking her back to the demon dimension.

INTRODUCING: Parker Abrams; Veruca.

ANALYSIS: While some college students become great friends with their dorm roommates, just as many find themselves suffering through a year of incompatibility. From the moment Buffy set eyes on Kathy, her Slayer instincts kicked up a notch—and it wasn't just Kathy's preference for Celine Dion.

Back at Sunnydale High, Giles and the others probably would have paid more attention to Buffy and taken her concerns more seriously. But because of Buffy's obvious difficulties adapting to college, everyone assumes she's just being oversensitive. Even after Buffy complains of nightmares in which a demon is sucking out her soul, the others refuse to point the finger at Kathy. And when Buffy's demeanor takes a *War of the Roses*-type turn toward her roomie, the others worry that Buffy may be dangerously close to the edge. While it's true that the whole college experience is threatening to suck the life out of Buffy, she knows the difference and is frustrated that the others doubt her.

After Kathy reveals her true demon self, the sense of vindication Buffy feels in discovering she's been right all along seems to give Buffy a new sense of purpose and a boost of confidence, evaporating much of her recent broodiness.

THE REAL HORROR: Feeling like Cassandra, the woman in Greek mythology who was given the gift of prophecy, along with the curse that nobody believed what she predicted. Instead of accepting Buffy's observation that Kathy must be a demon, Willow and the others assume Buffy is buckling under the pressure of college. Although they all apologize later, if one of Kathy's fellow demons had not appeared to drag Kathy back to the other dimension when he did, Buffy may have paid for Willow and friends' disbelief with her life.

BLOOPERS: When Giles and Buffy are talking, his towel moves around from one shot to the next.

When they get up to tighten the ropes holding her, Oz is on Xander's right. After Buffy knocks them out, the shot of them on the floor has Oz on Xander's left.

OF SPECIAL NOTE: Clayton Barber, who played demon #1, had previously worked as Angel's stunt double.

59. "The Harsh Light of Day"
(OCTOBER 19, 1999)

Director: James A. Contner
Teleplay: Jane Espenson
Recurring cast: Emma Caulfield (Anya); Mercedes McNab (Harmony); Adam Kaufman (Parker)
Guest cast: Jason Hall (Devon); Melik (Brian)
Music: "Dilate" (performed by Oz's band), by Four Star Mary, from *Thrown to the Wolves*; "Take Me Down," by Psychic Rain, from *Spun Out*; "Moment of Weakness" (at fraternity party), by Bif Naked from *I, Bifcus*; "Faith in Love" (as Harmony seduces Spike), by Devil Doll, from *Queen of Pain*; "Anything," by Bif Naked, from *I Bificus*; "Lucky" (as Buffy and Parker dance), by Bif Naked, from *I Bificus*; "It's Over, It's Under" (as Buffy looks for Harmony), by Dollshead, from *Frozen Charlotte*

Plot: Spike returns to Sunnydale with a new girlfriend, while Buffy looks for a new romance.

THIS WEEK'S VAMPIRE ACCESSORY: The Gem of Amara, which makes the wearer invincible.

INTRODUCING: Harmony as vampire vamp.

ANALYSIS: Angel has been gone long enough that Buffy is ready to try and get on with her life. So when the handsome Parker shows interest in her, Buffy responds—spurred on by Willow, who wants Buffy to be as happy romantically as Willow is with Oz. Meanwhile, Spike is back and, in his effort to get over Drusilla, has hooked up with Harmony, who was turned into a vamp during the melee following the mayor's Ascension. Although there is vigorous sexual heat between the two, it's obvious Spike isn't in love with Harmony, but is just using her to fill the void of being alone.

Unfortunately for Buffy, Parker isn't all that different from Spike. Once they finally have sex, Parker's interest in her dims. Buffy is shell-shocked. She had been the sole object of Angel's love and desire, so to find herself in a position of blatant rejection is new. But instead of feeling angry and telling Parker off, Buffy is engulfed with desperation and wants to get him back.

Also, Anya is trying to sort out her feelings for Xander. Her plan to get over him by having sex backfired, making her want him all the more. Although Xander is beginning to have feelings for Anya, he's hesitant about voicing them; but whether it's because of her past as a man-hating demon, or because the prospect of a serious relationship is a bit scary, is up for debate.

Buffy's distraction over Parker is almost fatal when she's blindsided by Spike, who's able to survive in sunlight thanks to the ring he's wearing. But, to Spike's utter frustration, Buffy proves she can still get the best of him and he narrowly avoids going up in a puff of smoke after she wrests the ring off his finger. Her decision to give the ring to Angel speaks not only of her desire for Angel to live a more normal life, but is a reflection of her new appreciation for just how special he and his love for her are. It's going to be tough for Buffy to find something that can ever come close to it.

THE REAL HORROR: Being used. The reason Buffy still wants Parker after he uses her for sex is that she doesn't want to feel discarded. If they continue to go out, in her mind it means their sexual encounter—and, by extension, Buffy herself—was as special to him as it had been for her. Buffy learns the sad lesson that just because she might fall for a mortal man, doesn't mean the road to romance will be any easier.

BLOOPERS: After Spike takes the necklace off, it reappears in the next shot.

OF SPECIAL NOTE: James Marsters was not listed in the opening credits when the episode first aired so as not to ruin the surprise of Spike being back. In reruns, his name is listed.

Originally this episode aired as part one of a *Buffy/Angel* crossover.

60. "𝔉ear 𝔌tself"
(OCTOBER 26, 1999)

Director: Tucker Gates
Teleplay: David Fury
Recurring cast: Kristine Sutherland (Joyce); Marc Blucas (Riley Finn); Emma Caulfield (Anya); Adam Kaufman (Parker); Lindsay Crouse (Professor Maggie Walsh)
Guest cast: Marc Rose (Josh); Sulo Williams (Chaz); Aldis Hodge (masked teen); Walter Emanuel Jones (Edward); Adam Bitterman (Gachnar); Michele Nordin (Rachel); Adam Grimes (lobster boy); Darris Love (hallmate); Larissa Reynolds (present girl)
Music: "Kool" (during party setup), by 28 Days, from *Kid Indestructible*; "Ow Ow Ow" (as party starts), by Third Grade Teacher, from *Greatest Hits Volume 1*; "Pretty Please" (as the group approaches the fraternity house), by Verbena, from *Into the Pink*

Plot: A Halloween frat party turns into a real haunted house.

THIS WEEK'S HALLOWEEN HORROR: Gachnar, a demon that feeds off people's fears.

INTRODUCING: Anya's fear of bunnies.

ANALYSIS: Parker's rejection still has Buffy depressed and withdrawn. Her emotional preoccupation with Parker is interfering with her Slaying. This is emphasized when she mistakes a student in a costume for a real demon. She's so wrapped up in her own angst that she doesn't notice that Xander is also fighting feelings of rejection, by Buffy and Willow, after they initially neglect to include him in a Halloween party thrown by a UC Sunnydale frat house. Anya doesn't help matters any by bluntly pointing out that Xander has nothing in common with the others—and on the surface, she is correct. But Anya, the still-developing human, fails to understand that people don't have to live the same lives to be friends; that friendship is based on kindred spirits caring and showing concern for each other.

Once they enter the frat house for the Halloween party, it's soon apparent the Hellmouth is at it again, as everyone's fears are coming true. Xander becomes invisible and Buffy gets angry because now she thinks Xander has bailed on her, too—just as dead bodies begin rising out of the ground to attack her. Oz's fear of losing control is made manifest when he starts to transform into a werewolf. And Willow's worry that she'll never be a good Wicca results in a spell backfiring—again. Eventually Buffy and the others overcome their fears and together they confront the demon controlling the frat house. In a clever twist, the demon itself turns out to be just a few inches tall. The only real power he had was the power given to him by people giving in to their fears. It's only by confronting fears that they can be overcome.

THE REAL HORROR: Feeling abandoned. Every time Buffy opens her heart to someone, they seem to leave. Parker's rejection opened old wounds for Buffy, who has never truly gotten over feeling abandoned by her dad after the divorce. Buffy is learning the hard way that the only way to find love is to open your heart—but by doing so, you also open yourself to hurt.

BLOOPERS: When Willow is checking Buffy's wound, the position of her left braid changes from one shot to the next.

OF SPECIAL NOTE: The title is taken from the famous line by Franklin Delano Roosevelt—"The only thing we have to fear is fear itself"—spoken during his inaugural address in March 1933, referring to America's struggle to recover after the Great Depression.

61. "Beer Bad"
(NOVEMBER 2, 1999)

Director: David Solomon
Teleplay: Tracey Forbes
Recurring cast: Marc Blucas (Riley Finn); Adam Kaufman (Parker); Lindsay Crouse (Professor Maggie Walsh)
Guest cast: Eric Matheny (main cave guy); Stephen M. Porter (Jack); Paige Moss (Veruca)

Music: "Overfire" (at the Bronze), by THC, from *Adagio*; "Nothing But You" (on the jukebox), by Kim Ferron, from the *Buffy the Vampire Slayer* soundtrack; "Ladyfingers" (in the dorm room), by Luscious Jackson, from *Electric Honey*

Plot: *Buffy drinks to drown her sorrows; she and her drinking buddies revert to cavemen.*

THIS WEEKS' WICKED BREW: Spiked beer that turns people into Neanderthals.

INTRODUCING: Oz's curious fascination with Veruca, who sings with a local Sunnydale band called Shy.

ANALYSIS: Buffy preoccupation with Parker borders on obsession, although reality does seem to be sinking in, slowly. After having fantasies of rescuing Parker, and his begging forgiveness, Buffy morosely concludes that she was an idiot for falling for his pickup line. When some self-important college guys ask her to join them for a beer, it seems like the perfect opportunity to get Parker off her mind. Like most college students, Buffy assumes she has it under control and sucks down beer after beer, oblivious to how it's affecting her and those she's with. All she knows is that it makes her troubles seem less important—even if the trade-off is a decidedly compromised mental acuity.

Across town, Willow's sense of security is rocked by Oz's fascination with a singer they hear at the Bronze. Up until this point, Oz never has seemed remotely interested in anyone else. But when Parker tries to put the moves on Willow, she accuses him of not being much different than a caveman, dragging a woman away by her hair to have sex. The heart of what Willow is saying—that, for all our civilization, our primal urges remain the same—will soon hit closer to home than she can imagine.

Although Buffy's beer binges have reduced her to a primitive state, her Slayer instincts aren't completely deadened and she manages to save several people, including Parker, from a fire started by her Neanderthal drinking buddies. As she slowly sobers up, it's apparent the experience has been cathartic. Buffy proves she now realizes it was Parker who was the jerk—by smacking him on the head with a club—and that she's ready to move on with her life.

THE REAL HORROR: Being a fool. Not only did Buffy let herself get talked into a one-night stand with Parker, but she compounded her misery by turning to alcohol for solace. The moral of this episode is clear and direct: The consequences of drinking can be fatal.

BLOOPERS: As Xander practices bartending, the two coffee cups on the table seem to change positions from one shot to the next.

OF SPECIAL NOTE: This episode received an Emmy nomination for "Outstanding Hairstyling for a Series" in the 52nd Annual Emmy Awards.

MUSICAL NOTE: Although Shy is the name of Veruca's band, the music they are performing actually performed by THC.

62. "Wild at Heart"
(NOVEMBER 9, 1999)

Director: David Grossman
Teleplay: Marti Noxon
Recurring cast: Marc Blucas (Riley Finn); James Marsters (Spike); Lindsay Crouse (Professor Maggie Walsh)
Guest cast: Paige Moss (Veruca)
Music: "Good Enough" (in the Bronze), by Eight Stops Seven, from *In Moderation*; "Dip" (song performed by Veruca), by THC, from *Adagio*; "Need to Destroy" (song Veruca rehearses), from *Adagio*

Plot: Oz makes a fateful decision after confronting his inner beast.

ANALYSIS: Oz takes center stage in this episode. Despite his seemingly thoughtful and introspective nature, Oz has never fully confronted exactly what it means to be a werewolf. Because he carefully locks himself away the three nights a month he transforms, he has fooled himself into believing he is in control of the wolf. But his close encounter of the erotic kind with fellow werewolf Veruca jolts him out of his complacency. His previous fascination with Veruca was based on mutual lupine recognition, and their sexual encounter while in their transformed state—has Oz taking a new look at himself. Veruca's embrace of the wolf, and its thrill of the kill, frighten Oz because up to now he has buried those thoughts. But he realizes that, although he transforms only three days a month, the wolf is part of who he is, daily.

After Willow discovers Oz and Veruca in his cage after an obvious night of passion, Willow feels betrayed and insecure about her own sex appeal. Buffy offers her a shoulder to cry on but, typically, the Slayer feels better taking action. In this case, Veruca not only broke her friend's heart but is a killer werewolf who needs to be stopped.

Veruca is simply doing what comes naturally and doesn't understand why Oz would want to fight the power that comes with their transformation, which she obviously finds to be a powerful aphrodisiac—similar to the way Faith finds Slaying a turn-on. Veruca believes all she has to do is kill Willow in order to set free the animal in Oz. But Veruca's threat to Willow so enrages Oz that he turns his transforming animal self on Veruca and kills her.

Although extremely hurt and disillusioned by Oz's indiscretion, it's not necessarily a relationship-breaker as far as Willow is concerned. So she is stunned when she finds Oz packing to leave Sunnydale. Buffy empathizes with her hurt and knows from her own sad experiences that it is going to take Willow a long time to recover.

THE REAL HORROR: Losing control. Even though Oz loves Willow, his inability to control the animal inside him puts their relationship at risk when he is seduced by the danger in Veruca. His decision to leave is prompted by his unwillingness to endanger Willow emotionally or physically, and his desire to understand the animal within himself in order to learn to control it. But as he drives away, it is clear he believes that day will be a long time coming.

OF SPECIAL NOTE: Seth Green and Paige Moss previously worked together in the 1998 film *Can't Hardly Wait.*

Whedon originally meant for the fiery relationship between Oz and Veruca to develop over most of the season, but the storyline was cut short after Seth Green's decision to leave the show.

63. "The Initiative"
(NOVEMBER 16, 1999)

Director: James A. Contner
Teleplay: Douglas Petrie
Recurring cast: Marc Blucas (Riley Finn); Mercedes McNab (Harmony Kendall); Adam Kaufman (Parker Abrams); Bailey Chase (Graham); Leonard Roberts (Forrest); Lindsay Crouse (Professor Maggie Walsh)

Guest cast: Mace Lombard (Tom); Scott Becker (lost freshman)

Music: "Welcome" (song Willow listens to when Riley visits), by Jake Lee Rau, from *Joy*; "Bodyrock" (at party), by Moby, from *Play*; "Never Say Never" (as Willow and Riley sit on the couch), by That Dog, from *Retreat*; "Fate" (at party), by Four Star Mary, from *Four Star Mary*

Plot: Spike is held prisoner. Riley figures out he's got a crush on Buffy.

THIS WEEK'S COVERT GOVERNMENT AGENCY: The Initiative. Riley Finn passes himself off as an unassuming teacher's aide, but in reality he's part of a secret government group operating in Sunnydale.

INTRODUCING: James Marsters as a series regular.

ANALYSIS: This episode sets the stage for the main story arc for the season. It becomes apparent the shadowy figures in black, who have been spotted running around campus, are hunting and capturing vampires for unexplained reasons. After being captured and finding himself locked in a sterile cell, Spike naturally blames the Slayer for all his troubles and keeps his spirits up by fantasizing how he's going to give her her overdue comeuppance.

For over a hundred years Spike has prided himself on being a literal terror; Buffy constantly bruising his demon-ego has grown very old. But when he discovers he can no longer bite anyone, courtesy of a chip implanted into his brain by the Initiative, Spike undergoes an identity crisis. Even worse, the commandos are chasing him and he's running out of places to hide.

Trying to figure out who exactly these men in black are, Buffy is unaware of Riley's growing attraction to her—in part because it takes Riley awhile to realize it himself. When working as a teacher's aide or on a mission for the Initiative, Riley is a take-command kind of guy. But when it comes to Buffy, his self-confidence deflates and he's like a tongue-tied schoolboy. That duality will eventually be the key to unlocking Buffy's heart.

THE REAL HORROR: Bad timing. Between Buffy's Slaying and his secret government work, it seems Riley never will find the right moment to finally ask Buffy out.

OF SPECIAL NOTE: The names on the dorm list include *Buffy* crew members like Jeff Pruitt and David Solomon.

It is revealed that Oz's real name is Daniel Osbourne.

MUSICAL NOTE: The song "Fate," by Four Star Mary, was previously featured in Episode 16, "Inca Mummy Girl."

64. "𝕻angs"
(NOVEMBER 23, 1999)

Director: Michael Lange

Teleplay: Jane Espenson

Recurring cast: Marc Blucas (Riley Finn); Mercedes McNab (Harmony Kendall); Emma Caulfield (Anya); Leonard Roberts (Forrest); Bailey Chase (Graham); Tod Thawley (Hus); David Boreanaz (Angel)

Guest cast: Margaret Easley (curator); William Vogt (Jamie); Mark Ankeny (Dean Guerrero)

Plot: Xander accidentally releases an Indian vengeance spirit. Angel secretly returns to Sunnydale to protect Buffy.

THIS WEEK'S UNWANTED THANKSGIVING GUEST: Hus, a Native-American vengeance spirit from the Chumash tribe, who seeks retribution for the death of his people.

ANALYSIS: Nothing puts a damper on Thanksgiving like a reminder of the Indians massacred at the hands of American settlers. Good and evil are often clearly delineated for Buffy, but from time to time she encounters moral shades of gray. While the Indian spirit released from the chamber must be stopped from killing any more Sunnydale residents, his rage and revenge are justified by the slaughter of his people. Willow represents the conscience of the group; although she doesn't want any more people to die, neither does she necessarily want to kill the Indian spirit, because he has a point.

Spike's ego has been thoroughly ground to dust and he finds himself in such desperate straits that he turns to Buffy for help, in exchange for information on the Indian spirit. Although he's treated with distrust, and trussed like a turkey to the chair just in case, Spike seems surprisingly comfortable among his former foes. Helpless, Spike finds himself in the unlikely position of desperately wanting the Slayer to win one for the good guys after Hus turns himself into a bear. Although Spike's not exactly a welcome guest, once Buffy sends Hus and his tribe back into the green ether, Spike is given refuge. He sits in his chair listening to the others go on about their typically complicated lives, and gets to see Buffy's life from her perspective, giving him a better insight into who she is.

THE REAL HORROR: Holiday dinners. Holidays can force a festive mood on us, which we often respond to with surliness. Although Thanksgiving is supposed to be a time of reflection and giving thanks for the blessings in our lives, whenever you get enough friends or family members around a dinner table, bickering inevitably ensues. But the tensions Buffy and her friends experience reflect just how much they've grown into a true family.

IT'S A MYSTERY: Why does Anya act as if she's never seen Angel before? She did meet him—when vampire Willow was sent back to the alternative universe. (see Episode 50, "Doppelgängland.")

BLOOPERS: After getting shot with arrows, Spike's shirt has no apparent holes in it.

OF SPECIAL NOTE: Angel returns to Sunnydale after his friend Doyle has a vision that Buffy is in danger, seen at the end of an episode of *Angel*, "The Bachelor Party."

65. "Something Blue"
(NOVEMBER 30, 1999)

Director: Nick Marck
Teleplay: Tracey Forbes
Recurring cast: Marc Blucas (Riley Finn); Emma Caulfield (Anya); Elizabeth Anne Allen (Amy)
Guest cast: Andy Umberger (D'Hoffryn)
Music: "All the Small Things" (as Willow dances), by Blink 182, from *Enema of the State*

Plot: Willow's magic has unintended effects on her friends.

THIS WEEK'S DILEMMA: A spell gone bad.

ANALYSIS: This time it's Willow's turn to wallow in self-pity. After discovering that Oz sent for all his things, Willow turns to Buffy for help but doesn't feel she's getting the degree of sympathy she deserves. Nor does she want to hear that it just takes time to get over being hurt. Because Willow has special powers, she decides to use them as self-help and casts a spell she hopes will mend her heart overnight.

Although she's powerful, Willow is a greenhorn. Like a beginning golfer who can hit the ball a country mile but can't control where it'll land, Willow's spell works, but not in the way she thought it would. She accidentally causes Giles to go blind, Buffy and Spike to get engaged, and Xander to be hunted by every demon in Sunnydale.

While it's easy to understand that she wants to make her pain go away, Willow is taking the first step down what will ultimately be a treacherous road. Using powers to help defeat evil is one thing; using powers to alter the natural emotional course of one's life is quite another. Anya seems to be the only one of the group who appreciates how powerful Willow must be for D'Hoffryn to offer Willow the vengeance-demon gig, but the others—too preoccupied by the spells they are under—don't pick up on it, nor do they effectively confront Willow after the spell is reversed. Perhaps because Willow has always been so grounded and steady, they miss some of the early warning signs foretelling dark times ahead.

THE REAL HORROR: Lashing out at those you love most. Because she is so hurt by Oz leaving, Willow inappropriately turns her pain and anger toward Buffy and the others. In real life you run the risk of alienating your friends; in Sunnydale such self-indulgence can result in your friends losing their lives.

IT'S A MYSTERY: Does D'Hoffryn have to get a person's permission before turning them into a demon, or is he just being polite?

BLOOPERS: Spoke's reflection is visible in Giles's glass bookcase.

OF SPECIAL NOTE: This episode introduces the idea of a Spike-Buffy romance.

REVELATION

As Willow and Buffy walk down the street after everyone's voice is stolen, they pass a man holding up a sign that says, "REVELATION 15:1." That biblical passage reads, "And I saw another sign in heaven, great and marvelous, seven angels having the seven last plagues; for in them is filled up the wrath of God." The Book of Revelation was written by John the Apostle and has been interpreted as being his divinely inspired vision of the end of the world.

66. "Hush"
(DECEMBER 14, 1999)

Director: Joss Whedon
Teleplay: Joss Whedon
Recurring cast: Marc Blucas (Riley Finn); Emma Caulfield (Anya); Leonard Roberts (Forrest); Phina Oruche (Olivia); Amber Benson (Tara); Lindsay Crouse (Professor Maggie Walsh)
Guest cast: Doug Jones (Gentleman); Camden Toy (Gentleman); Brooke Bloom (girl in Wicca group); Jessica Townsend (girl in Wicca group); Don W. Lewis (Gentleman); Charlie Brumbly (Gentleman); Carlos Amezcua (newscaster); Elizabeth Truax (little girl); Wayne Sable (freshman)
Music: "Danse Macabre" (during Giles's lecture in auditorium), by Camille Saint-Saëns

Plot: Buffy fights a silent enemy. Riley finally sees the Slayer in action.

THIS WEEK'S FAIRY-TALE MONSTERS: The Gentleman—demons who descend on a town and steal everyone's voices so they can cut the hearts out of seven people. They need their victims to be silent because the sound of a scream kills the Gentlemen.

INTRODUCING: Amber Benson as Tara, who meets Willow during an on-campus Wicca meeting.

ANALYSIS: Now that she is officially single, Willow looks to fill her free time by more aggressively pursuing witchcraft. But she is soon disappointed to discover the campus group is Wiccan in name only. The only one in the group who seems to share her interest is Tara. Shy and unassuming, Tara is also observant and can sense the power, and also the loneliness, within Willow.

Buffy wants to get closer to Riley but her secret life as the Slayer is a big obstacle. She doesn't want a relationship filled with lies and deceit, but at the same time, doesn't want to endanger Riley with her lifestyle. Ironically, Riley is confronting the same dilemma, unsure how he can keep his commitment to the Initiative secret and carry on a meaningful relationship at the same time.

Once the Gentlemen take away everyone's voices, Buffy and the others are forced to communicate either through writing, or expression and body language. Tara and Willow, though, can also communicate through their powers. In order to keep the Gentlemen from attacking them, Tara and Willow join hands and their combined power moves a soda machine to block the door. More than that, the touch of their hands sends a clear signal to both of them that there is something more powerful than witchcraft at work.

Riley and Buffy both finally end up battling the Gentleman, trying to release the stolen voices. After her earsplitting scream causes their heads to pop, Buffy must face an even greater challenge—explaining to Riley who she really is.

THE REAL HORROR: Being unable to find the words. At the end, when Buffy and Riley are confronted with having to be honest with each other about who they are, neither one knows what to say. As people get older and life gets more complicated, it sometimes can be difficult to say exactly what we mean, and out of fear of a negative reaction, we say nothing.

BLOOPERS: The tower clock switches between two different times from one shot to the next.

WHAT JOSS WHEDON HAS TO SAY: "The Gentlemen came from many storybooks and many silent movies and many horror movies and many nightmares—and Mr. Burns from *The Simpsons*."

DEGREES OF SEPARATION: The music Giles plays in the lecture hall, "Danse Macabre," is used as the theme for the British series *Jonathan Creek*. Anthony Stewart Head had a recurring role as a magician in *Jonathan Creek*, but he had to be replaced after the show's first season because of his *Buffy* commitments.

OF SPECIAL NOTE: this Episode was nominated for an Emmy Award in the "Best Writing in a Drama Series" category, and also received a nomination for "Outstanding Cinematography for a Single-Camera Series."

Lindsay Crouse and Amber Benson appeared together in the 1995 movie *Bye, Bye, Love*.

The newscaster seen in this episode, Carlos Amezcua, is the real-life co-anchor on KTLA's morning news. The weatherman from that same show, Mark Kriski, appeared in Episode 44, "Amends," in Season Three.

67. "Doomed"
(JANUARY 18, 2000)

Director: James A. Contner
Teleplay: David Fury and Jane Epsenson
Recurring cast: Leonard Roberts (Forrest Gates); Bailey Chase (Graham Miller), Ethan Erickson (Percy West)
Guest cast: Anastasia Horne (Laurie); Anthony Anselmi (partier)
Music: "Hey" (during party), by the Hellacopters, from *Payin' the Dues*; "Mouth Almighty" (while Willow is eavesdropping on Percy), by Echobelly, from *Lustra*

Plot: Buffy keeps Riley at bay while trying to prevent the end of the world. Again.

THIS WEEK'S APOCALYPTIC DEMONS: Vahrall demons, who plan to end the world with a recipe that includes the blood of a man, the bones of a child, a special talisman, and three sacrifices.

INTRODUCING: Riley as commando to the Scooby Gang. His cover is blown when he shows up to help fight the demons.

ANALYSIS: Instead of being relieved that Riley is in a similar line of work, discovering that he's a demon fighter causes Buffy to instinctively push him away. It's too similar to her relationship with Angel, and she's worried Riley will be a constant reminder of what she has lost if she works side by side with him the way she did with Angel. Plus, the idea of seeing someone she cares for injured or killed is a pain she doesn't want to set herself up for again.

Riley, though, doesn't worry about the "What if?"s. He knows how he feels about Buffy—and he feels pursuing a relationship with her is worth whatever risk they expose themselves to. He knows great joy doesn't come without the risk of also being hurt.

Spike, in the meantime, is finding his neutered vampire life not worth living. He has no purpose, and the humiliation of having to depend on Buffy's friends for everything makes him suicidal, but he can't even dust himself properly. Worried that he'll hurt himself, Willow drags Spike along on their hunt for the demons bent on ending the world. When he accidentally discovers that he can hurt evil without his head exploding, Spike becomes a new man, with a new sense of purpose, and helps Buffy and the others prevent the demons from making their sacrifice. Even though he has no moral commitment to "good" the way Angel does, Spike merely needs to feel alive, one way or another.

Coming to the brink of apocalypse yet again gives Buffy some newfound perspective. Life is too short to run away from the chance for love, even if it means making yourself vulnerable.

THE REAL HORROR: Having a bad premonition. It's unsettling when, for no concrete reason, we feel something bad is going to happen. It feels even worse when the premonition comes true, as did Buffy's portent of doom regarding the earthquake.

IT'S A MYSTERY: Why the rat playing Amy is a male.

BLOOPERS: The eyes of the dead boy Willow discovers, appear to open and shut from one shot to the next.

68. "𝔄 𝔑ew 𝔐an"
(JANUARY 25, 2000)

Director: Michael Gershman

Teleplay: Jane Espenson

Recurring cast: Robin Sachs (Ethan Rayne); Amber Benson (Tara); Emma Caulfield (Anya); Lindsay Crouse (Professor Maggie Walsh)

Guest cast: Elizabeth Penn Payne (waitress); Michelle Ferrara (mother)

Music: "In Good Time" (playing during Buffy's party), from *Dreamworks Demo Master*; "Over Divine" (during Buffy's party), by 12 Volt Sex, from *Pop Formula*

Plot: Giles's old nemesis Ethan Rayne is up to his old tricks.

THIS WEEK'S HANGOVER: After a night out drinking with Ethan, Giles is turned into a Fyarl demon. This species is spectacularly strong, spits paralyzing mucus, and has to be killed by something made of silver.

ANALYSIS: Giles is suffering a midlife crisis. For most of his adult life he has had a sense of purpose and knew what was expected of him. But, since being fired by the Watchers' Council and losing his job as librarian when he helped blow up Sunnydale High to kill the Ascended mayor, Giles has been living a day-to-day existence. Sure, he helps Buffy research each new evil as it arrives in town, but Buffy and the others are getting older and establishing individual lives. It stuns Giles to realize he's a middle-aged man with few friends his own age, and that his closest friends are young enough to be his children. He's also upset he's the last to know about Riley and the Initiative, and Professor Walsh adds to his feelings of uselessness when she caustically explains away Buffy's independence as a lack of a strong father figure.

Giles's brand of self-pity includes getting drunk, even if it is with Ethan Rayne, but he pays dearly for letting his guard down when he wakes up the next morning discovers he's been turned into a demon. Nobody except Spike can understand his demon dialect, so Giles is forced to ask for Spike's help. With his own recent groveling fresh in his mind, Spike agrees, but not before making Giles beg a bit, and making him agree to pay Spike money.

Now that Buffy is in a relationship with Riley, she wants to be accepted in his world and agrees to coordinate her efforts somewhat with Walsh and the Initiative. The others are wary of her getting too involved, because even though nobody can pinpoint why, something doesn't seem quite right with it. However, while Buffy may be on her best behavior, she is certainly not cowed by Walsh and refuses to let anyone interfere with her Slayer duties. So when she and the others mistakenly think Giles has been kidnapped—or worse—by a demon, Buffy is first in line to take the creature down.

Even though Buffy may have be too wrapped up in her new life with Riley to give Giles the time, attention, and respect he deserves, her connection to him remains intact. She stops herself from plunging a letter opener into his chest after one look into the demon's eyes because she immediately recognizes them as Giles's. The near-disaster makes Buffy pay better attention to keeping the lines of communication with Giles open. Lost in the chaos of getting Giles returned back to normal, however, is the bit of information passed on by Ethan Rayne, to be wary of 314. It's an oversight that will cost many lives.

THE REAL HORROR: Feeling superfluous. It's hard to feel you're making a valued contribution when you're out of work and unsure what direction your life is taking.

BLOOPERS: When demon/Giles is in Xander's room, the number of clothespins holding up the briefs on the line alternates between one and two.

MYTHOLOGICAL REFERENCE: Giles says he felt like Theseus and the Minotaur in the Labyrinth. In Greek mythology, King Minos of Crete sacrificed seven young men and seven young women to the Minotaur, a creature with the head and tail of bull and the body of a man, which lived in a maze called the Labyrinth. The Greek hero Theseus volunteered to be a victim, but when he arrived in Crete he fell in love with Ariadne, Minos's daughter. Ariadne gave Theseus a large ball of twine so he could find his way out. He tied one end to the entrance of the Labyrinth before entering, to trace his path. Once inside, he came upon the sleeping Minotaur and killed it, then followed the trail of twine back out.

OF SPECIAL NOTE: For those wondering about a body count, Buffy and her friends have killed at least one hundred vampires and fifty demons on-camera.

WICCA

Wicca is a modern "pagan" religion with roots in ancient European beliefs centered around a female fertility deity. Traditionally, many cultures have associat-  ed witchcraft with evil. But unlike those who use witchcraft as sorcery, Wiccans believe in using their magic only for the good of mankind. Their motto is, "If it harm none, do as you will."

"Wicca" is sometimes used synonymously with "witchcraft"; likewise, "witch" and "Wiccan" are often used interchangeably. But while all Wiccans are witches, not all witches are Wiccan.

The ethics of Wicca are based in personal accountability and respect for nature. The Law of Threefold Return warns that all actions, whether good or bad, will come back to the sender three times as strong. Environmental concern is also an important aspect. Because humans are of the earth, harming nature means harming ourselves—both individually and collectively—so each Wiccan strives to preserve the natural balance.

69. "The 'I' in Team"
(FEBRUARY 8, 2000)

Director: James A. Contner

Teleplay: David Fury

Recurring cast: Amber Benson (Tara); George Hertzberg (Adam); Leonard Roberts (Forrest Gates); Bailey Chase (Graham Miller); Jack Stehlin (Dr. Angleman); Emma Caulfield (Anya); Lindsay Crouse (Professor Maggie Walsh)

Guest cast: Neil Daley (Mason)

Music: "Trashed" (at the Bronze), by Lavish, from *Polaroid*; "Keep Myself Awake" (as Buffy enters the Bronze), by Black Lab, from *Your Body Above Me*; "Window to Your soul" (during both fight scene and later, in Riley and Buffy's love scene), by Delerium, from *Karma*

Plot: Buffy's involvement with the Initiative worries her friends.

THIS WEEK'S MAD SCIENTIST: Professor Maggie Walsh.

INTRODUCING: Dr. Angelman, Walsh's associate.

THE BIG BAD: Adam, a seemingly invincible new-millennium Franken-stein, fashioned out of spare demon parts.

ANALYSIS: After spending years fighting demons, vampires, and other evil creatures—with a bag of weapons and her wits—seeing the high-tech gadgetry wielded by the Initiative is awe-inspiring for Buffy. The entire operation seems so professional and organized that she's willing to accept official direction from Professor Walsh. Preoccupied with the importance of her new position, Buffy is oblivious to how much she hurt Willow's feelings by blowing off a planned girls'-night-out.

It's possible Willow is simply trying to use a night out with Buffy as a distraction. It's obvious there's an attraction between her and Tara, but at this point Willow seems frightened by it. That's why she doesn't invite Tara to the Bronze—she doesn't want other people to pick up on it because she hasn't come to terms with it yet. After Buffy shows up with a entourage of commandos, Willow takes off and ends up at Tara's door, asking if she wants to do some spells and conveying a more evocative undercurrent. Meanwhile Riley and Buffy build up so much sexual tension while fighting a demon that it serves as foreplay, and they finally consummate their relationship—under the watchful eyes of Dr. Walsh, who has planted a camera in Riley's room.

The problem with military operations is that, like the Watchers' Council, they operate by the book and don't allow for much leeway. To them, Spike is an anonymous enemy to be captured and used as a guinea pig. Xander and Giles find the Initiative even more abhorrent than Spike does, so they remove a tracking device from him and flush it down the toilet.

Even when she's trying to adhere to the official party line, Buffy's independence and Slayer experience can't be hidden, and Walsh immediately recognizes that Buffy is a threat to her secret plan to build the perfect soldier. Walsh sends Buffy into a trap but underestimates just how powerful the Slayer is when Buffy kills her would-be demon assassins, then puts Walsh on notice that she just made a very bad enemy.

Riley is shocked. He respected Professor Walsh and looked up to her, so her betrayal cuts deep. Forced to choose between his job and the woman he loves, the choice for him is easy.

THE REAL HORROR: Getting what you wish for—because it seldom turns out the way you'd hoped. Professor Walsh dreamed of creating the perfect soldier and killing machine. She did and it killed her.

70. "Goodbye, Iowa"
(FEBRUARY 15, 2000)

Director: David Solomon
Teleplay: Marti Noxon
Recurring cast: Amber Benson (Tara); George Hertzberg (Adam); Leonard Roberts (Forrest Gates); Bailey Chase (Graham Miller); Saverio Guerra (Willy); Emma Caulfield (Anya)
Guest cast: Amy Powell (reporter); Andy Marshall (scientist #1); Paul Leighton (rough-looking demon); Karen Charnell (shady lady); Jack Stehlin (Dr. Angleman); J. B. Gaynor (little boy)
Music: "Romeo Had Juliette" (at Willy's), by Lou Reed, from *New York*

Plot: Buffy uncovers the truth about 314.

THE WEEK'S ANTAGONISTS: It's Buffy versus the Initiative when Riley's men believe Buffy is responsible for Professor Walsh's death.

ANALYSIS: This episode features a frantic pace of action as everyone tries to figure out who, or what, is responsible for killing Professor Walsh. Riley, who doesn't realize he's undergoing withdrawal from a chemical cocktail Walsh had been secretly administering to members of the team, is confused and disoriented. Everything he believes in is methodically stripped away to reveal the lie the Initiative is based on. It's almost easier for him to believe Buffy is on the side of the demons than admit he's been manipulated and betrayed by his mentor, Walsh.

Buffy is hurt that Riley would think her disloyal but she doesn't have time to wallow in self-pity. She senses she's up against a profound adversary and knows that uncovering the truth will be the best antidote for the mistrust threatening to implode her relationship with Riley. When Adam finally shows himself and the extent of Walsh's deception is revealed, this sets the stage for Buffy's most formidable opponent yet.

THE REAL HORROR: Suspicion. Mistrust can undermine the strongest relationship, and is usually born of insecurity, jealousy, or misunderstanding.

All three play a factor in the finger-pointing that occurs after Professor Walsh's murder is discovered. Riley's peers don't like it that Buffy has disrupted the status quo and takes up so much of Riley's time and attention. Riley can't believe Walsh would do anything behind his back, and lashes out at Buffy in grief. And without Walsh to direct them, the other members of the Initiative feel anchorless and angry that their leader has been taken away. Everybody is so busy accusing Buffy, they fail to see what the real threat is.

BLOOPERS: When Riley and Forrest are arguing over whether Buffy was involved in Walsh's death, Riley points at Forrest with his left hand, but when the camera cuts to the next angle, his right hand is up.

OF SPECIAL NOTE: The word *cyborg* is a compound form of "cybernetic organism."

The Greek goddess Willow mentions—Thespia—was the daughter of the river god Asopus and his wife Metope.

71. "This Year's Girl (Part I)"
(FEBRUARY 22, 2000)

Director: Michael Gershman
Teleplay: Douglas Petrie
Recurring cast: Kristine Sutherland (Joyce Summers); Eliza Dushku (Faith); Harry Groener (Mayor Richard Wilkins III); Amber Benson (Tara); Leonard Roberts (Forrest Gates); Bailey Chase (Graham Miller)
Guest cast: Jeff Ricketts (Weatherby); Kevin Owers (Smith); Mark Gantt (demon); Kimberly McRae (visitor); Sara Van Horn (older nurse); Brian Hawley (orderly); Jack Esformes (doctor); Chet Grissom (detective); Alastair Duncan (Collins)

Plot: Faith wakes up from her coma and comes after Buffy, seeking revenge, with a little help from the mayor beyond the grave.

THIS WEEK'S ASTRAL PHENOMENON: Switching bodies. Once again showing his genuine concern for Faith, Mayor Wilkins left behind a magical talisman that allows her to switch bodies with Buffy and escape the consequences of her past evil deeds.

FORESHADOWING: In Faith's dream she remarks that Buffy has a lot to do to get ready for the arrival of "Little Sis."

ANALYSIS: Faith's dreams reflect the conflict raging inside her comatose head. On the one hand she obviously fears Buffy, but on the other, she covets all that Buffy is. Once she regains consciousness and learns the mayor is dead and that Buffy prevailed, Faith knows it's only a matter of time before either the police or the Council come after her again. Her only hope is to use the mayor's gift and get a second chance in someone else's body.

Having Faith back in the picture creates some dilemmas for Buffy. She's unwilling to open old wounds, and reticent to let Riley know too much about her relationship with Angel—out of fear he would never understand, and reject her. Buffy is vague with Riley about exactly why Faith hates her so much. Riley might press her further, except he's going through his own soul-searching. He's a soldier used to taking orders, so being on his own has left him feeling out of sorts.

His distraction plays into Faith's hands as she sets out to engage Buffy in a confrontation so she can initiate the switch. Once it's completed, Faith may look like Buffy, but she discovers that her soul will ultimately give her away.

THE REAL HORROR: Lack of personal responsibility. Unwilling to accept culpability for what she's done and all the hurt she's caused, Faith makes Buffy the object of her sins and plots to make Buffy take the fall instead by trapping Buffy in Faith's body and letting the Council's henchmen take Buffy away instead.

IT'S A MYSTERY: Exactly who calls Buffy to let her know Faith has escaped? And what happened to Faith's tattoo? It's not there when she's looking through Joyce's makeup.

BLOOPERS: When Buffy throws Faith across the dining-table during their fight, everything is knocked off, but in the next shot the tablecloth and some fruit are still there.

OF SPECIAL NOTE: Amber Benson previously worked with Eliza Dushku in the 1995 movie *Bye, Bye, Love.*

The expression "Five by five" is old radio jargon that means a signal is loud and clear. It has also come to mean, "Everything is all right."

72. "Who Are You? (Part II)"
(FEBRUARY 29, 2000)

Director: Joss Whedon
Teleplay: Joss Whedon
Recurring cast: Kristine Sutherland (Joyce Summers); Amber Benson (Tara); Leonard Roberts (Forrest Gates); George Hertzberg (Adam); Emma Caulfield (Anya); Eliza Dushku (Buffy)
Guest cast: Chet Grissom (detective); Alastair Duncan (Collins); Rick Stear (Booke); Jeff Ricketts (Weatherby), Kevin Owers (Smith); Amy Powell (reporter); Rick Scarry (sergeant); Jennifer S. Albright (date)
Music: "Vivian" (at the Bronze), by Nerf Herder, from *How to Meet Girls*; "Watching Me Fall" (in the Bronze as Spike and Buffy spar), by The Cure, from *Bloodflowers*; "Sweet Charlotte Rose" (at the Bronze during Willow and Tara's visit), by Headland, from *Headland 2*

Plot: After taking over her body, Faith prepares to take over Buffy's life. Adam goes on the offensive.

THIS WEEK'S CHALLENGE: Buffy has to convince people it's really her inside Faith's body, appearances notwithstanding!

ANALYSIS: From the beginning it has been known that Faith is a troubled young woman, but now she's clearly unstable. As she takes over Buffy's life, including her friends, her family, and her lover. Faith begins to believe she actually *is* Buffy, like someone suffering from multiple-personality disorder.

Buffy, on the other hand, is trying to keep her wits about her, knowing she's in danger of being locked away for the rest of her life. She must escape from the Council's men who want to take her back to London—in Faith's body, of course—and figure out a way to reverse the spell. The problem, of course, is that nobody believes a word she's saying.

But while Faith might have switched their bodies, she wasn't able to switch their respective souls—which, as the episode makes clear, is our true essence regardless of our appearance. It's Tara who recognizes this, and she helps Willow perform a spell to reveal what has happened and comes up with an antidote that will give Buffy back her rightful body. As Tara and Willow perform the magic together, their body language indicates their intimacy now extends beyond mere friendship. When, later, they walk into the Bronze, they are holding hands.

When Buffy is finally restored, and she learns how much of her life Faith experienced, she feels violated and a little disappointed that even in an intimate moment Riley couldn't tell something wasn't right. And although she never says it, you can't help suspecting that Buffy's head is telling her that Angel would have noticed.

THE REAL HORROR: Self-loathing. Faith freaks out when Riley tells her—as Buffy—that he loves her. And, when Faith-as-Buffy wails on Buffy-as-Faith, the depth of Faith's self-loathing is made uncomfortably clear. She tries to literally become someone else by switching bodies, but once she regains her true form, Faith is left alone with herself, which is more frightening than any creature she ever faced as a Slayer.

OF SPECIAL NOTE: The opening credits list Eliza Dushku as Buffy.

73. "Superstar"
(APRIL 4, 2000)

Director: David Grossman
Teleplay: Jane Espenson
Recurring cast: Danny Strong (Jonathan Levinson); Amber Benson (Tara); Bailey Chase (Graham Miller); George Hertzberg (Adam); Emma Caulfield (Anya)
Guest cast: Erica Lutrell (Karen); Robert Patrick Benedict (Adam's follower); John Saint Ryan (Colonel George Haviland); Adam Clark (cop); Chanie Costello (Inga); Julie Costello (Ilsa)
Music: "Trapped" (played by onstage band at the Bronze), by Royal Crown Revue, from *Walk on Fire*; "Serenade in Blue" (song Jonathan sings), by Royal Crown Revue

Plot: A lonely outcast turns into the world's most famous man.

THIS WEEK'S TRICKERY: One of Buffy's former high school classmates, Jonathan, casts a spell turning him into everyone's ideal. The only drawback is, the spell also creates a monster that is everyone's nightmare, to balance things out.

INTRODUCING: Colonel Haviland, the new leader of the Initiative.

ANALYSIS: This episode explores how easy it is to manipulate people, especially when they're willing. Logic would dictate that nobody could have accomplished as much as Jonathan claims to have done at his relatively tender age. Only Buffy begins to question just how perfect Jonathan is.

Even though Buffy still possesses all her powers, she is hesitant and uncertain. In the Jonathancentric universe, her leadership is unwanted by those around her, proving that ability is only one aspect of success; people also need encouragement to achieve their full potential. But even while under a spell, Buffy's Slayer instincts struggle to the surface and she doggedly questions whether Jonathan really is what he says he is. Ironically, the only person who even considers she might be right is Riley, the person who has known her the least amount of time.

Jonathan uses his status mostly for good, which is why he ultimately helps Buffy kill the monster, which breaks the spell, rather than allowing her to be injured or killed by it. Jonathan just wanted to leave his mark on the world and, unable to do it on his own, resorted to sorcery—not too dissimilar from what Willow did when trying to mend her broken heart. Both Jonathan and Willow underestimate the potential consequences of such power, which will one day change both their lives.

THE REAL HORROR: Going through life unnoticed. In high school Jonathan contemplated suicide because he felt like an outcast and found it too difficult to struggle to be accepted. Although he's now a young adult, emotionally Jonathan is still that lonely teenager who fantasizes about what it would be like to have friends, adventure, and plenty of sex. But he's willing to obtain his ideal life through mere trickery instead of working to cultivate real relationships. His preference for taking the easy way will be reinforced in later episodes.

OF SPECIAL NOTE: Jonathan's last name, Levinson. Though the Sunnydale High yearbook stated this, it's the first time it's been mentioned on the show.

MUSICAL NOTE: The vocals for the song sung by Jonathan at the Bronze were performed by Brad Kane, who played Tucker, the hellhound breeder, in Episode 54, "The Prom." Kane also provided the singing voice for Aladdin in all of the *Aladdin* movies.

74. "Where the Wild Things Are"
(APRIL 25, 2000)

Director: David Solomon
Teleplay: Tracey Forbes
Recurring cast: Amber Benson (Tara); Leonard Roberts (Forrest Gates); Bailey Chase (Graham Miller); Emma Caulfield (Anya)
Guest cast: Casey McCarthy (Julie); Kathryn Joosten (Mrs. Holt); Neil Daly (Mason); Jeff Wilson (Evan); Bryan Cuprill (Roy); Jeffrey Sharmay (drowning boy); Jeri Austin (running girl); Danielle Pessis (Christie); David Engler (Initiative guy); James Michael Conner (scientist)
Music: "Behind Blue Eyes" (at coffee house), sung by Anthony Stewart Head; "The Devil You know (God Is a Man)" (during party), by Face to Face, from *Ignorance is Bliss*

Plot: Buffy and Riley's sexual passion unleashes deadly poltergeists.

THIS WEEK'S DEADLY DISRUPTIONS: Poltergeists. The pent-up emotions of dead abused and sexually repressed children draw energy from Buffy and Riley's marathon lovemaking, slowly draining the life out of the passionate couple.

INTRODUCING: Safe sex. Although the use of birth control has been mentioned before, this is the first episode where we actually see condoms.

ANALYSIS: This somewhat graphic episode focuses on abuse and sexual repression. At first all Buffy and Riley know is that they are at that exciting point of a new relationship where physical passion is like an intense hunger. For Buffy, it's a chance to explore her sexuality freely, without worrying she will turn her partner into a murderous demon. And Riley's obvious love for her also gives her the emotional security to be uninhibited.

For Anya, sex isn't an expression or outgrowth of love, it *is* love. So when she and Xander skip lovemaking for a night, she assumes he doesn't love her anymore. Still new to this "human emotion" thing, she responds by immediately wanting to exact vengeance for her feelings of hurt and confusion. She finds a kindred spirit in Spike, who longs for the days when he had the power to cause damage. But Spike is a survivor and he is adapting to his new circumstances the best way he can—including going to a party thrown by Riley at Lowell House. If you can't bite 'em, you might as well drink their beer.

Willow and Tara's passion is more muted, in part because Willow hasn't revealed the nature of their relationship to anyone yet, but it is obvious they are intimately involved. So when Tara pulls back from Willow's touch during the party, it hurts and confuses Willow, who is still getting used to this new side of her sexuality.

Since Giles's midlife crisis, which ended with him being turned into a demon, he seems to have made an effort to get a life that includes other adults—and activities not dictated by the Hellmouth. While Buffy and her friends were in high school, Giles was primarily a "grown-up" authority figure. But now that Buffy and the others are on the cusp of being adults themselves, they start to see him in a different light. Although the females of the group seem to like it, Xander is unnerved by Giles as potential girl-magnet because up to now, he never thought of him as testosterone competition.

The episode also offers a glimpse at the fine line between passion and lust. While the former can inspire us, the latter can consume us. What started as a passionate encounter between Buffy and Riley is mutated by the supernatural forces in the house. Had not Xander and Anya broken the spell by hacking through the magically vine-covered door, Buffy and Riley's lust literally would have been the death of them.

THE REAL HORROR: Repressed anger—although it's never a pleasant experience, it's much healthier to express anger than to bottle it up inside. Spoken anger loses much of its power, but repressed anger gains in intensity until it can turn into an uncontrollable rage. The children abused by the former director of the orphanage that was previously located in Lowell House, Mrs. Holt, had been forced to repress not only their anger over being abused but their sexuality, too. Those pent-up emotions form the poltergeist that almost proves fatal to Buffy and Riley.

BLOOPERS: When Spike decides against entering Lowell House to save Buffy and Riley, his reflection can be seen both in the window and in the glass door.

LITERARY ALLUSION: This episode shares a title with the children's book *Where the Wild Things Are*, by Maurice Sendak, about a young boy named Max who gets sent to his room without supper and imagines that his room turns into a magical forest inhabited by monsters which make him their king.

OF SPECIAL NOTE: Some paranormal researchers believe the poltergeist phenomenon is most often associated with young women, and is the telekinetic manifestation of the stress of going through puberty.

MUSICAL NOTE: The song Giles performs at the Espresso Pump, "Behind Blue Eyes," was written by Pete Townshend and recorded by The Who on their 1971 album *Who's Next*.

75. "New Moon Rising"
(MAY 2, 2000)

Director: James A. Contner
Teleplay: Marti Noxon
Recurring cast: Amber Benson (Tara); Leonard Roberts (Forrest Gates); Bailey Chase (Graham Miller); George Hertzberg (Adam); Emma Caulfield (Anya); Seth Green (Oz)
Guest cast: James Michael Conner (scientist #1); Mark Daneri (scientist #2); Robert Patrick Benedict (Adam's follower); Conor O'Farrell (Colonel McNamara); Doron Keenan (commando #2)

Plot: Willow is forced to make a painful decision when Oz returns to Sunnydale a changed man.

THIS WEEK'S TURNABOUT: Oz has found a way to prevent transformation during the full moon through a combination of herbal and meditation techniques learned in the Himalayas.

ANALYSIS: When we see people every day, it's hard to notice how they change over a period of time. However, when you've been out of the loop for a while, the changes can come as quite a shock—the situation Oz finds himself in when he returns to Sunnydale.

For Oz, while he devoted himself to finding a way he thinks will enable him to control his inner animal, the rest of his life came to a standstill. But back home, Willow had no choice but to move ahead in order to get past the pain of being left behind. She discovered the truism when one door closes, often an unexpected door opens up. In her case, she found love with a soul mate who just happens to be another woman.

Complicating matters is the fact that Willow and Oz didn't break up because they stopped loving one another, but because Oz needed to be alone so as not to endanger her on the personal journey he needed to undertake. But, by leaving, he also ran the very real risk of letting Willow slip through his fingers.

The other thing Oz hadn't anticipated was what his response will be if things don't work out. He asks Xander if Willow has a new guy in her life, so he *is* realistic enough to consider the possibility. And Willow misses an opportunity to be honest with Oz when he brings it up, in part because she isn't sure herself how she feels about his return.

After one whiff of Tara's and Willow's mingled scents, Oz realizes why Willow preferred having breakfast over going to bed with him. Losing her to a woman means she has found something he can't possibly give her. Oz is so upset he transforms into a wolf in the middle of the day, which results in his being captured by the Initiative.

Meanwhile Riley is still trying to recapture his center. When he could view the world in black-and-white terms, his moral purpose was unambiguous. But meeting Buffy changed all that. Now, when he learns of Willow's love for a werewolf, Buffy interprets his surprise as coming from bias. She later realizes she judged him too harshly, when she reacts badly at first to Willow's admission that she and Tara are involved. It momentarily shakes up Buffy, to be confronted with a side of Willow she never suspected. It reminds us that, no matter how well we know someone, we never know everything about them.

The most important thing is the willingness to take a stand for what you believe in. Riley and Buffy run afoul of the Initiative and are branded traitors for freeing Oz, while Willow chooses the person she's in love with, Tara, over her first love, because she knows she and Oz aren't the same people they once were.

THE REAL HORROR: Jealousy. There's a reason they call it a monster. Oz's transforming in the middle of the day is a metaphor for how jealousy can turn the most rational person into a raving lunatic and replace civilized behavior with out-of-control, animal impulsiveness.

LITERARY ALLUSION: The comment about "pulling a William Burroughs" refers to the accidental shooting of his common-law wife, Joan

Vollmer Adams. Burroughs was a noted Beat writer, best known for his 1959 novel, *Naked Lunch*. While in Mexico, on the lam from authorities to escape drug charges, at a party he decided to show off his marksmanship by shooting a glass off Joan's head, William Tell style. He missed, and killed her. The moral about mixing drugs, drinking, and guns, seems pretty obvious.

OF SPECIAL NOTE: Shortly before this episode was filmed, Emma Caulfield signed on as a series regular.

76. "The Yoko Factor (Part I)"
(MAY 9, 2000)

Director: David Grossman
Teleplay: Dough Petrie
Recurring cast: Amber Benson (Tara); Leonard Roberts (Forrest-Gates); George Hertzberg (Adam); Emma Caulfield (Anya)
Guest cast: Bob Fimiani (Mr. Ward); Jade Carter (lieutenant); Conor O'Farrell (Colonel McNamara); David Boreanaz (Angel)

Plot: Adam recruits Spike in a game of divide-and-conquer between Buffy and her friends. Angel and Riley square off.

THIS WEEK'S NEMESIS REDUX: Spike, who agrees to alienate Buffy from her friends to make her an easier target for Adam.

ANALYSIS: Dr. Walsh was very successful in making Adam not only physically dominant, but astute as well. Adam knows the best way to defeat the Slayer is to take away her support group. And after studying human nature, he knows the way to do it is to attack their weakness—emotion. The stresses and tensions of all the changes Buffy and her friends have undergone since leaving high school finally boil over in this episode, with more than a little nudge from Spike acting as Adam's infiltrator.

Buffy has returned from visiting Angel in L.A., and is upset over an argument they had, over his helping Faith. Buffy feels betrayed; plus, just seeing him rekindled old feelings. With so much going on in her life, she hasn't been paying enough attention to how her preoccupation might be interpreted by others. She gets even more distracted when Angel shows up unannounced. His attempt to make amends with Buffy backfires as Riley gets territorial and he and Angel square off. Although the bond between Buffy and Angel is still very evident, she knows it's important she that direct her energies toward Riley.

The rest of the gang is confused, too. Willow assumes Buffy's distance is tacit disapproval of Tara. Because Xander hasn't found a trade or vocation that can give him a sense of purpose, he worries the others see him as superfluous. Giles, likewise, is still struggling to find his place with Buffy and the others as they become adults. These feelings are all really just projections of what they're feeling about themselves.

An argument finally erupts in which everyone vents their frustrations. Feeling that she's being unfairly accused and abandoned just when she needs her friends most, in the shadow of her pending showdown with Adam, Buffy storms out. In the cooling-off period that follows, everyone is left to reevaluate their relationships.

THE REAL HORROR: Lack of communication. The reason Spike is able to so effectively get Buffy and her friends to go at each other's throats is that he knows the right buttons to push, and plays on individual insecurities. He mixes just enough truth with out-and-out fabrication so that he easily manipulates all of them. It becomes a potential meltdown because nobody seems willing to sit down and talk it out. It's not until Buffy figures out what Spike's up to, and confronts the others about where they've been getting their information, that the misunderstanding is cleared up.

BLOOPERS: When Spike rushes into Giles's place with the discs, his reflection is visible the mirror behind Tara and Willow.

OF SPECIAL NOTE: The title of this episode refers to the way many Beatles fans blamed Yoko Ono for the band's breakup, viewing her as the instigator of bad blood, even though it was more a matter of the group having run its creative course.

MUSICAL NOTE: The song Giles is playing, "Free Bird," was originally written and recorded by Lynyrd Skynrd in 1973, and has become a classic-rock staple.

77. "Primeval (Part II)"
(MAY 16, 2000)

Director: James A. Contner
Teleplay: David Fury
Recurring Cast: George Hertzberg (Adam); Amber Benson (Tara);
    Leonard Roberts (Forrest Gates); Bailey Chase (Graham Miller);
    Emma Caulfield (Anya); Lindsay Crouse (Maggie Walsh)
Guest cast: Jack Stehlin (Dr. Angleman); Conor O'Farrell (Colonel
    McNamara); Bob Fimiani (Ward); Jordi Vilasuso (Dixon)

Plot: Adam initiates his plans to create an army of demon/human hybrids.

THIS WEEK'S FOLLY: Colonel McNamara loses almost half his commandos when Adam instigates a battle between captured demons and the Initiative in order to cull body parts for his hybrid soldiers.

INTRODUCING: The first Slayer. Buffy taps into the essence of the Slayer's primeval power through an enjoining spell that joins her spiritual forces with Giles, Willow, and Xander.

ANALYSIS: Buffy realizes she has been taking her friends for granted, and that she needs to do a better job of juggling her romantic life with her "family." When they were in high school, the close proximity of sharing every class together and being in a contained environment, made it easier to keep up with each other's feelings and moods. College is a much bigger environment. It's also a time when personal relationships tend to be more serious because people start contemplating life partners. Both Buffy and Willow come to realize that friendship is as much a commitment as a romantic relationship is, and how important their friendship is.

Right when he's thinking he's a worthless appendage, Xander once again proves his value. Just as he figured out how to destroy the Judge with a rocket launcher, his comment about combining their individual powers into a Super-Buffy is the key to the spell that endows Buffy with the necessary mystical power to defeat Adam.

Spike once again learns it's never a good idea to bet against the Slayer. Although he kills a demon threatening Giles, Willow, and Xander to make amends, you never get the sense he truly worries that Buffy will stake him. Already he's come to realize she only kills when necessary, and that she deeply values and respects life, even the undead variety. Although he finds the trait a potential weakness, he is also curiously intrigued by Buffy's character.

THE REAL HORROR: Ignorance. Colonel McNamara's arrogance and ego prevent him from giving Buffy any credibility. The result is the loss of many lives, including his own, and the dismantling of the Initiative as a failed experiment.

OF SPECIAL NOTE: This episode was originally intended to be the final episode for the fourth season before Joss Whedon added "Restless" as the finale.

78. "Restless"
(MAY 23, 2000)

Director: Joss Whedon
Teleplay: Joss Whedon
Recurring cast: Kristine Sutherland (Joyce Summers); Amber Benson (Tara); Emma Caulfield (Anya); Seth Green (Oz); Armin Shimerman (Principal Snyder); Mercedes McNab (Harmony); Phina Oruche (Olivia); George Hertzberg (Adam)
Guest cast: Sharon Ferguson (the First Slayer); David Wells (cheese guy); Michael Harney (Xander's dad); Rob Boltin (soldier)
Music: "The Exposition Song" (sung by Giles), by Anthony S. Head, Christophe Beck, and Four Star Mary.

Plot: The spirit of the original Slayer haunts the dreams of Buffy and her friends.

THIS WEEK'S UNEXPECTED THREAT: The original Slayer, who apparently is miffed about Buffy's use of Slayer power to defeat Adam.

INTRODUCING: Riley to Joyce. Having been involved with Riley for the past several months, Buffy finally introduces Riley to her mother for the first time. Riley stops by before leaving for a debriefing about the Initiative's demise in Washington, D.C.

ANALYSIS: The premise is that the original Slayer is so upset by her essence being summoned to defeat Adam, that she haunts the dreams of Buffy, Giles, Willow, and Xander. The dream sequences seem to be a way to drop in obscure clues about what is in store for the following season. Buffy is able to disarm, as it were, the First Slayer, by refusing to acknowledge it has any power over her and to sending her back to her primeval realm. The echoing message is that Buffy has no idea what is coming, and nothing can't prepare her for the impact of that truth.

THE REAL HORROR: Realizing we can't control what the future holds.

LITERARY REFERENCES: The Greek words Willow paints on Tara's back in her dream is the opening of a poem by Sappho. Sappho wrote ten books of verse, but over the ages the originals were lost. Scholars only know of her work through quotations used by other writers. Just one poem survives in complete form.

Sappho lived in Mytilene on the island of Lesbos, where women often congregated, and her poems usually focus on the relationships among women. The word *lesbian* is derived from the name Lesbos.

There are multiple references to C. S. Lewis's *The Lion, the Witch, and the Wardrobe.* Willow mentions it during her school report; Giles sings to Willow to "look through the Chronicles"; and Xander has to push his way through a closet in his never-ending basement.

WHAT JOSS WHEDON HAS TO SAY: "The cheese man means nothing. He is the only thing in the show that means nothing. I needed something like that, something that couldn't be explained, because dreams always have that one element that is just ridiculous."

OF SPECIAL NOTE: Tara's warning to Buffy, "Be back before dawn," has been interpreted as a foreshadowing of the sudden arrival of Buffy's sister Dawn, never seen before, in Season Five's opening episode, "Buffy vs. Dracula" (Episode 79).

The actor who plays Xander's dad is not the same actor who portrays that character in the sixth season, in Episode 116, "Hell's Bells."

MUSICAL NOTE: Accompanying Giles onstage at the Bronze are *Buffy* composer Christophe Beck on the piano and the band Four Star Mary.

✦ SEASON FIVE ✦

Fifth-year overview: Family takes center stage this year for Buffy as she juggles her education, Slaying, and family commitments. Although she's been burdened for years with the responsibility of being the Slayer, Buffy finds that dealing with family can be far more difficult than protecting Sunnydale from its assortment of vampires and demons—and far more emotionally draining. She also will encounter an adversary like none she's faced before, who will lead Buffy to a greater understanding of what it really *means to be the Slayer.*

SEASON FIVE REGULAR CAST

Sarah Michelle Gellar (*Buffy Summers*)
Nicholas Brendon (*Xander Harris*)
Alyson Hannigan (*Willow Rosenberg*)
Marc Blucas (*Riley Finn*)
Emma Caulfield (*Anya*)
Michelle Trachtenberg (*Dawn*)
James Marsters (*Spike*)
Anthony Stewart Head (*Rupert Giles*)

✦

79. "Buffy vs. Dracula"
(SEPTEMBER 26, 2000)

Director: David Solomon
Teleplay: Marti Noxon
Recurring cast: Michelle Trachtenberg (Dawn), Amber Benson (Tara), Kristine Sutherland (Joyce Summers)

Guest cast: E. J. Gage (mover #1), Scott Berman (mover #2), Marita Schaub (vampire girl #1), Leslee Jean Matta (vampire girl #2), Jennifer Slimko (vampire girl #3)

Music: "Finding Me" (as Buffy and Riley frolic on beach), by Vertical Horizon, from *Everything You Want*

Plot: Buffy comes face-to-face with the world's most famous vampire.

THIS WEEK'S STAR VAMPIRE: Dracula, who comes to Sunnydale, drawn by the dark power within Buffy.

INTRODUCING: Dawn, Buffy's younger sister, whose existence will be explained—all in good Hellmouth time.

ANALYSIS: the darkness within Buffy will become a recurring theme of the series. Ever since tapping into the essence of the First Slayer, Buffy feels increased power. But she doesn't understand where it comes from, or how to harness it. In some ways she feels as she did when she first came to Sunnydale and was still struggling to figure out how being the Slayer fit into the overall scheme of her life.

Although Dracula is temporarily able to exert power over Buffy, his comment that they are "kindred spirits" is perhaps why she is able to break his sway over her after she tastes his blood. She is able to absorb his power into her own and uses it to make her Slayer essence even stronger. Even though she's apparently unable to kill him permanently, she ends up shooing him away and her rejection is enough to send his vaporized self packing.

Compared to other vampires, such as the Master and Drusilla, Dracula seems less vicious. Although he turns Xander into his Sunnydale Renfield and keeps Giles busy fending off the three sisters, it seems Dracula could have done a lot more damage. But killing didn't seem to be his primary motive; instead he seemed to be looking for a soul mate as powerful as he himself.

THE REAL HORROR: Unwanted attraction. Although Buffy knows that Dracula is definitely not the kind of man you bring home to Mother, she can't help being intrigued by him.

BLOOPERS: During the dinner scene, the plate in front of Joyce turns into a bowl from one shot to the next.

LITERARY ALLUSION: The fictional Dracula story originated in Bram Stoker's 1897 novel, but his character was based on the historical figure Vlad the Impaler. (See Chapter 3, "A Brief History of the Vampire," page XXX.)

OF SPECIAL NOTE: Rudolf Martin starred on *All My Children* as Anton Lang, who had a brief affair with Sarah Michelle Gellar's character, Kendall. He also played Vlad the Impaler in the 2000 TV movie, *Dark Prince: The True Story of Dracula.*

Dracula is the first vampire in the series to shape-shift into an animal. Emma Caulfield has been added to the opening credits.

80. "Real Me"
(OCTOBER 3, 2000)

Director: David Grossman
Teleplay: David Fury
Recurring cast: Mercedes McNab (Harmony); Amber Benson (Tara); Kristine Sutherland (Joyce Summers)
Guest cast: Bob Morrisey (crazy guy); Brian Turk (Mort); Chaney Kley Minnis (Brad); Faith S. Abrahams (Peaches); Tom Lenk (Cyrus)

Plot: Dawn puts a crimp in Buffy's Slaying. A new vampire gang is in town.

THIS WEEK'S LEADER OF THE PACK: Harmony, out to prove she's a force to be reckoned with.

INTRODUCING: Giles as entrepreneur. Now that he's staying in Sunnydale and resuming his duties as Buffy's Watcher, he's decided to buy the magic shop, despite the disturbingly high mortality rate of previous owners.

ANALYSIS: Dawn is suffering the angst felt by many younger siblings. She's angry that Buffy is considered so important. Nobody seems to give her any respect and they treat her like a child. The truth is Dawn idolizes her sister but resents having to struggle to get noticed. She is living in Buffy's huge shadow.

For her part, Buffy feels saddled with and crowded by Dawn, and feels her sister doesn't appreciate all the responsibilities she has, between college,

Slaying, and babysitting Dawn. Buffy is used to people listening to her and being in command when it comes to Slayer matters, so she gets snappish when Dawn is not cooperative.

Tara seems to empathize with Dawn. Because Buffy and the others have been friends and Slayer partners for so long, Tara knows that sometimes, for any newcomer, being around them feels like being on the outside looking in.

Part of Buffy's frustration is that she needs to do her job and also wants to protect Dawn from being exposed to the horrors of the Hellmouth—a tough juggling act. Buffy really does know better when it comes to Sunnydale's dark side, but to Dawn her warnings are just so much noise. Dawn learns the hard way that she might not be as grown-up as she thinks is, when she mistakenly invites Harmony into the house and is kidnapped and used as bait to ambush and kill Buffy. Buffy is furious that Dawn broke a well-established house rule and feels more put-upon than ever. While Dawn feels Buffy gets to do whatever she wants, Buffy feels everybody else excuses Dawn's irresponsibility just because she's only fourteen. When Dawn runs out of the house in a snit and is captured by one of Harmony's gang, it seems to prove Buffy's point.

Like Dawn, Harmony has image issues. Alive and undead, she's always felt unfairly maligned and underappreciated, and plans to prove her mettle by being the one to bag the Slayer. All she's looking for is respect and to be *somebody*. Dawn shares that desire, unaware that what *she* is, isn't anything even she can imagine.

THE REAL HORROR: Impatience. Buffy is so irritated with Dawn that she runs the risk of being unreasonable.

IT'S A MYSTERY: How has Giles managed to afford rent and buy the magic shop after being unemployed for a year?

LITERARY ALLUSION: When Dawn mentions Hogwarts, she's referring to the School of Witchcraft and Wizardry that Harry Potter attends, from the hugely successful series of books by J. K. Rowling.

OF SPECIAL NOTE: The actor who plays Harmony's minion Cyrus, Thomas Lenk, will return in Season Six as Andrew Wells, one of the nerd trio.

The magic shop used to be called Uncle Bob's Magic Shop, but is now named the Magic Box.

81. "The Replacement"

(OCTOBER 10, 2000)

Director: James A. Contner
Teleplay: Jane Espenson
Recurring cast: Kristine Sutherland (Joyce Summers)
Guest cast: Kelly Donovan (Xander double); Cathy Cohen (building manager); David Reivers (foreman); Fritz Greve (construction worker)

Plot: A close encounter with a demon leaves Xander feeling like two different people.

THIS WEEK'S WOULD-BE SLAYER-SLAYER: Toth, the last of his demon clan, who wields a magic rod that splits an individual into two beings—one possessing their strongest traits, the other their weakest. If one dies, so does the other.

INTRODUCING: Anya's apartment is shown for the first time.

ANALYSIS: This episode touches on previously covered ground—how everyone must deal with the coexistence of disparate qualities within themselves. While more pronounced in Buffy's case, her friends also struggle with their own innate dichotomies. Xander's self-image has been skewed by his upbringing and by his lack of expectations. He knows he'll never be a college graduate and doesn't expect much opportunity to ever come his way. But the promotion he gets from the contractor makes him realize he finally might have found his calling in carpentry and building. And what his twin self proves is that underneath the self-deprecating humor is a young man confident in what he could achieve, given the chance. Xander's decision to move out of his parents' basement into his own apartment is a further sign that Xander knows it's time to start thinking more in terms of his future.

Up to now, Xander has not felt any sense of urgency as far as accepting more adult responsibilities. Anya, however, feels time is slipping through her hands. As a demon, she knew she had thousands of years to live, but humanity gives her a much smaller window and she's more cognizant than any of the others how precious time is.

Giles clears up the question of which one is the real Xander—they both are—and Willow easily reverses the spell once everyone is in the same room. Xander seems to suffer no lingering emotional effects from the experience, although it has made Riley thoughtful. He eloquently describes his love for Buffy to Xander, then almost offhandedly adds that despite the way he feels for her, he knows she's not in love with him. His lack of bitterness over this knowledge is the first indication that it's inevitable Buffy is going to break Riley's heart. But he is helpless to walk away until the relationship plays itself out to its end.

THE REAL HORROR: Confronting our weaknesses and learning to accept them as a part of us. What Xander learns from his literal better half is that our weaknesses are just as important as our strengths in determining who we are.

IT'S A MYSTERY: Why would Spike have an apparent tan-line on his arms?

FORESHADOWING: Joyce's headache.

BLOOPERS: There's no way Xander could own *Babylon 5* commemorative plates, because they were never released.

OF SPECIAL NOTE: Kelly Donovan is Nicholas Brendon's identical twin, and played the confident Xander. "Donovan" and "Brendon" are actually Kelly's and Nicky's middle names. Their real last name is Schulz.

WHAT NICHOLAS BRENDON HAD TO SAY: "Truth be told, I played both characters. It was very challenging and rewarding, and I must've done an okay job if you couldn't tell it was me. I had a blast working with Kelly, and he really deserves kudos for his work. He was never promised onscreen dialogue but they did end up using some and I think he did a stand-up job. In fact there was even one point where I had to rewind and freeze the tape to decipher who was who."

82. "Out of My Mind"
(OCTOBER 17, 2000)

Director: David Grossman

Teleplay: Rebecca Rand Kirshner

Recurring cast: Mercedes McNab (Harmony Kendall); Bailey Chase (Graham Miller); Charlie Weber (Ben); Amber Benson (Tara); Kristine Sutherland (Joyce Summers)

Guest cast: Time Winters (Initiative doctor); Dierdre Holder (hospital doctor)

Music: "Breathe" (as Riley plays basketball), by Nickelback, from *The State*

Plot: Buffy races the clock to save Riley. Spike is determined to regain his ability to kill but instead learns a shocking truth.

THIS WEEK'S DEADLY DOSE: Drugs previously administered to Riley by Dr. Walsh makes him think he's Superman.

INTRODUCING: Ben, an intern at Sunnydale General Hospital, who treats Joyce for an unexplained fainting spell. Ben will come to play a pivotal role in Buffy's and Dawn's lives.

ANALYSIS: A side effect of Walsh's previous experiments has left Riley on a constant adrenaline high. While it gives him superstrength and makes him impervious to pain, it will also destroy his heart if left untreated. But Riley doesn't want to be "just" normal. He is worried about being able to keep up with Buffy—he's worried that he won't keep up with Angel in her eyes. He wants to be her partner and her equal. He doesn't believe he can match her physical power. So even though his drug-induced stamina is killing him, he's reluctant to give it up. Like the husband whose ego can't take his wife earning more money than he does, Riley worries about being seen as an adornment on Buffy's arm. While it's acceptable in our society for women to be seen as trophies, most men can't handle a similar situation.

Spike is also feeling diminished by the chip in his head. Even though Buffy had nothing to do with his current condition, Spike has directed all of his anger toward the Slayer. She has become an obsession. It's almost as if he resents her for not having dusted him already. She leaves him alone because she doesn't see him as a threat and doesn't believe in killing just for the sake of killing. Being dismissed bothers him more than being hunted by her because at least then he felt like her peer. So when Buffy asks Spike for help in finding Riley so she can get him medical attention, Spike decides to undergo a little impromptu surgery. But his dream of giving the Slayer her comeuppance is dashed when the doctor fails to remove the chip and Spike is left to rant to the unholy gods.

It's only later, after an erotic dream, the true basis for Spike's obsessive hatred for the Slayer is revealed. The truth is, he's in love with the Slayer and hates her for having conquered him this way.

WEAPONS

In order to fight the variety of creatures the Hellmouth throws at her, Buffy has amassed a small arsenal of weapons. Among her favorites:

Crossbow: The crossbow's history dates back to ancient China. In Europe, where it was also called an arbalest, it gained popularity around 1000 A.D., particularly in England. It remained the weapon of choice until the fifteenth century, when firearms took its place.

Hunga-munga: A hooked throwing knife with a double-edged blade of African origin that comes in a variety of sizes.

Quarterstaff: A round pole of wood between six and nine feet long. Meant to be used with both hands, the quarterstaff got its name because the most effective technique was to have one hand grip the staff a quarter of the way from the bottom and the other grip it at the staff's midpoint.

Stake: Any wooden object with a pointed end. Buffy's sentimental favorite is Mr. Pointy, the good-luck stake given to Buffy by Kendra.

THE REAL HORROR: Your body failing you. Most people take their health for granted, especially young people. When something goes wrong, denial is a typical knee-jerk reaction because sickness leads to thoughts of our mortality. In Riley's case, he doesn't want to be fixed because he doesn't want to feel normal, and he kids himself into the near-fatal belief his body is strong enough to take the abuse.

IT'S A MYSTERY: Why has Spike waited until now to try and coerce a doctor into removing the chip? How could he have known there was a government-contracted doctor waiting for Riley?

83. "𝔑o 𝔓lace 𝔏ike 𝔥ome"
(OCTOBER 24, 2000)

Director: David Solomon
Teleplay: Douglas Petrie
Recurring cast: Clare Kramer (Glory); Charlie Weber (Ben); Kristine
   Sutherland (Joyce Summers)
Guest cast: Ravil Isyanov (monk); James Wellington (nightwatch-
   man); Paul Hayes (older nightwatchman); Staci Lawrence (cus-
   tomer); John Sarkisian (old monk)

Plot: Buffy learns a shocking truth about Dawn. Joyce's headaches are get-
ting worse.

THIS WEEK'S MYSTICAL TALISMAN: An orb called a Dagon's Sphere, which can repel nameless ancient evils.

INTRODUCING: The Key. Dawn is actually an energy called the Key, put into human form by a band of monks. The Key is a portal to another dimension which, if opened, will bring about apocalyptic destruction.

THE BIG BAD: Glory, who is not-so-affectionately referred to as "the Beast" by a cowering monk. We're not sure just yet who or what Glory is, but she wants the Key, and she wants it bad.

ANALYSIS: The beginning of what will become Buffy's most difficult Slayer struggle begins innocently enough on a relatively normal night out on patrol. A security guard hands her a strange orb he thinks she dropped, not knowing it belongs to a monk who is trying to hide from a power he calls "the Beast."

The Magic Box is jumping as its grand opening attracts half the population of Sunnydale. But Buffy's heart isn't in it because she's worried about her mother's health. She comes to believe Joyce's ailments aren't physical but mystical in nature. Or at least that's what she wants to believe, because if it's a creature Buffy can defeat it. The idea that something is wrong medically with her mom leaves Buffy feeling helpless and frightened.

Desperate to find the demon responsible, Buffy takes Anya's advice and performs a spell that's a kind of mystical Geiger counter. It can pick up remnants of spells cast in the past, which in turn should point Buffy in the right direction. But she is totally unprepared for what the spell reveals.

The frustration Buffy felt in general toward Dawn and her annoying adolescent behavior when Buffy thought she was her sister, turns to rage when she realizes Dawn isn't her sister at all. She mistakenly thinks Dawn is some kind of demon emissary responsible for making Joyce sick, with relentless headaches that have the doctors confounded. But once she learns the truth about the Key, who is now a helpless human child, Buffy knows keeping her safe from all harm is a responsibility she cannot shirk.

THE REAL HORROR: Family secrets. Even without mystical powers adding a whole other layer of ramifications, uncovering family secrets can rock everyone concerned, and leave a trail of mistrust and heartache. One might think that for Buffy, discovering that who she thought was her sister really isn't—and that all her memories of growing up together were planted in her brain by the monks seeking to protect the Key—might be a little easier to take because of her experience with the Hellmouth. But while Buffy is used to being in personal peril, she has managed to protect her family from being too exposed to the dangers inherent in Slaying. So she feels especially violated to learn that her family has been endangered by the Beast and the Key.

OF SPECIAL NOTE: The writer of this episode, Douglas Petrie, also wrote the screenplay for the 1996 Nickelodeon movie *Harriet the Spy*, which starred Michelle Trachtenberg.

Clare Kramer's character was almost named Cherry instead of Glory.

Clare Kramer appeared in *Bring It On* with Eliza Dushku, who plays Faith.

84. "Family"

(NOVEMBER 7, 2000)

Director: Joss Whedon
Teleplay: Joss Whedon
Recurring cast: Mercedes McNab (Harmony Kendall); Clare Kramer (Glory); Charlie Weber (Ben); Amber Benson (Tara)
Guest cast: Amy Adams (Cousin Beth); Steve Rankin (Mr. Maclay); Ezra Buzzington (bartender); Peggy Goss (crazy person); Torry Pendergrass (Damon); Megan Gray (Sandy); Brian Tee (intern); Kevin Rankin (Donny)
Music: "Tears Are in Your Eyes" (at Willy's), by Yo La Tengo, from *And Then Nothing Turned Itself Inside-Out*; "American Shoes" (during Tara's birthday party), by Motorace, from *American Shoes*; "Cemented Shoes" (during the birthday party), by My Vitriol, from *Cemented Shoes*; "I Can't Take My Eyes Off You" (as Willow and Tara dance), by Melanie Doane from *Adam's Rib*

Plot: Tara's family comes to town and threaten to reveal her secret. Glory convinces a clan of Lei-ach demons to find and kill the Slayer.

THIS WEEK'S WOULD-BE ASSASSINS: Lei-ach demons, who suck the bone marrow out of their victims.

INTRODUCING: Tara's family, an obviously conservative clan who come to fetch Tara on her twentieth birthday so she can return home and take care of the menfolk the way she's supposed to.

ANALYSIS: The complexities of family take center stage in this episode. When people used to live and die in the same hometown, or when generations of the same family lived under one roof, blood and marriage ties were most people's primary relationships. But our changing culture has brought an increasingly transient lifestyle, with divorce, freedom of travel, and professional mobility affecting our social structure. While blood kin form one type of family, the "family" afforded by friends has become increasingly recognized as being just as important and powerful. Which is why in a clever turnaround, it's now Xander and Buffy who feel slightly excluded by Willow, because of her relationship with Tara. They are adjusting to a new member of the family, going through the awkward stage when they don't really know her yet, but want to be welcoming for Willow's sake.

Spike is starting to accept his attraction to Buffy—enough so that now he allows himself to fantasize about her in an erotic fashion. More practically, he is starting to show signs of protectiveness both toward her and those she loves. Although Spike will always be the ultimate black sheep, he has been warily accepted by the others. Ironically, Tara's blood family seems to go out of their way to make her feel bad about herself, telling her she has a demon inside, just as Tara's mother did, which is the source of the powers her mother also had.

Tara's worry that she will be an embarrassment, or worse, in the eyes of Willow and Willow's extended family, prompts her to cast an ill-advised spell that prevents them from seeing the demon inside her. Unfortunately, it also blinds them from seeing the demons Glory has sent to kill Buffy—until Tara realizes her mistake and undoes the spell, resigned to the truth about herself.

In the confrontation between Tara and her family, who intends to force her back home, Tara is surprised when first Buffy and then the others stand up for her. While Buffy may not understand Tara and may not really know her, she knows that Willow loves her, and that's a good-enough reason to get involved. Ironically, it's Spike who figures out that Tara's father is lying about a family "demon legacy." His own undead issues aside, Spike shows respect for women as equals, and perhaps because of his age, recognizes old-fashioned male oppression against women when he sees it.

THE REAL HORROR: Deception. While family can be your most solid foundation, for some people it can also be destructive. For Tara, her Puritanesque family tries to control her, through lies and deception, by telling her powers come from evil and that nobody but the family will accept her. By isolating her, they can control her completely.

OF SPECIAL NOTE: The vampire who tries to pick Riley up at Willy's, Sandy, is the girl who was sired by vampire Willow in Episode 50, "Doppelgängland."

Amy Adams played Kathryn Merteuil in the sequel *Cruel Intentions 2: Manchester Prep*, a role originated by Sarah Michelle Gellar in *Cruel Intentions*. Amy also appeared with Nicholas Brendon in the 2000 horror-comedy flick *Beach Party*.

85. "Fool for Love"
(NOVEMBER 14, 2000)

Director: Nick Marck

Teleplay: Douglas Petrie

Recurring cast: Mercedes McNab (Harmony Kendall); Juliet Landau (Drusilla); Julie Benz (Darla); Kristine Sutherland (Joyce Summers)

Guest cast: David Boreanaz (Angel), Kali Rocha (Cecily Addams), Edward Fletcher (male partygoer); Katharine Leonard (female partygoer); Matthew Lang (2nd male partygoer); Chris Daniels (stabbing vampire); Kenneth Feinberg (chaos demon); Steve Heinze (vampire #1); Ming Liu (Chinese Slayer); April Wheedon-Washington (subway Slayer)

Music: "Balladovie" (at the Bronze), by the Killingtons, from *The Killingtons*

Plot: A near-fatal encounter sends Buffy on a quest to discover how other Slayers have been killed; Joyce undergoes tests to find source of her headache.

THIS WEEK'S UNDEAD HISTORY: Spike's backstory. Desperate to understand what fatal mistake other Slayers have made, in hopes of not repeating them, Buffy bribes Spike into telling her how he killed two Slayers.

INTRODUCING: Spike's Slayer victims. The first was a young Chinese girl who died in 1900; the other was killed in a New York subway in 1977.

ANALYSIS: Although she kills almost on a daily basis, Buffy has never really allowed herself to examine what her relationship with death is. She thinks hearing the stories of other Slayers' demises will help her avoid their mistakes. Spike humors her and weaves his own story in with his account of killing two Slayers.

What Spike understands and Buffy doesn't, is that the answer she is seeking can't be found in the stories of others. It resides inside her. He taunts Buffy by bluntly declaring that every Slayer has a death wish. Whether or not they do is debatable, but bringing death to so many in such an intimate fashion, up close and personal, often with her own hands, creates a morbid fascination with death and a desire to know it better. That desire eventually becomes a seduction to where, finally, they almost let themselves be taken, the way William allowed Drusilla to take him.

Spike has embraced the thrill of death, and over the years intentionally put himself at risk because the rush of survival was like a drug. But he also observes that Buffy's struggle is greater because, while one part of her is drawn to death, the other part clings to life because of the love she has for her friends and family. Unlike so many Slayers who are solitary hunters, Buffy's support group, while keeping her alive, also creates more anguish for her, and perhaps interferes with the natural life cycle of Slayers.

When she discovers Joyce is undergoing tests that indicate a possibly serious medical condition, the fear of losing her mother hits Buffy full-force. And, as always, the fragility of life remains a great unknown to Buffy.

THE REAL HORROR: Rejection. It could be argued that Cecily's rejection directly led to William being turned into a vampire. He was so heartsick that when Drusilla came along and tapped into his unhappiness, he succumbed willingly to her. A century later, Drusilla rejects Spike in part because she can sense his obsession with Buffy, and to prove her point, he's returned to Sunnydale. Although his given reason was to find the Gem of Amara which would make him invincible and allow him to kill the Slayer, Spike chose to stay in town. Now that he's acknowledged his love for Buffy, her Cecily-esque rejection reopens old wounds and Spike's knee-jerk reaction is scarily real: *If I can't have her, I'll kill her*—as if that would make up for all the rejections of his past. However, once he sees her by herself outside, afraid, crying over her mother's pending CAT scan, Spike's ego takes a backseat to his heart and his awkward attempts at comforting her, surprisingly, are not rebuffed. Whether she wants to admit it or not, hearing Spike's story has made Buffy realize, at least on some subconscious level, that she and Spike may have more in common than she ever dreamed.

MYSTERY EXPLAINED: Why Spike referred to Angel as his "sire" back in Episode 15, "School Hard," when it's now obvious Drusilla was the one to turn him. According to Joss Whedon, "Angel was Dru's sire and she made Spike. But sire doesn't just mean who made you; it means you come from their line. Angel is like a grandfather to Spike."

OF SPECIAL NOTE: According to this episode, Spike was twenty-five when he was turned in 1880.

The first Slayer he killed left him with a sword scar over his right eyebrow. The leather jacket Spike wears is a "memento" from the second Slayer he killed.

86. "Shadow"
(NOVEMBER 21, 2000)

Director: Daniel Attias
Teleplay: David Fury
Recurring cast: Kristine Sutherland (Joyce Summers); Clare Kramer
    (Glory); Charlie Weber (Ben); Amber Benson (Tara)
Guest cast: Kevin Weisman (Dreg); William Forward (Dr. Isaacs)

Plot: Glory sends an unholy emissary to sniff out the Key. Joyce gets a scary diagnosis.

THIS WEEK'S DEMON BLOODHOUND: A demon snake. Glory morphs a cobra into a demon using a long-lost Sobekian spell and a mystical amulet.

INTRODUCING: Oligodendroglioma. A brain tumor of unknown cause that is more common in men than women. Headaches are a typical symptom.

ANALYSIS: Joyce's illness is the latest emotional burden weighing on Buffy. She's spreading herself thin trying to protect Dawn from Glory and also being there for her mother after she's diagnosed with a tumor. In an effort to keep from falling apart, Buffy is walling up some of her emotions, and in the process Riley feels he's being pushed away. Dawn unwittingly reinforces his feelings of alienation when she comments on how calm Buffy is with Riley compared to Angel, whom she seemed consumed by. Although Dawn thinks she's giving Riley a compliment, Riley comprehends a passion Buffy had for Angel that she doesn't have for *him*. Spike, who always goes for the jugular, even in a metaphorical sense, further twists the knife by telling Riley that he's too "white-bread" for Buffy. Left alone, Riley begins to tiptoe toward a walk on the wild side. When he agrees to let Sandy bite him, it's hard to know if he's trying to understand Buffy's attraction to Angel or if he's becoming self-destructive. His indifferent dusting of Sandy speaks to the latter.

Buffy is oblivious to Riley's slipping away because she's too busy grasping at straws, like asking Willow to perform a spell to cure her mother. Giles gently tries to give Buffy some perspective, reminding her that a medical condition isn't a demon to be wished away or a spell to be broken.

Glory's latest attempt to locate the Key is foiled by Buffy, although the Slayer's most recent encounter with Glory confirms the sobering truth that there is no way Buffy is ever going to be a physical match for this adversary. Unless she finds out what exactly Glory is, and how to fight it, everyone she loves will remain in mortal danger.

THE REAL HORROR: Cancer. In a world of incurable diseases, cancer still evokes a special chill in our culture. The idea of our bodies turning on themselves in a deadly attack, adds to the helplessness of illness in general. Although the survival rate among cancer patients has improved significantly overall, any cancer involving the brain is especially worrisome since it's the seat of our consciousness. This is one enemy Buffy can't vanquish, regardless of her strength, and it engulfs her with a fear she's never known before.

BLOOPERS: It's been established Dawn was fourteen when she was introduced in 2000 so she couldn't have been nine years old when the family moved to Sunnydale in 1997; she would have been ten going on eleven.

During the fight with Glory, Buffy's right shoulder is injured, but at the hospital she's icing her left shoulder.

OF SPECIAL NOTE: There was an ancient Egyptian deity called Sobek, who took the form of a crocodile.

87. "Listening to Fear"
(NOVEMBER 28, 2000)

Director: David Solomon
Teleplay: Rebecca Rand Kirshner
Recurring cast: Charlie Weber (Ben); Amber Benson (Tara); Kristine
   Sutherland (Joyce Summers)

Guest cast: Nick Chinlund (Major Ellis); Kevin Weisman (Dreg); Randy Thompson (Dr. Kriegel); Paul Hayes (older nightwatchman); Keith Allan (skinny mental patient); Erin Leigh Price (vampire chick); April Adams (Nurse Lampkin); Barbara C. Adside (creature); Debbie Lee Carrington (creature)

Plot: There's an epidemic of madness sweeping Sunnydale. Riley reconnects with his military buddies.

THIS WEEK'S OUT-OF-THIS-WORLD DEMON: The Queller, an extraterrestrial demon that hunts down the insane and quells their ranting by regurgitating malodorous goo into their mouths to suffocate them. E.T., he ain't.

INTRODUCING: Ben's mysterious connection to Glory; Major Ellis, leader of the commando team Riley calls in to help with the alien.

ANALYSIS: Glory's practice of sucking the sanity of out people is beginning to take its toll on Sunnydale General's mental-health facility, now overflowing with deranged patients. The one interesting side effect of this mental illness is it brings out a kind of primal understanding that Dawn is not exactly human. Although Buffy does her best to downplay it, Dawn is beginning to sense that something really is different about her.

Buffy's Slaying is put on hold while she stays by Joyce's side in the days leading up to her operation. Without Buffy there to lead, Willow, Xander, and Giles take up the slack and go for strength in numbers—and somehow manage not to get themselves killed. Riley's unexplained absence is noticed, although nobody would ever guess he's finding dark solace with female vampires he's letting feed on his blood. Like men who find hiring street prostitutes excitingly dangerous, Riley's self-indulgence is turning into a risky habit.

The cockroach-looking alien stalking the insane doesn't seem to differentiate between those who have lost their minds to Glory and those who are having seizures due to physical illness. And Buffy's preoccupation with her own sadness and fear almost prevents her from saving her mother from the demon. Ironically, it's not Riley who shows up to help Buffy, but Spike, who's turned into a bit of a stalker himself. He keeps close to Buffy both because he wants to be near her but also because he's becoming more and more protective of her.

Although Giles and the others figure out what the demon is and why it's in Sunnydale, their assumption that Glory summoned the demon is unexpectedly off the mark. The episode's biggest surprise—that it was Ben who called for the demon and that he has some connection to Glory—also becomes the biggest mystery.

THE REAL HORROR: Losing your mind. As our population ages, more and more families are dealing with Alzheimer's and other forms of dementia. What begins as forgetfulness or confusion can degenerate into hallucinations, paranoia, and delusions. Although Joyce's symptoms are related to a brain tumor, becoming aware that you can't control your brain and are losing your faculties engenders feelings of fear and helplessness, both in the patient and in surrounding loved ones.

BLOOPERS: The Tunguska meteor explosion occurred in 1908, not 1917. In the early morning hours of June 30, local Siberians saw a huge fireball. It's estimated the object, now believed to be a stony asteroid or possibly a comet, broke up a little less than five miles above Earth before landing in a series of violent explosions. The power of the blast flattened trees over an area more than half the size of Rhode Island. The ensuing fires burned for over a week. By way of comparison, the force of the blast was estimated to have been two-thousand times that of the atomic bomb dropped on Hiroshima.

OF SPECIAL NOTE: This is the first time Buffy has encountered a demon of the extraterrestrial kind.

88. "Into the Woods"
(DECEMBER 19, 2000)

Director: Marti Noxon
Teleplay: Marti Noxon
Recurring cast: Bailey Chase (Graham Miller); Kristine Sutherland (Joyce Summers)
Guest cast: Nick Chinlund (Major Ellis); Randy Thompson (Dr. Kriegel); Rainy Jo Stout (Junkie vampire girl); Emmanuel Xuereb (Whip); Adam G. (tough vamp)
Music: "Summerbreeze" (as Riley and Buffy dance), by Emiliana Torrini, from *Love in the Time of Science*

Plot: *Riley and Buffy reach a turning point in their relationship. Joyce recuperates after her surgery.*

THIS WEEK'S UNHOLY PASTIME: Vampire brothels, where humans pay for the erotic thrill of having their blood sucked in a presumably controlled environment . . . Who knew?

INTRODUCING: A new military operation. Even though the Initiative has been disbanded, there still is a covert squad of commandos traveling the world putting out demon uprisings. Their next stop: Belize.

ANALYSIS: Even though Riley and Buffy spend a romantic night together after Joyce's successful surgery, there's an undercurrent of trouble. Little by little, each perceived slight Riley has felt is adding up to what may become an insurmountable mountain of hurt. Every time Buffy didn't think to turn to him for support and help further convinced him she doesn't need him. He not only wants her to love him and want him, but to *need* him. When Buffy doesn't give him that, Riley goes where he knows he's *desperately* needed.

Spike's motive for taking Buffy to witness Riley having his blood sucked by an anemic vampire is no doubt twofold: First, Spike wants Buffy, and with Riley out of the picture there's a better chance for the improbable miracle that Buffy would return any affection. Second, because he's in love with Buffy, Spike doesn't like Riley making a fool of the Slayer by getting off in vampire brothels.

Spike contends that Buffy's intimacy with death makes her crave a certain darkness in her intimate relationships, which means she's just biding time with Riley. Spike hits a button by telling Riley that while he may be sleeping with her, he still really hasn't gotten to her. Is that connection missing because she won't let herself feel it or because it simply isn't there? Buffy wants to believe it's the former, which is why she runs after Riley to try and stop him from taking off with the commandos on their demon mission in Belize. But she gets there too late and is left alone with her own internal demons.

THE REAL HORROR: How fast a relationship can fall apart. Even the seemingly strongest relationship can be stunningly fragile. All it takes is one secret or one issue that is allowed to fester and grow until it consumes the couple. Rather than confront Buffy earlier about his feelings, Riley took a self-destructive path that not only diminished him but humiliated her. Buffy wasn't blameless, either, taking Riley for granted and perhaps unfairly comparing him to Angel rather than embracing what was unique about him.

IT'S A MYSTERY: Why—after Riley stabs Spike with the faux stake—there's no visible hole in Spike's shirt.

BLOOPERS: In the first shot of Buffy punching the bag, both her hands are taped but when Riley walks in, only one is.

OF SPECIAL NOTE: The card at the end that reads "*In Memory of: D. C. Gustafson*" refers to a crewman who was a friend of Sarah Michelle's and who died of AIDS-related cancer in November 2000.

89. "Triangle"
(JANUARY 9, 2001)

Director: Christopher Hibler
Teleplay: Jane Espenson
Recurring cast: Kristine Sutherland (Joyce Summers); Amber Benson (Tara)
Guest cast: Abraham Benrubi (troll); Ranjani Brow (young nun)
Music: "There's No Other Way" (as Spike and Xander talk), by Blur, from *Leisure*; "Bohemian Like You" (as Olaf arrives at the Bronze), by the Dandy Warhols, from *Thirteen Tales from Urban Bohemia*

Plot: Willow and Anya's bickering is putting Xander in the middle. A spell gone wrong conjures someone from Anya's past.

THIS WEEK'S EX-BOYFRIEND: Olaf the troll. Originally a human, Olaf was Anya's boyfriend until she caught him cheating and turned him into a troll. This bitter act of vengeance and snappy magic is why she was offered the vengeance-demon gig.

ANALYSIS: The episode takes a lighter tone, departing for a bit from the darkness of Joyce's illness.

Although Glory has been lying low, Giles knows they need to find some answers for when she reappears, and decides to make a personal visit to the Watchers' Council to ask for help identifying her. During his absence, a power struggle over the shop ensues between Anya and Willow. But what they really are squabbling about is their insecurity and jealousies with each other over Xander.

Willow knows Xander in a way Anya couldn't, because they grew up together and are best friends. Anya worries that Willow could turn Xander against her, or seduce him. Willow worries that Anya is going to break Xander's heart—or worse. In their attempts to get affirmation for their places in Xander's life and heart, they are constantly putting him in the middle and trying to get him to pick sides. But all it does it make Xander annoyed at both of them. Worse, their bickering causes Willow to accidentally release a troll from a crystal in which some witches had imprisoned him. When the troll tries to make Xander pick whose life should be spared, Willow's or Anya's, Xander instead puts his own life on the line to save both. The point is, although he loves them in different ways, they are equally important to him.

Since the demise of her relationship with Riley, Buffy has gotten overly protective of her friends' happiness. She is obviously much more comfortable with Tara and now shares her feelings about things. Buffy is also more forthcoming with Dawn, realizing that her own inattentiveness was part of what undermined her relationship with Riley.

Spike is using every opportunity he can to get Buffy to notice him and to get on the Slayer's good side by being marginally more considerate to people when she's around. But what *is* genuine is his determination to watch her back, and he is gradually proving himself an important ally—who Buffy will come to depend on in ways she never imagined.

THE REAL HORROR: Being caught in the middle. Almost everyone knows what it's like to have two people you dearly love be at each others' throats, and the discomfort of being caught between the two.

IT'S A MYSTERY: How does Buffy know Riley went off to a jungle? We never see him give her any details of his mission.

BLOOPERS: In Episode 55, "Graduation Day (Part I)," Anya asked Xander to leave with her, mentioning her car is parked outside. That being the case, when she and Willow go after the troll in this episode, it couldn't be her first time driving.

OF SPECIAL NOTE: Abraham Benrubi is best known in the role of Jerry the desk clerk on *ER.*

90. "Checkpoint"
(JANUARY 23, 2001)

Director: Nick Marck
Teleplay: Douglas Petrie and Jane Espenson
Recurring cast: Kristine Sutherland (Joyce Summers); Clare Kramer (Glory); Charlie Weber (Ben); Amber Benson (Tara)
Guest cast: Cynthia LaMontagne (Lydia); Oliver Muirhead (Phillip); Kris Iyer (Nigel); Kevin Weisman (Dreg); Troy T. Blendell (Jinx); Harris Yulin (Quentin Travers)

Plot: The Watchers' Council tries to reassert control over Buffy, using their knowledge of Glory as leverage.

THIS WEEK'S MEDIEVAL REMNANT: Knights of Byzantium. An ancient order of soldiers that will do anything, including killing Buffy and Dawn, to keep the Key from falling into Glory's hands. In any other situation, they would probably be Slayer allies, but Buffy's protection of the Key has put her in the unusual position of being on opposite sides with a force of good.

INTRODUCING: Jinx, another of Glory's minions.

THE BIG BAD: Glory's no demon—she's a full-fledged god.

ANALYSIS: Buffy comes into her own in this episode, when she finally realizes the extent and depth of her power. Like most institutions, the Watchers' Council spends a lot of time justifying its existence, so when it comes to Sunnydale, Travers and his entourage make a big show of being there to review Buffy, her methods, Giles, and even her support group. But Buffy doesn't work for the Council; it works *because* of her and all the others who came before. Without a Slayer, the Council has no meaning. This sudden insight allows her to tap into her power even more, and to further establish her leadership.

An unexpected visit from Glory convinces Buffy that her family is in imminent danger so she turns to the only person strong enough to offer some semblance of protection—Spike. Although the outward antagonism is there, he knows she's entrusting him with the two people she loves most, and there is no doubt he will defend them to the death if need be.

THE REAL HORROR: Emotional blackmail. While efficient in the short run, such tactics usually backfire over the long haul, causing resentment and anger. Ever since Buffy quit the Council when fighting the mayor, they've had no leverage over her. Threatening to have Giles deported was one way of reasserting their control. But once again they underestimate Buffy's acumen and she quickly figures out they're bluffing, because she's the one with the actual power. Without Buffy, there is no hope in going up against Glory, especially since Faith is still missing in Slayer action behind bars.

OF SPECIAL NOTE: Anya's self-invented full name is Anya Christina Emmanuella Jenkins, and she was born on July 4, 1980, in Indiana.

91. "Blood Ties"
(FEBRUARY 6, 2001)

Director: Michael Gershman
Teleplay: Steven S. DeKnight
Recurring cast: Kristine Sutherland (Joyce Summers); Clare Kramer (Glory); Charlie Weber (Ben); Troy T. Blendell (Jinx); Amber Benson (Tara)
Guest cast: Justin Corence (Orlando), Michael Emanuel (burly guard); Joe Ochman (janitor); Paul Bates (crazy #1); Carl J. Johnson (crazy #2); Candice Nicole (young Buffy); Elyssa D. Vito (young Dawn)
Music: "Holiday" (during the birthday party), by Star Ghost Dog, from *The Great Indoors*

Plot: Dawn learns the truth about the Key.

THIS WEEK'S SPLIT PERSONALITY: Ben as Glory—or is it Glory as Ben? Ben and Glory reside in the same body and transform from one to the other, although people aren't able to remember it when they see the transformation.

THE BIG BAD: Glory is stuck on Earth after getting kicked out of her demon dimension by a couple of fellow gods. Although her powers have been greatly tempered on this mortal coil, she's still relatively invincible and slowly losing her mind, a side effect of her human form. This is why she needs to suck the sanity out of others—otherwise she wouldn't be able to function.

ANALYSIS: Finally everyone is on the same page regarding Dawn and the Key, though it's even more painful than Buffy anticipated.

Buffy confides to Willow and the others the truth about Dawn, but in their efforts to act normal around her, Dawn immediately knows something is wrong, aided by some fortuitous eavesdropping. Spike, who wants to give Buffy a birthday present but can't quite muster the nerve to come any closer to the house than the front yard, sees Dawn sneak out of the house and tags along, out of curiosity, and because he knows Sunnydale is not a safe place after nightfall.

Dawn is understandably upset after reading Giles's journals and finding out what, and who, the Key really is. Buffy naturally wants to take her frustration out on Spike, blaming him for Dawn's discovery, but her heart really isn't in it. She knows Spike is right—that honesty might have been the wiser course of action—but Buffy was afraid of Dawn's response, with good reason, as it turns out. When everyone breaks up into teams to go looking for Dawn after she runs away in a devastated snit, Buffy and Spike are paired up. It's as if, subconsciously, Buffy is able to let her emotional guard down a bit because she doesn't feel Spike's life depends on her; and in that way, they are more like equals. It gives Buffy a bit of a breather.

Despite her anger and confusion, whatever the Key once might have been, it is now a teenage girl who is frightened and needs her family and friends more than ever. Buffy once again goes to the heart of family by saying it doesn't matter how she came into her life, she is family because in Buffy and Joyce's hearts she is.

THE REAL HORROR: Finding out you really are adopted. At some point growing up, most people wonder if they really belong in the family they find themselves living with. There's a certain romance in thinking you were really born into some perfect family that exists happily, without bickering or tensions or money problems. But for those who do find out they were adopted, it can unleash a flurry of issues because their very foundation has been based on a false belief. Likewise, Dawn goes through an identity crisis when she not only finds out that she wasn't only not born into the Summers family, but that she wasn't really "born" at all.

BLOOPERS: In the scene where Dawn is tearing apart her diaries, a magazine on the wooden chest at the end of the bed disappears then reappears from one shot to the next.

92. "Crush"
(FEBRUARY 13, 2001)

Director: Daniel Attias

Teleplay: David Fury

Recurring cast: Mercedes McNab (Harmony Kendall); Amber Benson (Tara); Juliet Landau (Drusilla); Kristine Sutherland (Joyce Summers)

Guest cast: Frederick Dawson (porter); Greg Wayne (student); Joseph Digiandomenico (Matt); Walter Borchert (Jeff); Asher Glaser (boy in the Bronze); Jennifer Bergman (girl in the Bronze); Nell Shanahan (waitress)

Music: "Play It By Ear" (at the Bronze), by Summercamp, from *Pure Juice*; "Happy" (as Buffy and Ben talk), by Summercamp; "Key" (as Spike and Dru dance), by Devics from *If You Forget Me*

Plot: Spike professes his love for Buffy. Drusilla is not amused.

THIS WEEK'S WEAPON OF CHOICE: A stun gun used by Drusilla to immobilize Buffy.

INTRODUCING: The refurbished Bronze, which needed a makeover after Olaf the troll's demolishing act. Also, Sunnydale's train station.

ANALYSIS: Buffy's complex relationship with Spike gets more complicated. Dawn enjoys Spike's company because he treats her as an equal and doesn't talk down to her, and Buffy doesn't mind because she knows Spike can protect Dawn almost as well as she can. It isn't until Dawn tells Buffy Spike's in love with her that Buffy realizes it. Although she says the idea disgusts her, more frightening is that being with Spike would force Buffy to confront her own demons, and she isn't ready for that. Hurt by her rejection,

Spike is easy pickings for Drusilla, who has returned to Sunnydale to teach Spike how to ignore the pain caused by the chip. That said, she still kills the victim before Spike feeds.

Although Drusilla's "Evil is good" inspirational pep-talk works for a while, the sight of Buffy being knocked out by Drusilla snaps Spike out of it. Crazed with his unrequited love, Spike ties them both up in a desperate bid to prove his love for Buffy by offering to dust Drusilla—and Harmony, too, for that matter. Having bungled everything, all three women are furious at Spike and he ends up being rejected by all three. Although Buffy does her best to convince Spike to leave town, he's destined to become a central player in Glory's efforts to find the Key.

THE REAL HORROR: Being an unwanted object of desire. Most of us want to be wanted and want to be found attractive, but only by those we want or are attracted to in return. Although Spike has been effectively rendered safe to humans, he's not exactly harmless and Buffy has witnessed years of his bloody proclivities. Plus, allowing herself to feel any attraction to Spike would be a betrayal of her relationship with Angel, whose dark side was at least tempered by his soul (not to mention Spike and Angel were rivals when it came to Drusilla).

LITERARY ALLUSION: When Willow mentions Esmeralda, it's a reference to Victor Hugo's classic novel *The Hunchback of Notre Dame.* The horribly disfigured bell-ringer Quasimodo falls in love with the beautiful Gypsy girl Esmeralda. The parallel between Quasimodo's unrequited love for Esmeralda and Spike's for Buffy is fairly straightforward.

IT'S A MYSTERY: Why does Buffy let Drusilla get away, to kill again? It's more understandable in Harmony's case, because they went to school together and she's basically inept. But Drusilla has proven herself a deranged killer.

93. "I Was Made to Love You"
(FEBRUARY 20, 2001)

Director: James A. Contner
Teleplay: Jane Espenson
Recurring cast: Kristine Sutherland (Joyce Summers); Clare Kramer
(Glory); Charlie Weber (Ben); Amber Benson (Tara)

Guest cast: Shonda Farr (April); Adam Busch (Warren); Troy T. Blendell (Jinx); Amelinda Embry (Katrina); Paul Darrigo (driver); Gil Christner (resident); Kelly Felix (teenager); Paul Walia (friend)

Music: "Hidee Ho" (as Buffy and Xander dance), by Mellonova, from *Mellonova*; "OK Nightmare" (as Buffy sees Ben at the Bronze), by Caviar, from *Caviar*; "Kawanga!" (from when Spike leaves the Bronze to when he's tossed through the window), by Los Strait-jackets, from *The Velvet Touch of Los Straitjackets*

Plot: A jilted girlfriend goes on a rampage.

THIS WEEK'S MECHANICAL MALFUNCTION: April, a robot created to be the perfect girlfriend, short-circuits when dumped.

INTRODUCING: Warren Mears, a lonely engineering genius who loses control of his creation.

ANALYSIS: Spike's affections make Buffy contemplate the possibility that there is something dark within her that attracted him in the first place so she is still creeped out by his professions of love. Spike tries unsuccessfully to ingratiate himself with Giles and the others as a way of getting on Buffy's good side, but is soundly rejected. Considering they've previously accepted witches, vampires, and demons in their midst, their antipathy toward him is not just because he's one of the undead. There's a sense that subconsciously Buffy's friends worry she does have an attraction to the dark side and want to prevent her from walking down that path.

The challenges of being alone and not having an active romantic relationship are explored from a couple different angles. Warren represents one of the greatest ironies of human behavior. Often, when we finally get what we *think* we want—in his case, the perfect girlfriend—we find it's not what we wanted at all. While predictability can be comforting, it also can be boring.

THE REAL HORROR: Loneliness. Warren's way of dealing with it was to make a fantasy partner. Even if she wasn't real, it was better than being alone. Spike can relate. Besides his Buffy mannequin, he had Harmony dress up as the Slayer for some fantasy role-playing. Buffy deals with her loneliness by delving deeper into her work. Although she'd like to find someone, she doesn't want to feel like she needs a partner to validate her, which is why she ends up breaking off her coffee date with Ben. When she goes out with someone, she wants it to be because it's mutually desired, not because she feels under pressure. Before you can completely be with someone else, you have to learn to be alone with yourself—and Buffy will be taking a crash course.

IT'S A MYSTERY: How did Spike find the address where Warren was staying?

OF SPECIAL NOTE: Britney Spears was originally offered the role of April but, according to reports, backed out because of scheduling conflicts.

94. "The Body"
(FEBRUARY 27, 2001)

Director: Joss Whedon
Teleplay: Joss Whedon
Recurring cast: Amber Benson (Tara); Kristine Sutherland (Joyce Summers)
Guest cast: Randy Thompson (doctor); Kevin Cristaldi (first paramedic); Stefan Umstead (second paramedic); Loanne Bishop (911 operator); J. Evan Bonifant (Kevin); Kelli Garner (Kirstie); Rae'ven Larrymore Kelly (Lisa); Tia Matza (teacher); John Michael Herndon (vampire)

Plot: An unexpected tragedy leaves Buffy reeling.

THIS WEEK'S CRUSHING BLOW: The death of Joyce Summers from an aneurysm.

INTRODUCING: Willow and Tara's first onscreen kiss.

ANALYSIS: The death of a loved one immediately puts everything else in perspective. Parking tickets, material possessions, and even food, lose the importance they might otherwise have. Our focus turns to those we love and we draw them close. At the same time, there's a sense of isolation because, although grief can be shared, it is still a process that has to be experienced individually.

Buffy wanders through much of the episode in shock. She is so overwhelmed, her emotions are almost paralyzed. In addition to the grief she feels, she is crushed by the sudden awareness that she really is the grown-up of the family now—just when she needs her mother's advice and wisdom most. Although everyone wants to be there, only Tara can truly empathize, her own mother having died just a few years earlier when she was seventeen.

Giles instinctively takes on a more paternal, protective role for both Dawn and Buffy, like when he goes with the girls to speak to the doctor after the autopsy, and volunteering to fill out most of the necessary paperwork that accompanies death. Although Buffy and the others have seen far too much death in their young lives already, including the loss of friends such as Jenny Calendar, Joyce held a special place. Not only was she Buffy's mother, she was the voice of reason and Buffy's true emotional anchor.

THE REAL HORROR: Losing a parent. Although this is the way nature intended it, losing the person who has raised you inevitably leaves an indelible void. It means there is no longer parental comfort to fall back on; it also is a reminder of our own mortality and the fragility of life.

BLOOPERS: The picture Dawn is drawing in art class seems to change from one shot to the next without benefit of her having worked on it.

Unless Dr. Kriegel is a pathologist working for the coroner's office, it's doubtful he'd be performing the autopsy.

OF SPECIAL NOTE: This episode contains no background music apart from the opening titles. Nor was there a "Previously on *Buffy*" montage at the beginning of the episode.

The episode begins with the flashback of the gang's Christmas dinner because Joss Whedon didn't want the cast and crew credits to appear over the main scene of Buffy discovering her mother's body.

95. "Forever"

(APRIL 17, 2001)

Director: Marti Noxon
Teleplay: Marti Noxon
Recurring cast: Clare Kramer (Glory); Charlie Weber (Ben); Amber Benson (Tara)

Guest cast: David Boreanaz (Angel); Troy T. Blendell (Jinx); Joel Grey (Doc); Todd Duffey (Murk); Andrea Gall (customer); Alan Henry Brown (funeral director); Darius Dudley (minister); Annie Talbot (lady with baby); Noor Shic (lady with rosary)

Music: "Tomorrow We'll Awake" (as Anya and Xander talk in bed), by Splendid; "Tales of Brave Ulysses" (song Giles listens to), by Cream

Plot: Dawn casts a spell to bring Joyce back to life.

THIS WEEK'S INNOCENT DEMON: The Ghora, a three-headed demon whose eggs are needed to cast a resurrection spell.

INTRODUCING: Doc, an unspecified creature well-versed in the darker magics, such as bringing the dead back to life.

ANALYSIS: Buffy and the others are still coping with Joyce's death. Now that the initial shock and surprise has worn off, deeper issues are bubbling to the surface. Anya's revelation that death and life are actually part of the same life experience gives her comfort and helps her understand the synergy and symmetry of the natural human world. Giles seems to ponder, "What if?" as he listens to music that reminds him of Joyce. And Buffy is so afraid she will break down that she refuses to let herself feel at all, which in turn is alienating Dawn, who needs to share her grief with the only other person who can understand the immediate loss. Angel, who shows up after the funeral to comfort Buffy, gently tells her life has to go on. But all Buffy wants to do is go back in time—to when her mother was alive, there was no Glory, and Angel was there to hold her.

Although it's understandable that Dawn would want her mother back at any cost, it's surprising that Willow encourages that line of thought. This sets the stage for some serious philosophical differences down the road between Willow and Tara, over the moral issues and implications surrounding how witchcraft is used.

THE REAL HORROR: Having to confront loss. Buffy intentionally kept herself so busy arranging the funeral and dealing with the business of death, she was able to effectively shut down her emotions. But sooner or later she has to face her profound sense of loss and isolation. Buffy keeps telling Dawn that Joyce is gone and can't be brought back. But the hopeful expectation in Buffy's voice when she thinks her resurrected mother has come home, reveals that Buffy feels just as alone and lost as Dawn, if not more so.

IT'S A MYSTERY: Why is it that Jack, the zombie from Episode 47, "The Zeppo," is able to be brought back to life with so few effects that nobody seems to notice he'd ever been dead?

MUSICAL NOTE: The song Giles listens to after the funeral is the same one he played for Joyce during their night together in Episode 40, "Band Candy."

96. "Intervention"
(APRIL 24, 2001)

Director: Michael Gershman
Teleplay: Jane Espenson
Recurring cast: Clare Kramer (Glory); Amber Benson (Tara)
Guest cast: Adam Busch (Warren); Troy T. Blendell (Jinx); Sharon Ferguson (Primitive); Todd Duffey (Murk); Kelly Donovan

Plot: A new robot in town causes confusion. Glory mistakes Spike for the Key while Buffy ponders profound questions about her Slayer existence.

THIS WEEK'S PROPHETIC ENCOUNTER: Buffy's spiritual guide tells her "death" will be her gift.

INTRODUCING: Dawn as budding klepto, when she steals a pair of Anya's earrings.

ANALYSIS: Buffy worries that her Slayer strength and power is also making her emotionally distant from those around her. She worries the people she loves don't know just how much she loves them because she is usually so preoccupied facing evil threats and protecting everyone. Buffy's afraid that being in the Slayer mode will become the way she feels comfortable—that she will lose her humanity.

Buffy agrees to a kind of "Slayer retreat" in order to regain her focus as well as to understand how being a Slayer fits in with life. She's surprised to learn that it's not a matter of her lacking the capacity for love; rather, she loves so much that she sometimes pulls away because of the intensity. Love and pain are inextricably connected.

While Buffy is in the desert trying to understand her spiritual guide's teachings, Spike is enjoying his new toy: a special-order Warren-designed robot that looks just like Buffy, only it lives to please Spike. Their togetherness leads Glory's minions to mistakenly believe Spike is the Key. Glory knows he's not, but figures he probably knows who is. But not even the most brutal torture can get Spike to reveal anything, and it's clear he's prepared to die to protect Dawn, because he wouldn't be able to stand the pain Buffy would feel if anything happened to her.

Although Buffy is grossed-out by the thought of Spike and the 'bot together, it finally hits her that Spike is deadly serious about being in love with her—and it goes far beyond sexual lust. He loves without reciprocation and, when put to the test, selflessly, and in the process teaches Buffy an important lesson about the sacrifices of love.

THE REAL HORROR: Being proven wrong. Buffy didn't believe Spike capable of truly loving anyone, but he showed her otherwise with the beating he absorbed at the hands of Glory for refusing to identify the Key.

OF SPECIAL NOTE: Nicholas Brendon's twin, Kelly Donovan, was used as a double for a few scenes when Nicholas missed some filming due to illness.

The desert hilltop Buffy is led to is the same place she visited in her dream in Episode 78, "Restless."

Vampires can't have their brains sucked, nor can they house the Key, because of their impurity.

97. "Tough Love"
(MAY 1, 2001)

Director: David Grossman
Teleplay: Rebecca Rand Kirshner
Recurring cast: Clare Kramer (Glory); Charlie Weber (Ben); Amber Benson (Tara)
Guest cast: Troy T. Blendell (Jinx); Anne Betancourt (Principal Stevens); Leland Crooke (Professor Lillian); Todd Duffey (Murk); Alan Heitz (Slook)

Plot: Glory targets Tara.

THIS WEEK'S VENGEFUL WITCH: Willow. Glory mind-sucks Tara, and an enraged Willow recklessly sets up a confrontation using her darkest magic.

ANALYSIS: Dawn is beginning to crumble under the weight of responsibility, seeing the people around stopping their lives to protect her, and even getting hurt, as Glory continues her hunt. She begins to think that anything that can be the cause of such pain must be evil. Although Spike has no real answers, he's someone Dawn can talk to and she knows he won't placate her.

The latest victim is Tara. Glory thinks she must be the Key since she is the newest member of Buffy's group. When she realizes her mistake, she takes the opportunity to drain Tara's brain. Buffy barely saves Willow from a losing confrontation with Glory. As they gather in Tara's room, Dawn is guilt-ridden as she watches Willow tend to her now-befuddled lover. But because of her mental instability, Tara can now see the Key's aura. When Glory bursts in to finish what she started with Willow, she can tell by Tara's ramblings who the Key really is. Unless Buffy acts quickly, Dawn will be at Glory's mercy.

THE REAL HORROR: Angry words. When Willow and Tara exchange words because Tara's concerned about how powerful Willow is getting and how fast it's happening, Willow leaves in a huff. The last words they exchanged were harsh. It's a pointed reminder that we never can know for sure when we leave somebody, that we will see them again—especially in a place like Sunnydale—so we should always try to resolve issues and take the time to tell people we love them.

IT'S A MYSTERY: Glory's minions eavesdropping outside Buffy's house couldn't hear Dawn's conversation with Buffy that made it clear *she* was the Key.

WHAT REBECCA RAND KIRSHNER HAD TO SAY: "Conflict's good. Willow's getting really really powerful, and when you have those powers and they're growing, it's hard to know when to stop. Their argument was what happens when two people of varying powers are working together or working on a relationship together. At what point do you have to stop being powerful to let the other person feel all right, and at what point is being as powerful as you can be, the optimum thing for your relationship?"

OF SPECIAL NOTE: A blue-screen technique was used to achieve the brain-sucking effect. Clare Kramer (Glory) was filmed pushing her fingers into a dummy head (Tara) covered in blue material. Then in postproduction, the blue head was digitally replaced with Amber Benson's.

98. "Spiral"
(MAY 8, 2001)

Director: James A. Contner
Teleplay: Steven S. DeKnight
Recurring cast: Clare Kramer (Glory); Charlie Weber (Ben); Amber Benson (Tara)
Guest cast: Wade Andrew Williams (General Gregor); Karim Prince (knight of Byzantium); Justin Gorence (Orlando); Lily Knight (Gronx); Todd Duffey (Murk); Jack Donner (cleric #1); Bob Morrisey (crazy #1); Paul Bates (crazy #2); Carl J. Johnson (crazy #3); Mary Sheldon (nurse)

Plot: Buffy and Dawn flee Sunnydale with both Glory and the Knights of Byzantium on their heels.

THIS WEEK'S REVELATION: The link between Ben and Glory. After Glory was cast out of her Hell dimension, she was trapped inside the body of a newborn human boy. But because she's so powerful, she is periodically able to break out of her fleshly prison.

INTRODUCING: The purpose of the Key—to open the portals to all the dimensions. Not only will the portal to Glory's Hell dimension open so she can go home, but all realities will dissolve into each other, unleashing unimagined horrors.

ANALYSIS: It's hard to believe Buffy can continue to hold up under the pressure she has been under. It's been relentless, and her sudden reliance on Spike as she and the others run from Glory has Xander, for one, thinking she's cracking up. But once again Spike proves his loyalty—when the Knights of Byzantium attack their Winnebago and he's injured protecting the others.

After capturing the Knights' leader, Buffy finally learns why they are so determined to destroy the Key: because it will initiate the end of the world. Buffy is put in the most impossible position ever. Does she let the world be destroyed, or does she keep the promise she made to Joyce, that she would protect Dawn at all costs?

THE REAL HORROR: Running out of time. When Glory takes Dawn, Buffy feels she has failed and is so overwhelmed by having lost Dawn that she shuts down, paralyzed into inaction.

99. "The Weight of the World"
(MAY 15, 2001)

Director: David Soloman
Teleplay: Douglas Petrie
Recurring cast: Clare Kramer (Glory); Charlie Weber (Ben); Amber Benson (Tara)
Guest cast: Bob Morrisey (crazy #1); Joel Grey (Doc); Kristine Sutherland (Joyce Summers); Dean Butler (Hank Summers)

Plot: Willows tries to communicate with Buffy through her subconscious to snap her out of her catatonia.

THIS WEEK'S MENTAL OBSTACLE: Guilt. Buffy blames herself for Dawn's apparent fate.

ANALYSIS: Buffy's feelings of failure have reduced her to a zoned-out zombie, which seems completely out of character for Buffy. But she feels tremendous guilt for once having wished it would all be over—for wishing she didn't have to be the one to save the world and fight Glory—and now she believes that is what ultimately let Glory prevail.

But Glory is also acting out of character, struggling with unfamiliar feelings of human emotions as she prepares to sacrifice Dawn in order to open the portals. Apparently the barrier between Ben and Glory is slowly blurring so that some of his humanity is seeping into her consciousness. Unfortunately, Ben also fears dying. Although he wants to help Dawn, he ultimately can't sacrifice himself to do so.

Once Willow convinces Buffy she still has time to help Dawn and that she hasn't done anything wrong, Buffy snaps out it. Although she knows the odds are against her, she refuses to give up hope that somehow she can save both Dawn and the world. She has to figure out a way.

WHAT SCREENWRITER DOUG PETRIE HAS TO SAY: During this episode, producers were already working around her *Scooby-Doo* schedule, so making Buffy catatonic was a way of accommodating her absence. "We knew some weeks in advance what her schedule would be like, but we had the second-to-last episode of the season and no Buffy. What do you do? Joss and I were both big fans of the *Dr. Strange* comics. Dr Strange was a mystic magician who lived in Greenwich Village, New York, and could leave his body. His astral self would go off on these adventures."

IT'S A MYSTERY: Before the Key was human, how was it used to open the portal? With Dawn, it's her blood, but an energy ball wouldn't have blood.

BLOOPERS: After Glory has one of her minions put ash on Dawn's face, it disappears then reappears from one shot to the next.

OF SPECIAL NOTE: Ben is twenty-five years old.

100. "The Gift"
(MAY 22, 2001)

Director: Joss Whedon
Teleplay: Joss Whedon
Recurring cast: Clare Kramer (Glory); Charlie Weber (Ben); Amber
    Benson (Tara)
Guest cast: Joel Grey (Doc); Todd Duffey (Murk); Craig Zimmerman
    (minion #1); Josh Jacobson (teen); Tom Kiesche (vampire)

Plot: Buffy makes the ultimate sacrifice as her final gift to the world.

THIS WEEK'S APOCALYPTIC RITUAL: Dawn's blood will start the dissolution of the portal walls separating the dimensions and can only be stopped by her death.

INTRODUCING: Xander and Anya's engagement.

ANALYSIS: The loyalty of Buffy's friends is again reinforced by their willingness to face horrible death rather than just kill Dawn and stop the Glory threat in its tracks. Facing a common enemy, personal bickering is replaced by somber support and concern. Even Spike's contributions are welcome, as they realize what's at stake is bigger than all of them combined. And again, their combined strength as a team almost prevents the ritual from starting. Once Willow drains Glory's brain and channels it back into Tara, restoring her sanity, their combined powers keep the minions at bay while Buffy wails on Glory with Olaf's hammer. But even then, when Ben reappears, she simply can't bring herself to kill him and finish off Glory for good—in part because she probably believed the worst was over. But what slips the gang up was the unaccounted-for variable of Doc, whom Spike had left for dead, but who took it upon himself to start the bloodletting.

Dawn is ready to give her life to stop the apocalypse. But Buffy has an epiphany that, since Dawn was created out of her blood, she could stop the dimension-walls from breaking down. This suddenly gives Buffy a clear understanding of her life's purpose and what her true gift is meant to be.

THE REAL HORROR: Coming up short. Although Buffy soared into eternity without fear and in peace—in part, perhaps, because she believed her mother waited for her on the other side—those left behind were left in anguish, particularly Spike, who felt he'd failed to keep his promise to the lady he loved.

LITERARY ALLUSION: The Saint Crispin's Day speech mentioned by Spike is from Shakespeare's *Henry V*, Act IV, Scene III:

> *"But we in it shall be remembered—*
> *We few, we happy few, we band of brothers;*
> *For he today that sheds his blood with me*
> *Shall be my brother; be he ne'er so vile,*
> *This day shall gentle his condition;*

And gentlemen in England now-a-bed
Shall think themselves accurs'd they were not here,
And hold their manhoods cheap whiles any speaks
That fought with us upon Saint Crispin's Day."

OF SPECIAL NOTE: The "Previously on *Buffy*" montage contains images from all five seasons of the show.

This is the last original episode to air on the WB network. The WB added a note at the end of the episode thanking the cast and crew for their efforts.

SEASON SIX

Sixth-year overview: After giving her life to save Dawn, Buffy is res-urrected by Willow. However, being dragged away from the embrace of what Buffy believes was Heaven, leaves her initially resentful. Now forced to resume the daily struggle that is life, with bills to pay and responsibilities to keep, Buffy has just as many internal demons to confront as she does offered by the Hellmouth. But in the end, the greatest horrors Buffy sees this year are committed by very human adversaries, and her most powerful foe will come from her own inner circle.

SEASON FIVE REGULAR CAST

Sarah Michelle Gellar (*Buffy Summers*)
Nicholas Brendon (*Xander Harris*)
Emma Caulfield (*Anya*)
Michelle Trachtenberg (*Dawn*)
James Marsters (*Spike*)
Alyson Hannigan (*Willow Rosenberg*)

⁜

101. and 102. "Bargaining (Parts I and II)"
(OCTOBER 2, 2001)

Director: David Grossman
Teleplay: Marti Noxon (Part I); David Fury (Part II)
Recurring cast: Anthony Stewart Head (Rupert Giles); Amber Benson
   (Tara)

Guest cast: Franc Ross (Razor); Geoff Meed (Mag); Mike Grief (Klyed); Paul Greenberg (Shempy vamp); Joy DeMichelle Moore (Ms. Lefcourt); Bru Muller (teacher); Robert D. Vito (cute boy); Harry Johnson (parent #1); Kelly Lynn Warren (parent #2); Hila Levy (pretty girl); Richard Wharton (homeowner)

Music: "Permanence" (playing in the biker bar), by Static X, from *Machine*

Plot: Willow resurrects Buffy. Giles decides to return to England.

THIS WEEK'S LEATHER-CLAD FOES: The Hellions, a demon biker gang who terrorize Sunnydale after word spreads that the Slayer is really a robot.

INTRODUCING: The Urn of Osiris. Because Buffy did not die a natural death, but was killed by mystical energy, Willow performs a spell using the urn to resurrect Buffy from the grave. Buffy's new hair color is noticeably darker than in Season Five.

ANALYSIS: Spike feels he failed to keep Dawn from being cut by Doc, which directly led to Buffy's death. This is still a raw wound so Spike has become Dawn's most ardent protector. Spike is also obviously deeply pained by Buffy's death, which is why he has no interest in the Buffy-bot's affections: it's too painful a reminder that the real Buffy is no longer here. Likewise, Giles doesn't want to stay in Sunnydale for the same reason, compounded by his guilt over having failed his Slayer.

The decision to try and resurrect Buffy could be seen as selfish, but Willow's worries show their hearts are in the right place. The idea of Buffy possibly being stuck in the Hell dimension her death closed shut, suffering eternal agonies, is too much for them to bear. The major oversight is they neglect to realize that if she did reanimate, she would do so in a coffin buried six feet underground. So when the spell works, Buffy suddenly finds herself buried alive and the terror of it traumatizes her.

Buffy's question about whether she'd been sent to Hell as she looks down from the tower where she leapt to her death, is a good clue that wherever Buffy's spirit had been, she wasn't suffering. So being back on Earth, confronted with having to face the Hellmouth again, results in the rage she unleashes on the biker demons looting the town. It also is the source of the pain Buffy feels, realizing the struggle is about to start all over again.

DEMONIC POSSESSION

Someone who has their personality and body taken over by a demon is said to be possessed. Although most people still associate possession with projectile peasoup vomit and scary children with bad skin who can rotate their heads (thank you, Linda Blair), there are other, more accepted signs of demonic possession. In the Middle Ages, anyone displaying unusual behavior or a strange personality was often suspected of being possessed by the Devil. This is why so many old, ugly, or poor people were accused of being possessed.

The Catholic church still defines signs of true possession as someone displaying: superhuman strength, often accompanied by fits and convulsions; changes in personality; having knowledge of the future or other secret information; and being able to understand and converse in languages not previously known to them. Also on the list of other signs or symptoms for declaring demonic possession are having sexual thoughts; changes in the voice, becoming a deep, rasping, menacing, guttural croak; and, most important, a violent revulsion toward sacred objects and texts.

THE REAL HORROR: Having to start over. Whether it's losing everything to a natural disaster, getting fired, or ending a relationship, few people enjoy the daunting task of starting over. In Buffy's case, she has to resume the burden of being the Chosen One.

IT'S A MYSTERY: If they wanted to keep Buffy's death a secret, why would they bury her with a headstone announcing where she was buried? Even if it was in the woods, the Hellmouth has plenty of creatures who might lurk there.

OF SPECIAL NOTE: Osiris was the Egyptian god of the afterlife. After being murdered, Osiris was brought back to life by his wife Isis, who also happened to be his sister.

This is the first episode to air on UPN.

When aired in the U.K., several scenes were cut in their first showings: the snake, Willow killing the deer, and Buffy in her coffin. However, fans got a chance to see the full episode during a special "*Buffy* Night" on the Sky One network.

A scene where Willow kills a fawn to get the blood she needs for the spell, was edited out because producers thought it was too disturbing.

Anthony Stewart Head is now listed as a recurring "Special Guest Star."

Alyson Hannigan gets a credit promotion—now listed last: "And Alyson Hannigan as Willow."

103. "After Life"
(OCTOBER 9, 2001)

Director: David Solomon
Teleplay: Jane Espenson
Recurring cast: Amber Benson (Tara)
Guest cast: Lisa Hoyle (demon)

Plot: Willow's reincarnation spell has an unintended side effect. Buffy tries to readjust to life.

THIS WEEK'S MANIFESTATION: A bodyless demon created as a by-product of the reanimation spell takes turns possessing the bodies of the Scoobies. It is destined to die . . . unless it can kill Buffy.

ANALYSIS: Although there is still a below-the-surface tension between Xander and Spike, the others seem to have accepted him now, especially Dawn. Ironically, Spike is the only one Buffy can be honest and open with, because he didn't have anything to do with her reanimation, and because she doesn't have to worry about hurting his feelings. Plus Spike understands death in a way the others can't.

Buffy feels alienated from the world she once knew and is drawn to Spike as a result. When he finally gets to apologize for failing her, it's clear his feelings for her have evolved past the "lust" phase of first being in love. There's a depth in his response to her, although Spike *is* Spike, so there's little chance he's gone completely soft.

Because Willow mistakenly believes she saved Buffy from Hell, she doesn't understand why Buffy doesn't seem more appreciative at being brought back. Buffy finally understands that and tells them the lie they want to hear, swearing Spike to secrecy because she never wants them to know they dragged her out of Heaven.

THE REAL HORROR: Having to put up a false front. Sometimes, to spare the feelings of others, we have to pretend. Although part of Buffy wants to scream at losing Heaven, she doesn't, because she doesn't want to hurt the feelings of the people she loves.

104. "Flooded"
(OCTOBER 16, 2001)

Director: Douglas Petrie
Teleplay: Douglas Petrie and Jane Espenson
Recurring cast: Anthony Stewart Head (Rupert Giles); Danny Strong (Jonathan); Adam Busch (Warren); Tom Lenk (Andrew); Amber Benson (Tara)
Guest cast: Michael Merton (Mr. Savitsky); John Jabaley (Tito); Brian Kolb (bank guard)

Plot: Buffy discovers she's broke. Three friends aspire to be master villains.

THIS WEEK'S DEMON-FOR-HIRE: M'Fashnik, a mercenary demon who sells his services to the highest bidder.

INTRODUCING: The latest Sunnydale crime cartel. Sunnydale High's "Least Likely to Succeed" band together in a life of crime to keep themselves swimming in money, toys, and—hopefully—girls. The three include Jonathan—last seen in Episode 73, "Superstar"—the robot-building Warren, and Andrew, whose brother Tucker trained a pack of hellhounds to attack the prom during Buffy's senior year.

ANALYSIS: Her emotions aren't the only thing Buffy has to worry about. Now that her mother is no longer there to run the household, Buffy has to face the realities of paying bills. After taking care of hospital bills and expenses for almost five months, Buffy discovers she is almost broke. Not only is she overwhelmed by this unexpected pressure, she is spending so much effort trying to pretend she's happy to be back that she simply pulls away even more, emotionally, from the others.

Giles's confrontation with Willow about the forces she tampered with sets the stage for a growing uneasiness over Willow's reliance on magic and her fascination with the darker magics. Her upset at being harshly reprimanded by Giles also allowed us to see the first hint of the kind of anger Willow is capable of, if pushed. She knows she's powerful and she likes using that power.

Buffy, on the other hand, seems emotionally muted since her return. It's as if she has had to keep herself in constant check in order to avoid letting the truth slip out. More and more she finds a kind of solace with Spike, who at this point is demanding nothing of her—other than to be there if she needs him.

THE REAL HORROR: Debt. Buffy is more daunted by how she is going to keep a roof over her and Dawn's head than she's been by most anything the Hellmouth has thrown at her.

IT'S A MYSTERY: Why did Andrew just happen to have Buffy's address on a piece of paper in his pocket?

OF SPECIAL NOTE: Tom Lenk, who plays Andrew, was one of Harmony's minions in Episode 80, "Real Me," during Season Five.

105. "Life Serial"
(OCTOBER 23, 2001)

Director: Nick Marck
Teleplay: David Fury and Jane Espenson
Recurring cast: Anthony Stewart Head (Rupert Giles); Danny Strong (Jonathan); Adam Busch (Warren); Tom Lenk (Andrew); Amber Benson (Tara)
Guest cast: Paul Gutrecht (Tony); Noel Albert Guglielmi (Vince); Enrique Almeida (Marco); Jonathan Goldstein (Mike); Winsome Brown (woman customer); Christopher May (male customer); David J. Miller (rat-faced demon); Andrew Cooper Wasser (slime-cover demon); Richard Beatty (small demon); James C. Leary (Clem); Jennifer Shon (Rachel); Jabari Hearn (Steve); Derrick

McMillon (Ron); Clint Culp (bartender); Mark Ginther (horned demon); Alice Dinnean Vernon (mummy hand)

Music: "Kidnapper Song" (plays during bar scene), by the Masticators, from *Masticate!*; "Boom Swagger Boom" (also during bar scene), by Murder City Devils, from *Murder City Devils*

Plot: *Buffy is put through a series of frustrating tests by the Trio. Also, Buffy gets drunk.*

THIS WEEK'S REALITY-ALTERING TOYS: Through a combination of witchcraft and high-tech gizmos, Warren, Jonathan, and Andrew put Buffy through a series of "tests" and compete to see who can give the Slayer the most fits.

INTRODUCING: Kittens as the ante of choice for demon poker.

ANALYSIS: Buffy feels as if she's failing at everything. She feels out of her intellectual league when she tries to audit some college classes; she can't keep the job Xander got her because her strength causes resentment among the other laborers; and something is messing with her by altering reality.

Buffy just wants to escape and since death isn't really an option anymore, she ends up at Spike's and gets drunk. Spike believes what Buffy really needs is to get back in touch with the Slayer within and to worry less about the niceties, and aggravations, of everyday life. He knows the reason she feels out of place in the regular world is because she *is* out of place. Buffy has become more at home in the dark, fighting monsters, than dealing with such life basics as financial obligations and holding down a paying job. Slaying is her calling and vocation and takes up most of her emotional energy.

As the Trio is able to confound Buffy with their "tests," their confidence grows and they begin to believe they aren't just playing at being supervillains, but cumulatively are a worthy opponent for the Slayer. To them, it's like a real-life video game, but they play with no regard for the consequences their actions might bring.

THE REAL HORROR: Feeling ill-equipped. It's one thing to take on a challenge when you feel up to the task; quite another when you feel as if you don't even possess the necessary tools to succeed. While Buffy may have superhuman strength and impeccable Slayer instincts, she feels she lacks everyday skills.

106. "All the Way"

(OCTOBER 30, 2001)

Director: David Solomon

Teleplay: Steven S. DeKnight

Recurring cast: Anthony Stewart Head (Rupert Giles); Amber Benson (Tara)

Guest Cast: John O'Leary (Kaltenbach); Kavan Reece (Justin); Amber Tamblyn (Janice); Dave Power (Zach); Charles Duckworth (Glenn); Dawn Worrall (Christy); Emily Kay (Maria); Adam Gordon (Carl); Steven Anthony Lawrence (chunky kid); Sabrina Speer (girl); Chad Erikson (guy); Dominic Rambaran (paramedic #1); Anthony Sago (paramedic #2); Lorin Becker (witchwoman); Lily Jackson (witchy-poo)

Music: "Body of Binky" (in the park), by Coin Monster, from *Schematic*; "Make Me a Star" (as Xander and Anya make wedding plans), by Strange Radio, from *Pre-Release Pop Radio*; "Everybody Got Their Something" (as Xander, Anya, and Willow dance), by Nikka Costa, from *Everybody Got Their Something*; Even If (It Is Love), by Lift, from *September*; "Around My Smile" (when Dawn and Justin kiss), by Hope Sandoval and the Warm Inventions, from *Bavarian Fruit Bread*; "Just as Nice" (at the Bronze), by Man of the Year, from *The Future Is Not Now*; "The Sun Keeps Shining on Me" (when Dawn realizes the truth about her date), by Fonda, from *The Strange and the Familiar*

Plot: Dawn sneaks out on Halloween, and gets more excitement than she'd reckoned for.

THIS WEEK'S UNDEAD BAD BOYS: Teenage vampires out to score—blood, that is.

INTRODUCING: Dawn as rebellious teen.

ANALYSIS: Buffy is still adjusting to the new path her relationship with Spike has taken. He has become a comrade-in-arms as well as a sort of family friend. The reason she thinks it was easier when they were adversaries was because she didn't have to worry about any hidden meanings. She knows he's in love with her, but since she's been back among the living, he hasn't pressed her about it the way he did before her run-in with Glory.

While on the one hand Dawn's kleptomaniacal tendencies and lies may be seen as typical teenage behavior, there's also a dark side to Dawn. We see this when she and her friends are callously cruel to an old man who wants to give them special Halloween cookies he's baked. Although Buffy frequently lied to Joyce about where she was as a teenager, it usually involved her saving the world. Dawn knows how special her sister is, but it's hard growing up in such a looming shadow. Dawn steals as a way of making herself feel special and to give her an identity outside of being just "Buffy's little sister."

Buffy has turned much of her parental authority over to Giles. Buffy either ignores or doesn't see that he feels it's really her responsibility. But what troubles Giles most is Willow's growing dependence on witchcraft—and the way she mindlessly resorts to it. Rather than saving it as a tool for fighting Hellmouth creatures, it's becoming a habit and she is using it to control others.

THE REAL HORROR: Sibling rivalry. Like most teenagers, Dawn thinks she is far more capable than anyone gives her credit for, and doesn't understand why Buffy seems to get to do whatever she wants. But Dawn doesn't realize just how much Buffy and the others run interference on her behalf, protecting her from the dangers of living in Sunnydale. When Dawn finds herself making out with a vampire who wants to turn her, she has to be saved by Buffy. The downside is she gets caught big-time in her lie that she was at her friend's house for a sleepover, which just further proves everyone's point that she's too young to be on her own.

IT'S A MYSTERY: Why didn't Dawn notice that Justin's face and lips were unnaturally cold when they kissed?

BLOOPERS: If Dawn was in the ninth grade last year, this year she should be a sophomore.

Buffy's comment to Xander she was gone three months isn't correct. Spike has previously noted Buffy was dead 147 days, which would be almost five months.

OF SPECIAL NOTE: As a young girl, Amber Tamblyn played Emily Quartermaine on *General Hospital.* She is the daughter of *West Side Story* and *Twin Peaks* star Russ Tamblyn.

107. "Once More, With Feeling"
(NOVEMBER 6, 2001)

Director: Joss Whedon
Teleplay: Joss Whedon
Recurring cast: Anthony Stewart Head (Rupert Giles); Amber Benson
    (Tara)
Guest cast: Hinton Battle (musical demon); David Fury (mustard
    man); Marti Noxon (parking-ticket woman); Daniel Weaver
    (handsome young man); Scot Zeller (henchman); Zachary
    Woodlee (demon/henchman); Timothy Anderson (henchman);
    Alex Estronel (henchman); Matt Sims (college guy #1); Hunter
    Cochran (college guy #2)

*Plot: A mysterious force causes everyone to reveal their deepest feelings
through song, exposing some unpleasant truths.*

THIS WEEK'S MUSICALLY INCLINED MEDDLER: A fashion-
conscious demon named Sweet, who was summoned by the misguided Xander,
who thought a little music would add some much-needed cheer to the group.

ANALYSIS: Besides being a marvel of ingenuity, this episode allows for
vital dramatic development, to move the series and the characters' relationships along. Forcing everyone to reveal their innermost, most closely
guarded feelings put everyone on the same page—Buffy and the others
respond to what they've learned and/or revealed.

At first the singing seems cheerful as mostly-happy emotions are shared
when everyone is together as a group or paired off in couples. Tara tells Willow that the greatest magic of all is the transforming power of love, and their
nature walk leads to them making love. Meanwhile Xander and Anya come
to grips with all the questions and worries they've been keeping hidden from
each other and themselves, revealing their worry that they might not truly be
meant for each other. Giles finally admits to himself and Buffy that she will
never grow as a person unless he leaves and forces her to deal with problems
herself; while he has been Watcher to her Slayer, he cannot be Watcher for
her life.

Buffy's revelation that she was plucked from Heaven, and the difficulty she's had in finding any meaning being back, leaves the others, especially Willow, stunned. But it's Spike who prevents Buffy from dancing herself into spontaneously combusting, by telling her the only way to get past the pain of losing Heaven is to live, and not just go through the motions. She takes his advice and starts by reaching out to him and they embrace in a passionate kiss. But Buffy's struggle to conquer her demons isn't ending, it's only just beginning.

THE REAL HORROR: Brutal honesty. Although we like to think we can handle the truth, few people are secure enough, or masochistic enough, to really want to hear what other people are thinking.

BLOOPERS: One of Sweet's puppet demons appears to be moving after he's been killed during Buffy's speed-dancing moves.

OF SPECIAL NOTE: The original broadcast of this episode ran 68 minutes long. For future airings, the show would be edited down to fit an hour-long time slot.

The "mustard man" was played by co–executive producer David Fury and the "parking-ticket woman" was played by executive producer Marti Noxon.

Even the Mutant Enemy logo sings the *"grrr-arg"* at the end of the episode.

Alyson Hannigan requested to have no individual songs and as few singing lines as possible.

At one point, there was the possibility of Sarah Michelle using a singing double but she decided against it because she decided she needed to convey the intense emotions expressed in the songs.

MUSICAL NOTE: The soundtrack to this episode is available on CD. In addition to the songs from the episode, the tracks also include the demo of "Something to Sing About," performed by Joss Whedon and his wife Kai Cole. Here is the chronological list of songs featured in the episode:

"Overture/Going Through the Motions"; "I've Got a Theory/Bunnies/If We're Together"; "The Mustard (fragment)"; "Under Your Spell"; "I'll Never Tell"; "Parking Ticket (fragment)"; "Broomdance"; "Rest in Peace"; "Dawn's Lament"; "Ballad"; "What You Feel"; "Standing"; "Under Your Spell/Standing (reprise)"; "Walk Through the Fire"; "Something to Sing About"; "What You Feel (reprise)"; "Where Do We Go from Here"; "Coda".

108. "Tabula Rasa"

(NOVEMBER 13, 2001)

Director: David Grossman

Teleplay: Rebecca Rand Kirshner

Recurring cast: Anthony Stewart Head (Rupert Giles); Amber Benson (Tara)

Guest cast: Raymond O'Connor (loan shark); Geordie White (vamp #1); Stephen Triplett (vamp #2); David Franco (vamp #3)

Music: "Goodbye to You" (at the Bronze), by Michelle Branch, from *The Spirit Room*

Plot: Willow accidentally gives everyone amnesia.

THIS WEEK'S DEMON DEBT-COLLECTOR: Sharky, to whom Spike owes a gambling debt of forty kittens.

ANALYSIS: In an effort to make Buffy forget she has lost Heaven, Willow uses a spell. But she accidentally makes everyone forget who they are and what their relationship to one another is.

It's just the latest example of how Willow is now using magic to deal with all of life's problems and hurdles. While she may be growing ever more powerful as a witch, she is losing touch with how to cope as a human, and is stunting her personal growth. Although magic seems easy, Willow still fails to understand that by using magic she puts herself and everyone around her at risk because it is not an exact science. Tara soon suggests that she doesn't know if she can continue their relationship unless Willow deals with her directly and not through magic. Willow sees it simply as Tara leaving her, instead of realizing that her obsession with magic is driving Tara away.

Likewise, Buffy accuses Giles of abandoning her. She doesn't understand that he loves her enough to leave, thereby forcing her to deal with the issues she's been studiously avoiding.

Once everyone gets their memories back, there's still plenty of awkwardness to go around. Tara is heartbroken that Willow couldn't keep her promise to not do magic for a week, and breaks off their relationship. Giles leaves Sunnydale with a heavy heart. Despite knowing he's doing what's best, it pains him that Buffy is angry with him and he goes on his way carrying a sense of loss. Buffy feels abandoned and, remembering the freedom from pain she felt when she lost herself and didn't know who she was, Buffy turns to Spike in a bid to lose herself again, just for a while, in his kiss.

THE REAL HORROR: Having to live with yourself. Willow is left with the consequences of her reliance on magic, while Buffy turns to Spike in an effort to forget who she is and what's expected of her.

OF SPECIAL NOTE: *Tabula rasa* is Latin for "blank slate." The expression has come to mean "starting from scratch."

MUSICAL NOTE: Michelle Branch performs onstage at the Bronze at the end of the episode.

109. "Smashed"
(NOVEMBER 20, 2001)

Director: Turi Meyer
Teleplay: Drew Z. Greenberg
Recurring cast: Danny Strong (Jonathan); Adam Busch (Warren); Tom Lenk (Andrew); Elizabeth Anne Allen (Amy Madison); Amber Benson (Tara)
Guest cast: Patrice Walters (woman); John Patrick Clerkin (man); Jack Jozefson (Rusty); Rick Garcia (reporter); Kelly Smith (innocent girl); Jordan Belfi (Ryan); Adam Weiner (Simon); Melanie Sirmons (Brie); Lauren Nissi (girlfriend)
Music: "Vermillion Borders," "Parachute," and "Here" (at the Bronze), by Virgil, from *Virgil*; "Run Away" (by girl band onstage at the Bronze), by the Halo Friendlies, from *Halo Friendlies Ghetto Demo*

Plot: Willow turns Amy back to normal and they go on a magic spree.

THIS WEEK'S CURIOUS TWIST: Spike discovers he can hit Buffy without his feeling pain, leading him to believe she came back to life less human than when she left it.

INTRODUCING: Amy. Willow manages to finally de-rat Amy after she spent nearly three years in rodent mode.

ANALYSIS: Without Tara around to curb Willow's use of magic, Willow is further seduced by her power, and gets even more careless with it—urged on by Amy, who uses her powers with reckless abandon. Although the others, especially Xander, are worried about her, and Anya knows how seductive this kind of power can be, Buffy wants to believe that Willow's innate levelheadedness will win.

Buffy also wants to believe that her kissing flings with Spike are aberrations and that she really isn't drawn to him for some more primal reason. But after Spike taunts her about perhaps not being so much better than he is, as evidenced by his ability to hit her without causing himself pain, Buffy loses her cool and her control, and finally gives in to her emptiness and loneliness by finding violent comfort in Spike's arms. Their lovemaking is so raw and fierce that it literally brings down the abandoned building they are in. While this may be love for Spike, for Buffy it's not about passion, it's about the desperate desire for release.

Each in her own way, both Willow and Buffy have gone and crossed over to embrace the darkness within, in an effort to rid themselves of the pain that's enveloping them.

THE REAL HORROR: Losing yourself. Doing something completely out of character, just as a way of *not* dealing, will only lead to more alienation because the outcome inevitably will be self-loathing.

IT'S A MYSTERY: Why is Amy's hair a different color from when she originally turned herself into a rat?

OF SPECIAL NOTE: Andrew claims to have seen every episode of *Doctor Who* which began in 1963. However, the BBC purged their archives (for unexplained reasons) sometime during the 1970s, and about a hundred early episodes of *Doctor Who* were destroyed. Clearly Andrew isn't old enough to have seen them prior to the purge.

MUSICAL NOTE: The band Virgil is performing onstage at the Bronze, before Willow turns them into a girl group.

110. "Wrecked"
(NOVEMBER 27, 2001)

Director: David Solomon
Teleplay: Marti Noxon
Recurring cast: Elizabeth Anne Allen (Amy Madison); Jeff Kober (Rack); Amber Benson (Tara)
Guest cast: Fleming Brooks (Mandraz); Mageina Tovah (jonesing girl); Michael Giordani (jonesing guy); Colin Malone (creepy guy)
Music: "Black Cat Bone" (while Willow is at Rack's), by Laika, from *Good-Looking Blues*

Plot: Willow's addiction to the dark magics has near tragic consequences. Buffy must deal with the emotional consequences of having sex with Spike.

THIS WEEK'S MIND-ALTERING FORCE: Magic that can be as addictive as drugs.

INTRODUCING: Rack, who is kind of a dealer—except here the drugs are magic spells; Anya's new hair color.

ANALYSIS: Buffy is horrified at having slept with Spike, so she lashes out at him in anger when she's really upset with herself. She knows she doesn't love Spike, and while the sex may be physically pleasing, she knows she is complicating her life in unnecessary ways.

Willow is beginning to suffer the effects of her magic binges, which take a physical toll. After Amy introduces her to Rack, whose spells are nothing short of drug highs, Willow is terrified because she knows she's out of control, but at the same time she can't stop herself from going back for more, like any addict. She misses Tara so much, she wants something to fill the void, even though by using magic she is only further alienating the woman she loves.

After Willow crashes a car with Dawn in it, Buffy finally realizes that Willow indeed has a problem and confronts her on it. Willows promises to stop, horrified that she put Dawn in danger—but it's a promise Willow knows she may not be able to keep.

THE REAL HORROR: Addiction. The first step is admitting to yourself that you have a problem. Willow is at that stage, but now the hardest part is being strong enough to keep from slipping back into whatever has control over you.

OF SPECIAL NOTE: This is Jeff Kober's second appearance on *Buffy*. He previously played vampire Zackary Kralik in Episode 46, "Helpless," in Season Three.

The cartoon playing on TV is *Ding Dog Daddy*, made by Warner Brothers in 1942 and directed by Friz Freleng.

111. "Gone"
(JANUARY 8, 2002)

Director: David Fury
Teleplay: David Fury
Recurring cast: Danny Strong (Jonathan); Adam Busch (Warren); Tom Lenk (Andrew)
Guest cast: Jessa French (Cleo); Kelly Parver (girl in park); Jeffrey Jacquin (meter man); Dwight Bacquie (security guard); Lyndon Smith (little boy); Melina Webberley (little girl); Elin Hampton (co-worker)
Music: "I Know," by Trespassers William, from *Anchor*

Plot: The Trio turn Buffy invisible. Social Services threatens to take Dawn away from Buffy.

THIS WEEK'S HI-TECH SURPRISE: An invisibility ray. Warren builds it using the mystical diamond they stole from the Sunnydale Museum. Unfortunately, it causes whatever it has turned invisible to eventually dissolve into nothingness.

INTRODUCING: Warren's dark side. Unlike Jonathan and Andrew, Warren wants to know the power of taking a life, and has set his sights on the Slayer.

ANALYSIS: In another attempt to enhance the Trio's criminal profile, Warren builds an invisibility ray-gun and accidentally zaps Buffy with it.

Buffy relishes the sense of freedom it gives her and she delights in some mischief, including getting back the Social Services caseworker who'd threatened to take Dawn away if Buffy didn't prove herself a more fit guardian.

Willow distracts herself from going cold-turkey on the magic by investigating what exactly happened to Buffy. She uses the old-fashioned methods of computer- and legwork, and eventually tracks down the Trio's lair. Jonathan and Andrew simply want to get Buffy to meet them so they can make her visible again. They are not killers, and neither wants anything to happen to her. But Warren shows his true colors when he tries to zap Buffy into oblivion. After Willow uses the ray-gun to make everyone visible again, Buffy is stunned to see who has been behind the strange things that have been happening. She doesn't take the Trio very seriously, and considers them mostly a nuisance. But she will soon find that she tragically underestimates the evil in Warren's soul.

THE REAL HORROR: Lost time. Once she's confronted with the possibility of fading away, Buffy finally realizes she really doesn't want to die, and that she wants to be there for Willow and the others, because life is precious.

LITERARY ALLUSION: Warren calling Jonathan "Frodo" refers to Frodo Baggins, the Hobbit hero of J. R. R. Tolkier's trilogy, *The Lord of the Rings*, who stands only about three feet tall.

112. "Doublemeat Palace"
(JANUARY 29, 2002)

Director: Nick Marck

Teleplay: Jane Espenson

Recurring cast: Elizabeth Anne Allen (Amy Madison); Kali Rocha (Halfrek)

Guest cast: Pat Crawford Brown (old lady); Brent Hinkley (Manny); Kirsten Neilson (Lorraine Ross); T. Ferguson (Gary); Marion Calvert (Gina); Douglas Bennett (Phillip); Andrew Reville (Timothy); Kevin C. Carter (Mr. Typical); John F. Kearney (elderly man); Sara Lawall (housewife type); Victor Z. Isaac (pimply teen)

Music: "The Twist" (during the training video), by Warren Bennett, from *Jukebox Anthology*

Plot: Buffy gets a job at a burger joint and suspects the secret ingredient may be human flesh.

THIS WEEK'S FAST-FOOD-JUNKIE DEMON: An old woman who has a six-foot snake living in her head.

INTRODUCING: Halfrek, an old "vengeance buddy" of Anya's.

ANALYSIS: Both Buffy and Willow are attempting to reintegrate themselves back into a more normal routine. Willow, who turned to magic in part to feel special, is reminding herself that there are non-spell ways to fight the Hellmouth. Likewise, Buffy has taken a job at a burger place to earn some money. Although the idea of only being able to work in a fast-food restaurant is a bit depressing, Buffy chooses to see it as a temporary, stop-gap measure. The listlessness of her co-workers makes Buffy suspect there's some evil force at work, though Xander assures her that's just a typical response to working a boring job. But when Buffy finds a severed finger, she suspects that the establishment's "secret ingredient" is processed humans. About the only thing that distracts Buffy from her investigation is a quickie with Spike out in the garage. She can't seem to keep herself from craving the physical release that sex with Spike gives her. Plus, in those moments she's coupling with Spike, she gets a break from being everyone's savior and can just concentrate on fulfilling her basic needs.

Amy proves to be not just a bad influence, but also a bad friend, when she gets Willow high on magic against Willow's will. Amy needs to validate her addiction by trying to get Willow to partake with her. Although it leaves her shaky and wanting more, Willow keeps her focus and determines that the real secret the burger chain is hiding is that their meat patties are really veggie burgers.

Buffy learns the truth about the missing Doublemeat Palace employees when she comes face-to-face with a regular customer who prefers eating from her own personal human menu. When Willow is able to kill this snake through her own ingenuity, it gives her a sense of accomplishment—and the hope she really will be able to wean herself off magic. She is so determined to reclaim her life—and perhaps win Tara back in the process—that she tells Amy to stay away from her. But the real threat to Willow's "sobriety" will come from a completely unexpected source.

THE REAL HORROR: Punching a clock. One thing about being the Slayer is that you never know what evil you'll be fighting from one day to the next. Working in a fast-food joint can be mind-numbing, but Buffy is willing to endure being intellectually stultified in exchange for a steady income.

113. "Dead Things"
(FEBRUARY 5, 2002)

Director: James A. Contner

Teleplay: Steven S. DeKnight

Recurring cast: Amber Benson (Tara); Danny Strong (Jonathan); Adam Busch (Warren); Tom Lenk (Andrew)

Guest cast: Amelinda Embry (Katrina); Marion Calvert (Gina); Rock Reiser (desk sergeant); Bernard K. Addison (cop #1); Eric Prescott (cop #2)

Music: "Boo Wah Boo Wah" (at the Bronze), by Red and the Red Hots, from *Gettin' Around*; "Out of this World' (in the cemetery), by Bush, from *Golden State*

Plot: The Trio tries to frame Buffy for murder. Buffy discovers why Spike can hurt her.

THIS WEEK'S DATE-RAPE INVENTION: The cerebral dampener: Warren's latest gizmo will turn any woman into a willing sex slave.

INTRODUCING: Warren crossing the line. After the cerebral dampener loses its effect and Katrina realizes what they were planning, she is justifiably furious and tries to leave. Although Warren may not have intended to kill her, once he does, he shows no remorse and the destructive side of him is finally set free.

ANALYSIS: Buffy is softening her attitude toward Spike, but his characterizations of her still bother her. And while she may enjoy sex with him, Buffy doesn't really trust him. She refuses to validate their physical attraction, by thinking of it as anything but sex—because to her it's really not; it's an escape. But Spike will take what he can get, and having at least a little of Buffy is better than none at all, plus he seems to hold out hope that she will come around. Despite Spike's love for Buffy, their lovemaking seems to lack the emotional connection that Buffy had with Angel, or with Riley—no doubt in part because, for all his emotion, Spike still lacks a soul.

Buffy wants to believe she came back wrong somehow, because then she would have something to explain her desire for Spike. But when Tara confirms that the only reason Spike can hurt her is because of the physical side effects of reanimating—not anything soul-related—Buffy breaks down, ashamed at giving her body so freely to Spike. Tara is completely nonjudgmental but astutely points out that Buffy feels so bad partly because, deep inside, she knows she's using him with little regard for his feelings, undead or not.

No matter how many times she pushes him away, Spike is doggedly there for her. When the Trio summons a demon with time-altering side effects and Buffy thinks she accidentally killed Katrina in the heat of battle, Spike tries to dispose of the body. Spike doesn't understand why Buffy can't just chalk it up to collateral damage, but she is mortified at taking a human life. Dawn is especially outraged that Buffy would even consider turning herself in. It was one thing to go away because she had no choice but to save the world—but Dawn sees Buffy's decision to turn herself in as a direct reflection of how unimportant Dawn is to her, since Buffy might be voluntarily putting herself in the position of being taken away again. Buffy seems driven by the overall guilt she's feeling and is looking for some sort of absolution.

Once she realizes who the dead girl is, she also realizes she was set up. It finally sinks in that perhaps Warren and his nerdy friends are a lot more dangerous than she first thought, and that she'll have to expand her definition of evil adversaries to include humans.

THE REAL HORROR: Date rape. Jonathan is horrified when Katrina points out that what they are doing is akin to rape. He didn't appreciate that they are using high-tech wizardry to make women do things they would never do otherwise—which is no different ethically than slipping a drug into her drink so she'll be so spaced she won't resist.

IT'S A MYSTERY: What happened to Buffy's scar from when Angel bit her? It looked big and permanent during her first year of college and now it's nowhere to be seen.

BLOOPERS: During one of Warren's scenes, a lock of hair appears and disappears from his forehead from shot to shot.

114. "Older and Far Away"
(FEBRUARY 12, 2002)

Director: Michael Gershman
Teleplay: Drew Z. Greenberg
Recurring cast: Amber Benson (Tara); Kali Rocha (Halfrek)
Guest cast: Ryan Browning (Richard); Laura Roth (Sophie); James C.
  Leary (Clem); Elizabeth Cazenave (teacher)
Music: "Rock and Roll Bar," by Mint Royale, from *Rock and Roll Bar*;
  "Seconds," by Even, from *A Different High*; "Pictures of Success,"
  by Rilo Kiley, from *Takeoffs and Landings*

*Plot: Another birthday, another crisis. Anya confronts Dawn about her
stealing.*

THIS WEEK'S MEDDLING DEMON: Halfrek. Unlike Anya, whose
vengeance-demon gig was limited to unfaithful men, her buddy Halfrek has
branched out and specializes in avenging children. Drawn to Sunnydale by
Dawn's unheard cries for help, Halfrek poses as a guidance counselor and
grants Dawn her fondest wish, which has claustrophobic consequences when
Buffy's party guests discover they can't leave the house.

INTRODUCING: Spellcasters Anonymous, a self-help group for addicted
witches and warlocks. Willow has started attending meetings as part of her
magic rehab.

ANALYSIS: While Dawn might have a point that people aren't paying as
much attention to her as she wants, she also comes across as more than a little unreasonable. She is stealing from people who not only take care of her,
but also periodically quite literally put their lives on the line for her. But
Dawn doesn't seem to appreciate that the world doesn't revolve around her
anymore the way it did when she was the Key. Dawn isn't volunteering to get
a part-time job on the weekends or after school to help pay any of the bills,
and yet she seems to resent Buffy for always being busy.

On the other hand, Buffy feels guilty not because of the work or the Slaying, but because of the time she is devoting to her secret affair with Spike,
and her preoccupation with how much she hates herself. So not only is Buffy

not there physically for Dawn and, more importantly, she is emotionally absent. Dawn feels alone because she feels invisible—the little sister nobody really listens to whose opinion really counts. Unlike Buffy, who had Willow, Xander, and Giles when she was that age, Dawn doesn't seem to have the same kind of support group.

Although Dawn is understandably upset after being suspected, falsely, of casting some sort of spell to keep everyone in Buffy's House, she is caught red-handed when Anya finds her stash of stolen goods. Not only is Anya angry, she is hurt that Dawn would betray everyone this way. Although Buffy tries to deflect some of the blame onto the mysterious guidance counselor, who Anya quickly figures out is Halfrek, it's clear that Dawn's troubles will not go away quickly. Parenthood was thrust on Buffy with little warning—with a teenager no less—so Buffy realizes she's going to have to make some significant adjustments in her own life to help Dawn work this out.

THE REAL HORROR: Feeling forgotten. When Joyce was alive, Dawn always felt there was someone around who put her first. Being raised by a sister, who is trying to work out her own life, is very different, because Dawn isn't Buffy's child, so the emotional bond, while strong, is different. And with Giles leaving, Dawn is left with no true parental figure, and so she feels she is being forgotten by everyone around her because they are so wrapped up in their own lives.

BLOOPERS: While at Buffy's, Spike's reflection is visible in the hall mirror as he passes it.

When the demon in the opening scene vanishes, Buffy assumes it ran away. But when it's in her house, she identifies it as being the one she killed the night before.

OF SPECIAL NOTE: Kali Rocha, the actress playing Halfrek, also played Cecily, the woman who broke William's heart, leading to his fateful run-in with Drusilla. Spike and Halfrek apparently recognize each other, so this could be foreshadowing of a plot line to come.

115. "As You Were"

(FEBRUARY 26, 2002)

Director: Douglas Petrie
Teleplay: Douglas Petrie
Guest cast: Marc Blucas (Riley Finn); Ivana Milicevic (Sam Finn); Ryan Raddatz (Todd); Adam Paul (skanky vamp); Marilyn Brett (lady); Alice Dinnean Vernon (baby demon puppeteer)
Music: "Sound of the Revolution," by Lunatic Calm, from *Breaking Point*; "Washes Away," by Trespassers William, from *Anchor*

Plot: Riley returns to Sunnydale, and brings his new wife. Buffy comes to a decision about Spike.

THIS WEEK'S FERTILE THREAT: The nearly extinct Suvolte demon, a species that breeds alarmingly fast, and which finds humans a favorite snack. Riley has tracked a Suvolte-eggs dealer to Sunnydale and must destroy the eggs before there's a Suvolte population explosion that could be apocalyptic to the human race.

INTRODUCING: Sam Finn, Riley's fellow demon hunter, and new wife, whom he met shortly after leaving Sunnydale for Belize.

ANALYSIS: Ever since returning to Earth, Buffy hasn't been able to tap into her emotions. Grieving and depressed over the loss of Heaven, she feels dead inside, which makes her feel less than human, which is what drew her to Spike. Previously, when Buffy was beating on Spike, telling him he had no soul and was unable to truly love, she really had been talking about herself.

Seeing Riley and the solid relationship he has with Sam, and the inner peace it has given him, makes it very clear just what is missing from Buffy's life, and how far she still has to go before she is capable of having that kind of relationship. It's not so much a matter of if she does or doesn't love Spike in one fashion or another, but whether she *can* truly love him or anyone else. Trite as it may be, the truth is, she can't love anyone until she starts liking herself.

Everyone has been giving Buffy the benefit of the doubt and trying to comprehend what she's been through, but there comes a point when it passes from understandable trauma to self-indulgence. Spike is quite right that Buffy needs to finally decide what she wants and get on with it. Buffy is embarrassed when Riley catches her and Spike in bed—and when it's discovered that Spike's the mysterious "Doc" who's trading in Suvolte eggs, Buffy's humiliation is complete. However, one can't help but wonder if Spike embarked on the big-money plot in order to help Buffy allay some of her financial concerns.

After they blow the eggs to bits with a grenade, Riley and Buffy have a heart-to-heart and he refuses to put her down or try to make her feel ashamed. In his mind, she is doing whatever she needs to at the moment—whether it be seeing Spike or working at a hamburger joint—but ultimately it has nothing to do with who she is inside, nor will it detract from it.

Riley's unconditional support for Buffy is cathartic, and for the first time since her return she feels ready to stop hiding from life and to start meeting it head-on. The first step on the road to reclaiming herself is to stop using

VAMPIRE MAKEUP

When one of the show's vampires gets angry, its face abruptly changes, revealing the demon inside its body. The transformation takes mere seconds. Fans took to calling this physical manifestation of vampirism a "game face," and that term was picked up for occasional use on the show. However, it takes considerably more time than that to turn *Buffy*'s actors into their vampire alter egos: on average, about an hour and twenty minutes to put it on, and forty minutes to take it off.

The vampire makeup, designed by John Vulich is a prosthetic piece of latex that fits around an actor's nose and creates the wrinkled-forehead look. Then they paint on the face by using makeup to blend it in, which is what takes most of the time. The final touches are contact lenses and fake teeth.

Spike as an escape. She breaks it off with him gently and walks out feeling freer than she has since her death. But losing Buffy will send Spike into an emotional tailspin.

THE REAL HORROR: Self-destructive behavior.

IT'S A MYSTERY: Why wouldn't Riley notice Joyce wasn't around and ask about her?

BLOOPERS: Buffy's rejection for readmission to UC Sunnydale lists her address as 1630 Crestview instead of 1630 Revello Drive.

116. "Hell's Bells"
(MARCH 5, 2002)

Director: David Solomon
Teleplay: Rebecca Rand Kirshner
Recurring cast: Amber Benson (Tara); Kali Rocha (Halfrek)
Guest cast: Sander (Tony Harris); Andy Umberger (D'Hoffryn); Lee
    Garlington (Jessica Harris); Jan Hoag (Cousin Carol); George D.
    Wallace (old Xander); Steven Gilborn (Uncle Rory); James C.
    Leary (Clem); Daniel McFeeley (warty demon); Rebecca Jackson
    (Tarantula); Mel Fair (tentacle demon); Nick Kokich (demon
    teen); Robert Noble (night manager); Julian Franco (young bar-
    tender); Susannah L. Brown (caterer girl); Joey Hiott (Josh, age
    ten); Abigail Mavity (Sara, age eight); Chris Emerson (Josh, age
    twenty-one); Ashleigh Ann Wood (Sara, age eighteen); Megan
    Vint (Karen)

Plot: Xander leaves Anya at the altar. Buffy and Spike try to be friends.

THIS WEEK'S PAYBACK DEMON: One of Anya's former victims pretends to be the Xander of the future and shows him a nightmare vision of
what married life with Anya would be like. Buffy kills the interloper but not
before he has convinced Xander he's not ready for marriage.

INTRODUCING: Xander's parents, Tony and Jessica Harris, and his
uncle Rory.

ANALYSIS: People often cry at weddings because it's a day filled with such hope for the future and it signifies a new beginning. Seeing Xander and Anya prepare to exchange vows has breathed some much-needed life into Buffy. Now that she's broken off her sexual relationship with Spike, she seems better able to talk with him amiably and not verbally attack him. When Spike shows up at the wedding with a date, Buffy is surprised by how hurt she is to see him with someone else. Even though she broke it off, nobody likes feeling they are so quickly replaceable.

Spike admits he was trying to make her jealous, probably hoping it might win her back. But when he sees she is hurt, he cares for her too much to keep up the charade, and leaves—but not before telling her how much it means to him to see her looking happier.

Like most families who are thrown together by marriage, Xander's relatives and Anya's close friends circle each other warily, trying to curb their obvious dislike and/or suspicion of one another. Watching his parents' obnoxious behavior, which Xander realizes stems from deep unhappiness with their lives, also pushes his emotional buttons. He loves Anya but can't ignore the doubts he feels, even when it becomes clear that he was tricked and lied to by a demon bent on ruining Anya's life. Xander doesn't want the two of them to end up like his bitter, depleted parents.

Although Xander doesn't say they will never get married, for Anya there's no going back once left at the altar. So when D'Hoffryn offers to give her old job back, Anya has a decision to make.

THE REAL HORROR: Family legacies. Had Xander been raised in a loving home with parents who liked each other, rather than in a household consumed by drunken arguments and bitterness, he very well might have handled his doubts better. There's hardly a person alive who doesn't have some doubt before getting married—forever is a long time. And even though divorce is always an option, most people go into marriage with the intent on it truly being for good. If the wedding had taken place, it's easy to believe that Xander and Anya could have built a good life together, but Xander was too afraid to try and now he might never know.

117. "Normal Again"

(MARCH 12, 2002)

Director: Rick Rosenthal

Teleplay: Diego Gutierrez

Recurring cast: Danny Strong (Jonathan); Adam Busch (Warren); Tom Lenk (Andrew); Amber Benson (Tara)

Guest cast: Dean Butler (Hank Summers); Michael Warren (doctor); Kirsten Nelson (Lorraine Ross); Kristine Sutherland (Joyce Summers); Sarah Scivier (nurse); Rodney Charles (orderly); April Dion (kissing girl)

Plot: After being stung by a demon summoned by the Trio, Buffy believes Sunnydale is all a bad dream.

THIS WEEK'S PSYCHOSIS-INDUCING DEMON: The Glarghk Guhl Kashma'nik. Its poison induces hallucinations. Because Buffy has been feeling so removed from her life since returning, the poison has a particularly dramatic effect on her because it gives her the opportunity to leave all her troubles behind.

INTRODUCING: Buffy's time in an institution. For the first time she reveals that back in Los Angeles her parents institutionalized her the first time she tried to tell them vampires were real.

ANALYSIS: All of Buffy's adjustment problems, crushing responsibilities, and feelings of inadequacy come together in a perfect emotional storm in this episode. Her previous experience in a mental institution serves as the foundation for Buffy's delusion that in fact Sunnydale is one big hallucination. The appeal, of course, is that if she can stay in her fantasy "real-world" world, then she won't have to deal with all of her current problems.

It's a good thing Buffy has built up so much goodwill. Also, that Willow, Xander, and the others have had firsthand experience with spells and various Hellmouth ailments that can make people do things that are completely out of character—like when Buffy tries to kill all her friends and Dawn in order to stay in her alternative-world fantasy.

Much was made of the final scene, in which Buffy is seen looking catatonic in the hospital room. Some thought the writer was suggesting that this was really all a bad dream (like the infamous *Dallas* stunt of bringing a dead character back to life by presenting the entire previous season as his wife's nightmare). But it can also be seen that even though Buffy chooses to not let the poison overtake her, and eventually wills herself back to the real world, a part of her mind still yearns for an escape.

THE REAL HORROR: Feeling trapped. Seemingly hopeless situations can lead to depression and other disorders that shut down a person's ability to cope. When Buffy is poisoned by the demon, she retreats to a place in her mind where she won't have to be brave, responsible, or even try to find her place in the world anymore. Her imagined world—in which her parents are both alive, still married and taking care of her—is an escape from the feeling of being in over her head.

LITERARY ALLUSION: When Jonathan calls himself "Jack Torrance," he's referring to the protagonist in Stephen King's *The Shining*, who becomes possessed and tries to kill his own family.

OF SPECIAL NOTE: This episode was originally scheduled to be broadcast as the eighth episode of the season, but was pushed back.

118. "Entropy"
(APRIL 30, 2002)

Director: James A. Contner
Teleplay: Drew Z. Greenberg
Recurring cast: Danny Strong (Jonathan); Adam Busch (Warren); Tom Lenk (Andrew); Kali Rocha (Halfrek); Amber Benson (Tara)
Guest cast: Edie Caggiano (mother)
Music: "Sao Paulo Rain" (while Xander mopes), by Tom McRae, from *Tom McRae*; "That Kind of Love" (at the end of the episode), by Alison Krauss, from *Forget About It*

Plot: Buffy discovers the Trio has been spying on her. Spike and Anya turn to each other for comfort.

THIS WEEK'S BIG-BROTHER ACCESSORY: The Trio's surveillance camera, which Buffy discovers after Xander accidentally demolishes a stone statue in her front yard. Willow, now more comfortably relying on computers again, later discovers that the camera is part of an entire network that has been monitoring every move Buffy makes, in every place she's likely to go.

INTRODUCING: Willow and Tara together again as a couple.

ANALYSIS: Spike's frustration, and desperation, at Buffy's having called off their relationship is starting to show—to the point where he tries to blackmail her by threatening to tell her friends about their affair. Buffy is still dealing with the remorse of having attempted to kill her friends and her sister, and their forgiveness has had a calming effect on Buffy and she's not so afraid about the truth of her affair with Spike coming out. If they could deal with her as a would-be mass murderer, they can probably deal with her surprising choice of comforter and sex partner—the term "boyfriend" simply doesn't fit in this case. Even so, she'd rather not have to go through what would still be an uncomfortable situation if she can avoid it.

Xander is trying hard to make amends with Anya, though the last thing she wants to hear is that he wants to keep going steady. She has also channeled her hurt into vengeance, having taken D'Hoffryn up on his offer to give her back her powers. Unfortunately, she can only conjure vengeance on behalf of others, so all her plans to make Xander suffer unspeakable horrors are foiled, especially since she can't manage to trick anyone into making such a wish against him.

In a somewhat unlikely pairing, Anya and Spike end up sharing drinks while commiserating over their respective crummy love lives. Both are highly charged sexual beings and, combined with the drinks, it's inevitable they would turn to each other for physical comfort and release. Because they both feel awkward and uneasy about it afterwards, this indicates their tabletop tryst will have to remain a closely guarded secret between them. But Willow taps into the Trio's camera network just in time to catch them in the act, which leaves both Xander and Buffy reeling.

It's understandable why Xander is enraged. But it's more surprising to see how affected Buffy is, especially since she's been the one insisting all along she has no feelings of love for Spike. Even if that is true, she at least *needed* his love and attention, so she feels betrayed on a different level. Interestingly, it's Dawn who immediately picks up on what Buffy's reaction means, and is the least surprised of anyone, probably in part because Dawn likes

Spike and is aware that Spike is in love with Buffy. Dawn hasn't been exposed to the vicious Spike, so she has no negative history with him.

Willow is shocked, although she quickly gets over it because she herself has been in a position in which she kept a relationship quiet out of fear of people's rejecting her because of it. But for Xander, the double-whammy of Buffy's and Anya's betrayals makes him want to have nothing to do with either of them.

THE REAL HORROR: Being cheated on and seeing it firsthand. Even though Buffy never admitted to a real relationship with Spike, and Xander had called the wedding off at the worst possible moment, both feel crushingly betrayed by Spike and Anya's having sex. It would be bad enough had they merely learned of it after the fact, but to see it live, courtesy of the Trio's surveillance cameras, makes the cut that much deeper.

IT'S A MYSTERY: Why does Anya's hair seem to curl and uncurl randomly throughout the episode?

119. "Seeing Red"
(MAY 7, 2002)

Director: Michael Gershman

Teleplay: Steven S. DeKnight

Recurring cast: Danny Strong (Jonathan); Adam Busch (Warren); Tom Lenk (Andrew)

Guest cast: Amy Hathaway (woman in bar); Nichole Hiltz (Frank's girlfriend); James C. Leary (Clem); Garrett Brawith (Frank); Tim Hager (administrator); Stefan Marks (guard #1); Christopher James (guard #2); Kate Orsini (girl at the Bronze)

Music "The Leaves," by Daryll-Ann, from *Happy Trauma*; "Stranded," by Alien Ant Farm, from *ANThology*; "Displaced," by Azure Ray, from *Azure Ray*

Plot: Buffy finally confronts the Trio. A tragedy changes everyone's lives forever.

THIS WEEK'S MYSTICAL WHEATIES: The Orbs of Nezzla'khan, which give the possessor strength and invincibility. Warren plans to use the orbs for a robbery but when Buffy shows up, he decides to make himself a reputation by being the one to kill the Slayer.

INTRODUCING: Jonathan's conscience. Whatever mischief Jonathan has gotten into, it's clear he's doesn't want anyone to get hurt and he's still horrified by Katrina's death, even if he's convinced himself Warren didn't mean to do it. When he sees Warren looking to kill Buffy, however, Jonathan manages to tell her the secret of his power so she can stop Warren. But the humiliation drives Warren to an unimaginably violent act of revenge.

ANALYSIS: This episode drives home the need to live life as fully as you can, and to keep those you love close to you, because life can change—or end—without any warning.

Dawn's happiness over seeing Tara and Willow back together as a couple is refreshing because she simply sees them as two people in love, not two women in love. Sexual preference matters about as much as what brand shoes they wear, and it sends a strong message about tolerance and acceptance. With Tara back, Willow feels a renewed determination to stay clean and sober from magic. Tara's love makes her feel special and important and worthy—more so than the magic ever could.

Once he's had time to digest the truth about Buffy and Spike, Xander is more disgusted with Buffy than he is with Anya, because in his heart Buffy is still his dream woman. Plus his ego doesn't understand why she would get involved with Spike, but never wanted him the same way. So it's not just concern for Buffy, but his own long-held feelings of sexual rejection, that bubble to the surface when Buffy tries to talk to him.

When he finds out from Dawn that what he did with Anya had been broadcast live, Spike feels even more desperate. He thinks that if he can just get Buffy to make love again, all will be forgiven because she'll feel how much he loves her. Plus, he thinks that because everyone knows, there's no reason for her to hold back. But he handles it badly and ends up trying to force himself on her in an ugly confrontation. Spike doesn't realize the line he's crossed until Buffy, bruised and traumatized, manages to push him off. Spike can't believe what he's done and in his guilt, blames Buffy for making him so crazed and decides he has to do something drastic to get his self-respect back.

After Willow figures out the heist the Trio is planning, Buffy sets out to stop them. With a little help from Jonathan, she succeeds. Warren manages to escape, while Jonathan and Andrew are carted off to jail, an unusual sight, considering most of Buffy's foes are the type to explode into dust or get tossed into the Hellmouth's compost heap.

When given time to reflect, Xander realizes that perhaps Buffy would have been more honest had she trusted him not to react badly—which he did. But when he does react badly, it's because nobody matters to him more than Willow and Buffy, and the idea of losing either of them is unthinkable. However, as Warren sprays Buffy's backyard with bullets in a deranged attempt to avenge her foiling his heist, Willow has the most precious thing in her life taken away.

THE REAL HORROR: Senseless violence. Of all the horror seen in Sunnydale, none is more disturbing than when one human kills another. Tara's death is particularly poignant because it is accidental and because Warren's motives are driven by greed and ego. They're still terrible, but somehow people understand crimes of passion more than crimes of indifference or self-aggrandizement. So, while despicable and inexcusable, people may better understand Spike's actions than they do Warren's.

WHAT JAMES MARSTERS HAD TO SAY ABOUT SPIKE'S ATTEMPTED RAPE. "I can't even watch a movie where that's in there. I get up and want to kill the guy. It's my personal issue. So, that was one of the hardest things I've ever done in my life, not even as a job, because Sarah and I are friends. I told Joss, "Nobody's safe around here. You cut right to the bone, dude. This is not a safe show."

BLOOPERS: When Spike is in Buffy's bathroom, his foot is briefly seen reflected in the mirror.

OF SPECIAL NOTE: The attempted robbery scene was filmed at Six Flags Magic Mountain theme park in Valencia, California.
Amber Benson is in the main credits for the first time.

120. "Villains"

(MAY 14, 2002)

Director: David Solomon

Teleplay: Marti Noxon

Recurring cast: Danny Strong (Jonathan); Adam Busch (Warren); Tom Lenk (Andrew); Jeff Kober (Rack); Amelinda Embry (Katrina)

Guest cast: James C. Leary (Clem); Steven W. Bailey (cave demon); Tim Hodgin (coroner); Michael Matthys (paramedic); Julie Hermelin (clerk); Alan Henry Brown (demon bartender); Mueen J. Ahmad (doctor); Jane Cho (nurse #1), Meredith Cross (nurse #2); David Adefeso (paramedic #2); Jeffrey Nicholas Brown (vampire); Nelson Frederick (villager)

Music: "Die, Die My Darling" (in the demon bar), by the Misfits, from *The Misfits*

Plot: Willow resorts to magic to avenge Tara's death.

THIS WEEK'S HORROR: Magic abuse. Instead of using her powers for the good of humanity, Willow sets out on a murderous mission to employ all the power she can summon to execute not just Warren—who is directly responsible for Tara's death—but also his cohorts, who she feels are guilty by association.

INTRODUCING: Willow as villain vigilante. Her grief has sent Willow into a paroxysm of revenge, prompting her to resort to the darkest of magics and to take the law into her own hands.

ANALYSIS: The devastating power of grief and revenge are vividly depicted in this episode. Willow shuts out the pain of watching Tara die in her arms by letting the dark side take over, which has the unfortunate side effect of shutting down her humanity and conscience as well.

After Willow saves Buffy's life by removing the bullet in her chest and healing her wounds, she embarks on her mission to make Warren pay. Buffy, especially, knows that while killing Hellmouth creatures and vampires is her calling, they must not break the laws of society by becoming vigilantes. Not only is it illegal, but it will put Willow at risk of losing her humanity, as it did Faith. As far as Willow is concerned, she feels she died when Tara did; she has no interest of going on with life as she knew it and is willing to bury the old Willow. There is no incentive for her to sit back and let justice take its course, so she tracks down Warren and, to Buffy and Xander's horror, skins him alive. As gruesome as the death is, what is more disturbing is watching their friend's soul dying in front of their eyes.

THE REAL HORROR: Being blinded by hatred. Willow is so devastated and angry and lost at having lost Tara that she risks forever losing herself, and her soul, when she exacts sadistic revenge against Warren.

OF SPECIAL NOTE: Amber Benson's name has been removed from the opening titles and although her body is seen, she's uncredited.

Because Tara's death was not caused by mystical forces, the spell that brought Buffy back won't work.

121. "Two to Go"
(MAY 21, 2002)

Director: Bill Norton
Teleplay: David Fury
Recurring cast: Anthony Stewart Head (Rupert Giles); Danny Strong (Jonathan); Tom Lenk (Andrew); Jeff Kober (Rack)
Guest cast: Steven W. Bailey (cave demon); Jeff McCredie (officer); Damian Mooney (patrol cop); Michael Younger (truck driver)

Plot: Buffy must protect Jonathan and Andrew from Willow.

THIS WEEK'S MAGICAL POWER SURGE: Willow can only go into magical overdrive for so long before she depletes her power, like a battery that needs recharging. Thus she absorbs all of Rack's dark energy into herself, which has the unfortunate side effect of draining the life out of him.

INTRODUCING: Anya using her powers for good instead of vengeance. Despite her continued upset at Xander, Anya comes through when Buffy asks for her help against Willow, and joins the effort to protect Jonathan and

Andrew, as well as Buffy and Xander, while hoping to bring Willow back to her senses.

ANALYSIS: Xander is once again feeling those "I'm a mere mortal" blues. His best friend is on a murderous rampage and he can't keep up with Buffy trying to help her stop it. He feels powerless and helpless to make a difference, but keeps plugging along.

Watching Willow immerse herself in dark magic is almost as painful as when Angel turned; perhaps more so because Willow isn't under the influence of a curse, but wracked with grief and fury. But Buffy knows (besides not wanting Willow to hurt herself or anyone else) that when Willow does snap out of her maniacal trance, she will loathe herself for what she's done. The only way to save Willow is to stop her, but Buffy is no match for Willow's power.

Some long-hidden resentment bubbles to the surface during their confrontation at the Magic Box, such as Willow's old feelings of insecurity and feeling unimportant when measuring herself against the Slayer. The appeal of witchcraft was to be someone special, but now that the dark side has taken over, the power is seductive and addictive. As she becomes more consumed, and because she is in such immeasurable pain, Willow wants everyone else around her to suffer as well.

Just when it seems that nobody has the power to stop her, the unexpected arrival of Giles, and a blast of his own power, sets the stage for a do-or-die confrontation.

THE REAL HORROR: Being unable to reach a friend. It's oh-so-frustrating when someone you care for simply won't listen to reason. Willow takes this scenario to murderous heights when she ignores everyone's pleas to not give in to the dark side.

BLOOPERS: When Willow is chasing Warren through the woods, you can see the cables that are pulling the tree branches away from Willow.

OF SPECIAL NOTE: When originally broadcast, this and Episode 122, "Grave," were aired as a special two-hour episode.

Anthony Stewart Head was not credited in the guest-cast list to keep his return appearance a surprise.

122. "Grave"

(MAY 21, 2002)

Director: James A. Contner
Teleplay: David Fury
Recurring cast: Anthony Stewart Head (Rupert Giles); Danny Strong
    (Jonathan); Tom Lenk (Andrew)
Guest cast: Brett Wagner (trucker)
Music: "Prayer of St. Francis" (at the end of the episode), by Sarah
    McLachlan, from *Surfacing Extended*

Plot: Willow decides to end the world. Buffy finally sees the light.

THIS WEEK'S TEMPLE OF DOOM: The temple of Proserpexa. Proserpexa was a powerful female demon devoted to the destruction of the Earthly dimension. Her effigy shows her as having two mouths with forked tongues, and snakes for hair. Her followers had planned to end the world by funneling the Earth's life force into the effigy and in turn using that force to immolate the Earth. An earthquake foiled that plan by burying the temple, but Willow plans to resurrect the site to finish the job.

INTRODUCING: The great and powerful Giles. Giles returns to Sunnydale after being imbued with powers by a coven of witches who had sensed the dark forces being unleashed by Willow. Spike with a soul. After enduring numerous, torturous tests, a demon grants Spike's wish that he be turned back to how he was before.

ANALYSIS: Willow is now so consumed by her power that she responds to Giles as a rebellious teenager would. Part of her knows what she's doing is wrong, but she also knows nobody can stop her for long. Plus she's still smarting over the way Giles scolded her previously about her use of magic. Somewhere inside, though, Willow must also blame herself for Tara's death because, for all her powers, Willow was unable to protect her from Warren's stray bullet.

While Willow is briefly incapacitated, Buffy and Giles catch up, Buffy confessing that things have been bad since he left. But instead of being upset with her over Spike, Giles starts laughing at the absurdity—and that burst of affectionate emotion seems to be the key to unlocking Buffy's angst. Giles's mirth reminds her that if things are kept in perspective, there's very little that can't be overcome. While sleeping with Spike might have been emotionally self-destructive, it truly wasn't life and death. But Willow's magical bender *is*.

After Willow escapes from Giles's mystical binds, she unleashes a torrent of fury-driven magic on him and eventually drains his power the way she did Rack, although Giles survives. After a momentary high, having so much power within her, Willow suddenly feels all the pain in the world. But instead of it bringing her back in touch with her humanity as Giles and the Coven hoped it would, it convinces her that the best way to stop everyone's pain is to end the world.

In the end it isn't Buffy's Slayer superabilities or Anya's demon powers or Giles's Coven-imbued magic that brings Willow back from the apocalyptic edge, it's Xander, who uses the greatest power of all—love. Although he was unable to stop Warren from shooting Buffy and killing Tara, he is able to save Willow from destroying the Earth, although it remains to be seen if anyone is able to put the pieces of Willow's shattered life back together.

THE REAL HORROR: Suicide. For some people who can only feel desperation, loneliness, or extreme sorrow, suicide seems the only way to stop the pain. Unable to deal with the loss of Tara, Willow chooses to end her own life along with everyone else's. But while it was the loss of her true love that set Willow on this death-filled, destructive path, it is the unconditional love shown by Xander that finally reaches her heart and breaks through the emotional barrier created by the dark magics. Once the fury subsides, Willow's loss and despair washes over her in a flood of pent-up emotion and her humanity is restored. But Willow's road to recovery, and her redemption for having taken human lives, will undoubtedly be a long and painful process.

Buffy, too, is on the road to emotional recovery and realizes that in her efforts to protect Dawn, she's been stifling her. She knows it's time to show her love by teaching Dawn the world, good *and* bad, because we have to make the best of our time on it.

BLOOPERS: Willow's nosebleed appears and disappears from shot to shot.

OF SPECIAL NOTE: The tattoo visible on Sarah Michelle's back when she climbs out of the hole is the Chinese symbol for "integrity."

Seventh-Year overview: Life comes full circle for Buffy as she finds herself back at the newly rebuilt Sunnydale High, this time keeping the Hellmouth in check while Dawn attends school. Although still finding her way as a single parent to Dawn, Buffy is less angst-ridden than she was last year and, through an unexpected opportunity, finds that in addition to helping mankind as the Slayer, she can also help people on a more personal level through her new job as guidance counselor.

REGULAR CAST:

Sarah Michelle Gellar (*Buffy Summers*)
Nicholas Brendon (*Xander Harris*)
Emma Caulfield (*Anya*)
James Marsters (*Spike*)
Michelle Trachtenberg (*Dawn Summers*)
Alyson Hannigan (*Willow Rosenberg*)

✛

123. "Lessons"
(SEPTEMBER 24, 2002)

Director: Joss Whedon and David Solomon
Teleplay: Joss Whedon
Recurring cast: Anthony Stewart Head (Rupert Giles); Kali Rocha (Halfrek); D. B. Woodside (Principal Robin Wood)
Guest cast: David Zepeda (Carlos Trejo); Jeremy Howard (dead nerd); Ken Strunk (dead janitor); Rachael Bella (dead girl); Ed F.

Martin (Mr. Lonegrin); Simon Chernin (student); Jeff Denton (vampire); Alex Breckenridge (Kit Holburn); Mark Metcalf (The Master); Juliet Landau (Drusilla); Harry Groener (Mayor Wilkins); George Hertzberg (Adam); Clare Kramer (Glory); Adam Busch (Warren)

Music: "So High" (at the coffee shop) by Strange Radio from *Pop Radio*

Plot: Something big and bad is brewing in the Hellmouth; Sunnydale High reopens.

THIS WEEK'S IMPENDING DOOM: The Ultimate Big Bad: An unidentified evil, which has the power to take the form of every Big Bad known to Buffydom, is brewing beneath Sunnydale. In this episode, it raises the spirits of former Sunnydale High school students Buffy failed to save.

INTRODUCING: The rebuilt Sunnydale High; Principal Robin Wood; a rehabilitating Willow.

ANALYSIS: Buffy and the others are still dealing with the aftermath of the emotional devastation caused by Warren's murder of Tara and his own subsequent murder at the hands of a witched-out Willow. But life—and the Hellmouth—go on. Comparing Dawn's first day of school at Sunnydale High with Buffy's reflects just how much time has passed and how much Willow, Xander, and Buffy have matured. Although still ultimately optimistic, they've faced so much evil and experienced so much personal loss it's hard to believe they were ever as fresh-faced and naïve as Dawn and her classmates are now.

Buffy is still trying to balance her fears for Dawn's well-being with the need to let Dawn be her own person, but it's clear Buffy has regained some much-needed self-deprecating humor. So, instead of obsessing on her inner demons, Buffy is more attuned to fighting whatever evil is stirring in the Hellmouth. Whatever it is, it's so powerful that Willow literally can hear it all the way in England, where she's rehabilitating with Giles and learning to control her powers, which are now as much a part of her as her eye-color or her ability to taste. Although her family is a bit fragmented at the moment, Buffy is back on solid emotional ground and better prepared to deal with whatever life and the Hellmouth throw at her.

THE REAL HORROR: Being reminded of past failures, such as when the spirits of former students confront Buffy and accuse her of failing to save them. Buffy has always had a heightened sense of responsibility, even when she's tried to deny it or run away from it, so despite all the lives she has saved, she still feels a nagging sense of failure for every life lost. This is the first indication that whatever evil is lurking beneath Sunnydale, it has the ability to play on someone's fears and weaknesses.

IT'S A MYSTERY: Why does Dawn refer to this as her first day of high school since it was stated in the Season Six episode "Older and Far Away" that she was in high school.

FORSHADOWING: The mysterious pursuit and killing of a Slayer-aged young woman at the beginning of the episode indicates that whatever evil Buffy will face next has an influence far beyond the Sunnydale city limits.

LITERARY REFERENCE: When Willow refers to Giles as Dumbledore, she is referring to the powerful and wise headmaster of Hogwarts School of Witchcraft and Wizardry in J. K. Rowling's *Harry Potter* books.

OF SPECIAL NOTE: The scenes with Willow and Giles were filmed in England to accommodate Anthony Head; Joss Whedon directed the scenes filmed in England while David Solomon directed the rest of the episode, which was filmed in Los Angeles; in the new high school, Xander built the Principal's office over the Hellmouth instead of having it under the library.

WHAT JOSS WHEDON HAS TO SAY: "The reopening of the high school is where we're starting, and it represents a lot of what we're talking about in terms of getting back to the very first mission statement of the show, which was the joy of female power: Having it, using it, sharing it.

"We'll deal with issues, but we won't be hitting the incredibly depressing reality of being grown up quite so hard," he said. "Those things will still be issues, because Spike is still in the mix, and he did try to rape Buffy. Willow has been addicted, and both of those people have to be in the mix, so we'll deal with those issues, and things are still going to be scary, depressing, and confusing for our characters. It's going to be tough for them, but at the same time, they're going to reclaim that essential notion of the beauty of power, and of their mission, and not get so caught up in questions."

MUSICAL NOTE: Strange Radio is playing in the Espresso Pump café while Anya and Halfrek are having coffee.

124. "Beneath You"

(OCTOBER 1, 2002)

Director: Nick Marck
Teleplay: Douglas Petrie
Recurring cast: Anthony Stewart Head (Rupert Giles); DB Woodside
   (Principal Robin Wood)
Guest cast: Kaarina Aufranc (Nancy); Tess Hall (punk girl); Benita
   Krista Nall (young woman); Jack Sundmacher (Ronnie)

Plot: Buffy's troubling dreams hint at a pending evil; Anya finds that her heart just isn't into revenge the way it used to be.

THIS WEEK'S SIDEWALK BUSTING DEMON: Anya turns a caddish boyfriend into a worm-like Sluggoth demon, capable of eating through concrete with its huge mouthful of teeth.

INTRODUCING: Buffy as high school guidance counselor; Spike's realization he can hurt a human without blinding head pain.

ANALYSIS: While on one level this episode has Buffy confronting a powerful demon, it also serves to further the season story in a number of ways.

Xander's attraction to Nancy, who is being stalked by the giant worm, indicates he is ready to try and get on with his life. But Nancy's mutual attraction goes cold after she discovers that Anya is a demon—and Xander's former girlfriend. Xander is reminded once again why relationships with "civilians" are going to be difficult if not impossible.

Although Anya thought being a vengeance demon again would fill the void left by her breakup with Xander, she is as miserable as ever. Not even turning Nancy's boyfriend, Ronnie, into a vicious giant worm lifts her spirits; it's clear the thrill of vengeance is gone, but she isn't about to admit it since it's all she has to hold on to right now.

Spike's am-I-crazy-or-just-feeling-incredibly-sorry-for-myself mood swings are either a genuine cry of pain, or he's being tormented and manipulated by some dark force. Buffy's failure to tell anyone that Spike was living in the school's labyrinth basement either indicates a subconscious protectiveness on her part—or denial. Although he was criminally wrong to try to rape her,

Buffy still feels a modicum of responsibility for having used Spike to escape her own demons.

More troubling to Buffy at the moment are her disturbing dreams in which she sees another young woman killed by the mysterious men in robes. Before the woman dies she says, "From beneath you, it devours." Although she doesn't understand what is happening, Buffy knows it means death for others like the girl.

THE REAL HORROR: Getting what you asked for. Both Nancy and Spike deal with the consequences of having their wishes granted. For Spike, it was a soul that he thought would turn him into the man Buffy wanted. Like Angel. He seems to have forgotten that it took Angel a hundred years to deal with his guilt and use his immortality for good instead of wallowing in self-loathing. Instead of becoming a man worthy of Buffy, Spike has been reduced to a near-animal and has become vulnerable to the evil lurking beneath them.

Nancy simply wished for her abusive boyfriend to go away, but despite whatever rancor they had, she was still horrified that he was turned into a monster.

Anya wanted her powers back, but now that she has them, she has too much human compassion to enjoy them and sets herself up for some serious consequences when she reverses the wish in order to save Nancy and the others.

BLOOPERS: While at the Bronze, Buffy puts her sword on the table but during the fight scene it's gone.

OF SPECIAL NOTE: Principal Wood is a vegetarian.

125. "Same Time, Same Place"
(OCTOBER 8, 2002)

Director: James A. Contner
Teleplay: Jane Espenson
Guest cast: Camden Toy (Gnarl); Matt Koruba (teen boy); Anthony S. Johnson (father); Nicholette Dixon (sister); Marshe Daniel (brother)

Plot: Willow returns to Sunnydale but is rendered invisible to her friends; when a skinned corpse is discovered, the Scooby gang is afraid Willow has turned evil again.

THIS WEEK'S FLESH-EATING DEMON: Gnarl, a sadistic, green-skinned demon who paralyzes his victims with his poisonous fingernails before slowly eating their flesh, strip by strip.

INTRODUCING: A demon immune to magic. Willow's magic is useless against Gnarl.

ANALYSIS: As difficult as it has been for Willow to come to grips with having taken human life and spiraling out of control with her magic after Tara's murder, the prospect of going back to Sunnydale and facing her friends has been almost more stressful. She is terrified that she won't be forgiven, in part because she still hasn't truly forgiven herself. In the past, Giles had primarily been a father figure, but now he's also taken on the guise of spiritual advisor having overseen Willow's recovery.

Back home, Xander and Buffy are nervous about Willow's return, worried she may not have her magic completely under control, but they want Willow to feel welcome and their desire to welcome her back wins out over their fears. They plan an airport reception and are deflated when Willow fails to get off the plane. Likewise, Willow feels the pain of rejection when she gets off the plane and doesn't see anyone she knows. What she doesn't realize, is that in order to avoid the possibility of rejection she has subconsciously cast a spell that makes her invisible to Buffy, Xander, and Dawn, and they invisible to her. Because Anya and Willow have a relationship that has turned frosty on occasion, they can see each other just fine.

Although they feel guilty suspecting her, Xander and Buffy assume the worst when a skinned corpse turns up and they suspect Willow has gone evil again, unaware it's really Gnarl.

When Willow gets captured by Gnarl, she considers it exquisite karma that she should be facing a slow, painful death by flaying. Part of her seems to accept her fate, believing she has little to live for now that it looks as if Buffy and Xander have rejected her. However, when Buffy, Xander and Anya show up at the cave and Buffy kills Gnarl, Willow realizes that they haven't abandoned her, causing the spell to lift and allowing her to see and be seen.

Although they started off as the Scooby gang, it is more clear than ever that Buffy, Xander and Willow are a close family, with an unconditional love that comes from the emotional glue that bonds them together.

THE REAL HORROR: Being rejected by the people you love. Willow is so consumed by guilt and self-loathing over her actions after Tara dies, that she doubts Buffy and Xander could ever really forgive her. Fear of their rejection causes Willow to literally become invisible—we can't reject who can't see. Had she followed Giles' advice to trust herself, thereby allowing others to follow, she would have spared herself both emotional grief and her near-death encounter with Gnarl.

OF SPECIAL NOTE: In an online posting at the Bronze Beta, writer Jane Espenson admitted Gnarl was inspired by a *Lord of the Rings* character. "There was some Gollum in the history of Gnarl."

Camden Toy, who plays Gnarl, was one of the gentlemen in the season four episode, *Hush.*

126. "Help"
(OCTOBER 15, 2002)

Director: Rick Rosenthal
Teleplay: Rebecca Rand Kirshner
Recurring cast: D. B. Woodside (Principal Robin Wood)
Guest cast: Azura Skye (Cassie Newton); Zachary Bryan (Peter); Glenn Morshower (Cassie's father); Rick Gonzalez (tough student); Kevin Christy (Josh); Sarah Hagan (Amanda); Jarrett Lennon (tattle tale); J. Barton (Mike Helgenburg); Daniel Dehring (red robed #1); A. J. Wedding (red robed #2); Marcie Lynn Ross (dead woman)

Plot: Buffy is determined to save a student who believes she only has a week to live; a cult of high school boys plan to use magic to become rich.

THIS WEEK'S GREED DEMON: Avilas, who will give infinite riches in exchange for a human sacrifice.

ANALYSIS: Buffy always feels better when she's actively fighting an adversary because it makes her feel in control of the moment and, on another level, her destiny in general. So when she is confronted with Cassie's calm revelation that she will die within the week, Buffy's instinct is to find whoever, or whatever, is threatening her. But while Slayer Buffy gets to use brute force to defend the world, School Counselor Buffy has to use a more conventional approach, which she finds extremely frustrating.

Because they live in Sunnydale, it's not unreasonable to suspect that the danger stalking Cassie is of a mystical nature. So it isn't too surprising to discover that a group of high school boys are planning to bring forth a demon who would grant them fabulous wealth in exchange for a human sacrifice. Although there's no explanation as to how Buffy just so happens to infiltrate the ceremony, she incinerates the demons and saves Cassie—only to have the girl die of heart failure, the result of a genetic disorder.

Being reminded again, as she was with her mother's death, that there are some things she is powerless to stop, Buffy must accept that sometimes, the victory is in simply making the effort.

THE REAL HORROR: Early death. Most teenagers assume they have a whole lifetime in front of them to look forward to. And while death is always sad, it seems particularly tragic when a young person dies, because they haven't had a chance to experience many of life's more wonderful moments, or had the opportunity to fulfill whatever their potential might have been. Cassie's monologue about why she wants to lives, even though she knows she won't, was a poignant poem regarding the desires of the heart.

LITERARY REFERENCE: The book Cassie is reading, *Slaughterhouse Five*, by Kurt Vonnegut, is about a young soldier named Billy Pilgrim who travels through time, experiencing his life in a kind of nonlinear chronology. Because of this, Billy experiences his death numerous times and comes to accept it. He also encounters the Trafalmadorians, aliens from the fourth dimension, who can see the future, the past, and the present but are powerless to change it.

OF SPECIAL NOTE: Cassie's Web site really exists. It was built by the production teams and can be found at http:; sh/www.geocities.com/newcassie. Principal Wood reveals he's from Beverly Hills. When Willow visits Tara's grave, her birthdate on the tombstone is October 16, 1980.

127. "Selfless"

(OCTOBER 22, 2002)

Director: David Solomon

Teleplay: Drew Goddard

Recurring cast: Andy Umberger (D'Hoffryn); Kali Rocha (Halfrek)

Guest cast: Abraham Benrubi (Olaf); Joyce Guy (professor); Jennifer Shon (girl); Taylor Sutherland (villager #1); Marybeth Scherr (villager #2); Alessandro Mastrobuono (villager #3); Daniel Spanton (viking #1); John Timmons (viking #2)

Music: "Mrs." (the song Anya sings during the "Once More, With Feeling" flashback) by Joss Whedon.

Plot: A deadly vengeance wish leaves Anya so wracked with guilt that she decides to sacrifice her own life in order to undo the spell.

THIS WEEK'S HEART-SEEKING DEMON: Anya summons a spider-like Crimslaw demon, which rips the hearts out of a dozen fraternity brothers.

INTRODUCING: Anya's backstory.

ANALYSIS: Even since getting back her vengeance demon stripes, Anya has been lost in a kind of netherworld. Her heart isn't into granting wishes the way it used to be, because she feels human compassion, and yet she feels alienated from the gang because of her break up with Xander. She has no place she feels she really belongs. And after a wish she grants ends in the deaths of a dozen frat boys, Anya is ready to leave this world. She decides she will reverse the spell, although it means sacrificing her own life, rather than live with the guilt.

Although Buffy has put up with Anya's return to demonhood because of their personal relationship, the deaths cross the line and Buffy feels she has no choice but to kill Anya before her wishes can harm anyone else. But the idea of Anya being killed is unacceptable to Xander and his reaction reveals he is still in love with her. While Xander and Buffy have had arguments in the past, he's never before had so much personally at stake.

The situation forces Willow to tap into her magic, which frightens her because she knows she could still spin out of control under its power. She summons D'Hoffryn to negotiate an out for Anya, explaining to him that she isn't cut out for the vengeance life anymore. She succeeds, although Anya will pay a steep price for D'Hoffryn letting her go.

THE REAL HORROR: Unexpected consequences. While Anya was willing to sacrifice her own life in order to reverse the deaths of the frat boys, she wasn't prepared for Halfrek to die in her place. Now that her wish to undo

SLAYER MUSIC

One of the most distinctive aspects of the series is the music. In addition to supplying soundtrack cuts, the groups that contribute music to *Buffy* often appear on stage during scenes at "the Bronze." Joss Whedon says he likes to have some of the lesser-known bands provide music for the episodes in order to give them a little exposure. "And I like hiring the un- signed bands because they're cheap," he laughs. "No, not really. A lot of great bands just don't get enough expo- sure. And for some reason, all these bands sent in tapes of music for us to use." That's how the Nerf Herder song was chosen for the *Buffy* theme.

The bands are selected on an episode-by-episode basis. Whedon says he'll sometimes write a scene around a particular song he's just heard. "I'll hear the music then get a picture in my mind of what the characters will be doing."

Because of the strong fan response to the music, *Buffy* has gone multimedia: The first soundtrack, *Buffy the Vampire Slayer: The Album* was released in 1999, and a second, *Once More with Feeling*, which included the soundtrack of the musical episode, was released in 2002.

the deaths of the boys is granted, Anya has to suffer the pain and guilt of being the cause of her friend's death for the rest of her life.

IT'S A MYSTERY: Why Anya's real name is said to be Aud when in the season five episode, "Triangle," Olaf refers to Anya as Anyanka, not Aud.

LITERARY ALLUSION: When Spike makes the comment, "Scream Montresor all you like, Pet," he's referring to Edgar Allan Poe's *The Cask of Amontillado*, in which a man is sealed alive inside a wall by his adversary.

OF SPECIAL NOTE: Anya's real name was Aud and she became a demon in 880 A.D.; Willow reveals she used magic to gets A's on all her finals the previous year.

The girl who has her wish granted, Jennifer Shon, previously appeared in the "Life Serial" episode as one of Buffy and Willow's classmates.

MUSICAL NOTE: The song seen during the flashback didn't appear in the original episode. According to a post by Drew Goddard at the Bronze Beta, Joss Whedon wrote Anya's song, called "Mrs.," overnight: "We were on the set of *Firefly* when Joss was directing "The Train Job," we were talking and he said something like, 'What if we flash back to the musical' . . . And the very next morning he walked in and said, 'I've got the song.' Sometimes I think you can start car batteries with his brain."

128. "Him"

(NOVEMBER 5, 2002)

Director: Michael Gershman
Teleplay: Drew Z. Greenberg
Recurring Cast: D. B. Woodside (Principal Robin Wood)
Guest Cast: Brandon Keener (Lance Brooks); Thad Luckinbill (R. J. Brooks); Yan England (O'Donnell); Angela Sarafayan (Lori); David Ghilardi (teacher); Riki Lindhome (Cheryl)
Music: "A Rush of Blood to the Head" (while Dawn's at school) by Coldplay from *A Rush of Blood to the Head*; "Little Fury" by The Breeders from *Title TK*

Plot: The Sunnydale High School quarterback is irresistible to any woman he meets; Spike becomes Xander's new roommate.

THIS WEEK'S MYSTICAL ACCESSORY: R. J.'s magical letterman's jacket, that causes every woman to fall in love with him.

INTRODUCING: Dawn as love-struck teenager.

ANALYSIS: This episode takes a break from the unidentified impending doom rumbling beneath Sunnydale and takes a mostly light-hearted look at infatuation. Like most teenagers, Dawn is a mass of contradictions. On one hand, she wants to assert her individuality and be treated like a grown up; on the other, she is still insecure about her appeal to the opposite sex. She wants to be seen as a sexual being and yet, is inexperienced in the ways of physical relationships. So when Buffy falls under R. J.'s spell and goes after him, Dawn feels completely outclassed as well as betrayed.

Like Buffy before her, Dawn is searching for her place to fit in. Unlike Buffy, she doesn't have a higher Slayer calling to give her a boost of self-confidence. Although Dawn is devoted to Buffy, the difficulties of living in such a large shadow are reflected in Dawn's desperate desire to have some-thing—or in this case, someone—to call her own.

While the girls are trying to outmaneuver each other, Xander and Spike are settling into an uneasy alliance as roommates. Although Buffy is still keeping her distance from Spike, both physically and emotionally, she har-bors compassion for him and the torment he has endured since regaining his soul. The only way to get him out of the basement was to find a place for him to live and Xander drew the short straw. Part of Spike hates being somewhere he knows he isn't wanted, but at the same time, he's desperate to get away from the voices he hears talking to him in the basement. Nobody is quite sure whether he's truly going mad or is simply experiencing appropriate guilt for the sins of his past.

THE REAL HORROR: Finding out that what you thought was love, really wasn't. Nobody wants to hear that the rush of emotion they are feeling isn't as real as it first appears because everyone likes to think they're in better control of such things. Dawn believes she is in love with R. J. but the more she tries to convince Buffy of it, the more apparent it becomes that her emotions aren't genuine. When Xander and Spike mug R. J. to steal and destroy his jacket, the spell is broken, leaving Dawn with an odd emptiness at how fleeting such feelings can be.

MUSICAL NOTE: The Breeders appears in this episode playing at the Bronze while Dawn dances with R.J.

129. "Conversations With Dead People"
(NOVEMBER 12, 2002)

Director: Nick Marck
Teleplay: Jane Espenson and Drew Goddard
Recurring Cast: Danny Strong (Jonathan); Tom Lenk (Andrew)
Guest Cast: Kristine Sutherland (Joyce Summers); Adam Busch (Warren); Azura Skye (Cassie Newton); Jonathan M. Woodward (Holden "Webs" Webster); Stacey Scowley (young woman)
Music: "Blue" (at the beginning and end of episode) by Angie Hart from *The Angie Hart Project*; "Never Never Is Forever" (while Dawn is at home) by Scout from *Drummer on the Cover*

Plot: Some unknown evil taking the guise of dead people is trying to manipulate Buffy and her friends' emotions; Jonathan and Andrew return from Mexico.

THIS WEEK'S REVELATION: The force that "from beneath, devours" is trying to diminish the Slayer's strength by attacking her support group.

INTRODUCING: Andrew as a killer. Spurred on by a vision of Warren, Andrew murders Jonathan in the basement of Sunnydale High.

ANALYSIS: It's clear that something is intentionally messing with the heads of Buffy and the Scooby gang using a sort of divide-and-conquer strategy. Up to now, Spike has been the primary target, most likely because he's the most vulnerable as he readjusts to having a soul with the guilt and anguish that comes with it.

A half a world away, Giles has been doing research and trying to figure out what is brewing. The murder of his associates indicates he is close to the answer. Before his fellow Watcher dies, he tells Giles "it" has begun. Back in

Sunnydale, a spate of visitations from the dead leaves a wake of emotional destruction.

Home alone, Dawn is terrorized by an invisible force and traumatized by a vision of her mother telling her not to trust Buffy. Buffy spends the night being psychoanalyzed by a former, now-vamped, classmate named Holden. Before dusting him, Holden reveals that he was sired by Spike. Willow is visited by Cassie, who brings greetings from Tara from beyond. Despite her desire to believe Tara is trying to communicate with her, Willow is smart enough to know that Tara would never wish her harm. When "Cassie" suggests Willow commit suicide to prevent a relapse into Evil Willow, Always the Smartest One in the Room Willow realizes the deception and for the first time we get a glimpse of the real evil behind the apparitions.

Like a moth drawn to fire, Jonathan can't seem to stay away from Sunnydale. But it's more than just his desire to devise another scam. In his heart, he cares about the people there, especially Buffy and the Scoobies, and is hoping to make amends for the pain and havoc he previously helped cause. Jonathan is essentially a decent person who would happily fight the good fight against evil, while Andrew has always been morally borderline. So it's not surprising when Andrew falls under the sway of "Warren" and stabs Jonathan.

THE REAL HORROR: Having your emotional buttons pushed. What makes the force stalking Sunnydale so formidable is that it seems to know Buffy and the others, and uses this knowledge to play on their deepest fears and insecurities. Buffy's biggest strength has always been her support group. By targeting those around Buffy, either by trying to drive them insane (Spike), make them reluctant to use their powers (Willow), or cause distrust (Dawn), her overall power as the Slayer is diminished.

OF SPECIAL NOTE: This is the first episode of the series in which Nicholas Brendon does not appear; Holden's revelation that Buffy's former beau, Scott Hope, played by Fab Filippo, is now openly gay is a sly reference Filippo playing a homosexual on the Showtime cable series *Queer as Folk*.

MUSICAL NOTE: Angie Hart is performing at the Bronze; the song she is singing was written by her and Joss Whedon; Hart is from the band Splendid.

130. "Sleeper"
(November 19, 2002)

Director: Alan J. Levi

Teleplay: David Fury and Jane Espenson

Recurring Cast: Anthony Stewart Head (Rupert Giles)

Guest Cast: Robinne Lee (Bronze vampire); Rob Nagle (Robson, the Watcher); Linda Christopher (Nora); Stacey Scowley (young woman); Kevin Daniels (bouncer); Lisa Jay (Linda)

Music: "This Is How It Goes" (at the Bronze) by Aimee Mann from *Lost in Space*; "Pavlov's Bell" (at the Bronze) by Aimee Mann from *Lost in Space*

Plot: Buffy worries that Spike has started killing again.

THIS WEEK'S EVIL TWINS: Spike is being driven to kill by a vision of his former evil self, who seems to have complete control over him.

ANALYSIS: Although still shaken by the experiences of the previous night, Willow and Buffy are able to try and put it in perspective. This is where their experience dealing with evil is an advantage. Dawn is more freaked out and has a harder time getting over the visitation from "Joyce." Willow's insight, that there are elements of truth interspersed in the lies, is reminiscent of how Spike put a wedge between Buffy and the others back when he was in cahoots with Adam.

The most immediate problem is whether or not Spike has started killing again. On one hand, he seems genuinely remorseful but on the other, Buffy senses something is going on he's not telling her. The irony is, Spike himself doesn't know what he's doing and it's not until Buffy confronts him in the basement, where he's been burying his victims, that his recent killings come back to him and he begs for death.

Although Buffy abhors the killings, she is also aware of something powerful and evil manipulating Spike. Instead of killing him, which Xander is naturally in favor of, Buffy realizes that the best way to learn about her nemesis is to get close to Spike, who has confronted it more than anyone.

Willow's reaction after her encounter with "Cassie" reflects her recovery. Rather than devastate her, it makes Willow more focused and gives her a sense of purpose. The best way to atone for her previous evil acts will be to vanquish the evil at hand.

THE REAL HORROR: The morning after. Spike is so totally controlled by his visions that it seems as if he's having blackouts, the way a drunk does. He has flashes of what he's done but no clear cut memory of exactly what happened.

IT'S A MYSTERY: Does the chip still cause Spike pain or not? If yes, why didn't he howl in pain when killing? If no, why was he yelping when pummeling on Peter, the riches-seeking student who kidnapped Cassie in "Help?"

MUSICAL NOTE: Amy Mann appears at the Bronze; The song the shape-shifter hummed before Spike started attacking people was the English folk song, "Early One Morning."

131. "𝔑ever 𝔏eave 𝔐e"
(NOVEMBER 26, 2002)

Director: David Solomon
Teleplay: Drew Goddard
Recurring Cast: Danny Strong (Jonathan); Tom Lenk (Andrew); D. B. Woodside (Principal Wood); Harris Yulin (Quentin Travers);
Guest Cast: Camden Toy (ubervamp); Adam Busch (Warren); Cynthia LaMontagne (Lydia); Oliver Muirhead (Philip); Kris Iyer (Higel); Donald Bishop (butcher); Bobby Brewer (Hoffman); Roberto Santos (Grimes)

Plot: Buffy keeps Spike under guard; The Scoobies interrogate Andrew; a powerful evil is unleashed from beneath Sunnydale High.

THIS WEEK'S BEARERS OF ILL WILL: The Harbingers, or Bringers, who summon the ultimate evil by pouring Spike's blood on the Seal of Danzalthar.

INTRODUCING: The destruction of the Watcher's Council. Tight-lipped as always when it comes to helping Buffy, Quentin Travers declines to share any information with her, such as the systematic killing of future Slayers-in-waiting around the world and Giles's disappearance. But his silence proves self-indulgently misguided when he and the rest of the Council are blown to bits after their building is bombed.

THE BIG BAD: The First Evil. Buffy realizes the same essence of absolute evil that tried to destroy Angel in the season three episode "Amends," is back and able to assume the appearance of any dead person. In the end, the First Evil is revealed to be an ancient vampire, quite possibly the first pure vampire ever to stalk the earth.

ANALYSIS: When the First Evil tried to get Angel to kill back in season three, Angel decided he'd rather die first. But Angel had a hundred years to adjust to the constant guilt he endured over past sins as well as weaning himself off feeding on humans. Spike has been thrown completely off balance not just by regaining his soul, but by the realization that the only reason Buffy was physically involved with him was because she hated herself, not because she loved him. He's too emotionally weak to fight the First Evil and instead, when the Bringers use his blood in a ritual, Spike becomes the instrument through which First Evil vampire is freed.

Although Buffy now knows who her adversary is, she still hasn't grasped his ultimate goal—to completely wipe out the Slayer lineage so that he and his kind can rule the earth without interference.

THE REAL HORROR: Mind control. As Xander figures out, it's the song sung by the First-Evil-as-Spike that triggers Spike's killing sprees.

IT'S A MYSTERY: When the First Evil initially appeared to torment Angel, Giles said there were only three Harbingers but there now appears to be many more. Also, one of the hallmarks of the Harbingers was that "nothing will grow above or below them," and yet in this episode, there are plenty of plants above their lair.

OF SPECIAL NOTE: Camden Toy makes his third appearance on *Buffy*, this time as the ultimate vampire freed by the Harbingers. He previously appeared in season four's "Hush" and earlier this season as Gnarl in "Same Time, Same Place."